ALL THE DEVILS ARE HERE

ALL THE DEVILS ARE HERE

American Romanticism
and Literary Influence

DAVID GREVEN

UNIVERSITY OF VIRGINIA PRESS
Charlottesville and London

University of Virginia Press
© 2024 by the Rector and Visitors of the University of Virginia
All rights reserved
Printed in the United States of America on acid-free paper

First published 2024

9 8 7 6 5 4 3 2 1

Library of Congress Cataloging-in-Publication Data

Names: Greven, David, author.
Title: All the devils are here : American romanticism and literary influence / David Greven.
Description: Charlottesville : University of Virginia Press, 2024. | Includes bibliographical references and index.
Identifiers: LCCN 2023049031 (print) | LCCN 2023049032 (ebook) | ISBN 9780813951010 (hardcover ; acid-free paper) | ISBN 9780813951027 (paperback ; acid-free paper) | ISBN 9780813951034 (ebook)
Subjects: LCSH: American literature—19th century—History and criticism. | American literature—20th century—History and criticism. | Romanticism—United States—History—19th century. | Romanticism—United States—History—20th century. | Influence (Literary, artistic, etc.) | Gender identity in literature. | Sex in literature. | Race in literature. | Shakespeare, William, 1564-1616—Influence. | Milton, John, 1608-1674—Influence. | LCGFT: Literary criticism.
Classification: LCC PS169.R6 G74 2024 (print) | LCC PS169.R6 (ebook) | DDC 810.9—dc23/eng/20231206
LC record available at https://lccn.loc.gov/2023049031
LC ebook record available at https://lccn.loc.gov/2023049032

Cover art: "Edgar," from *Twelve Characters from Shakespeare*, John Hamilton Mortimer, 1775. Etching. (Metropolitan Museum of Art, Rogers Fund, 1968)

FOR MY UNCLE LEONARDO GREVEN, AUTHOR OF *CUENTOS DE NUEVA YORK: EL PADRE QUE SE FUE Y OTROS CUENTOS* (1978), WHO TAUGHT ME THE TRADITION OVER FRANKS AND BEANS

The other side of the water
makes a figure of me. Who listens,

at dusk, now I can no longer
pretend no one is there.
—JAMESON FITZPATRICK, "Address"

CONTENTS

Acknowledgments | xi

Introduction: The Intertextual Image	1
1 The Stranger Maiden: *The Last of the Mohicans,* Shakespeare, and Milton	33
2 Incest and Intertextuality: *The House of the Seven Gables* and Milton	59
3 "To Veil Full Purpose": *The Blithedale Romance* and Shakespeare	89
4 Survivors and Stepmothers: *Moby-Dick* and *King Lear*	121
5 "Faltering in the Fight": *Pierre* and *Hamlet*	145
6 "A Jewish Aspect": *The Marble Faun* and *The Merchant of Venice*	173
Epilogue: Douglass and Influence	207

Notes | 221
Bibliography | 267
Index | 293

ACKNOWLEDGMENTS

These acknowledgements have deep roots. I must first thank the professors at CUNY Hunter who saw something in me worth encouraging and did so with love and rigor: Louise De Salvo, Jane Benardete, and Marlies K. Danziger.

In graduate school, I was fortunate to have the dissertation adviser *par excellence* in Michael T. Gilmore. Timo, I miss you every day. I also greatly benefited from working with John Burt, Wai Chee Dimock, Mary Baine Campbell, Paul Morrison, and Eugene Goodheart.

This book began its life in an issue of *The Nathaniel Hawthorne Review* that I guest-edited, "Hawthorne and Influence," *The Nathaniel Hawthorne Review* 42, no. 1 (2016): 1–15, 147. Julie Hall was as supportive an editor as one could hope for. Andrew Hadfield, Michael Jonik, Joan Curbet, Geoff Bender, Christopher Stampone, and Renée L. Bergland all contributed superb essays.

In a joint venture between the Milton Society and the Nathaniel Hawthorne Society, Ann Baynes Coiro and I cochaired a panel, "Hawthorne and Milton: Remapping Intertextuality," at the Modern Language Association Convention, Austin, January 7–10, 2016. This was a heady experience, and I thank all the superb contributors, and Ann especially. I also thank Feisal G. Mohamed for his support.

Many friends have made meaningful contributions to my thinking on this project. I thank Lina Perkins Wilder for reading the *Hamlet* portions of the chapter on *Pierre* and for her insights; I have also greatly benefited from her erudite and illuminating Shakespeare scholarship. Anne Dunlop has been an invaluable guide on art history. John Bryant has been unfailingly insightful about Melville. And Barry McCrea has given me hope that my scholarly dreams are not mine alone.

Wyn Kelley is not only a superb critic and scholar, but also one of the most genuinely giving and thoughtful people I have ever known. Words fail, but will have to suffice: my deepest thanks to you, Wyn. Maria DiBattista brought out the best in my scholarship. Christopher Ohge sounded new depths in my readings of Melville and Shakespeare. Leanna Herbert has been a superb research assistant. I thank the English department at the University of South Carolina for giving me a research leave through the Morrison Fellowship, and I thank the university for granting me a sabbatical leave in the same academic year, all of which went considerably toward allowing me to realize this project. I also humbly and deeply thank the Dean's Office, Dean Joel Samuels, Vice President for Research Prakash Nagarkatti, and my colleague and former chair as well as eminent Shakespeare scholar Nina Levine for support in completing this project.

Eric Arthur Brandt, my editor at the University of Virginia Press, has been as insightful as he has been supportive in his stewardship of the publication process. I want to thank him and the deeply thoughtful and incisive anonymous readers for their invaluable help. One could not work with a better press. I thank Fernando Campos, too, and the entire team at the press.

Throughout my years as an academic, I have counted myself fortunate when encountering like-minded and sympathetic souls. With apologies to any friends I have failed to mention, I thank the following for their kinship: Rasmus Rahbek Simonsen, Jennifer Greiman, Russell Sbriglia, Ronan Ludot-Vlasak, Monika Elbert (an editor to whom one remains forever grateful), Leland Person, Alexandra Urakova, Paul C. Jones, Jonathan Schroeder, Brenda Wineapple, Lisa Ruddick, Julie Rivkin, Jana Jennison Argersinger, Geoff Bender, Renée Bergland, Rob Tally, Wesley Scott McMasters, Brian Yothers, Matthew Rebhorn, and Dana Rilke. My life would also be considerably impoverished without the friendship of Catherine Keyser, Paul Famolari, Hunter Gardner, Thomas Lekan, John Lane, Allen Miller, Ann Poling, Marc Démont, Brian Glavey, Eleanor Stein, Yvonne Ivory, Jenny Pournelle, Jie Guo, Gretchen Woertendyke,

Tony Jarrells, David Lee Miller, Esther Gilman Richey, Michael Gavin, and Rebecca Coughlin Gavin. Special mention to esteemed Renaissance scholars David and Esther for being so inspiring in their work and our conversations. James Bogdanski and Robert Simonson, you get a shout-out of your own.

Viki Zavales and Ben Schreier are my family. Immeasurable thanks and love to them always. And thanks to Sarah Koenig for reminding me to tell Captain Picard, "Blow up the damn ship, Jean-Luc!"

My beloved parents, Florence and Oswald Greven, and maternal aunts continue to be inspirations and sources of profound love and sympathy. My eternal thanks to them all.

Deepest, most lasting, most ardent thanks go to my partner and love of my life, Alex Beecroft, now and always.

Portions of this manuscript, in earlier and often quite distinct forms, have been published in the journals *Memoria Di Shakespeare. A Journal of Shakespearean Studies*, *The Nathaniel Hawthorne Review*, *ESQ: A Journal of Nineteenth-Century American Literature and Culture*, and *The Journal of American Culture*, and in the 2002 second edition of *A New Companion to Herman Melville* in the Blackwell Companions to Literature and Culture series, edited by Wyn Kelley and Christopher Ohge. To all these journals and editors, I offer my profuse thanks.

ALL THE DEVILS ARE HERE

INTRODUCTION

THE INTERTEXTUAL IMAGE

OUR AGE IS NOT RETROSPECTIVE. We view the past through the prism of contemporary concerns, rendering it primarily useful as a forerunner to present ails. This is not the perverse presentism that some critics celebrate, but rather a normalizing one, making the past continuous with our moment through the political questions that guide, shape, and determine our relationship to what came before. When the questions are not overtly or manifestly political, they cease to get raised. Hence the moribund status of influence in nineteenth-century Americanist literary criticism, an inquiry seldom pursued because answers seem so readily available and transparent.

This book returns to influence, having faith in fresh responses. While the course of influence studies has seemed to move from the pathbreaking to the rigidly standard-bearing, I argue that influence still has something to say to us about creativity, artistic passion, and the historical emergence of American literature.

To demonstrate this claim, I consider the American Romantics' uses of Shakespeare and Milton, whose foundational works provided a template for later authors' depictions of sexual desire, gender and racial identity, and the intricate hazards of prejudice. Clearly, the reliance on British literary tradition necessarily restricted the scope of influence and reflected highly specific attitudes, so my reader may rightly wonder at the idea that dead white males taught future dead white males about identity, race, and desire. Nevertheless, that is the gist of my argument—that American Romantics, specifically James Fenimore Cooper, Nathaniel Hawthorne, and Herman Melville, modeled these forebears when it came to depictions of subjectivity, and that their relationship to them requires attention if we are to understand romanticism's representational practices.

SHAKESPEARE AND MILTON IN ANTEBELLUM AMERICA

There are numerous ways that one could productively approach the question of influence in nineteenth-century American writing. To begin with, many authors and works from the British tradition were influential.[1] Works within the European tradition such as Dante's epic *The Divine Comedy*, Cervantes's *Don Quixote*, and Goethe's *Faust* and *The Sorrows of Young Werther* were crucial as well. The classical literature that was foundational to the Western tradition seized the imaginations of a wide range of writers, especially during the antebellum period's Greek revival. And many non-Western works (Arab, Vedic, Hindu, African) were shaping forces: Emerson, Thoreau, and others made notable use of translations of the Qur'an and the Gita.[2]

Arguably, Shakespeare and Milton were the best-known and the most ardently embraced literary influences for American writers at this point. I follow critics such as F. O. Matthiessen in focusing on their significance to the making of an American literary tradition.[3] "Americans' participation in Shakespeare studies in the nineteenth century," writes Nancy Glazener, was "an important marker of national cultural achievement, an effort contributing to the American institutionalization of English literature. Responses to American texts were affected, in turn, by this sense of the literary, and American literature ultimately was installed in the academy as a 'subdiscipline' of English literary studies."[4] Maria DiBattista, in the enthralling and comprehensive introduction to the special issue she edited of the Italian publication *Memoria di Shakespeare. A Journal of Shakespearean Studies*, "American Shakespeare," locates the relevance of Shakespeare's work to issues of diversity within the work itself. Referencing Harold Bloom, she observes:

Following Dr Johnson, Bloom locates the grandeur and astonishing fecundity of Shakespeare's all-too human / superhuman art in the number of these transformations, in his "diversity of persons": "No one, before or since Shakespeare, made so many separate selves" (1). Although this claim is made in exploring Shakespeare's universalism, it reflects an American preoccupation with the allure, but also the challenge of diversity, connecting as it does the notion of a changeable and changing selfhood with the social advantages and cultural splendors of difference, of separate selves each with their individualizing language, each intent on exercising their inalienable right to pursue their own sweet (or foul, as the case may be) will.[5]

As in Victorian England, Shakespeare's progress in Victorian America was vertical: "assessments of the value of his work rose and rose";[6] his work achieved the same canonical status as the Bible.[7] Shakespeare emerged as a suitably popular hero who resonated with the masses of the United States; moreover, his works were exceedingly popular with women readers:[8] "By the nineteenth century a familiarity with Shakespeare was expected of every educated person; the sooner aspirant middle-class children could acquire such knowledge, the better."[9] Given the pervasiveness of Shakespeare's influence, it is unsurprising that American authors alluded to his works frequently. The authors discussed here submitted his schemas to a constant revision, transforming his material into fodder for their own concerns.

While Shakespeare was clearly enshrined, Milton's relevance to the American experiment, the way his work was co-opted as a model for the building of a new Edenic nation, makes him a close influential rival: "Associated with *Il Penseroso* and *Comus,* the profligate ease and pleasure pictured in *L'Allegro,* and the 'scorned delights' and serious devotion described in *Il Penseroso,* point clearly in *Comus* to the poet armed with Puritan armor."[10] Reviewing a volume of Milton's prose works edited, with a biographical introduction, by Rufus Griswold, the great Transcendentalist Margaret Fuller writes, "Mr. Griswold justly and wisely observes:—'Milton is more emphatically *American* than any author who has lived in the United States.' He is so because in him is expressed so much of the primitive vitality of that thought from which America is born ... He is the purity of Puritanism.... He is one of the Fathers of this Age ... But the Father is still far beyond the understanding of his child."[11] Fuller's presentation of Milton as a wily father whose knowingness exceeds that of his child is suggestive. K. P. Van Anglen observes that "late eighteenth-century and antebellum bourgeois novelists such as Brocken Brown, Cooper, Stowe, Hawthorne, and Melville, and poets and critics like Whittier, Lowell, and Longfellow . . . [as well as] the Transcendentalists and their predecessors (as from very different perspectives Whitman and a number of subversive female and African-American authors)" all grappled with Milton's legacy. Milton influenced "primarily as a presence who focused their thoughts and feelings on issues of authority and legitimation."[12] The Milton that I will be evoking in this book has an uncanny power to dramatize the American scene. A discrete study of Milton's complicated support for Puritanism and his influence on the development of not only American literature but also American society, while beyond the scope of this book, is a topic that hovers over it.

American Romanticism inherits British Romanticism's investments in Milton. In "The Voice of the Devil" in *The Marriage of Heaven and Hell*, William Blake famously opined, in reference to Milton's epic poem *Paradise Lost*, that the "reason Milton wrote in fetters when he wrote of angels and God and at liberty when of Devils and Hell is because he was a true poet and of the Devil's party without knowing it."[13] Blake's commentary has historically been taken as a Romantic credo, summarizing this literary movement's investments in Satan's stature as romantic rebel.[14] Versions of the influential Satan recur in American romanticism—Cooper's Huron villain Magua, Melville's antihero Ahab. As I will show, however, Milton's Eve also exerted a powerful influence. Through Satan and Eve, Milton allowed American Romantics, female and nonwhite authors included, to identify with the wronged, outcast other and with the woman striving for autonomous freedom, respectively.[15]

AMERICANIST ANXIETIES OF INFLUENCE

F. O. Matthiessen's contemporary Marius Bewley identified "the largest problem that confronted the American artist in the nineteenth century, and which still occupies him" as "the nature of his separateness, and the nature of his connection with European, and particularly with English, culture." For Bewley, the American artists who principally embodied this dynamic of grappling with American separateness were Cooper, Hawthorne, Melville, and Henry James. "They form a tradition," Bewley argues, one centered in a "finely critical consciousness of the national society," a focus on "the American scene." They were "seriously concerned with the new nation in a way that European novelists are rarely, or never, concerned with theirs."[16] The centrality of nineteenth-century American writers' engagement with literary forebears, particularly from the British literary tradition, offers a sharp contrast to Americanist literary criticism's emphases of the present, which seldom include the question of literary influence. Gay critics whose works call to my own, Matthiessen, Bewley, and Newton Arvin are my precursors. I self-consciously align myself with their goals, approaches, and example, while focusing, as they did not, on the politics of gender and sexuality as they intersect with questions of race, class, and national consciousness.[17]

All the Devils Are Here resituates these postwar critics' concerns within a transatlantic literary system that focused, however uneasily and unstably, on frequent points of exchange; it was by engaging with precursors that the American romantics found a means of capturing and critiquing the American scene. Contemporary transatlantic literary studies of the nineteenth century have illuminated these concerns but eschewed questions of influence. For example, Meredith L. McGill makes explicit the role that influence will *not* play in the collection she edits, *The Traffic in Poems: Nineteenth-Century Poetry and Transatlantic Exchange* (2008): "Studies that focus on authors' influence on one another or on transatlantic reception—the identification of American 'Wordsworths' or the study of 'Wordsworth in America'—can significantly enrich our genealogies, but they do not do much to change them.... Extended comparisons of British and American texts, such as Robert Weisbuch's *Atlantic Double-Cross* (1986) and Paul Giles's *Transatlantic Insurrections* (2001), tend to confirm the distinctiveness of the cultures they are comparing and to reinforce the idea of a national literature, if only through the evenhandedness they bring to the work of comparison."[18] In many respects, my argument adheres to her guidelines in contending that considerable overlaps exist between the British and nineteenth-century American literary traditions. I disagree, however, with her view of the inertness of influence, that it "does not do much to change" our understanding of transatlantic exchanges.

Robert Weisbuch implicitly echoes Harold Bloom and his theory of the agon, or conflict, at the heart of influence: the "keynote of Anglo-American literary relations in the mid-nineteenth century" is "enmity."[19] As I will expand upon, I do not see enmity at work in American writers' uses of British source material or, indeed, in influence generally. Certainly, anxiety was present, given the profound obstacles early American authors faced in gaining international credibility. But a more accurate term than *enmity* is *collaboration,* a sense that their precursors gave nineteenth-century authors license to reimagine. American authors shared and took in idiosyncratic directions what British literary tradition made possible.

Far from constituting a worshipful reiteration of existing themes, the American Romantics' engagement with British literary tradition was active and unpredictable, shaping the way that US authors approached representation, in particular issues of gender, sexuality, and race. And yet, influence has been ignored in Americanist literary study for some time, rarely mentioned in scholarly databases and the conference proceedings of organizations like C19 and the Futures of American Studies Institute. Ideological, archival, and historicist approaches, for all their considerable insights, have not paid sufficient attention to the aesthetic and affective dynamics of literary influence and intertextuality, though more and more scholars have begun to revisit this question. Even taking the last decade as an example, one searches contemporary scholarly treatments of nineteenth-century American literature and discovers little to no consideration of influence. For example, the collection *Turns of Event: Nineteenth-Century American Literary Studies in Motion* (2016), edited by Hester Blum, addresses the subject of "literary and cultural influences" once, within the introduction's discussion of current efforts at "canon reformation ... recognizing the artificiality and intellectual limitations of certain kinds of boundaries (whether national, political, linguistic, physiological, or temporal)," reflective of "turns" in literary study such as "the linguistic, transnational, hemispheric, postnational, spatial, temporal, religious or postsecular, aesthetic, and affective turns."[20] Similarly, *Unsettled States: America and the Long 19th Century* (2014), edited by Dana Luciano and Ivy Wilson, does not address influence (there is one reference to "aesthetics"). Even the new turn to aesthetics, focusing primarily on the reconstruction of historical milieus and their attitudes toward the aesthetic, has not taken up influence: the topic never arises in *American Literature's Aesthetic Dimensions* (2012), edited by Cindy Weinstein and Christopher Looby, despite the collection's wide-ranging purview.

Foregrounding leftist ideological critique, Americanist literary criticism avoids the topic of influence, given its associations with Harold Bloom. Gary Schmidgall's book on Whitman and British literary tradition makes ominous reference to Bloom as "the critic who must now be named."[21] Caroline Chamberlin Hellman's *Children of the Raven and the Whale* identifies Bloom's famous study *The Anxiety of Influence* as "notorious" and notes that the study of influence "was out of vogue for some time, in part owing to perceived paternalist or imperialist presumptions with regard to issues of race and gender."[22]

While opposition to Bloom is a key factor in the shunning of influence, it reflects a larger antihumanist trend. The Shakespeare scholar Neema Parvini has located this trend in academic criticism since the 1980s. In his *Shakespeare's History Plays: Rethinking Historicism* (2012), Parvini writes that antihumanist critics read Shakespeare "diagnostically, as mere products of their time and place which reflect only ideas of that time and place. This effectively limits Shakespeare's authorial agency to a set of established positions attributable to other sources in the period." Parvini argues that it is precisely what Shakespeare's critical intelligence accomplishes that the "anti-humanist modes of thought find inconceivable": "a scope for the role of the individual and individual agency in history."[23] In so writing, Parvini clarifies patterns in Americanist literary criticism.

In his 1990 study *Shakespeare's America, America's Shakespeare*, Michael D. Bristol takes humanism to task as "conservative rather than critical" because it denies "historically distant contexts" and also because it is nostalgic for "various forms of archaic repression."[24] While I recognize that one must be vigilant regarding such dangers, Bristol's argument needs to be updated (while remaining accurate as an overview of the antihumanism position). To begin with, the critique of humanism has resulted in the avoidance of topics associated with it, such as influence. Because I believe influence and intertextuality are central not only to American romanticism but to writing generally, the lack of attention paid to it is worrisome. To ignore engagements with precursors denatures and distorts literary works, rendering them cultural documents with no historical underpinnings, a strange development given the pervasive emphasis on historicism in Americanist literary theory of the present.

While I hope to revive influence as a critical question, I do not want to reinscribe the problematic cultural attitudes and practices often associated with influence and humanism.²⁵ To study influence is not inherently racist, sexist, or classist, though it can have that aim or produce that effect. To consider influence and its significance is not an explicitly and intentionally conservative act of canon-building and canon-preserving, though it can certainly be these things. To believe in a literary tradition is not implicitly to believe in a white, male, European literary tradition, though some critics have insisted precisely on that view. In revisiting the question of influence, especially in Americanist literary practice, I am reframing the question. Far from being opposed to the perspectives that have enriched criticism since the 1980s, influence intersects with them. Far from obscuring or deferring topics such as race, racism, gender, sexuality, feminism, class, queer sexuality, and homophobia, influence illuminates their presence in literary works, allowing us to see both the perpetuation of long-standing phobic attitudes and the intermittent resistance against them by authors of historical texts.

A better term than *canon* (with its distracting religious connotations) is *dialogue*. Authors are always in dialogue with one another, often across the expanses of geographical and temporal space, exchanges that John Hollander calls "intertextual echoes." As he explains, using poetry as his model, "a poem treats an earlier one as if it posed a question, and answers it, interprets it, glosses it, revises it in poetry's own way of saying, 'In other words.'" Approached this way, the history of poetry "may be said to constitute a chain of answers to the first texts—Homer and Genesis—which themselves become questions for successive generations of answerers." The answers that are provided, or better put, offered, constitute the history of literature. But this expanse narrows down to the minute particular: "Intertextual answer can often be the minute matter of a single word or scheme taken up by another writer and used significantly, particularly with respect to its original use."²⁶ Hollander helps us to understand literature as a system of question-posing and -answering, without any stipulation that the answer provided is definitive or anything but provisional. The idea that literature raises questions that subsequent literature answers (again, in the sense of "tries to answer" or provisionally answers) has a deep relevance to questions of the politics of identity. The unresolved but vital questions of an earlier work, for example its take on social conflicts, impel the answering writer to reflect on the previous writer's situation and her own. At least, such exchanges can happen. Artists' attempts to respond to, break free of, surpass, or simply simulate the work of their predecessors are endlessly fascinating, but I am specifically interested in the answer/question model reconceived as an ongoing discussion about the politics of identity.

While Americanist scholars have deemphasized influence as a topic, a similar, if also distinct concept, literariness, has gained traction.[27] In his remarks about Richard Poirier's well-known study *A World Elsewhere,* Leo Bersani writes, "Recent attempts to define the 'literarity' of literature through certain regularizing motifs, forms, and structures miss what I take to be" Poirier's central truth: "an ontology of literature must be grounded in a recognition and demonstration of language seeking to break its relations with the environments—both historical and textual—in which it is performed."[28] In responding to precursor texts, American authors found a way to ground their work in a national identity and at the same time to "break relations" with their "historical and textual environments."

INTERTEXTUAL POSSIBILITIES

While influence has lost its grip on the critical imagination, its more sophisticated, rigorous cousin, intertextuality, a concept with roots in Saussurean linguistics and coined by the leading French feminist psychoanalytic theorist, Julia Kristeva, in the 1960s, has received extensive treatment.

Kristeva introduced the term *intertextualité* in her 1966 essay "Word, Dialogue, and Novel," defining it as "a mosaic of quotations; any text is the absorption and transformation of another. The notion of *intertextuality* replaces that of intersubjectivity, and poetic language is read as at least *double.*"[29] Marjorie Garber highlights Leon Roudiez's impatience with the reception of Kristeva's term: "It has nothing to do with matters of influence by one writer on another, or with the sources of a literary work"; rather, Roudiez corrects, it involves "the components of a *textual system* such as the novel."[30] That having been said, Kristeva's 1966 essay models influence, being a nearly feverish riff on the writings of the Russian Formalist Mikhail Bakhtin.

Writing roughly two decades later, another French theorist, Michael Riffaterre, offers a quite exacting view:

Let me first anticipate and so avoid possible confusion in my terms. Some scholars glibly mistake the intertext for sources and seem to think that intertextuality is just a newfangled name for influence or imitation. We must be clear that intertext does not signify a collection of literary works that may have influenced the text or that the text may have imitated. . . . In contrast, intertextuality is not just a perception of homologues or the cultivated reader's apprehension of sameness or difference. Intertextuality is not a felicitous surplus, the privilege of a good memory or a classical education. The term indeed refers to an operation of the reader's mind, but it is an obligatory one, necessary to any textual decoding. Intertextuality necessarily complements our experience of textuality. It is the perception that our reading of the text cannot be complete or satisfactory without going through the intertext.[31]

Linda Hutcheon, in her well-known essay "Literary Borrowing," parses Riffaterre thusly: "from the perspective of a theory of intertextuality, the experience of literature consists only of a text, a reader, and his or her reactions that take the form of systems of words, which are grouped associatively into the reader's mind. . . . the locus of textual appropriation is the reader, and not the author." Hutcheon doubles down on this Barthesian position: "Texts do not come to life, texts do not generate anything—until they are read."[32]

Jay Clayton and Eric Rothstein, in "Figures in the Corpus," the introductory essay to their reader *Influence and Intertextuality in Literary History* (1991), identify influence as "a literary history about agents" and intertextuality as "a literary history of meshing systems," noting that the terms "preside more as rival subjugators in various kinds of commentary than as co-workers in a continuous, flexible scheme."[33] While appreciatively noting Roland Barthes's theory of intertextuality in *S/Z*, Clayton and Rothstein add a cautionary note: "The infinite circularity of codes makes every text, potentially, the intertext for every other text."[34] Following Clayton and Rothstein, I use *influence* to refer to the overall question of texts having an impact on other texts, and intertextuality to refer to the complex dynamic among texts across time, cultures, and related phenomena. Caroline Chamberlin Hellman, addressing Bloom's "notorious" stances, notes in *Children of the Raven and the Whale* that it is possible to view both influence and intertextuality "through a less defensive lens."[35] She works within the parameters of intertextuality rather than influence, focusing on writers such as Chang-Rae Lee, Jhumpa Lahiri, Ta-Nehisi Coates, and Junot Díaz and their reception of canonical nineteenth-century American authors. Hellman notes that influence "supposes conscious borrowing from a master author, dominant source text, or tradition, whereas intertextuality is less concerned with hierarchies of textual relations." Some scholars use the terms *influence* and *intertextuality* interchangeably, as Hellman observes, and my approach reflects this, given that I find both terms equally useful. That said, influence is irreducibly at the heart of this psychoanalytically inflected book. I emphasize the affective, personal aspects of both the scene of writing and the experience of reading. Taking Marjorie Garber's lead, I encourage us to allow "influence to flourish—we might even say, to bloom."[36]

Graham Allen links Harold Bloom's influence theory to intertextuality: "Bloom's characteristic method of reading involves an intertextual assessment of the patterns of misreading" active in comparisons between a studied poem and its precursor texts. "Bloom's intense awareness of canonical literature opens this procedure out into a wider framework," one that "includes the precursor's own misreading of previous figurative patterns."[37] This last point demands emphasis. The study of influence extends beyond the writer being studied—it impinges on the precursor's own work, activating its distinctive patterns of disturbance and contingency, allowing us to see the studied work *and* its precursors in a mutually illuminating relation. As Paul H. Fry, blending Bloom and T. S. Eliot, puts it in his *Theory of Literature* (2012), the key aspect of the relationship between tradition and the individual talent "is that it reconstitutes tradition. It doesn't just innovate. It makes us see tradition itself in a different way. . . . it's a dynamic, mutual relationships that exists between tradition and the individual talent *or* between the strong precursor and the belated poet that seems to be in play."[38]

Marko Juvan (originally writing in Slovenian) describes intertextuality thusly in his *History and Poetics of Intertextuality* (2008): "Intertextuality is essentially a cross-cultural phenomenon linking together not only one national literature with other—including marginal, peripheral—literatures and cultures, but also, within a given semiosphere, mainstream literary production with its past, forgotten forms, and marginal, subaltern, or emergent subsystems; finally, intertextuality structures the text's affiliation and response to its cultural contexts—of other arts, social discourses (from politics to science), sociolects, ideologies, ways of living, and media."[39] The wide-ranging engagement with literary forms is not bound to but, if anything, liberated by temporality in intertextuality. The more we begin to understand intertextuality *and* influence as dynamic and cross-cultural and deeply various, even if the influenced and the influencing texts are recognizably Anglo-American and European, the closer we will be to a new theory of influence as the study of the series of exchanges, challenges, provocations, and reworkings inherent in the creation of the literary (in this case, certainly, and the same principles apply to other forms of representation).

Influence studies can facilitate the recognition of literary deep time, the central concept of Wai Chee Dimock's book *Through Other Continents*, which refers to the residues, traces, and repositories of older literary cultures, sometimes quite ancient ones, in modern literary works. Influence studies enable a productive merger between formalism and historicism, long seen as fundamentally opposed, an opposition maintained, until recently, by warring critical camps. As Rónán McDonald writes in the introduction to *The Values of Literary Studies: Critical Institutions, Scholarly Agendas* (2015), "a generation ago formalism was seen as an ideologically naïve approach to literary studies and close textual study the preferred method of the reactionary criticism that occluded the politics and exclusionary discourses of written texts. Now diverse scholars are challenging the antagonism traditionally asserted between historicism and formalism."[40] McDonald, drawing on the work of Jacques Rancière and Derek Attridge, points to the "new attempt to engage with the literary as a category, while also maintaining faith with the inextricability of literary works from historical formations."[41] Influence contributes to this new framework.

Despite the seeming indifference or hostility to the topic, a growing body of new work on influence has emerged: Michaela Bronstein's *Out of Context: The Uses of Modernist Fiction* (2018); *Alan Hollinghurst: Writing Under the Influence* (2016), edited by Michèle Mendelssohn and Denis Flannery; and *Katherine Mansfield and Literary Influence* (2015), edited by Sarah Ailwood and Melinda Harvey. Studies published in the last decade of most relevance to *All the Devils Are Here* include Reginald Wilburn's *Preaching the Gospel of Black Revolt: Appropriating Milton in Early African American Literature* (2014); Caroline Chamberlin Hellman's *Children of the Raven and the Whale* (2019), an examination of the impact of nineteenth-century American authors on contemporary multiethnic ones; Daniel Hack's *Reaping Something New: African American Transformations of Victorian Literature* (2017); Gary Schmidgall's *Containing Multitudes: Walt Whitman and the British Literary Tradition* (2014); *Transatlantic Women: Nineteenth-Century American Women Writers and Great Britain*, edited by Beth Lynne Lueck, Brigitte Bailey, and Lucinda L. Damon-Bach (2012); Páraic Finnerty's *Emily Dickinson's Shakespeare* (2008); and Renée Bergland's essay "Emily Dickinson 'In the Other's Eyes—,'" published in *Women's Studies* (2018). I edited a special issue of the *Nathaniel Hawthorne Review* from 2016, "Hawthorne and Influence: Reframing Tradition."[42] Promisingly and excitingly, a 2022 edition of *Leviathan: A Journal of Melville Studies*, guest-edited by the French scholars Ronan Ludot-Vlasak, Édouard Marsoin, and Cécile Roudeau, focuses on Melville's "intertextual veerings" among other topics.

INTERTEXTUAL DESIRE

Kevin Ohi notes of Shakespeare's valedictory play *The Tempest*, "The question of Prospero's power... is also the question of the play's relation to literary tradition. Prospero's power need not be understood as purely invidious, just as it need not be understood as purely redemptive."[43] The doubleness, neutrality, or irresolvability of Prospero's status allegorizes several themes within the present study. First, the precursor text is always itself under pressure from its position within literary tradition, its own unstable properties and unresolved conflicts. Second, the strong poet who grapples with the precursor text does not relieve this text of its inherent difficulties or conflicts; much less does the strong poet produce a work free of these. Rather than a Bloomian agon, an intergenerational oedipal conflict, the strong poet maintains something of a meditative and contemplative relationship to the precursor; rather than an agon, ambivalence inheres within the act of influencing and revision, the translation of a prior's work's character or qualities into a present idiom. The term that Ohi favors for this process is not *influence* but "transmission." Specifically, he refers to "queer transmission," defined as "the transmission... of a minority queer culture, of the modes through which queer forms of life and specialized knowledge move from generation to generation." How does this happen in a culture "inhospitable to queer forms of life," and how do "texts encode queer meaning in contexts that often forbid explicit mention of queer concerns"?[44]

Engaging with Ohi's concerns, *All the Devils Are Here* explores the intersections among identity and influence in the making of American literature. Feminist, anti-racist, and queer perspectives intersect in this endeavor. Encounters with precursor texts and the desire to reimagine their visions; impulses to inhabit and discover oneself in the precursor text and to convey this discovered self in a new literary form: these are dynamics I call *intertextual desire*.[45] This dynamic can be studied in myriad ways; my effort in this book is to consider the implications of intertextual desire for literary depictions of gender, sexuality, and race. I seek to illuminate and evoke what the intertextual moment yields in terms of gendered, sexual, and racial representation. Influence accrues a radical potentiality when considered, as it should be, a key element in the depiction of otherness and the vexations of difference, never more vexing than to the historical white Protestant author contemplating the specters of nonwhite and non-Protestant identity.

BLOOM AND AMERICAN ROMANCE: MISREADING AND BELATEDNESS

Bloom's concepts of *misprision* (misreading) and *belatedness* are useful for the main subject of this book: a discussion of the centrality of Shakespeare and Milton to the development of the form of American romance, in formal terms and regarding depictions of gender, sexuality, and race. As indicated by the furor they continued to generate at the time of his death, Bloom's ideas and political positions remain controversial. My use of Bloom's paradigms should not be taken as an endorsement of his larger political attitudes (or personal behavior). Writing as a multiracial gay man whose parents are immigrants and working-class, I am hardly inclined to support Bloom's race-baiting provocations, misogyny, or elitism. Along the same lines of difficulty, the Freudian sensibility I bring to bear on my study of influence does not imply an adoption of all of Freud's ideas, especially regarding female sexuality.[46] Reading Bloom and Freud reparatively, I propose a theory of influence that speaks to its sexual politics, which stem from its foundational qualities as a narcissistic encounter haunted by belatedness. The basis of my reparative approach is Eve Kosofsky Sedgwick's model of reparative reading, her essay "Paranoid Reading and Reparative Reading; or, You're So Paranoid, You Probably Think This Introduction

Is about You," drawn from the work of the psychoanalyst Melanie Klein. (Sedgwick explicitly challenged the hermeneutics of suspicion—in a word, paranoia—in queer theory, leading some theorists to dissent.[47]) Sedgwick notes that "among Klein's names for the reparative process is love."[48] Given that on many levels what I foreground here is a love for the texts under study, Sedgwick's model seems especially apt.

As I will have frequent opportunities to note, Milton's Satan is, for Harold Bloom, the definition of the strong poet, strenuously fighting against belatedness. If this is so, several episodes in *Paradise Lost* are germane to a theory of literary influence and American romantic literature's relationship to British literary tradition. In book 4 of Milton's epic, Satan, expulsed from Heaven and curious about the wondrous new creatures God has created and given dominion over the earth, stares at the human pair Adam and Eve. Named as such, the grief in Satan's reaction to their prelapsarian beauty is palpable:

> O Hell! What do mine eyes with grief behold . . .
> Not Spirits, yet to heavenly spirits bright
> Little inferior; whom my thoughts pursue
> With wonder, and could love, so lively shines
> In them divine resemblance (4.358–64)[49]

These nonangelic creatures have been given the right to reflect God, which wounds the fallen angel who once enjoyed the status of being the morning star, yet Satan confesses that he "could love" them, "so lively shines / In them Divine resemblance." Saying that their happy days are numbered due to his infiltration of their realm, Satan notes that he could pity them even though he is himself "unpitied: league with you I seek, / And mutual amity so strait, so close, / That I with you must dwell, or you with me / Henceforth" (4.374–780). Heather Love, in *Feeling Backward*, insightfully frames Satan as an important queer figure, embodying the "intimate link between defiance and abjection."[50]

"Throughout *Paradise Lost*," Lacey Conley argues, "Satan uses artful rhetoric to create relationships with other characters. He manipulates language to convince them that to join in 'league' with him will be mutually advantageous—but this is, of course, never the case. Through offers of flattery and false hope, the Fiend employs the rebel angels, Sin, Chaos, and finally Eve in his futile mission to frustrate God's omnipotence."[51] Giving the fallen archangel's duplicity its full due, we can nevertheless recognize in Satan an ardent, transgressive desire for connection with forbidden objects, creations made by and belonging to the ultimate original author, God, the strong poet Satan's chief adversary. If we read Satan and God as rival authors, we can read Satan's league-seeking with Adam and Eve as a testament of desperate longing to influence them as they—and he, however intransigently resistant—are influenced by their author-creator. This is to suggest that in warring against the precursor, the strong poet seeks not to overthrow the precursor but to see themselves in the precursor's image. Milton extends this allegory when Eve, in the narrative she gives of her nativity in book 4, beholds her own image in the water and is instantly beguiled by it. *Paradise Lost* has a special poignancy for any theory of literary influence. As I will discuss, both Satan and, especially, Eve plangently figure influence, the longing to see one's own image in the precursor's original.

At the heart of Bloom's theory of influence is the oedipal battle waged by "strong poets," those who "wrestle with their strong precursors, even to the death."[52] Poetic influence goes beyond "source-study," "the history of ideas," and "the patterning of images"; instead, "poetic misprision," Bloom's preferred term, "is necessarily the study of the life-cycle of the poet-as-poet."[53] Misprision chiefly takes six forms: *clinamen*, the poet's "swerve" away from the dominating precursor; *tessera*, the process through which a poet "antithetically 'completes' his precursor"; *kenosis*, "a movement towards discontinuity with the precursor"; *daemonization*, a complex means of creating a "Counter-Sublime" in which the poet assimilates the precursor's work into "a range of being just beyond [the] precursor" in order to "generalize away the uniqueness of the earlier work"; *askesis*, a "self-purgation" that impinges on the precursor's work as well, rendering it similarly "truncated"; and *apophrades*, "or the return of the dead": in the poet's last phase, "the poem is now held open to the precursor," a more deliberate gesture of openness than the earlier phase in which the poem simply "*was* open." This gesture produces an "uncanny effect." The "later poet" seems to have "written the precursor's characteristic work."[54] Bloom argues that most readings of poetry fall under the category of *clinamen*, being "more or less creative or interesting mis-readings."[55] Indeed, any poem is its poet's "deliberate misinterpretation, as a poet, of a precursor poem or of poetry in general."[56] Hence Bloom's famous theory of the poet's agon, or conflict, with the precursor.

A "strong misreading," an especially forceful swerve, creates something distinctively the poet's own. Clearly, Bloom's masculinist biases need to be challenged—the royal "He" dominates his prose and thought. But the core ideas remain valuable. Indeed, it is worth considering that what may be Bloom's most ingenious critical insight, his early emphasis on the *clinamen*, has been popularized not by him but by his chief rival Shakespeare-idolater Stephen Greenblatt, in his immensely successful 2011 book *The Swerve: How the World Became Modern*.[57]

While describing Bloom's criticism as "bracing" and "rousing," Gary Schmidgall in his study *Whitman and British Literary Tradition* concludes that Bloom is "deeply un-Whitmanic in the negativity of his vocabulary."[58] Schmidgall's reasons for concluding that *The Anxiety of Influence* does not offer the right critical paradigm for studying Whitman is worth considering since my study takes the opposite view: "[The strong poet] must indulge in *misprision, misreading, mistaking / taking amiss,* and *misinterpretation.* [Bloom's] pivotal interchapter begins with the notion that 'to imagine is to misinterpret' (93). Bloom's reiteration a few pages later—'poetry is misunderstanding, misinterpretation, misalliance' (95)—seems utterly at odds with... Whitman[, who] thought a great poet's work was to strike up for a new kind of poet and poetry; why need it be seen as an act of misprision?"[59] American authors such as Cooper, Hawthorne, and Melville joined Shakespeare and Milton in working within the formal category of the romance. American writers, in developing the romance as a distinctively American form, were using the romance elements in Shakespeare and Milton (and other precursors such as Spenser and Walter Scott) as a foundation. That they did so vexes the question of misprision being inapplicable to their efforts to produce "a new kind of" American writing. It was precisely by working within the tradition already established by Shakespeare and Milton and offering strong misreadings of these precursors, reworking and reimagining preexisting themes and materials and adapting them to their national idiom, that the American romancers created the American Newness.

Paul H. Fry glosses Bloom on belatedness: "once the belated text is written by a strong poet, we can never read the precursor text in the same way again." To take the example of "Tintern Abbey," Wordsworth's revision of Milton's poem "Lycidas," "Wordsworth's strong misreading of the precursor text is so powerful" in Bloom's view that "it becomes our own strong misreading. We just can't think about 'Lycidas' in the same way after we've read 'Tintern Abbey.'" The belated poet has "an organic priority" because the belated poet asserts "I am doing something new, I'm going where no one has gone before."[60] Fry continues: "the strong precursor emphasizes a rhetoric of literal originality, in the sense of being first, while acknowledging that earlier poets have always already said everything." For Bloom, tradition and the innovation of tradition are both equally important (and in this manner Bloom's theory accords with T. S. Eliot's views even if Bloom frames his work in opposition to Eliot's).[61]

In *A Map of Misreading*, Bloom identifies Milton's romantic rebel Satan in *Paradise Lost*, who refuses to believe that God is prior to him and vengefully vows to undermine God's rule, as the prototypical strong poet who chafes against the "psychology of belatedness." Satan's strategy is "to become a rival creator to God-as-creator. He embraces Sin as his Muse, and begets upon her the highly original poem of Death, the only poem that God will permit him to write." The triad of Satan-Eve-Death inhabits Nathaniel Hawthorne's characterological schema in *The House of the Seven Gables*, as I discuss in chapter 2. Bloom, always with an eye on American belatedness, identifies Ralph Waldo Emerson and Emily Dickinson as Americans who wrote in a nation "that needed, for a while, to battle against the European exhaustions of history." Dickinson, an Emersonian heretic against orthodoxy, "recognized in Satan a distinguished precursor gallantly battling against the psychology of belatedness."[62] Bloom identifies Milton as an incomparable poet by nature of the "intensity of [his] self-consciousness as an artist," one who was in "direct competition with Homer, Virgil, Lucretius, Ovid, Dante and Tasso," a competitiveness that brought him "very close to Spenser," who exerts an immense influence on *Paradise Lost*.[63] For our purposes, here is Bloom's most relevant finding: "The Romantic tradition differs vitally from earlier forms of tradition, and I think this difference can be reduced to a useful formula. Romantic tradition is consciously late, and Romantic literary psychology is therefore necessarily a psychology of belatedness." A "guilt of belatedness haunts" American literature, Bloom argues, as evinced (pace Gary Schmidgall) by Walt Whitman's attempt to "follow" Emerson by "[striking] up for a new world."[64]

A Map of Misreading situates Freud's concept of the primal scene as crucial to literary influence. Recasting the Freudian primal scene as "The Scene of Instruction," Bloom discusses "Milton's Satan, who remains the greatest really Modern or Post-Enlightenment poet in the language": "The ultimate Scene of Instruction is described by Raphael in book V of *Paradise Lost*, where God proclaims to the Angels that 'This day I have begot whom I declare / My only son' and provocatively warns that 'him who disobeys / Mee disobeys . . . / and . . . falls / Into utter darkness.' We can describe this as an imposition of psychology of belatedness, and Satan, like any strong poet, declines to be merely a latecomer" (37). The position of the writer who attempts to enter and remake tradition in her own image, however much one resists the political entrapments of the Bloomian agon, inevitably corresponds to the latecomer's status. While this is inevitably to succumb to the kind of fallen readings Stanley Fish consistently warns against from his early to his most recent work on Milton, I argue that the lingering, languorous regard for the beauty of the image of the self, usually but not always refracted through the image of the Divine Maker (crucially in this regard, Eve longs for her own image independent of God or Adam's seeming presence within it), makes of the latecomer something of the one who got there first.

I discuss Satan as a cohesive figure and symbol for Cooper, whose villain Magua in *The Last of the Mohicans* closely resembles Satan in being sinister and sympathetic at once; and the deeply influential confrontation among Satan, Sin, and Death in book 2 of *Paradise Lost*, for Hawthorne. Moreover, while the titular protagonist of *King Lear* looms large in my discussion of *Moby-Dick*, Melville's Ahab, in his grandiloquence and a perpetual attitude of revolt, is always already haunted and shaped by Satan. As I will have frequent opportunities to discuss, Milton's Eve is an equally resonant, impelling, and defining figure for American romance. Her description of her nativity, of initially becoming entranced by her own image and being disciplined into normative heterosexual desire by Adam and God, provides a powerful allegorical basis for American romantic writers' own narcissistic encounters with precursor texts where they discover their own image, an allegory given articulation in Melville's *Moby-Dick* and *Pierre*. Cooper's heroine Cora, Hawthorne's Hepzibah and Alice Pyncheon, and Melville's Isabel all proceed from an Eve-like basis. Moreover, Eve's encounter with Satan in the guise of a seductive serpent provides a powerful model of submission to influence.

To recapitulate, I do not theorize the interactions between antebellum authors and their British precursors as a Bloomian agon, an oedipal battle between the precursor and his influenced and rebellious literary son. By emphasizing, as I do, influence as a narcissistic encounter, I am consciously eschewing the patriarchal, oedipal cast of Bloom's thought and emphasizing its queer potentialities, rooted in narcissism and melancholia. Bloom's central idea of an anxiety within the scene of influence retains a resonance for thinking about the nineteenth century's forging of a distinctively American literature through a sustained engagement with the long-standing British model. Antebellum authors' anxieties, however, stemmed less from oedipal battles and more from the particulars of the American scene: the difficulties of getting American literature noticed at all and the lack of commercial success their art-fictions encountered. When these authors were undertaking efforts to put American literature on the map, the very idea of an American literature struck some commentators as ludicrous. The English clergyman Sydney Smith's infamous screed against the United States in his 1820 review of Adam Seybert's *Annals of the United States* is characteristic of the bewilderment and scorn the emergent American writer faced: "In the four quarters of the globe, who reads an American book? Or goes to an American play? or looks at an American picture or statue?"[65] A network of material anxieties shaped the creation of a distinctively American literary art, a set of obstacles ranging from cultural hierarchy to piracy to mainstream indifference.[66]

Far from being hampered by anxiety, antebellum authors were impelled to defy elitist standards that they associated with Europe. They viewed Europe's vaunted links to tradition and history as a hindrance to present-day achievement, contentions shared and prominently registered in print by Emerson and Melville especially. In terms of American opposition to European cultural hegemony, Emerson's rhetoric in his 1837 lecture "The American Scholar" is exemplary: "We have listened too long to the courtly muses of Europe.... We will walk on our own feet; we will work with our own hands; we will speak our own minds. The study of letters shall be no longer a name for pity, for doubt, and for sensual indulgence." Melville's review "Hawthorne and His Mosses" simultaneously likens Hawthorne to Shakespeare, claims the American author as nearly the Bard's equal, and expresses a rivalrous distance from English literary tradition.[67]

One might argue that antebellum authors shared their British counterparts' anxiety about posterity.[68] But their chief anxiety was related to making American literature happen in the present. In terms of encountering precursor texts and making use of them as foundations for a new literary tradition, antebellum authors vigorously accepted the challenge to add their links to the "long chain" of influence, as John Hollander has described it.[69]

NARCISSISM, MELANCHOLIA, AND INFLUENCE

The oedipal cast of Bloom's theory has helped to imprison it within its late-adopted carapace of ideological intolerance. Freud's metapsychological articles "On Narcissism: An Introduction" (1914) and "Mourning and Melancholia" (1917 [1915]), written at an extraordinarily fraught moment in world history, disrupt the Bloomian agon. I argue that influence has a narcissistic and melancholic basis.

Freud distinguished mourning, or traditional grief, from melancholia, a mourning without end. One of several possible strategies that the melancholic ego pursues to compensate for loss is to masquerade as the lost, still-desired object. Love me, whispers the ego to the bereft id, I am so much like the object. Certain aspects of this emotional strategy inhere in influence, which might be said to offer a counterlure, leading the writer to find themselves, their image, in that of the precursor. Influence is an inherently melancholic process. The writer of the present attempts to create out of her own work an object that mimics and simulates the contours and qualities of the precursor and solicits the reader with the promise that this new work is attractively similar to that of the precursor.[70] Melancholic separateness allows for—rather than requires or produces—an empathy for the estranged, because the writer, call her a strong poet or a belated poet or simply an author, occupies a position of cultural and temporal estrangement simply by writing *after* the precursor, whose work holds a value meaningful enough to be influential.

Influence is a narcissistic encounter, the strong poet's intertextual desire to locate their own image in the face of the precursor. When the strong poet encounters a precursor, her response, strategy, entanglement, is not to wrestle down and defeat the precursor—not necessarily this—but rather to discover her image in the face of the precursor's work. The strong poet's effort to write proceeds from the narcissistic basis of finding their like within the precursor, rather than in trying to overthrow the precursor. This proposition immediately evokes Lacan's theory of the mirror stage, wherein the child, with an encouraging mother behind them and prodding them on, sees themselves in the image of the mirror and mistakes that illusion for an image of wholeness.[71] The scene of influence is not immune to the anxieties inherent in the mirror stage.[72] Nor is the mirror stage synonymous with narcissism. If we imagine the strong poet using the precursor as mirror, we evoke both the mirror stage and the mythic basis of psychoanalytic theories of narcissism, Narcissus mesmerized by his reflected image.

The question of the image immediately intersects with feminist and queer concerns. Women's relationship to the image has been well documented, to say the least, a cultural history we address in chapter 2.[73] In terms of the Narcissus myth, it has had a particularly powerful resonance for gay male sexuality, as has also been well documented, within a continuum of uses of the myth as expressive of gendered subjectivity and the problematic relationship between self and desire. As outlined in chapter 2, narcissism and incest work together as figures for intertextuality in literary tradition.

While Satan's mighty rebellion against a patriarchal God in *Paradise Lost*—his refusal to believe that he is belated, made by God and thus secondary—powerfully underscores Bloom's concept of belatedness, another episode from the same work speaks to the melancholic and narcissistic dimensions of influence, Eve's own account of her birth in book 4. To evoke the narcissistic and melancholic qualities of influence is to suggest that the scene of writing while engaging with the precursor is one of languorous self-reflection, a self-lulling contemplation of the self as image within the prior text.

As Jeffrey S. Shoulson observes of Eve's nativity, it

> plays out the virtually irresolvable conflict between two divergent sides of Milton's creative and interpretive inclinations. As she reflects on her image in the pool, Eve stands as the figure for imagination, and hence self-generated thought. But the warning voice, never fully identified, represents divine inspiration reinscribing sexuality—specifically female sexuality—within a larger authoritative framework of biblical stricture. Milton has the opportunity to pose simultaneously as the playful, imaginative spectator, having his origins in the feminized classical texts of Ovid, and as the authoritative, inspired law-giver, whose antecedents are to be found in the biblical text.[74]

Eve refers to her first moments of life as "that day I oft remember, when from sleep / I first awak't" (4.449–50). As she narrates, she came into consciousness and immediately felt disoriented, "much wondring where / And what I was" (4.451–52). Exploring her surroundings, she discovers the source of the sounds of running water emanating from a cave and spreading out into a "Plain," a "Smooth Lake, that to me seemed another Skie" (4.459). She stares into the lake:

> As I bent down to look, just opposite,
> A Shape within the watry gleam appeard
> Bending to look on me, I started back,
> It started back, but pleas'd I soon returnd,
> Pleas'd it returnd as soon with answering looks
> Of sympathie and love; there I had fixt
> Mine eyes till now, and pin'd with vain desire,
> Had not a voice thus warnd me. (4.460–67)

What this mysterious voice, presumably that of God, warns her is that "What thou seest, / What there thou seest fair Creature is thy self" (4.467–68). Eve is in imminent danger of falling in love with herself. Memorably and ambiguously, Eve in the present observes of her past actions, "what could I doe, / But follow strait, invisibly thus led?" (4.475–76). The person to whom she is led is Adam, whom she finds "less winning soft, less amiablie milde, / Then that smooth watry image; back I turnd," (4.479–80), to which she attempts to return, only to be warned now by Adam, who cries out, "Return faire Eve."

In *Milton's Eve* (1983), Diane Kelsey McColley argues that "the scene in which Eve is tempted to prefer herself to Adam is a textual remedy for a narcissistic reading of the poem," a warning to us that we should not fall in love with the watery image of ourselves we see reflected in the Smooth Lake of the poem.[75] Milton's revision of the Latin poet Ovid's depiction of Narcissus in book 3 of *The Metamorphoses* both typifies and heightens Milton's intertextual sensibility, on such consistent and description-defying display in *Paradise Lost*. Ovid's story of Narcissus contains the story of Echo, a poignant female character stripped of her autonomous voice and pining, in her own fashion, with vain desire for the beautiful boy in love with his own reflection in the water. She mirrors his abject frustration and witnesses his pining despair in the face of an impossible desire and unreachable object.

Feminist scholars have found much to discuss in both poets' depictions of Narcissus as well as in Freud's interpretation of female narcissism; Kaja Silverman and Sara Kofman have located a surprising possibility for female agency in Freud's figure of the narcissistic woman who can wield some control over the sexual sphere of appearances and surfaces.[76] Drawing on Jane Gallop's analysis of the Lacanian resonances in the story of Adam and Eve's fall in Genesis, Lee Edelman has explored the complexities of Eve's narcissism in *Paradise Lost,* establishing the episode as richly suggestive for queer theory, especially given the cultural pathologization of homosexuality as narcissistic. As he outlines, the text contrasts Eve's and Adam's narcissisms, figuring hers as pathological. In a particularly incisive interpretation, he writes, "Eve's narcissism, justly so called since it alludes to Narcissus, must be sacrificed to legitimize, or at least to obscure, what the text seems to want us *not* to construe as *Adam's* narcissism." Eve's narcissism is "characterized pejoratively as antithetical to Adam's—much as gay sexuality is characterized, both in psychoanalytic discourse and in the Western imagination, as narcissistic and therefore as structurally distinct from heterosexual eros." While Edelman and I have points of disagreement about psychoanalytic theory, especially when he links queer sexuality to the death drive in his later work, his main point about the queer resonances of this Miltonic episode are well-taken.[77]

TOWARD A MELVILLIAN-MILTONIC THEORY OF INFLUENCE

Unlike Hawthorne, who in his two collections of Greek myth retold for children never even mentions Narcissus by name, Melville explicitly does so, in a queer-forward manner, in *Moby-Dick:*

> Why is almost every robust healthy boy with a robust healthy soul in him, at some time or other crazy to go to sea? Why upon your first voyage as a passenger, did you yourself feel such a mystical vibration, when first told that you and your ship were now out of sight of land? Why did the old Persians hold the sea holy? Why did the Greeks give it a separate deity, and own brother of Jove? Surely all this is not without meaning. And still deeper

the meaning of that story of Narcissus, who because he could not grasp the tormenting, mild image he saw in the fountain, plunged into it and was drowned. But that same image, we ourselves see in all rivers and oceans. It is the image of the ungraspable phantom of life; and this is the key to it all.[78]

Melville figures the scene of influence and intertextuality as homoerotic tableau: a "robust healthy boy" offers a fitting and suggestive counterpart to Narcissus, a mythic icon frequently depicted as a smooth, lithe, contemplative slender youth. Melville's contemporaries certainly did so, even depicting him as a sensual boy, as the Welsh sculptor John Gibson does in his 1838 sculpture, and as William Theed the Younger does in a similar incarnation. (Queen Victoria purchased Theed's 1845 sculpture of Narcissus in 1847 and placed it in the Principal Corridor, Osborne; it now resides at Buckingham Palace.) The Melvillian rough falls prey to the image of Narcissus fixated by his own image, their frisson producing a "mystical vibration." Customarily, Melville injects a quality of the sacred, establishing the sea as a site of reverence for the "old Persians," linking the Narcissus myth to the Zoroastrian beliefs of the Parsee Fedallah (the Parsees being Persians who settled in India and retain their Zoroastrian heritage). Extending the homoerotic and homosocial associations, the narrator reminds us that the Greeks deified the sea, implicitly identifying Poseidon as this deity and the "own brother of Jove." Narcissus and all his associations provide the "still deeper" meaning, not just of Narcissus but also his "story" of self-fixation unto death.

Ovid's definitive account of Narcissus (*Metamorphoses*, 3.339–510) provides Melville's intertext. He read the "Garth translation" translated by John Dryden, Alexander Pope, Joseph Addison, William Congreve, "And Other Eminent Hands"; Addison translated book 3, which includes the Narcissus story. In Ovid, Narcissus, even on his way to the underworld, cannot resist staring at his image in the river Styx. As Addison translates it, "Then on th'wholesome earth he gasping lyes, / 'Till death shuts up those self-admiring eyes. / To the cold shades his flitting ghost retires, / And in the Stygian waves it self admires" (3.621–24).[79] Melville theorizes the cause of Narcissus's death as an inability to "grasp" something, explicitly the "tormenting, mild image" that fixates him, implicitly the meanings of his own myth. Because the Melvillian Narcissus cannot grasp the "ungraspable phantom of life," and of his own desire, he entombs himself in the fountain of his own fascination, into which he "plunged . . . and was drowned," new details Melville adds.

Bloom's focus on Satan in *Paradise Lost* as the key figure for influence is understandable, but it is Eve's self-mesmerized image-encounter that rivets the American romantics, who devise key episodes where female and male characters encounter their own image with mingled desire and dread. Cora Munro sees a version of herself in villainous Magua's face, the telltale "rich blood" they share seeping through their visages; Alice Pyncheon experiences the sternest form of male rebuke of her desire to look in *The House of the Seven Gables;* Isabel Banford in Melville's *Pierre* falls prey to the siren-call of self-reflection. Intertextually echoing Milton's Narcissus-like Eve, Isabel recalls having stared at her reflection in a smooth lake when she was a girl. She then sees that reflected image of herself in the face of the man who speaks the word "Father" to her and that she is made to feel is her father (*Pierre,* 124).[80] When Pierre brings Isabel and Lucy into an art gallery and they discover a portrait of a man that recalls the image of Pierre's father—"A stranger's head, by an unknown hand," Isabel exclaims—"'My God! see! see!' cried Isabel, under strong excitement, 'only my mirror has ever shown me that look before! See! see!'" (349–50). Isabel's ability to look upon herself and other objects of desire faces the challenge of patriarchal control and censure, just as Alice Pyncheon's does. In the same work, Hepzibah Pyncheon's ability to look with desire faces a different, not unrelated challenge, the prohibition placed on her desiring looking by the ban of incest, given that the object of her gaze is her brother, the forlorn, ghostly Clifford. Hepzibah's vigilant lonely gaze conveys that sense of interminable mourning and longing that Freud would later identify as melancholia. Though providing a melancholic model of the intertextual image, Milton revising Ovid just as Melville revises Milton and Ovid, Eve's encounter with her image, defined by its punitive outcome, places a prohibition on melancholia, disallowing her to linger over her alluring reflection, correcting her languorous languishing as soon as it commences.

To recapitulate, influence is not enmity. It is not an agon. Rather, it is a contemplative collaboration, a reverie of self and text that allows for and is created through sustained immersion in and lingering attention to the object that is the precursor. Influence encompasses event and duration, the event being the encounter with the precursor, duration being the encounter's experience.

Let me hasten to add, and by doing so to acknowledge, that a tremendous dearth of feminist agency inheres in the examples I have given, though not in the theory of influence as narcissistic and melancholic lingering over the precursor-image. To begin with, the crucial figure of Echo demands analysis and must be incorporated into any discussion of Narcissus. Knitting together a dazzling range of figures—Derrida, Wilde, Rilke, Lou Andreas-Salomé, Derek Jarman—Elizabeth Richmond-Garza revisits the Narcissus myth and its theoretical elaborations for the purposes of theorizing translation. Parsing Derrida's commentaries on Echo's role, she writes, "Derrida's Ovid creates a myth of two lovers, both blinded by language, whose love story is that of language itself, love of the self and of the other respectively. For Derrida, Echo's repetition is actually a voicing of herself, made possible by the incorporation of the *différance* of the other. Her love translates the other into the self and reveals the other that is already present, just as all translations are supplements, changing both the original (since they are always nonequivalent) and the target language (adding to its intertextual and semiotic fields)."[81] While my argument here is not focused on the issue of translation, I believe that these findings dovetail with my concerns. In this parsing of Derrida, I recognize a thematic similar to my theory of influence: Echo's "love translates the other into the self and reveals the other that is already present." Which is to say, the strong poet writes from the position of Echo, contemplating Narcissus and incorporating him, revealing him as already present within herself.

As I do, Eyal Peretz disputes the oedipal cast of Bloom's theory: "[The] drama played out between the 'tradition' and any strong newcomer is not an Oedipal drama (or not only), but more profoundly a drama of witnessing where the newcomer witnesses/acts the tradition, which can only happen if the tradition witnesses/acts the newcomer's wounding event. The newcomer should be understood as exactly that, as the one whose arrival is absolutely new and unforeseen, an absolute surprise, a surprise witness who is the only one able to testify to the unforeseen excess kept alive only within literary history."[82] While I do not share Peretz's unyielding sense of the absolute newness of the newcomer, I do share his sense of the strong poet–newcomer as witness, watcher, rapt audience. For these reasons, Echo seems to me an apt figure for the writer of the present, fixatedly beholding the Narcissus-like precursor.

To theorize her role thusly is not to reify Echo's role as supplement to the male subject. Rather, it is to emphasize Echo's active role as desiring subject who, though suffering imposed impediments—Hera's having taken away her power to speak; Narcissus's scornful indifference—nevertheless finds a means of registering and articulating her desire, of making the object her own. For it matters little if Narcissus recognizes her desire or acknowledges it, much less if he returns her love; he is there to be contemplated, and in contemplating him and answering him (whether he answers back or hears her), Echo performs a feat of desire that records her experience and expresses her longing. The strong poet contemplates the Narcissus-like text and answers it with her own intertextual echoes.

Richmond-Garza's analysis of Andreas-Salomé's response to Rilke's first Narcissus poem, which he sent her in handwritten form, contains language eloquently germane to the present discussion. Andreas-Salomé responded to the poem with this reading: Narcissus "may have seen not only himself reflected in the pool but also himself-as-still-all . . . Does not his face show both rapture and melancholy?"[83] Rapture and melancholy summarize the encounter and the experience of influence.

One might find that Melville in his famous review "Hawthorne and His Mosses" evokes the competitive language of the Bloomian agon, as he pits a nearly Shakespeare-like Hawthorne against the Bard, finding the contest almost evenly split. Overall, however, as his Narcissus passage in *Moby-Dick* attests, he views the precursor as a fascinating, flickering shadow on the water that beguiles the contemplative writer of the present. Throughout this book, I will be referring to Melville and Milton as theorists of influence. While the bulk of the chapters focus on Shakespeare as intertext, all the readings flow from the basis of a Miltonic-Melvillean theory of influence.

CHAPTER DESCRIPTIONS

Chapter 1 focuses on James Fenimore Cooper's novel *The Last of the Mohicans* (1826) and lays the groundwork for studying the American romance as a dialogue with Shakespeare and Milton. Set during the Seven Years' War, Cooper's mythic romance has often been read as a version of *Paradise Lost*, with the villain Magua, a Huron hell-bent on revenge against the British Colonel Munro, seen as a Satan figure. In addition, Cooper makes frequent allusion to Shakespeare's play *The Merchant of Venice,* signaling a self-conscious reworking of Shakespeare's themes of antisemitism for the American racial context. Chapter 1 explores these intertextual echoes in *The Last of the Mohicans,* arguing that Cooper's revision of Shakespeare and Milton places equal emphasis on matters of race and femininity. Cooper places his depiction of femininity in contrastive relation to racial otherness. Portia's central role in defeating the Jewish Shylock in *Merchant of Venice* and Miranda's conflict with the Indigenous subject Caliban in *The Tempest* provide models for Cooper's exploration of the fraught dynamics in the relationship between his mixed-race heroine Cora Munro and Magua. I am particularly concerned with Cooper's reworking, in his depiction of the agonized relationship between Cora and Magua, of the conflict between Portia and Shylock and Miranda and Caliban. While the readings of Milton's influence on this text have consistently focused on Magua as Satan, I give equal focus to considerations of Cora as a version of or complement to Milton's Eve, especially in her encounter with Satan. Cora emerges as Eve-like in her valiant, forthright, and autonomous position in a male-dominated narrative.

In chapter 2, *Paradise Lost* provides a particularly illuminating point of contrast for Nathaniel Hawthorne's 1851 novel *The House of the Seven Gables*. This chapter analyzes Hawthorne's depiction of female and queer characters and focuses on the theme of incest, which links Hawthorne's novels to British Romanticism as well as Milton. Incest functioned in British Romanticism as a language for self-exploration, and narcissism as its mirror. Incest functions as an allegory for intertextuality, the blending of like texts. Milton foregrounds incest in book 2 of *Paradise Lost* through tableaus with important feminist implications. Considering the ambivalence with which Milton depicts Sin, the incestuously conceived daughter of Satan, I consider the analogously ambivalent, but also sympathetic, characterization of Hepzibah Pyncheon, the elderly spinster at the center of *Gables,* as a woman motivated by incestuous love and desire for her brother, Clifford, whom I read as a protohomosexual character. Milton's revision of the Ovidian Narcissus myth in his account of Eve's nativity provides a foundation for Hawthorne's extensive exploration of the female gaze through his characterizations of desiring women who look upon male objects of desire, Hepzibah and the historical figure of Alice Pyncheon, punished for her active sexual gaze.

Both Hawthorne and Herman Melville engaged deeply in their fiction of the 1850s with the works of Shakespeare and Milton. While the study of this mutual engagement could easily be a book-length one, chapter 3 focuses on a specific figure that synthesizes these intertextual concerns: the veil. While numerous influences, such as Spenser's *The Faerie Queen*, Milton's masque *Comus*, and the Bible inform Hawthorne's 1852 novel *The Blithedale Romance*, I focus on his uses of Shakespeare's veil imagery, especially prominent in the comedy *Much Ado about Nothing*, an important intertext for *Blithedale*. Considering Shakespeare's use of the veil in *Much Ado*, I discuss the trope of the veil as it pertains to femininity, figured here as "The Veiled Lady," revealed to be the character of Priscilla in disguise. Hawthorne's reworking of Shakespeare preserves *Much Ado*'s thematization of female sexuality as "veiled" and therefore exploitable by misogynistic males, but refuses the comedic resolution of this play, substituting a tragic and ambivalent one instead. I argue that one of the chief ways in which antebellum authors made use of precursor texts was to critique their gendered depictions, especially depictions of female characters. The theatricality associated with the Veiled Lady allegorizes the work's relationship to Shakespearean drama, while the veiled-woman trope allows Hawthorne to explore constructions of femininity in a transatlantic context. A through line exists in these works: the theme, present in Spenser as well, of the unmasking of a woman in order to expose her hidden perfidy. While clearly a misogynistic gesture, the unmasking of woman in both Shakespeare and Hawthorne's works allows for an exposure of the accusing male's lack of empathy for woman as well as his duplicity and self-infatuation. *Measure for Measure*, another work in which veiled women confronting male misogyny make a climactic stand, proves a useful counterpoint for *The Blithedale Romance* as well. The considerable ambivalence in Shakespeare's mordant comedies and in Hawthorne's tragicomic novel over the status of the veiled woman involves not only male suitors but also ambiguous patriarchs, fallen fathers or would-be protectors. This last theme allows me to include a discussion of another work Hawthorne evokes, *King Lear*, and its themes of agonized, possibly incestuous father-daughter relationships.

Ever since Charles Olson's brilliant study *Call Me Ishmael*, published in 1947, the importance of *King Lear* as an intertext for Melville's magisterial *Moby-Dick* has been well known. Hoping to break new ground in oft-trodden territory, I focus in chapter 4 on, as Olson put it, the simultaneously "implicit" and "pervasive" presence of *Lear* in *Moby-Dick*: survival and femininity. In terms of survival, I consider the analogous roles of Ishmael and Edgar. *Lear*'s Edgar, the son and heir of the Earl of Gloucester, a nobleman loyal to King Lear, is cast out into the wilderness through his illegitimate brother Edmund's duplicitous stratagems and his father's rejection of him as a traitor. The implicit relation between Ishmael and Edgar is their shared status as survivors and symbolic orphans. The ultimate survivor, Ishmael famously quotes Job in the epilogue: "And I only am escaped alone to tell thee" (Job 1:14–19). Thinking of Edgar and Ishmael as *queer* survivors, wayward sons cut off from the father's economic, social, and personal power, dovetails with current interest in the concept of survival in both queer theory and Shakespeare studies. Less explicit yet also highly significant, the vexed issue of *Moby-Dick*'s treatment of the feminine indexes intertextual concerns. *Moby-Dick* reimagines *King Lear,* a work that foregrounds its powerful female characters, as a world seemingly devoid of the feminine. Yet, as I discuss, the novel includes recurring and resonant thematizations of femininity, particularly in the figure of Ishmael's stepmother and in the generalized theme of the "step-mother world." *Moby-Dick*'s stepmother, the nonbiological mother with the power to reject, abandon, and replenish the subject, a figure of rejection and abandonment, echoes the themes of motherlessness and misogyny in *Lear.*

Melville's 1852 novel *Pierre; or, The Ambiguities* foregrounds its intertextual link to Shakespeare's *Hamlet,* and chapter 5 closely examines this literary relation. The first half of the chapter reads *Hamlet* closely in terms of several key themes of particular relevance to *Pierre* and American Romantic writing generally: incest, framed as an all-encompassing allegory for the problems within and posed by the family (continuing the discussion of incest and intertextuality in chapter 2); sexual ambivalence, which the play thematizes in its hero's horror at the thought of adult genitality; and an episode that combines distinct concerns with Hellenism and dismemberment, the reference to the myth of the amputated giant Enceladus, which links *Hamlet* to *Pierre*. The second half of the chapter analyzes *Pierre*'s reworking of *Hamlet,* with special attention paid to incest, but specifically the relevance of this motif to the depiction of female sexuality in the novel. The titular hero's possible half-sister, Isabel, represents Melville's most sustained portrait of femininity. She can be considered a version of Shakespeare's Ophelia, just as the character of Mary Glendinning, Pierre's mother, revises Hamlet's mother, Gertrude. Melville's transformation of Shakespeare's female portraits is fascinatingly problematic, as he both daringly uses the precursor text to imagine forms of subversive female power but also reifies images of the woman as, respectively, narcissistic and siren-like, a doom to men. At the same time, Melville, as Cooper did before him, reimagines Milton's Eve, specifically in the moment in Isabel's chapter-spanning narrative in which she ponders her own reflection in a pool. The novel's most resistant element is its *Hamlet*-like depiction of masculinity as "faltering in the fight," always already compromised and embattled. Melville's Shakespearean and ekphrastic uses of the Enceladus myth allow him to develop an allegorical register for his mutually illuminating explorations of the failure of the artist and the failure of American masculinity.

Chapter 6 brings the ongoing concerns of the study to bear on Hawthorne's last published novel in his lifetime, *The Marble Faun*. This chapter builds on Sacvan Bercovitch's suggestive essay on overlaps between Shakespeare's Shylock, a character we discuss in chapter 1 in relation to Cooper's Magua, and Hawthorne's heroine Miriam Schaefer, considering the depiction of the Jewess as highly significant in both racialized and gendered terms in Victorian America. On a parallel track, Hawthorne's reworking of Milton's central preoccupation with the felix culpa, or Fortunate Fall, speaks to antebellum writers' ambitious efforts to comment on the history of Western tradition and the future of art, characteristically imagining the agonized yet resolute final stance of a female artist as embodiment of these concerns and a figure of mingled pessimism and possibility.

1

THE STRANGER MAIDEN

The Last of the Mohicans, *Shakespeare, and Milton*

EARLY AMERICAN WRITERS needed to establish American literature as legitimate and recognizable. They did so in an international atmosphere of hostility to the very idea of American literature. The English clergyman Sydney Smith's infamous screed against the United States in his 1820 review of Adam Seybert's *Annals of the United States* contains an oft-cited passage. The first line of the passage is the most well known, but the last line is the most telling:

> In the four quarters of the globe, who reads an American book? Or goes to an American play? or looks at an American picture or statue? What does the world yet owe to American physicians or surgeons? What new substances have their chemists discovered? or what old ones have they advanced? What new constellations have been discovered by the telescopes of Americans? Who drinks out of American glasses? or eats from American plates? or wears American coats or gowns? or sleeps in American blankets? Finally, under which of the old tyrannical governments of Europe is every sixth man a slave, whom his fellow-creatures may buy and sell and torture?[1]

Smith links the American lack of cultural vitality to the horrors of slavery, which both explains and exemplifies this cultural lack. The implicit suggestion is that for an American literature to come into being, it would need to tell the story of America's relationship to race and racial conflicts.

American authors of the nineteenth century made use of literary tradition to establish their independent and dynamic status as authors and tell a distinctively American story. When that story involved race, authors drew on tradition to tell it. Cooper's novel-romance *The Last of the Mohicans* (1826) is instructive in this capacity. English literary tradition provided a template for his explorations of social problems besetting the United States, chiefly the racism predominant in histories of nonwhite experience. Of the epigraphic references to *The Merchant of Venice* that abound in *Mohicans,* perhaps the most crucial is the epigraph for the novel itself: "Mislike like me not for my complexion, / The shadowed livery of the burnished sun" (2.1.1–2).[2] Galvanizing forces, Shakespeare and Milton hover over *Mohicans,* with *The Merchant of Venice, The Tempest,* and *Paradise Lost* being particularly salient. Satan's fall from Heaven and his seduction of the first human woman, Eve, in *Paradise Lost;* antisemitism and the irreconcilability of the racial or ethnic other in *Merchant of Venice;* the relationship between Caliban, the quasi-Indigenous subject, and Miranda, the daughter of the European ruler of the island, in *The Tempest:* all provided vital models for Cooper's complex and controversial racial schemas. (This is not to discount important intertexts such as Homeric epic, which Cooper cites in "Preface to the Leather-Stocking Tales" [1850].[3]) Along with the difficulties of representing race, the author's depictions of femininity, especially when enmeshed with racial anxieties, stemmed from his engagement with English literary models. Taking Shakespeare's and Milton's ideas about race and gender further, Cooper presages Harriet Beecher Stowe's similar intertextual practice in *Uncle Tom's Cabin.*[4] Influence, however, has not frequently been addressed in the treatment of these matters.[5]

Cooper's works are crucial to the development of American romance while being reflective of an agon with English precursors. As Cooper wrote in his 1828 *Notions of the Americans,* "the literature of England and that of America must be fashioned after the same models. The authors, previously to the revolution, are common property," and the American has "as good a right to claim Milton, and Shakspeare [*sic*], and all the old masters of the language, for his countrymen, as an Englishman."[6] He added later, "Shakspeare [*sic*] is, of course, the great author of America, as he is of England, and I think that he is quite as well relished here as there."[7] Challenging "the

"Macklin and Mrs. Pope as Shylock and Portia" in *The Merchant of Venice*, William Nutter, 1789. Engraving. (Library of Congress)

calumny England has undeniably heaped upon America," Cooper avers that England can "boast" of almost no past accomplishments in which "America may not claim to participate. The arms of our ancestors were wielded in her most vaunted fields; the geniuses of Shakspeare [sic] and Milton were awakened in the bosom of a society from which we received our impressions"; they join inheritances such as "liberty and the law" that we claim "as the portions of a birthright."[8] English culture is our culture, not a tradition imposing its will on us but a continuously fecund resource to which Americans have equal right. Shakespeare and Milton loom large as the cynosures of this birthright and aptly inform Cooper's work, nowhere more prominently than in *Mohicans,* arguably his most distinctive achievement.[9]

COOPER AND SHAKESPEARE

Shakespeare's centrality for Cooper has been well established since the publication of *Pages and Pictures from the Writings of James Fenimore Cooper, with Notes by Susan Fenimore Cooper* (1861), compiled by the author's daughter after his death. (Author of several books herself, Susan Fenimore Cooper's books include the highly regarded *Rural Hours, a Nature Diary of Cooperstown, New York* [1850], an influence on Henry David Thoreau as he wrote *Walden* [1854]). Cooper kept his eight-volume "travelling set" of Shakespeare by his side from 1826 forward.[10] He also frequently mentioned that Shakespeare should have written *Paradise Lost,* given that he was a much more pleasurable read than Milton.[11]

W. B. Gates summarizes Cooper's "indebtedness" to Shakespeare thusly:

> More than forty percent of the quoted chapter headings in the novels are from Shakespeare (395 out of 939), and there are more than a hundred additional verbal allusions or quotations. The novelist sometimes lifted an incident from Shakespeare almost bodily; at other times he combined incidents or expanded one episode into two; in the creation of some characters he leaned heavily upon their Shakespearean prototypes. In several of the novels the framework of the plot is apparently from Shakespeare, the borrowed material sometimes being introduced early in the story and then kept submerged in a rolling sea or obscured in a majestic forest until near the end of the novel.[12]

George Dekker, perhaps Cooper's most incisive critic, notes, "It is rather to Shakespeare than to Pope, to *The Merchant of Venice* and *The Tempest* than to *The Rape of the Lock,* that Cooper is most indebted."[13] On the subject of the "disguises, transformations, ruses" that pepper the "old romancers'" works and Cooper's emulative own, Dekker expands: "he differed from most other writers of romance in that his almost childish addiction to these devices was countered by a no less strong attachment to frankness, truth, 'simplicity.'" Dekker continues, "If with one part of his being he reveled in the intricate dissemblings of Shakespeare's comedies—and Shakespeare was certainly the romancer who most influenced him—with another part he stood allied with Cordelia and Kent against a world of duplicity, error, and illusion."[14] Cooper, as his epigraphs adumbrate, evokes *A Midsummer Night's Dream* when Natty Bumppo dresses as a bear and Chingachgook as a beaver in *Mohicans*. Wayne Franklin advises that these episodes' "startling comic implications" demand recognition. "One endures here by assuming what would destroy one's life . . . the very principle which underlay Cooper's lasting call for a sharp attention to the given world."[15] The pattern of inversion of Shakespearean source material Dekker and Franklin locate in Cooper, his transformation of Shakespearean comedy into American tragedy, links Cooper to Hawthorne, who turns *Much Ado about Nothing*'s comic notes to tragic in *The Blithedale Romance*.

THE TEMPEST AND *THE MERCHANT OF VENICE*: TEMPLATES OF RESISTANCE

The Last of the Mohicans does not refer to *The Tempest* (1610–11), Shakespeare's valedictory play, either epigraphically or in the main text, but the play's significance to his works has long been noted by critics.[16] The sorcerer Prospero and his daughter, Miranda, live on the island that has been their refuge since Prospero, the rightful Duke of Milan, and his infant daughter were set adrift by Prospero's brother, Antonio, who deposed him. The island had been ruled by the witch Sycorax, herself an exile. Mother to the half-human Caliban, Sycorax died before Prospero and Miranda arrive. Prospero frees the spirit being Ariel from the tree where Sycorax had imprisoned the sprite, only to enslave Ariel himself. Caliban, often represented as devil-like, bestial, a kind of feral merman, lives with the sorcerer and his daughter in a permanent state of enmity. By his own account, Prospero initially attempted to befriend the creature, but subjugated him after he attempted to rape Miranda.[17] The vexed relationships among Prospero, Miranda, Caliban, and the unfree spirit Ariel provide a telling backdrop for and a pointed contrast to Cooper's gender and sexual configurations in *Mohicans*. His mixed-race heroine Cora Munro and her fraught relationship with the villain, Magua, a Huron who loathes her father, Colonel Munro, a Scot working for the British during the Seven Years' War, parallels and critiques Shakespeare's character schema in *The Tempest*, with Cora in Miranda's role, Magua in Caliban's, Munro's in Prospero's, and, perhaps, the dream-prone musical psalmodist David Gamut filling in for the sexually ambiguous Ariel.

Important to the play's reception, Miranda impressed nineteenth-century critics as representative of Shakespearean femininity generally. Samuel Taylor Coleridge in his *Lectures on Shakespeare* applauds the "simplicity and tenderness of her character." Contemplating her as exemplary, he muses that "in Shakespeare all the elements of womanhood are holy"; women embody the "the sweet, yet dignified feeling of all that continuates society," possessing an admirable "equipoise." Coleridge identifies this as a laudable "want of prominence": the harmonious moral nature of women combines head and heart and results in "the blessed beauty of the woman's character."[18]

Making a feminist intervention, Elaine Showalter observes in *Sister's Choice* that *The Tempest* has inspired American women writers such as Margaret Fuller, Stowe, Louisa May Alcott, Katherine Anne Porter, Sylvia Plath, and Gloria Naylor. The theater and film director Julie Taymor adds to this list, for her 2010 film version of the play features Helen Mirren as "Prospera." Showalter discusses the extraordinary moment in the play when Miranda contemplates her female identity. Ferdinand, the son of the King of Naples and amongst those who have washed up on the island's shore, praises Miranda as "perfect and peerless" (3.1.47), indicating the enthusiasm that will intensify into a marriage proposal by the end of the play (although one could argue it is she who proposes to him[19]). Miranda, of whose mother very little mention is made in the play, responds thusly to his encomiums: "I do not know / One of my own sex, no woman's face remember / Save, from my glass, mine own" (3.1.48–50). Showalter contends that this moment exemplifies the play's importance to American women writers as "a metaphorical account of the woman artist or intellectual."[20] American women writers gravitate toward "Miranda's role as motherless daughter of the Father who falls in love with his language and power."[21] Her situation is heightened by her lack of any familiarity with another woman, even her mother, whose fate remains unknown. Miranda recalls Lear's daughters, and her experience resonates with the theme of motherlessness in *King Lear*. Crucially, neither Milton's Eve nor Satan's daughter Sin have any biological mother or relationship with one. These intertexts find their complement in the slew of motherless women, such as Cora Munro, in the American romantic texts we examine here. The theme of motherlessness resonates in *Moby-Dick, The Blithedale Romance, Pierre,* and *The Marble Faun.*

Caliban's lines about having learned to curse resonate in postcolonial theory, which has enshrined the play as exemplary of its concerns.[22] He famously retorts, "You taught me language; and my profit on't / Is, I know how to curse. The red plague rid you / For learning me your language!" (1.2.364–66). His lines are typically read as a rebuke of Prospero and his imperial rule. Implicitly, they are; but Caliban is responding not to Prospero but to Miranda, who has just spoken thusly to the creature:

> Abhorred slave,
> Which any print of goodness wilt not take,
> Being capable of all ill; I pitied thee,
> Took pains to make thee speak, taught thee each hour
> One thing or other. When thou didst not, savage,
> Know thine own meaning, but wouldst gabble like
> A thing most brutish, I endow'd thy purposes
> With words that made them known. But thy vile race,
> (Though thou didst learn), had that in't which good natures
> Could not abide to be with. (1.2.353–61)

The white woman's embattled relationship with the racial and species other in *The Tempest,* related to themes in *Merchant,* involves the threat of sexual violence. Prospero remarks that he treated Caliban ("Filth as thou art") with kindness, and "lodged thee / In mine own cell, till thou didst seek to violate / The honour of my child" (1.2.344–47). For Ronald Takaki, Caliban embodies the colonial encounter: "Belonging to a libidinous race, in Shakespeare's portrayal, Caliban was driven by the passions of his body. Prospero saw him as a sexual threat to the nubile Miranda."[23] The English fear of sensuality embodied, Caliban reflects the English colonists' fears of Native Americans and Black people and the dread of a loss of self-control.

The scenes between Prospero and Caliban and between Caliban and Miranda provide the foundation for Cooper's depiction of the tortured antagonism and connection between Cora Munro and Magua in *The Last of the Mohicans*. Echoing the threat of Caliban's intended rape of Miranda, *Mohicans* foregrounds the sexual dynamics of Cora and Magua's relationship from the moment that the heroine first appears. Magua makes Cora the object of his displaced aggression, forcing her to bear the brunt of his anger against her father. Whereas Miranda speaks contemptuously toward Caliban, Cora generally speaks unsentimentally but respectfully toward Magua. The threat of sexual violation combined with Prospero's control over his daughter, whom he often expediently causes to sleep, inform and perhaps determine Miranda's attitudes toward Caliban. Cooper, as I see it, continues the conversation between them and renews their opportunities to voice positions.

Edward P. Vandiver Jr. noted in 1940: "The play from which Cooper chiefly quotes is *The Merchant of Venice;* then come *The Tempest, Hamlet,* and *Macbeth.*"[24] George Dekker highlights *The Merchant of Venice* (1596–99) as particularly significant to Cooper's interests in "racial relations and particularly in racial or tribal revenge."[25] *Merchant* has been read as the ur-antisemitic work and as a work that opposes antisemitism. Some find Shylock an antisemitic caricature, while others find him sympathetically or at least ambivalently drawn. Having lent money to the prosperous but cash-poor Venetian merchant Antonio, Shylock demands an unusual compensation should Antonio fail to pay him back, the infamous "pound of flesh" to be literally extracted from Antonio. Antonio has borrowed the money so that he can help out his young friend Bassanio, who wishes to woo a particularly elusive woman, Portia.[26] Her late father devised a most unusual scenario of courtship: Portia's suitors must choose among three different caskets, one gold, one silver, one lead. Many fail, but Bassanio correctly guesses that the right casket is the lead one and wins his beloved's hand in marriage. When the time comes to repay Shylock, Antonio, having discovered that his ships are lost at sea, cannot do so. Because his daughter has run away with a Christian and a large amount of her father's money, and because Antonio has antisemitically abused him in the past, Shylock wants revenge. He insists on getting Antonio's pound of flesh as payment despite Bassanio's offers to give him ample financial recompense. Portia, disguised as a young male legal expert, accompanied by her waiting maid Nerissa, also in male disguise, intervenes in the trial and successfully argues against Shylock. Her efforts result in a judgment that forces Shylock to give half of his wealth to the government and the other half to Antonio, and to bequeath his estate to his daughter and her Christian husband. In addition, Shylock must convert to Christianity. The vengeful villain must succumb utterly to the state, the religion, and the men who wronged him.

Portia is ostensibly presented as the heroic savior of her fiancé and his friend. But it can also be argued that she is a less sympathetic character than she initially appears. At the same time, though the villain, Shylock has ample opportunity to remind the audience of what he has suffered as a Jew, specifically from the antisemitic Antonio; ultimately, Shylock is a pitiable figure in his ingeniously crafted defeat. The showdown between Shylock and Portia haunts the relationship between Cora and Magua. While ostensibly positively valued for rescuing Antonio, Portia is at best an ambiguous character. Her uneasy relationship to Shylock, whose defeat she successfully engineers, echoes in Cora's mingled sympathy for and revulsion toward Magua.

Magua is, like Shakespeare's Jew, at once villainous and sympathetic. Magua's claim for justice against English and European rule and against Colonel Munro echo Shylock's grievances against Christianity and Antonio. Most ingeniously, by reimagining Portia as the mixed-race Cora, Cooper draws surprising connections between his Shylock-like Magua and the woman who opposes and, at least morally, defeats him. In Cooper's hands, the Portia-Shylock relationship bespeaks a mutual experience of racial prejudice and ambivalence toward white European rule. Cooper reinserts the central issue of racial and antisemitic prejudice in *The Merchant of Venice*, which was largely deemphasized in the broader context of the play's nineteenth-century reception in Europe and the United States.

John Stokes notes of the nineteenth-century European reception, "One might have expected race to have been an important element in relation to *The Merchant of Venice*, but, in fact, productions outside of England and Germany were extremely rare," and the most salient element was commonly seen to be Shylock's role as a usurer rather than his status as a Jew. The deemphasizing of racial matters "could, perhaps, be seen as implicitly racist itself."[27] In the United States, race did return as a concern of the play, but in the inherently caricatural form of the minstrel show. Blackface minstrelsy, which began its heyday in 1843, made frequent use of Shakespeare. George W. H. Griffin's version of *Merchant of Venice*, titled *"Shylock," A Burlesque*, "had Griffin impersonating 'Shylock (Dealer in Old Clothes)' and reciting his rhymed speeches in a mock-Yiddish accent. Although this play is listed among the company's Ethiopian dramas, there is no indication that the actors used blackface or pseudo-African American speech... In other respects, however, this skit fits the minstrel genre." The skit contains racist and antisemitic caricatures, includes the pound-of-flesh punishment, and preserves Portia's role as Shylock's inquisitor.[28]

PORTIA AND CORA

Shakespeare's Portia is, on the one hand, thrillingly intelligent and daring and, on the other hand, suspect in her pitiless decimation of Shylock. Shylock's insistence on getting the pound of flesh from Antonio, which will doubtlessly result in grievous injury if not death, demands that he receives a comeuppance. But the one Portia delivers strips bare Shylock's very identity. Though female and therefore subordinate to the masculinist state, Portia comfortably embodies state power while working in the service of men. She inflicts a deeper, more absolute punishment on Shylock than the state had envisioned. And nowhere does her vulnerable status as woman, which she acknowledges, lead her to feel sympathy for the equally vulnerable status of the outcast Jew.

Cooper's conceptualization of Cora Munro emphasizes the porous boundaries between the heroic woman and the racial-ethnic other. Her Scottish father, Colonel Munro, met and married Cora's mother in the West Indies. Munro explains this to the Southern colonist Duncan Heyward, whom Munro mistakenly assumes wants to marry Cora but has marital eyes on her younger, blond, unambiguously white half-sister Alice. This conversation among the men takes place later in the novel (156–66).[29] Munro loves both his daughters ardently and angers at the thought that Heyward views mixed-race Cora as inferior. Cooper consistently demonstrates that Heyward does indeed hold this view, though he frequently soft-pedals his racism when talking to Munro and Alice.

The novel introduces Cora and her sister at the end of chapter one. The first chapter ends with a much-discussed, almost hallucinatory descriptive passage signaling Cora's mixed-race heritage. Her visual scan of the treacherous Magua provokes this description. Falsely pretending to lead Heyward and Munro's daughters to Fort William Henry, where the colonel is stationed, the Indian runner Magua makes a sudden movement that startles the women. Alice cries out; Cora does not, but "in the surprise her veil also was allowed to open its folds, and betrayed an indescribable look of pity, admiration, and horror, as her dark eye followed the easy motions of the savage." Cora's "tresses . . . were shining and black," resembling "the plumage of the raven." Highlighting one of its central themes early on, the novel muses of Cora that her "complexion was not brown, but it rather appeared charged with the color of the rich blood, that seemed ready to burst its bounds."[30]

As she surveys the runner, Cora feels "pity, admiration, and horror." This indelible mixture of responses reworks Aristotle's theory of tragedy, the spectator's feelings of terror and pity in response to the protagonist's sufferings leading to catharsis.[31] Cooper thereby alerts us to his racial themes' ineluctably tragic nature. George Dekker notes, "Cora's emotions upon first seeing the man who will cause her own death are, almost exactly, those of classical tragedy." It also presages "her love for a man of another race," Uncas, and is therefore "an image of transgression."[32]

Immediately, the visual appraiser becomes the visually appraised. Cora's features fall under the narrator's scrutiny, particularly the darkness of her hair (in contrast to the pristine blondeness of Alice), the "rich blood" that momentarily browns her skin and threatens to burst its bounds, the immaculate ivory of her teeth, and the equally immaculate symmetry of her features overall. Cora and Magua share the status of being objects of the gaze, as will the "good" Indian characters, the Mohicans Chingachgook and Uncas. This is not to suggest that only the nonwhite characters undergo such visual scrutiny. David Gamut, the Christian psalmodist and eccentric who joins the group, is also visually perused and found a highly singular object.[33] Significantly, the sight of Magua turns *Cora* into a sight; as the passage adumbrates, the complexity of her responses to him stems from the complexity of her racial intermixture. The next chapter immediately deepens these impressions. Cora chastises Heyward for casting mild aspersions on Magua's trustworthiness. "Should we distrust the man, because his manners are not our manners, and that his skin is dark!" Cora "coldly" asks (21). Cora will be persecuted by Magua, made to suffer his lurid sexual advances. But she crucially defends his honor before his villainy is revealed, a villainy qualified by Magua's account of the abuses he suffered at Munro's hand.

To return to Portia: Charlotte Artese in her essay "'You Shall Not

Know': Portia, Power and the Folktale Sources of *The Merchant of Venice*" (2009) has demonstrated that Shakespeare borrows both the pound of flesh and the casket-test in *Merchant of Venice* from folktale traditions. Crucially, however, he reduces "the heroine's power" by substituting the casket test for the folk motif of the bed test, in which a prospective bride tests her suitor's sexual power, thus emasculating him: "Portia is even more disempowered than most noble, marriageable ladies, and she resents it. She laments, 'I may neither choose who I would nor refuse who I dislike; so is the will of a living daughter curbed by the will of a dead father. Is it not hard, Nerissa, that I cannot choose one nor refuse none?' (1.2.22–26). The law of the father, his last will and testament, overrides the (sexual) desire of the daughter, her will: Portia's wordplay emphasizes both the difference between her father's power and her own, and the absurdity, in her view, that his should triumph."[34]

Cooper envisions a similarly frustrating sexual scenario for his heroine, one compounded by her mixed-race background. Cora, a nominally white woman of marrying age, cannot marry the Mohican Uncas despite his elegance and grace. Hints of their rapport only deepen the sense that she cannot easily marry *any*one: however much the two may be drawn to one another, the fear of miscegenation, even with Cora's mixed-race considered, impedes union. (As I discuss below, critics have overblown the idea that Cora is in love with Uncas.) And she neither wants nor could want marriage to the Huron Magua. Cora's compassion for Magua offers a humane and thoughtful contrast to Portia's attitude towards Shylock, an adversary ultimately given no quarter. Efrain Kristal succinctly puts the matter: "Shylock was resentful before the beginning of the play, and his resentment makes him cruel; likewise, in the trial scene the audience witnesses the birth of Portia's resentment, and her turn to cruelty. In the trial scene, the two are aligned in their resentment and in their cruelty, and in the play, they are also aligned in the irony that their beautiful speeches (Portia's speech about mercy, and Shylock's famous speech about the shared humanity of Jews and Christians) are undermined by their cruelty."[35] Cooper's Cora never strikes a cruel note, however. Magua frequently does, yet he remains a reminder of grievous wrongs done to him and his people.

William Greenslade notes that "the period from the early 1810s through to the mid-1830s was peculiarly turbulent, characterized by political censorship ... Shakespeare's plays, together with the figure of Shakespeare himself, were to be drawn on in support of both radical and conservative positions during this period."³⁶ Cooper's use of Shakespeare's cultural authority reflects the conservative position, but his retooling of the plays in *Mohicans* cannot be so described. As John McWilliams observes, "for his novel's epigraph, Cooper chose the plea of the Prince of Morocco to Portia . . . : 'Mislike me not for my complexion / The shadowed livery of the burnished sun' (2.1.1–2). Morocco, whom the stage directions describe as a 'tawny Moor dressed all in white,' warns 'fair Portia' not to condemn him for his skin color and thereby deny his inner valor. Morocco's words anticipate the sexual attraction between Uncas and Cora, but they also prompt the reader to question—much as Shylock will—all kinds of racial labels."³⁷ Cooper emulates Shakespeare's humanizing of Shylock by sympathetically depicting the Shylock-like Magua's suffering and its cause. But I contend that Cooper's revision of Portia, a woman compromised in sexual desire and in defiance of the threatening male Other, is equally significant. In Cora, Cooper reimagines Portia as nonvengeful. Moreover, Cora's chief motivations stem not from a more conventional heterosexual desire but rather a sororal protectiveness. Rather than defeating the villain because he endangers her marital prospects, Cora fights him in order to shield her sister and herself from his sexual violence. Granted, Cora's lack of heterosexual motivation reflects antebellum America's fears of miscegenation, or amalgamation, as it was called. Nevertheless, Cooper sees her as noble and makes her selflessness commensurate with this quality.

Some readers see Portia as benevolent, associated with a Christ-like mercy, which her most famous speech adumbrates ("The quality of mercy is not strain'd, / It droppeth as the gentle rain from heaven" [4.1.183–84]). Yet, as Charlotte Artese argues, in the folktale traditions Shakespeare draws on, "the analogue to Portia is undeniably a trickster figure. Shakespeare augments the folktale tradition in order to suggest that the law is leveraged against the outsider. . . . Only Portia knows the Venetian law's bias against the alien."³⁸ In his spellbinding *Shylock Is Shakespeare,* Kenneth Gross reinforces the point: "The association of Portia with a riddling enchantress comes out more strongly at the trial, in her way of managing the death and life of Antonio and Shylock, and her showing of what tricksy, vengeful logic subtends her call for mercy."³⁹

Portia manipulates Venetian law's arcane dimensions to defeat Shylock, so deftly that she devises a defense that startles Antonio, Bassanio, the judge, and the audience. Cora need not resort to chicanery to hold her own against Magua. When he presents his grievance with her father, Cora does not deny the validity of his accusations but instead steadfastly appeals to logic. Her father Colonel Munro "made a law," as Magua describes, "that if an Indian swallowed the fire-water, and came into the cloth wigwams of his warriors, it should not be forgotten." Magua, recalling the incident in which he drunkenly broke Munro's law and was publicly whipped as a result, taunts Cora thusly: "Was it the fault of le Renard that his head was not made of rock? Who gave him the fire-water? who made him a villain? 'Twas the pale-faces, the people of your own color." To which accusation Cora replies, "And am I answerable that thoughtless and unprincipled men exist, whose shades of countenance may resemble mine?" (102–3). Tellingly, Cora "calmly [demands]" this of her interlocutor; Cooper frequently emphasizes her quiet resolve.

"To turn *The Last of the Mohicans* into a vehicle for racial hatred has proved regrettably easy," John McWilliams notes. "All one needs to do is to forget, as Cooper's book never allows us to do, why Magua acts as he does." One of Cooper's finest critics, McWilliams is on very steady ground here. But his reading of Cora's responses to Magua fails to recognize her consistent integrity. Regarding Magua's specific charges against Munro, McWilliams argues that "Cora tries to avoid [them] by forcing it back entirely to personal grounds," noting that her father kept his word and had the offender, Magua, punished. Then McWilliams writes, "But Magua will not permit her narrow view to prevail."[40] Perhaps Cora's response might be called bloodless; like Portia, she sticks to the letter of the law. But unlike Portia, Cora does not proceed to envision a punishment for Magua that exceeds her father's edict. If anything, Cora has a Cordelia-like parsimoniousness, according Magua no more and no less sympathy than she believes he deserves.[41]

COOPER AND MILTON

Cooper's reworking of Milton naturally arises. Robert Milder observes of *Mohicans* that the "Miltonic references are particularly important both in patterning the action of the book and in shaping the reader's response."[42] George Dekker asks of Cooper, "Is he of the Devil's party without knowing it? (There are many echoes of *Paradise Lost* in this novel [*Mohicans*].)"⁴³ When Milton's influence on *Mohicans* has received critical attention, the Satan-like Magua dominates the discussion. David Kesterson's reading of the passage where Magua is called the Prince of Darkness exemplifies this typical focus.⁴⁴ John McWilliams, as Milder, Donna Richardson, and Kesterson do, likens Magua to Milton's towering antihero in *Paradise Lost*: "John Milton's Satan . . . in his pride, eloquence, and drive for revenge, is Magua's prototype in previous epic literature." McWilliams points out the moment when, near the close of chapter 27, Cooper remarks of Magua that "it would not have been difficult to have fancied the dusky savage the Prince of Darkness, brooding on his own fancied wrongs, and plotting evil" (284).⁴⁵ McWilliams observes, "If Milton was, as William Blake claimed, of the Devil's party without knowing it, we may also say that Cooper knowingly gave a red Satan just cause for revenge and then shuddered at the consequences."⁴⁶

Cooper's reimagining of Milton's Eve in Cora Munro demands scrutiny and poses a significant challenge to the view of the novel as reactionary. The Shakespearean echoes in Milton's depiction of Eve—especially Miranda's fraught relationship with Caliban and his threat of sexual violence against her, less so Portia's eloquent outmaneuvering of Shylock—reverberate in the portrayal of Cora.

WHEN CORA READS MILTON

In the introduction, I argued that Eve's account of her nativity in book 4, a reworking of the Ovidian Narcissus myth (itself a reworking of several versions), is a template for the narcissistic basis of literary influence as well as symptomatic of male authors' displacement of anxieties of influence and authorship on to female subjects. Here, I want to compare the scene of Satan's seduction of Eve and Eve's transformation after she has fallen with Cooper's depiction of Cora, Magua, and an analogous scene of seduction.

In book 4 of *Paradise Lost,* Satan spies on the newly created human couple Adam and Eve and discovers them "Imparadis't in one anothers arms" (4.506–619). It is precisely their "mutual love" that "so pains Satan as he watches them from his solitary viewpoint," as Paul Hammond writes.⁴⁷ Conflicted, tormented, but resolved, the fallen angel decides to destroy their prelapsarian bliss. In book 9, Satan, in the form of a serpent, tempts Eve to eat the Fruit of the Tree of Knowledge despite God's edict that she and Adam must not do so. When Satan appears before her, Eve is gardening alone, having successfully persuaded Adam to allow her this freedom despite Satan's threat. Not some low slithering thing, "prone on the ground," but a regal and resplendent creature, "his Head / Crested aloft, and Carbuncle his Eyes; / With burnisht Neck of verdant Gold, erect / Amidst his circling Spires," the serpent rises to hail the woman in the garden (9.495–502).

The wide-ranging, long-standing commentary on the Eve-Satan-serpent encounter in *Paradise Lost* defies summary. I want to underscore readings that directly concern the sexual aspects of Eve's seduction by Satan because, I argue, these elements inform Cooper's depiction of the Cora-Magua relationship. Judith Yarnall, in her study *Transformations of Circe*, suggestively reads Eve once she eats of the fruit as a version of Homer's sorceress Circe, infamous for her ability to transform men into animals subservient to her. "Eve's tasting of the fruit," she writes, "upsets the hierarchical relationships that Milton, with his Platonized Christianity, has presented as proper and ordained . . . Eve's act asserts human will above divine will, the feminine above the masculine, appetite over reason. Her plucking of the apple gives her the power to alter the order of Creation and transforms her—temporarily—from a patriarchal woman to a Circean figure."[48] The reference to Circe here—in the description of Eve as accustomed to the rustlings of wildlife "more duteous at her call, / Than at Circean call the herd disguised" (9.520–22)—"is ironic, for Eve is in no way in control of the serpent" though it demonstrates Milton's awareness of these linkages. The animality of Cooper's Indian characters has long been noted, highlighted by their mythic monikers: Le Gros Serpent (the Big Snake) for Chingachgook, Le Cerf Agile (The Agile Stag) for Uncas, Le Renard Subtil (The Subtle Fox) for Magua. If Cora is an American version of Milton's Eve, her intimate relations with these were-men echoes Eve's familiars and the serpent in her midst, and as we have noted Magua is frequently associated with the latter.

Satan-as-serpent tempts Eve by appealing to her intellectual hunger. After eating the fruit, he promises her, "your eyes that seem so clear, / Yet are but dim, shall perfectly be then / Opened and cleared, and ye shall be as gods" who know "both good and evil" (9.706–9). The serpent successfully persuades Eve to reach for and eat the fruit, and when she does so, a change comes over her: she begins speaking in language that strikingly reveals awareness of her enforced status as the second sex. In her much-debated inner monologue, Eve wonders if she should withhold knowledge of her "change," to "keep the odds of knowledge in my power / Without copartner? So to add what wants / In female sex, the more to draw his love, / And render me more equal, and perhaps, / . . . sometime / Superior; for inferior who is free?" (9.816–25). Eve muses thusly, writes Michael Schoenfeldt in his chapter "Gender and Conduct in *Paradise Lost*," because she cannot "imagine the coexistence of hierarchy and freedom" and "desires a superiority that Adam ostensibly possesses but seems neither to want nor to be capable of maintaining."[49]

There are many ways of interpreting the turn Eve's thinking takes. Jeffrey Shoulson offers the possibility that Eve's rhetoric reflects Milton's knowledge of midrash: "Many commentators on *Paradise Lost*, especially those who have been interested in the epic's Hebraism, attribute some of Milton's less conventionally Christian views on sexuality to his familiarity and sympathy with Jewish thought."[50] A key parallel between midrash and "Milton's Ovidian story of Eve" is "their shared interest in sexuality . . . The very site of corruption becomes the site of restitution and healing. If sexuality is the form in which the rabbinic Fall occurs, then sexuality—specifically female sexuality as allegorized in the fig tree—is also the specific form in which we may look to 'repair the ruins of our first parents.'"[51] Critics such as Gary Dyer have discussed the linkage between Walter Scott's Jewish heroine Rebecca in *Ivanhoe*, published seven years before *Mohicans*, and Cora.[52] Looking ahead to our discussion of Miriam Schaefer in *The Marble Faun* as a figure of the Jewess and remembering Shoulson's findings, we can establish Milton's Eve as an elaborate reminder that the biblical Eve is the first literary representation of the Jewess.

Numerous scholars have debated the question of Milton's purported misogyny. Perhaps Julia M. Walker makes the most thoroughgoing case for his misogyny in *Medusa's Mirrors*, in the chapter "Eve: The First Reflection."[53] My views align with other critics'. Jeanie Grant Moore observes that "between the Eve of Genesis and Milton" intervened "a centuries-old hermeneutic that clouded her image and permeated the contemporary consciousness about all women. Not only was the fallen Eve seen as the incarnation of evil, but the prelapsarian Eve was also seen as infected."[54] Moore persuasively argues that while Milton does not condone Eve's disobedience, "the construction of Satan's argument to Eve allows the reader to understand her being duped. The ploy that wins her over is not flattery to her own person; rather, it is his appeal to her desire to know the forbidden: knowledge reserved for gods."[55] Michael Schoenfeldt writes, "Satan's flattery stirs the desire for autonomy" that she has just expressed to Adam when arguing that they should divide their gardening labors equally. Adam, for his part, far from protecting Eve by patronizing her, only renders her "more susceptible to Satan's flattery, and especially to his offer of independence and self-improvement."[56] If one views Milton as unsympathetic to Eve, her Narcissus-like vanity makes her susceptible to Satan's seduction. If, as I do, one views Milton as sympathetic to Eve, she emerges as an eloquent, courageous figure victimized by the hypercunning fallen angel. I argue that Cooper extends Milton's sympathy for women to Cora, who shares Eve's eloquence.

One of the most remarkable aspects of Cooper's characterization is his refusal to make Cora's responses to Magua sexually motivated. My reading of Cora's relationship to desire opposes the nearly consistent reading of her in criticism from Cooper's time to our own as tied to both Magua and Uncas by levels of mutual sexual attraction, whereas Cooper emphasizes Cora's reserve, composure, dignity, punctiliousness, and courage. While Cooper offers hints of an attraction between Cora and Uncas, these largely occur after both have been killed and during their mutual funerals, as Nancy Armstrong and Leonard Tennenhouse point out, and none are offered regarding Cora's attraction to Magua beyond her first apprehension of him, in which admiration plays a role.[57] Critics ranging from those of Cooper's own time to Dana Luciano in *Arranging Grief* have either relied on critical commonplaces about the love between Cora and Uncas and her attraction to Magua or overinterpreted passages in the novel that associate Cora with an explicit sexual desire directed towards the Indian males in her midst.[58] Or, they have given her short shrift as yet another of Cooper's self-sacrificing white virgins. Or, they have viewed her as a necessary capitulation to Cooper's rabid fear of miscegenation, given her mixed-race identity. I find no evidence in Cooper's text to support these negative and, in some cases, distorted views of Cora. In emphasizing Cora's punctiliousness and related qualities, Cooper challenges the long misogynistic tradition, centered in the biblical and, more uneasily (because the depiction is so debatable), the Miltonic Eve, of the knowing, appetitive, carnal, lustful, destruction-causing woman. J. Gregory Harding observes, in a reading I support, that Cooper establishes "a two-way dynamic, in which movement from savagery to civility runs from one end to the other, but movement toward the ideal is toward the center of the scale from either end, toward the standard set by Cora Munro."59

As we have noted, chapter 1 of *The Last of the Mohicans* emphasizes Cora and Magua as objects of the gaze, united as nonwhite personae by their shared status as visual spectacles, even if that includes their own participation in the othering gaze. Despite the overlaps between them, Cooper determinedly eschews suggestions that a mutual sexual attraction between Cora and Magua exists; her feelings toward him are not conveyed in a sexual register but instead one of mingled compassion, disapproval, and revulsion. Cooper's decision not to sexualize Cora's responses to Magua is remarkable because of his equal insistence on making Cora a mixed-race character. The nineteenth century, especially in the antebellum period, was rife with images of the black female or mulatta "Jezebel" figure, overpowering in and overpowered by her avid sexuality, phobic typing supported by scientific racism.60 Cooper's last Leather-Stocking novel *The Deerslayer* (1841) concludes the five-book series with the image of Natty Bumppo as a young man. Cooper depicts Judith Hutter, the would-be heroine, as a fallen but very sympathetic figure. As I have argued, Judith's ardent desire for Natty, at his youngest and most marriageable and as sexually inviolate as he is desirable, palpably infuses the novel and imbues his resolutely unattainable persona with a new pitilessness.61 In contrast, Cora is a "chaste" woman who cannot easily endure Magua's sexual provocations. Magua challenges Cora to "live in his wigwam for ever [*sic*]" to pay off the debt of her father's crimes against him (104). He intensifies his intimidation by bending "his fierce looks on the countenance of Cora, in such wavering glances, that her eyes sunk with shame, under the impression, that, for the first time, they had encountered an expression that no chaste female might endure" (105).

Chaste though she is, Cora Munro vexed the critics of Cooper's day, who found her a wanton. W. H. Gardiner, in a review in *North American Review* in July 1826, offered an assessment that takes the contemporary reader by surprise: he faults Cooper for creating in Cora "quite a bold young woman," who "makes rather free, we think, with the savages. This, probably, she felt the better title to do, in respect of the dark blood which flowed in her own veins."62 Finding in Cora, however austerely depicted, the stereotype he expects to discover, Gardiner imposes his own sense of how such a character *would* be expected to behave in a conventional portrayal. An unsigned review in the March 1826 edition of *New York Review and Atheneum* criticized Cooper for "the management of his female personages; a nice matter for Shakespeare before him has been accused of want of knowledge in this province of poetry."[63] At least Cooper was in good company in his apparent bewilderment over femininity.

The issue of whether Milton's Eve was a suitable model for women was being debated in Cooper's time. Specifically evoking Milton, the antebellum Southern author William Gilmore Simms, whose novels such as *The Yemassee: A Romance of Carolina* (1835) established him as Cooper's rival author of historical, epic, Indian romances, firmly situates *Paradise Lost* within the misogynistic tradition of setting limits on women's autonomy. In his revision of Milton, Simms describes the Eve-like woman of the present as

> A frail, weak thing, who never struggles long,
> When once her pride has told her, she is strong;
> Never so much in danger, as when pride
> Asserts the privilege to wander wide;
> To trust herself, nor, with a holy fear,
> Remember Eve in that serener sphere,
> Where but one serpent, hid beneath the flowers,
> Beguiled her to assert her fancied powers,
> And left her wreck'd,—the ruin of her race,
> Still falling from the garden and the grace![64]

Simms evokes Milton's poem as cautionary tale, claiming that the modern woman, unlike Eve, who argued that she and Adam should divide their labors and she should have the right to tend the garden on her own, is not "deluded" with "maxims false as these, / That women still may do as she may please; / By instinct taught, impossible to err, / With man, submissive still, her worshipper."[65] Cooper envisions a very different Eve than Simms's phobic one, who flaunts ill-advised "instinctive" freedoms, swooning with vain ambitions. Cora Munro positively recalls Milton's Eve in being forthright, self-sufficient, and eloquent.

Intertextual echoes abound: the Miranda-Caliban interaction haunts Milton's reworkings of Shakespeare, and Cooper's melding of both. If we recall Miranda's remarks to Caliban, whom she addresses as "abhorred slave," Cora's interaction with Magua eschews such direct verbal abuse. When, in chapter 11, Magua proposes that she live in his wigwam, Cora feels a "powerful disgust," but she does not exhibit it. "However revolting" the proposal, she maintains her "self-command" and offers a rational counterargument: how could Magua take pleasure in sharing his life "with a wife he did not love"? (104). Interestingly, Cora places the emphasis on his emotional life, not her own feelings. She then reminds Magua that a racial barrier exists between them, that she is "of a nation and colour different from his own" (104). It is at this point that Magua inflicts "an expression that no *chaste* female might endure" on Cora (105; emphasis added). Magua's look infuses her with sexual shame. Magua then makes it clear that preying on Cora in perpetuity once he enslaves her as his wife will chiefly be a means of tormenting Munro, which suggests that his desires for her stem primarily from vengeance and sadism. That is Cora's understanding, clearly: she rails venomously at her captor: "Monster! well dost thou deserve thy treacherous name!" for having devised "such a vengeance!" (105).

Cooper here imagines a moment that might have occurred in *Paradise Lost*. What if Eve had confronted Satan after he enacted his vengeance and tricked her into sinning? What would Eve say to Satan after he beguiled her, effecting not only her fall but also her husband's, leading Adam bitterly and cruelly to castigate her? Milton's Adam relinquishes any sense of his own responsibility when he denounces Eve as herself the "serpent," accusing her of being "leagued" with Satan, "thyself as false / And hateful; nothing wants, but that thy shape, / Like his, and colour serpentine may show / Thy inward fraud" (10.867–71). When envisioned as complicit with Satan, Eve undergoes a diminution of her worth in Adam's eyes.[66]

This darkening of man's estimation of woman dovetails with Heyward's appraisal of Cora's lesser value. In Heyward's eyes, Cora's moral inferiority and her racial inferiority fatally intertwine. Cooper's direct handling of the Southern colonist Duncan Heyward's racism addresses the issue of racial prejudice head-on and thereby undercuts the seeming authority of white masculinity. Munro correctly deduces that it is Heyward's racism that dictates his preference for Munro's younger daughter, an allegation that Heyward unconvincingly disputes. He makes his racism explicit when he woos Alice during battle with the Hurons. "This is neither the place nor the occasion to detain you with selfish wishes," Heyward tells Alice, "but what heart loaded like mine would not wish to cast its burthen!" Casting his heart's burden includes explaining to Alice that Cora's worth in his eyes is inevitably lessened by her racial intermixture. He reveals this even while noting Munro's lack of prejudice: "Your venerable father knew no difference between his children; but I—Alice, you will not be offended, when I say, that to me her worth was in a degree obscured—" (260). Alice, for her part, immediately counters Heyward's assessment of Cora. As the dash at the end of his sentence indicates, she cuts him off with the rebuke "you knew not the merit of my sister" (260). Heyward, of a younger generation than Munro and about to marry Alice, with whom he will preside over the imminent establishment of a nation, represents an intensifying racist sensibility rather than progress. Less enlightened than the older Munro, the seeming hero Heyward cannot appreciate his future sister-in-law's value. That Cooper clearly appreciates it goes a long way toward establishing *Mohicans* as an anti-racist text despite its traces of racism.

Though Natty Bumppo is the Cooper creation that R. W. B. Lewis, in his famous 1955 formulation, described as the "American Adam," "the hero in *space*" who "seems to take his start outside of time, or on the very outer edges of it, so that his location is essentially in space alone" and whose "initial habitat is spaciousness, as the unbounded, the area of total possibility," it is Heyward who dimly recalls Milton's Adam in his worst moments. Heyward echoes Adam's scorn of the autonomous woman, both Eve and Cora being associated with self-sufficiency and independence.[67] Satan and Magua, ruined and rejected sons, exploit women in their campaign against the Father who created conditions for their inevitable abjection (in Satan's case, God's exaltation of the Son, provoking Satan's intense envy; in Magua's, Munro's having issued an edict against intoxication while making it possible for Magua to imbibe to the point of drunkenness, and publicly punishing and humiliating him for this drunkenness). Well might Eve, given the opportunity to confront her abuser, rebuke the serpent by calling him "Monster!" and scorning him for his successful revenge plot and for so expediently using her as a tool.

Cora steadfastly maintains her autonomy and independence without succumbing to pride or wantonness. In putting the matter this way, I am not attempting to justify the misogyny that for some critics informs Milton's depiction of Eve. My chief intention is to highlight the quiet radicalism in Cooper's reworking of Milton. In strictly theological terms, Milton adheres to the biblical account in casting Eve in the role of seduced-woman-turned-seducer. In the misogynistic reception of Eve, one that I believe Milton counters or at least complicates, her lush sexuality ensures her fall and, in her pernicious influence on him, Adam's. Cooper's response to this misogynistic tradition is to depict a heroine who does not succumb to Satanic seduction. Cora appeals to God in the face of Magua's life-threatening command, during the climactic action, that she choose to go with him or die. Refusing to submit to him or to look at him, Cora drops to her knees and stretches "her arms towards Heaven, saying, in a meek and yet confiding voice—'I am thine! do with me as thou seest best!'" (337). Cora performs the Christian duty of appealing to God in the face of evil and of, to the last, resisting her imminent harm by a rapist. Even with this austere portrayal of a chaste female character, Cooper incurred, as we have noted, the ire of contemporary reviewers for creating an overly sexualized femininity. However one feels about the entire schema in feminist terms, Cooper envisions the redemption of Eve, creating a contemporary version who, in the scene of seduction, effects a covenant with God rather than a radical break from his commands. To be sure, the subsequent action of *Paradise Lost* details the excruciatingly complex, devastating process of reestablishing the human covenant with God, a profound chastening of, and inexpressibly hard-won redemption by, Adam, Eve, and their progeny. I do not mean to suggest that Cooper's reworking of Milton's vision matches its scale or complexity, only that Cooper daringly responds to Milton's own critique of misogynistic tradition.

In her well-known essay "The Women of Cooper's Leatherstocking Tales," Nina Baym discusses Cooper's depiction of the heroine Mabel Dunham, with whom the frontier hero Natty Bumppo falls unrequitedly in love in *The Pathfinder* (1840). Baym writes, "Cooper tries to show that Mabel is a truly noble woman" by "giving her qualities which transcend her sex: stamina, boldness, resourcefulness, enterprise."[68] She argues that Cooper maintains an attitude of ambivalence toward his heroines. Seeing Cooper as a conservative who upholds the status quo in his fictions, she notes that his female characters are among "his more memorable creations," but also that "the conception of a flexible social structure evaded him"; in his work, "order is achieved only at the cost of a social submission that falls with particular completeness and severity on women."[69] Baym's point is a persuasive one, and far fairer than Richard Chase's assessment, in his famous

The American Novel and Its Tradition, of the inadequacy of Cooper's (and Hawthorne's!) female portrayals. But Cooper's pessimism also allows him to envision—or does not prevent him from doing so—a female agency within the structures of masculinist authoritarian rule. Through Cora and Magua's relationship, Cooper reexamines the already established patterns of the Miranda-Caliban relationship, giving Caliban a new opportunity to plead his case, and Miranda a fresh opportunity to articulate her own position. Cooper's revisiting of Eve and Satan's encounter in the garden similarly revisits the question of female agency. Wayne Franklin, in the first volume of his biography of Cooper, observes:

> It may be that Cooper's most talked-about female figure in his forest romances [is Cora Munro] ... As a woman of both Afro-Caribbean and Euro-American heritage who falls in love with and dies with the Mohican warrior Uncas, Cora is often taken as little more than a piece of racist apologetics. She is seen as representing a wish that black and red peoples might equally exit the American scene and leave the field to white actors. That Cora is an exceptionally strong and capable woman ... that Cooper conceives of her and Uncas as "high" figures fully capable of tragedy—should temper this argument.[70]

Influence plays a central role in the treatment of such controversial subjects, tempering any argument that Cooper's characterization of Cora was in service to his era's gendered status quo.

THE STRANGER MAIDEN

Cooper's Cora provides this study's foundational figure, a female character associated with unknowability and elusive meaning, hidden not from view but from understanding, enigmatic and distant in a manner that evokes long-standing views of women as such, and their sexual allure as flowing precisely from these qualities. This enigmatic quality also indicates, on the part of these female personae, a resistance to *being* understood, to being contained by masculinist forms of knowledge and inquiry.

The chapters that follow theorize the portrait of femininity in these antebellum writings as both intertextual and consistent. One of the most significant dimensions of this portrait is that it hinges on mystery. The Delaware women who movingly and musically mourn for Cora and Uncas reverently memorialize the slain pair with their "thrillingly soft and wailing" "sounds." When they turn specifically to Cora, the women change "their tones to a milder and still more tender strain," and allude "with the delicacy and sensitiveness of women, to the stranger maiden," whose departure from the earth so soon after Uncas's "[renders] the will of the Great Spirit too manifest to be disregarded" (342). Later, observing the shattered aspect of Uncas's father, Chingachgook, the women "seemed to bestow all their thoughts on the obsequies of the stranger maiden" (345).

To describe Cora in such a manner is to convey a sense of her containing the distinct meanings of the stranger and the maiden at once. The *Oxford English Dictionary* defines maiden, a word inherited from the Germanic, as "a girl; a young (unmarried) woman . . . maid . . . Also: a female infant (obsolete). Now chiefly *literary, archaic,* and *regional*" (original emphasis). Evocative of the long-standing romance tradition that Cooper inherits and newly envisions, the maiden connotes premarital chastity. The novel's narrator affirms the view of Cora as chaste by translating the Delaware women's apprehension of Cora as a maiden. But why a *stranger* maiden, beyond literal diegetic reasons?

The figure of the stranger immediately evokes the New Testament in the King James version:

> for I was an hungred, and ye gave me meat: I was thirsty, and ye gave me drink: I was a stranger, and ye took me in: naked, and ye clothed me: I was sick, and ye visited me: I was in prison, and ye came unto me. Then shall the righteous answer him, saying, Lord, when saw we thee an hungred, and fed thee? or thirsty, and gave thee drink? When saw we thee a stranger, and took thee in? or naked, and clothed thee? Or when saw we thee sick, or in prison, and came unto thee? And the King shall answer and say unto them, Verily I say unto you, Inasmuch as ye have done it unto one of the least of these my brethren, ye have done it unto me. (Matthew 25:35)

In light of key biblical references to Jesus as both advocating his disciples to welcome the stranger and as the stranger himself, waiting to be welcomed, Cooper's description of Cora alludes to her having attained a Christ-like stature, thereby transcending associations with the fallen Eve, which I note once again, not to endorse misogynistic reading traditions but to emphasize Cooper's positive valuation of his heroine.

The enigma of femininity in the male writerly mind is a theme that links the chapters of this book, in which woman's status as "maiden" is forever contested, women are viewed as duplicitous and veiled, and the wrenching loose of the female veil of deception and illusion is framed as goal and triumph. The authors under discussion both support these ideas and counter them, consistently depicting these ideas as motivating but illusory and futile, leading to the destruction of women who wield an agency that defies male rule. The influence of Shakespeare and Milton most keenly manifests itself in American Romanticism's depictions of femininity as simultaneously unknowable—the stranger—and egregiously violated—the endangered and defamed maiden. Influence allows us to theorize the implications for femininity in these writers' intertextual negotiations of ceaselessly preoccupying and shared themes.

2

INCEST AND INTERTEXTUALITY

The House of the Seven Gables *and Milton*

NATHANIEL HAWTHORNE'S ENGAGEMENT with John Milton's writings, specifically his epic, *Paradise Lost* (first printing 1667), informs Hawthorne's treatment of gender and sexuality. Both Hawthorne's uses of Milton and his exploration of the incest theme, which Milton treats as well, link him to English Romantic writers. Hawthorne evokes and reinterprets his predecessor repeatedly in tales such as "The May-Pole of Merry Mount" (1837), "The New Adam and Eve" (1843), and "Rappaccini's Daughter" (1844) and in his novel romances. Hester Prynne recalls Milton's Eve in *The Scarlet Letter* (1850), the 1634 masque *Comus* informs the *The Blithedale Romance* (1852), and the felix culpa, or Fortunate Fall, theme resurfaces in *The Marble Faun* (1860). Moreover, Milton's own intertextual writings (inflecting Ovid, Virgil, Spenser, Shakespeare, and other key precedents) offered later authors such as Hawthorne a crucial archive of images, themes, and structures that enabled him to develop a literary art sensitive to gender and sexual identity dynamics.

While critics have taken various approaches to Hawthorne's 1851 novel *The House of the Seven Gables,* this chapter highlights what we might call its queer and feminist ethics in relation to influence. Hawthorne's commitment to undesirable characters—the elderly, scowling Hepzibah Pyncheon and her similarly aged, manic brother Clifford—evinces the author's interest in the marginalized and the silenced. His concerns include not only the novel's personae (which include the would-be reformer and dilettante Holgrave, a young daguerreotypist; the Pyncheons' country cousin Phoebe; the lively and cheerful old neighbor, Uncle Venner; the historical Alice Pyncheon; and the novel's villain, the outwardly gregarious and smooth-talking but almost transparently malevolent Judge Pyncheon) but also its affective dimensions, specifically how it evokes and explores desire's transgressive forms. Hawthorne's frequent depictions of male narcissism typify the agonized gendered relationship to vision throughout his work.[1] I argue that female, queer, and incestuous desires centrally inform how *The House of the Seven Gables* depicts various strategies the abject devise for deriving pleasure despite a repressive social order. I argue that these dynamics emerge from Hawthorne's intertextual poetics, central to his significance within transatlantic Romanticism. Before turning to *House of the Seven Gables*, I want to lay the groundwork for a consideration of Hawthorne and influence generally.

HAWTHORNE'S READING

To think about Hawthorne's work in terms of influence and intertextuality, we must first think about the works that shaped his intellectual, creative, and emotional life. Philip Young locates Hawthorne's intertextual basis in his intense reading during adolescence, augmented by his relationship with his sister and fellow bibliophile Elizabeth ("Ebe"). During the young Nathaniel's two-year convalescence after a leg injury, he and Ebe "read all they could, the boy taking on Spenser, Bunyan, Shakespeare, Boswell's Johnson, almost all of Scott's fiction, and, in translation, Rousseau's *Nouvelle Héloïse*."[2] Edwin Havilland Miller notes that Hawthorne's childhood poems included imitations of Milton.[3] Of Hawthorne as a representative young man of his time, Brenda Wineapple writes, "he consumed Walter Scott, Ann Radcliffe, *The Arabian Nights*, Tobias Smollett, William Godwin, Rousseau's *La Nouvelle Heloise*, the poet James Greenland, Samuel Johnson, James Hogg, Oliver Goldsmith, Byron, Southey, Burns, and Henry Fielding.... And there was Ebe. With her he could share his reading and with her aspire to great verse."[4] The child Nathaniel "drank in the lilting cadence of Scripture and stored up its parables."⁵ And when Hawthorne and his wife, Sophia Peabody, married in 1842 and moved into the Emerson-owned Old Manse in Concord, Massachusetts, the author would read Spenser, Shakespeare, and Milton aloud to his new bride as they "sat in Hawthorne's study beneath the astral lamp," "the happy couple criticizing Milton's God but not his earth."⁶

Marion L. Kesselring details the books that Hawthorne took out of the venerable New England library, the Salem Athenaeum. Unlike his more business-minded Manning uncles, Hawthorne's Aunt Mary Manning was "perhaps more sympathetic" to his authorial ambitions, and it was she who transferred her borrowing privileges to him in May, 1828 (the year of Hawthorne's first novel, *Fanshawe*). In addition to works by Increase and Cotton Mather and the early American historian William Douglass, Hawthorne read tomes such as Snow's *History of Boston* and, especially, Felt's *Annals of Salem,* and several works on witchcraft.⁷ Hawthorne did read American literature—collections of poems, the works of Charles Brockden Brown. But the lion's share of his reading (if we can assume he read what he borrowed) was in English literature. Poets such as Dryden, Prior, Gay, Blackmore, Crabbe, Burns, Hogg, Coleridge, Keats, Shelley, Wordsworth, and Byron; dramatists such as Shakespeare and Marlowe; and the prose of Carlyle, Charles Lamb, Harriet Martineau, and Coleridge (*Table Talk*) as well as novels by Defoe and Scott were all in the burgeoning young author's purview.⁸ Hawthorne also displayed a great fondness for travel literature, including a work he borrowed in 1836, Hiof Ludolf's 1682 *A New History of Ethiopia*.⁹

George Woodberry, in his 1902 *American Men of Letters* study of Hawthorne, makes an interesting observation about Hawthorne's literary friendships in life: "His own genius was solitary, and in his friendships literary sympathy had no share, for he neither received nor gave it; in fact, if he became familiar with an author, such as Thoreau or Ellery Channing or Herman Melville, it was with the man, not the author. The terms on which he stood with Longfellow and Emerson are those on which, at the happiest, he might have met Thackeray, Tennyson, or Carlyle; but, though speculation must be vain, it is far more probable that he would have found little congeniality with any of the three."¹⁰ Woodberry's observations are suggestive. Was it possible that for Hawthorne a strict demarcation existed between life and art, and that art-making was an essentially private experience, not a shared or collaborative one? We can't help but think of the unrealized possibilities of artistic collaboration between Hawthorne and Longfellow and also with Melville (the Agatha story), the planned collaboration with Poe when he invited him to join the literary journal Poe hoped to create, *The Stylus* (which, sadly, never materialized), or of the chilliness of Hawthorne's relations with Emerson. We might imagine influence facilitating Hawthorne's stated hope of achieving "intercourse with the world," an act of community-building that took place, could only take place, on the page. George Parsons Lathrop, in his landmark 1876 *A Study of Hawthorne*, discusses the author's ties to Bunyan and Milton.[11] F. O. Matthiessen observes that what Melville and Emerson identified as Hawthorne's realism stems from his engagement with these authors.[12] For Lathrop, "Hawthorne is vastly more an adept than either Milton or Bunyan in keeping the creatures of his spirit separate, while maintaining amongst them the bond of a common nature; but besides this bond they are joined by another, by something which continually brings us back to the author himself. It is like a family resemblance between widely separated relatives, which suggests . . . some strong, far-back progenitor."[13] The idea of influence as a genealogical tie, a matter of shared sinew, is intriguing, especially when we consider that while on a visit to London in 1871, Lathrop married Hawthorne's daughter Rose, his second daughter (after the firstborn, Una) and his youngest child of three (Julian, the boy, was the middle child).[14] Given the deep preoccupations with family ties and their agonizing aspects in Hawthorne's fiction, and how closely related his work was to that of his fellow allegorists Spenser, Bunyan, and Milton, we might begin to understand influence as a means of simultaneously acknowledging and disavowing propinquity, of merging and separating literary bloodlines. Perhaps the aspect of influence that makes this an especially charged metaphor for Hawthorne lies in his "most valuable inheritance from the seventeenth century tradition," in Matthiessen's view: "his comprehension of the dependence of the body on the mind," especially evident in the ego's power to "warp man's physical constitution to its own savage bent."[15] Hawthorne locates the mind's and the romancer's struggles alike in the body's maddening corporeal crucible. His characters' personal torments and internecine conflicts always manifest in the body. At the same time, the carnality in Milton, the palpable physical splendor and immediacy of the prelapsarian Adam and Eve, finds a complement in Hawthorne's evocation of the desirable body—Coverdale's openly erotic appreciation for Zenobia's sensual form in *Blithedale,* the equally sensual form of the faun-like Donatello in *Marble Faun*—even as its antithesis, the undesirable body—Chillingworth's misshapen figure, modeling his suspect nature in *The Scarlet Letter;* Hepzibah Pyncheon's involuntary scowl, emblematic not of a bad character but rather of her hopelessly frustrated spinster's longing—does the same work through negation.

Lathrop's idea of influence as a form of consanguination, "a family resemblance," inevitably evokes the intense racial anxieties of American culture in the nineteenth century and especially its fears of "amalgamation" (miscegenation). One Hawthorne work acutely allegorizes influence along these lines, his 1844 tale "Rappaccini's Daughter."[16] If we think of Milton as a central influence for Hawthorne, and for other antebellum authors as well, Melville especially, we can consider Hawthorne's reworking of the Puritan poet as exemplary of his intertextual practice (though hardly exhaustive of it). In "Rappaccini's Daughter," Hawthorne's emphasis on Miltonic themes and imagery is particularly acute, allowing us to consider the implications of influence for questions of race, gender, and sexuality.

Perhaps the most evocative allegory of influence in literature, Milton's depiction of Eve's seduction by Satan in the form of the serpent in *Paradise Lost* recurs in reimagined form in several Hawthorne works. Eve, the first woman, created by God from the first man Adam's left rib, intransigently questions male rule, as evinced by the married couple's argument over the division of labor, for which Eve advocates. Her dissent precipitates her solitary position when Satan as serpent seduces her into eating from the Tree of Knowledge. The eating of the Fruit at the serpent's behest—"Greedily she engorged without restraint, / And knew not eating death..." (4.791–92)— produces a remarkable clarity for Eve about her social position. This clarity seems to intensify and reawaken the earlier indications of her intransigence, such as the moment when the newly born Eve fled Adam in their initial encounter. Narrating her nativity, Eve explains that she became entranced by her own reflection in the water, Adam seeming a less desirable option (4. 440–91). (God and Adam command her to renounce her self-desire and to accept Adam as her mate; Milton reworks Ovid's Narcissus myth into a cautionary tale of female vanity, albeit quite ambivalently rendered as such, as I have noted.) What was her initial position of resistance to and ambivalence towards heterosexual relations with Adam becomes a much more direct and resistant clarity about her gendered subject position once she eats the Fruit. During her impassioned apostrophe to the Tree that has given her the "Experience" that wipes out her "ignorance," Eve begins to ponder Adam's possible responses to her transformation.[17]

While Eve's expressed views towards Adam have been heretofore marked by ambivalence, here she reveals the depth of her feelings for him, even as she evaluates the politics of her own subordinated social position through a surprisingly feminist lens, asking, "for inferior who is free?" (4.824–25). She decides that Adam will be with her even if he is against her, in bliss or woe, life or death. The startling clarity Eve experiences here turns her into a cunning strategist who will do anything to keep Adam for herself, even defy God. The fusion of death and eroticism, the willingness to imagine death as the only province in which desire can live, directly anticipates Hester Prynne's actions and words in the forest scene in *The Scarlet Letter;* it also informs, to a certain extent, Beatrice Rappaccini's situation, which, despite typical readings of her as an Eve-like fallen woman and seducer, Hawthorne depicts as her victimization by corrupt and weak-minded men. (Both Milton and Hawthorne, as I see it, invest considerable power and poignancy in depictions of female intransigence.)

Rappaccini, the dark and dubious scientist, has created in his daughter Beatrice an invincible young woman. Splicing her blood with that of the poisonous plants in the garden, Rappaccini makes Beatrice a creature "as terrible as thou art beautiful," as he describes her in response to her protestations. Telling her father that she is "miserable" at the discovery of his perfidious experiments, Beatrice rebukes him: "wherefore didst thou inflict this miserable doom upon thy child?" Rappaccini will have none of this: "Wouldst thou, then, have preferred the condition of a weak woman, exposed to all evil, and capable of none?" (127).[18]

Hawthorne reworks Milton by making it much clearer that Beatrice does *not* want the enhanced clarity and power, especially given its costs, that comes from being rendered a superior being, whereas Milton carefully prepares us for Eve's seduction, her willingness to eat of the Fruit, by consistently depicting her as longing for agency, ambivalent about her relationship to Adam, and narcissistic. Similarly, Hawthorne frequently depicts a Satan-like seducer—a Spenserian magus such as Chillingworth in *The Scarlet Letter,* Westervelt in *The Blithedale Romance,* and the Model in *The Marble Faun*—who promises the fruits of dark knowledge or seems to embody it.

Satan specifically appeals to Eve's desire for knowledge, tricking her into believing that God has placed an embargo on eating from the Tree of Knowledge because he jealously wishes to prevent the humans from being gods. Throughout Hawthorne's work, women strive to level the gendered playing field. Even the impecunious highborn spinster Hepzibah Pyncheon enters the marketplace in her twilight years and defies the masculinist oppression of her evil cousin Jaffrey. For all the controversies over not only Hawthorne's female portraits but also his attitudes toward women, he consistently explored female rebellion and intransigence. Zenobia in *The Blithedale Romance* is Hawthorne's fictional portrait of "the high-spirited Woman, bruising herself against the narrow limitations of her sex" that he describes in the preface (2).

I would argue that Beatrice Rappaccini is a volatile allegory for influence. Her mingled poison blood suggests the intermarrying of traditions brought together to form a new being; her bewilderment and horror when made aware of her origins evokes the anxieties that writers of the period may have felt as they strove to create an American literary form.[19] Hawthorne swerves from Milton by imagining that the scene of seduction *gives birth* to the woman rather than leading to her corruption and fall. The biological product of her Satan-like father's schemes, Beatrice, in her body and blood, incorporates the deadly properties of the Fruit that Eve greedily engorged along with her death. Hawthorne's ultimate swerve from Milton—and from Genesis—is his heroine's rebuke of male authority. "I would fain have been loved, not feared," Beatrice, dying into freedom (to echo Bloom on *Hamlet*), challenges her father, reversing Machiavelli's paradigm. "I am going, father, where the evil, which thou hast striven to mingle with my being, will pass away like a dream—like the fragrance of these poisonous flowers, which will no longer taint my breath among the flowers of Eden" (127). The volatility of Hawthorne's swerve lies in his insistence that the woman's only recourse from oppression lies in death, a fate similarly chosen by *Blithedale*'s heartbroken and defiant Zenobia. Beatrice's death also evokes the figure of the tragic mulatta who so often meets a fatal end in nineteenth-century fictions. We have only touched on a few of the possibilities of thinking about Hawthorne in terms of influence here (especially given the polyglot nature of the tale's literary borrowings).[20] But if we think of influence as volatile—unstable and unclassifiable, reflective of textual and cultural tensions and disturbances—we gain a renewed sense of its importance to the creation of an upstart literary project such as American romanticism.

ROMANTIC POETICS: INCEST AND NARCISSISM

The theme of incestuous desire is one of the clearest linkages between Milton and Hawthorne and among the most important Romantic tropes, a crucial allegorical and, occasionally, material figure in works by Percy Bysshe Shelley, Lord Byron, Samuel Taylor Coleridge, Edgar Allan Poe, and Herman Melville.[21] Incest preoccupied American Romanticism no less than its British counterpart, as borne out by famous works such as Poe's "The Fall of the House of Usher" (1839), Melville's *Pierre: or, The Ambiguities* (1852), and Hawthorne's *House of the Seven Gables* and *Marble Faun*. Critics such as Diane Long Hoeveler, James D. Wilson, and Edwin Haviland Miller have emphasized its importance to Hawthorne.[22]

Using incest as a literary figure allowed nineteenth-century authors to register unrepresentable and unimaginable affiliations. Incest functions both allusively, signaling intersubjective dynamics among fictional characters that authors cannot explicitly name, and allegorically, suggesting other dynamics, such as the political and the social. As I will show, it also figures the practices of literary romance and literary intertextuality.

Gillian Harkins notes that literary depictions of incest helped consolidate "an early Anglo-U.S. national literature." The subject usefully encoded the US as a divided family "whose racial and territorial boundaries were perceived to be terrorized" by menacing external and internal forces. "Twinned with 'miscegenation,' incest figured the dangerous intersection between family and nation across literary genres and periods," emerging in works such as Charles Brockden Brown's 1798 *Wieland*, Melville's *Pierre*, Pauline Hopkins's 1903 *Of One Blood*, William Faulkner's 1929 *The Sound and the Fury*, Ralph Ellison's 1952 *Invisible Man*, and Vladimir Nabokov's 1955 *Lolita*.[23] Discussing *Pierre*, Paul Hurh emphasizes how the subject fosters critiques of American familial relations. Installed as the model for political stability, the family is the locus of sentimental fantasies of political order. Familial sympathy has the potential to "redraw class and social inequalities into a fable of communal domesticity," yet also threatens, if heightened, to expose "the sexual dynamics underpinning the familial unit and the ambiguous authority of the taboos that either police or exhibit them."[24]

Melville wrote *Pierre* after having read and commented on *The House of the Seven Gables* in an 1851 letter to Hawthorne.[25] *The House of the Seven Gables* foregrounds Hepzibah's feelings for Clifford, insinuating an incest theme. We might note here that Melville's ironically pitched sentimental novel concerning a failed young male literary artist and his (possible) half-sister Isabel, for whose protection he essentially wrecks his life, seemingly remakes—or parodies—Hawthorne's novel. Cindy Weinstein observes of *Pierre* that incest defines nearly all its characters' relationships: "The only choice one has is whether the relationship is chosen to be biological or is biological, whether one is to commit incest knowingly or unknowingly."[26] The strange, brooding Isabel regards the incest taboo as meaningless. The only distinction she makes, Weinstein observes, is "a general feeling of my humanness among the inhumanities."[27] Incest therefore emerges as the norm for human interactions, not an aberration. Claiming herself to be not of woman born, Isabel provides a dangerous example for Pierre, who cannot unknow this knowledge and who chooses to dissolve himself and those he loves into nothingness.

Hawthorne's depiction of ardent, if vexed, sibling bonds resonates with the antebellum era's affective trends. As C. Dallett Hemphill observes, the antebellum period promulgated "the ideal of pure sibling love" to reassure Americans "that it was not dangerous" and to help "remove the taint of incest."[28] Nevertheless, as she also discusses, the fear of incestuous relations haunted American culture from its Puritan beginnings forward. Hawthorne's own family history no doubt informed—although to what extent remains debatable—how he depicted such matters. His maternal Manning family history, as Cecile Anne de Rocher notes, includes the 1681 conviction of two sisters, Margaret and Anstice, for "'whorish carriage' with their brother. Margaret, Anstice, and Nicholas Manning serve as the real-life precedents to Hester Prynne... forced to wear paper signs describing their crime."[29] Noting that incestual motifs recur in Hawthorne "between brothers and sisters, fathers and daughters, and sisters," Edwin Haviland Miller posited that the theme has biographical roots in the author's relationship with his sister Elizabeth, whom he called "Ebe."[30]

Incest mirrors narcissism and allegorizes homosexuality (a complex and unsettling exchange, to be sure). Discussing Romantic poetics, Camille

Paglia notes that incest may "reflect a desire to copulate with the self in sexually transmuted form."[31] In *The House of the Seven Gables,* incestuous female desire intersects with a narcissistic, protohomosexual male sensibility. Hepzibah's incestuous desire provides a location for experiments in form and feeling, intertextuality and sentimental attachment. Her desiring gaze finds a surprising complement in the colonial-era episode of Alice Pyncheon, whose transgressive sexual appraisal of the carpenter Matthew Maule's body incites the strapping young mesmerist's punitive wrath (he entrances her and forces her to do his bidding). Hepzibah reverences the portrait of her forlorn, once-beautiful sibling Clifford's younger self; Alice's fate concretizes the lurking impropriety in Hepzibah's visual fixations. Pyncheon women across the centuries desire transgressively and face punitive consequences, thematizing the female sexual gaze as threatening. Simultaneously, Hawthorne's depiction of Clifford prefigures psychoanalytic readings that link male homosexuality and narcissism. In the previous chapter, I explored the ways in which Cooper's intertextual poetics allowed him to conceptualize a resistant model of mixed-race femininity; here, I propose that Hawthorne uses intertextual poetics to explore how female and queer desire might surface in a homophobic and misogynistic culture.

Two key episodes from *Paradise Lost* strikingly dovetail with *The House of the Seven Gables.* The incest theme emerges in Satan's encounter in book 2 with his daughter, Sin, who burst Athena-like from his head when he had his first rebellious thought, and their son, Death; homoerotic narcissism and the female gaze appear in Eve's nativity narrative, where she describes her narcissistic encounter with her own reflection (4.440–91). The Sin episode provides a comparative framework for Hepzibah's incestuous desire and Clifford's narcissistic persona, as does Eve's nativity narrative for the tale of Alice Pyncheon.

MILTON'S SIN

Regarding uses of Milton by antebellum authors, Hawthorne and Melville have attracted the most critical attention.[32] While Melville's intertextual engagements continue to spark vigorous scholarly discussion—for example, new digital technologies that feature Melville's marginalia reveal a more precisely nuanced response to Milton—Hawthorne's revisions of his

"Satan, Sin and Death," William Hogarth, etched by Samuel Ireland, 1788. *Paradise Lost*, bk. 2 (Metropolitan Museum of Art, Harris Brisbane Dick Fund, 1932)

predecessor, once a critical trend, have infrequently interested contemporary critics.[33]

Given Hawthorne's deep interest in Puritan ideology, Milton understandably fascinated him; the two authors shared a central preoccupation with the Adam and Eve narratives, including their creation, marriage, encounter with Satan as the serpent, fall into sin, expulsion from the Garden, and hard-won redemption. Both authors highlighted the felix culpa concept, which posits that, however arduous the expulsion from Paradise was for the first human pair, the fall was worthwhile, a necessary catalyst for spiritual development and journey toward oneness with God. Seeking redemption and grappling with sin's enormity, humans ultimately learn from their mistakes and, however agonizingly, regain their divine stature. Hawthorne reprises this Miltonian theme in *The Scarlet Letter* (Hester realizes and atones for her errant desire, at least insofar as critics traditionally interpret this gendered narrative) and *The Marble Faun* (Miriam and Donatello recognize their sinful act, the murder of the Model, and seek repentance). Milton's *Paradise Lost* created the ultimate rebel, Satan, whom Romantic poets extolled. Joseph Anthony Wittreich illuminates the significance that Romanticism's valorization of the villainous Satan holds for literary interpretation. William Blake's famous line that Milton "was a true Poet and of the Devils party without knowing it" is the "key sentence of Romanticism . . . not because of its implied Satanism but because of its open acknowledgment of conscious versus unconscious meanings in *Paradise Lost,* its admission of inconsistencies and contradictions, which an earlier criticism nearly succeeded in silencing."[34] Given that Milton's epic exemplifies intertextual practice, famously referencing and revising scores of literary precedents, it serves us well as a framework. Milton intertwines the concepts of incest and narcissism, a thematic that Hawthorne extends and revises.[35]

After his fall and expulsion from Heaven, the rebel archangel Satan makes his way through Chaos and flies toward Earth planning to seduce the first humans into their fall. He encounters two formidable creatures flanking Hell's gates: his daughter, Sin, and Death, the product of his incestuous union with Sin. Richard Allen Shoaf discusses how incest figures the literary itself, signifiers mating with the signified, the poet making love to his imagery. Incest exemplifies narcissism: "in incest, the image in the water (or the glass) is made flesh, and Narcissus's desire is realized, or better, reified . . . incest is the parody of production."[36] This description also points to Eve's later account that depicts her entrancement by her own image. While Shoaf highlights how Satan allegorizes suspect authorship, Maggie Kilgour observes that Milton revises Ovid's version of the Narcissus myth to thematize the fallen angel's creativity: "In some ways Satan seems an ingenious and perceptive adapter of Ovid's story, which he ominously turns into an *aition* [cause] of the origins not of poetry, but of sin. The emergence of Sin from Satan's head as he contemplates rebellion combines the myth of the birth of Athena/Minerva, wisdom, with that of Narcissus and the tales of incest in *The Metamorphoses*."[37]

Luridly described, Sin seems like "woman to the waist, and fair, / But ended foul in many a scaly fold / Voluminous and vast, a Serpent armed / With mortal sting." (*PL,* 2.760–65). What's more, a litter of "hell hounds," their "Cerberean" mouths agape, throng about the creature, barking loudly and making a "hideous peal"; when any noise disturbs them, they burrow back into her womb and "kennel" there, still howling (*PL,* 650–60). Milton likens Sin to Ovid's Scylla in *The Metamorphoses*, a beautiful nymph that Circe transforms into a monstrous creature whose lower body consists of thrashing, noisy hounds, and to Spenser's Error in *The Faerie Queen*, a monster who is also woman to the waist and snake below and kennels a hideous brood. Sin eloquently narrates her own story, revealing both her resilience and her shocking sexual agency. Like Pandora, she disrupts the Golden Age of male rule that a homosocial space, Heaven as Milton depicts it, enables. Bursting out of Satan's head, Sin produces an "amazement" that "seized / All the host of heaven; back they recoiled afraid" (*PL,* 2.758–59). But Sin wins, or woos, them over, as she quickly describes: "familiar grown, / I pleased, and with attractive graces won / The most averse, thee [meaning Satan] chiefly, who full oft / Thyself in me thy perfect image viewing / Becam'st enamored" (*PL,* 2.760–65). Having his way with his daughter, he impregnates her with Death. Enflaming his lust for her, Sin reflects Satan's image back to him; narcissism mirrors incestuous sexual violence, which emerges from narcissistic desire.

Aspects of book 2 resonate in *The House of the Seven Gables.* Satan's impaired luster anticipates the once-beautiful Clifford's shattered image. His revulsion when he sees Sin prefigures Clifford's involuntary recoil at scowling Hepzibah. Despite Sin's hideous appearance and decisive role in humanity's downfall, Milton treats her sympathetically and allows her to tell her own story. Hawthorne's depiction of Hepzibah reflects a similar sympathetic ambivalence. Most strikingly, her affect when she defends Clifford against Jaffrey Pyncheon evokes how Milton describes Sin's physical body. Mortally afraid of allowing the brutal Jaffrey to approach her vulnerable brother, Hepzibah literally blocks his path. When the "vibrations" of her menacing cousin's voice reach her, she issues forth, "as would appear, to defend the entrance, looking, we must needs say, amazingly like the dragon which, in fairy tales, is wont to be the guardian over an enchanted beauty" (126). Her ferocious protectiveness poignantly masks "the native timorousness of her character" (127). Much like the dragon woman Sin, who pleads that her vain and contemptuous father recognize her and who intercedes on her monstrous son's behalf when Death and Satan battle, Hepzibah combines outward monstrosity and plangent vulnerability, as she protects someone even more defenseless than herself. Associated with the law, business, capital, and the public sphere, Judge Pyncheon emerges as a postlapsarian secular God who menaces the pitiable, Sin-like Hepzibah and the deteriorated, Satan-like Clifford.[38] Though very clearly a victim of male narcissism, Sin sinks into gratifying revenge along with her father-lover and brother-son. While Hepzibah's dragon-woman body signals her perceived spinsterish monstrousness, she is a positive character whose protective efforts ennoble her. For Nina Baym, Hepzibah's resistance to Jaffrey Pyncheon's tyrannical hold on the weak Clifford is a "specifically female or womanly" heroism, "action taken on behalf of another and involving significant self-abnegation."[39] Nevertheless, the novel suggests that she, too, sins, incestuous desire the common thread.

HEPZIBAH IN THE MIRROR

So impecunious that, as the narrative begins, she establishes a cent-shop, the aged gentlewoman Hepzibah Pyncheon seems quite distinct from Hawthorne's dark, sensual, sexually charged heroines such as Hester Prynne in *The Scarlet Letter*, Zenobia in *The Blithedale Romance,* and Miriam Schaefer in *The Marble Faun*. Yet, like them, she pines with desire for an unavailable male, her aged brother Clifford. Alternately somnolent and manic after his wrongful incarceration because his cousin, Judge Jaffrey Pyncheon, framed him, Clifford has been newly released from prison. Hepzibah's age and disposition has obscured her importance within the context of Hawthorne's anguished, volatile representations of transgressive female sexuality in his novels of the 1850s. Though critical readings consistently emphasize Hepzibah's status as postmenopausal woman and sexless spinster, she merits reconsideration as one of Hawthorne's sexually oriented heroines.[40]

Hawthorne's exploration into sexual matters often manifests as coy deferrals and protestations that stress embarrassed decorum. Both surface when the narrator nears Hepzibah's fleshly form. Before sunrise on the day that she haplessly opens her business, the impoverished Hepzibah begins "what it would be mockery to term the adornment of her person" (30). Crucially, this description establishes an early linkage between the elderly spinster and the young Alice Pyncheon, the victim of a sadistic mesmerist, Matthew Maule, who delights in humiliating the haughty, highborn woman. The narrator quickly adds, "Far from us be the indecorum of assisting, even in imagination, at a maiden lady's toilet!" (30). Hawthorne evacuates Hepzibah's corporeality from the text. Specifically, it is her naked self that he obscures from both us and the narrator; "disembodied listener[s]" (30), we become as immaterial as the elderly spinster. Hepzibah's body returns from its temporary hiatus, emerging as a riotous zone of auditory effects. She emits "gusty sighs"; her "stiffened knees" creak (30). Yet because she is alone in the house—save for the daguerreotypist Holgrave, who apparently hears her not—her creaks and especially her sighs are "inaudible," heard only in heaven (30). Simultaneously, the striking scowl that distinguishes her face, the part of herself she advances most prominently to the public, marks her as a fascinating and freakish visual spectacle. Clearly, parodic aspects characterize this lengthy description, redolent of the anxieties that the aging female body evokes.[41] Hawthorne will take the entire novel to achieve empathy for his heroine: much like Hepzibah's toilette itself, his empathy is a work in progress.

Significantly, this depiction evokes, even if comically, one of the most consistent and famous images in the Western art canon: the vain woman obsessively regarding herself in the mirror. This figure increasingly suggested female narcissism's pernicious aspects, which Milton in *Paradise Lost* both foregrounds and deconstructs in Eve's nativity scene. Hepzibah "give[s] heedful regard to her appearance, on all sides, and at full length, in the oval, dingy-framed toilet-glass, that hangs above her table" (31–32). John Berger asserts that "the mirror was often used as a symbol of the vanity of woman."[42] Addressing the reader and making them complicit by using second-person, Berger deflates the hypocritical moralizing that characterizes art tradition: "You painted a naked woman because you enjoyed looking at her, you put a mirror in her hand and you called the painting *Vanity*, thus morally condemning the woman whose nakedness you had depicted for your own pleasure." In Berger's famous aphorism, "To be naked is to be oneself. To be nude is to be seen naked by others and yet not recognised for oneself."[43] We never know if Hepzibah is naked, even to herself. Yet, even as he emphasizes how it unseemly it would be to denude her, the narrator does so. By making Hepzibah elderly and emphasizing her agedness, Hawthorne verges on offering his most sustained caricature of the older woman; his work, which contains many disquieting images of older women, ranging from the grandmother obsessed with her imagined image after death in "The Ambitious Guest" (1835) to *The Scarlet Letter*'s cackling, brazen witch, Mistress Hibbins, eager to mentor the sprite-like Pearl. But Hawthorne presents Hepzibah's distress and strangeness with a sympathy—evoking the feminine sentimental genre—that gathers intensity and clarity as the romance unfolds.

Hepzibah may be a satirically drawn figure, but she is also, I believe, the most developed and nuanced female character of Hawthorne's 1850s romances, which abound with indelible female portraits. Moreover, as a figure of the artist who conceives her, Hepzibah emerges as Hawthorne's opportunity to imagine his own predicaments through a specifically detailed female perspective.[44] His heroine's anguished, awkward attempts at opening the cent-shop mirror the romancer's struggles to enter realist literature's harsher, more exacting world, a transition the author dramatizes in the famous preface to *Gables* and its "claim" for "a certain latitude" that would be unavailable to him "had he professed to writing a Novel" (1). Hepzibah's allegorical role as artist deepens and subverts Hawthorne's satirical yet poignant rendering of misogynous Western art's traditional figure, woman before the mirror.

Gen Doy notes that gender differences inhere in artistic self-portraits involving the mirror: "When a woman artist looks in a mirror, she encounters not just a technical aid to making a self-portrait, but a whole tradition which invites her to see herself as an object, as sexually attractive (or not), as slender (or not), or as vain and narcissistic (always)."[45] To consider Hepzibah's potential narcissism, we must begin with the understanding that vision's tyrannical regime enslaves all Hawthorne's subjects. Hester Prynne on the scaffold, a scorned spectacle, comes immediately to mind, and Minister Hooper and Feathertop, alternately gaped at and self-regarding, do as well. The question to ask may not be, what is Hepzibah's relationship to vision, but instead, what is vision's relationship to her? Her encounter with the looking glass allegorizes the far more glaringly public and sustained encounter she will have with the marketplace, which subjects her most vulnerable moments of self-regard to collective, unflinching, and repeated judgments. Her scowl aptly emblematizes the torments of the modern visual subject, appraised for surface-level commodity value. This symbolic encounter also metaphorizes the intertextual gesture, seeing a "whole tradition" in one's literary reflection.

SEX AND SCRUTINY

Hawthorne counterbalances Hepzibah's image with that of a beautiful young man. Done by the notable artist Edward Greene Malbone (1777–1807), a Boston-based American painter, the miniature portrait that Hepzibah treasures—Clifford before his imprisonment—contrasts poignantly with the aged yet childlike man who returns home upon his release. The disparity between Clifford's youthful beauty and his ruined present image; his horror at his sister's scowl and his love of idealized beauty, indicating his status as "Sybarite" (108), a term that connotes gender and sexual ambiguity; Hepzibah's preoccupation with the loveliness he once possessed: these obsessions with *visual identity* constitute a discourse of narcissism that Hawthorne links to incestuous desire. As elaborated in my book *The Fragility of Manhood,* I define visual identity as the gender and sexual politics of cultural notions of beauty that are socially enforced and made manifest in the body's corporeal surfaces.

George Ripley's character descriptions in his 1851 review of the romance indicate that antebellum readers could detect these dynamics; he foregrounds "Old Maid Pyncheon, concealing under her verjuice scowl the unutterable tenderness of a sister—[and] her woman-hearted brother, on whose sensitive nature had fallen such a strange blight."[46] Antebellum writers, Emily VanDette observes, could "count on their contemporary readers to recognize the codes of sibling love, and to identify and sympathize with brother-sister pairs, making that mode of affiliation an especially powerful and salient device for imagining civic unions." Brothers' and sisters' increasingly distinct lives reflected the period's gender ideologies. The emphasis on crucial differences between the sexes defined "a system that demanded, basically, protection from brothers, moral guidance and domestic servitude from sisters, and a solid pact of mutual confidence between a brother and a sister."[47] Hawthorne ironizes this relationship's typical idealization in children's literature and conduct books, which aimed to inculcate these values in their target audiences, by making his brother-sister pair elderly and appointing Hepzibah as her ostensibly defenseless brother's protector.[48]

Hepzibah's preoccupation with Clifford's sensually beautiful youthful image suggests that he kindles her desire. He maintains a complex relationship to images, his own and others', reveling in Phoebe's soft beauty, shrinking from Hepzibah's scowl. Hawthorne's depiction of his narcissistic sensibility prefigures Freudian theories of male homosexuality. Like incest, homosexuality in the nineteenth century was often (though not exclusively) rendered nameless and unnamable: both sexual practices eschew conventional moral law that legitimizes only heterosexual marriage. Teresa Goddu has argued that incest symbolizes the torpid Pyncheon family's aversion to democracy and that Hepzibah embodies the family's incestuous dynamics. Much like Chanticleer, the family rooster, "who mates both with his wife and his sister, Hepzibah's passion is not for a lover but for her brother.... Her seclusion heightens her sole sentiment." Her incestuous feelings, however, do not symbolize so much an "illicit longing" as a desire to withdraw from the social order and "worldly transactions."[49]

Goddu asserts that Hawthorne uses the gender significance of femininity—the traffic in women—to suture the disparate conflicts that bind together the antagonistic but mutually unhappy Pyncheons and Maules. Both families are locked into generations-spanning conflict once a colonial-era Pyncheon falsely accuses a Maule of witchcraft so that he can steal Maule's land, leading the latter, his execution imminent, to curse the Pyncheons. Incest figures the fatal longevity of crime and curse; the novel's climactic "alliance," the marriage between country cousin Phoebe Pyncheon and Holgrave, a Maule, effects a compromise that simultaneously preserves incestual intimacy and facilitates free exchange.[50] Hawthorne's 1850s heroines yearn for inaccessible men, such as *The Scarlet Letter*'s Arthur Dimmesdale, *The Blithedale Romance*'s Hollingsworth, and *The House of the Seven Gables*'s Clifford, who ultimately reject the women who love them. Clifford's horror at the turban-headed and helplessly scowling Hepzibah literalizes this spurning attitude. Gender ambiguity and fluidity characterize these much-desired men: the young minister Dimmesdale, whose hand continuously and tremulously flutters over his heart, and who begs Hester to protect him from the intimidating little girl Pearl, their daughter: "Pacify her, if thou lovest me!" (210); the bear-like yet sensitive Hollingsworth, who tenderly ministers to the ailing first-person narrator Coverdale; and the young Clifford, who evinces "feminine traits, moulded inseparably with those of the other sex!" (60). Clifford's beauty evokes his mother's, which has "perhaps some beautiful infirmity of character" that only augments her and Clifford's appeal. Hepzibah appreciatively connects gender fluidity and her brother's youthful beauty to their mother. And she links the two in a shared oppression: "'Yes,' thought Hepzibah, with grief . . . 'they persecuted his mother in him! He never was a Pyncheon!'" (60). Asserting this connection, she dissociates herself from their circuit of desire—oppressive family members persecuted his, not their, mother, in him. As Freud will later do, Hawthorne affiliates the mother with male homosexuality. (Freud theorizes male homosexuality as the result of a negative Oedipus complex: the male identifies with the mother, inhabits *her* desire rather than the father's.[51])

Notably, all Hawthorne's heroines are motherless, even if, like Hester, they are mothers. While this point deserves more development than I can provide here, the incestuous possibilities that his fiction frequently foregrounds most likely emerge from maternal absence. As Juliet Mitchell notes, an affirming mother fulfills a crucial "need for primary recognition: for, necessarily and essentially, the mother to see her infant for what it is"; "without this maternal recognition there will be a sense of emptiness within the infant and a sense of void without."[52] Most saliently, sibling incest provides solace in a world lacking reassuring resources such as maternal love. Perhaps sibling love provides a potential "refuge in a too traumatic world? Repeated trauma leaves too little of the self—can the sibling replenish it?"[53] Mitchell's questions find an ambiguous and ambivalent response in *The House of the Seven Gables*. Clearly, for the ruined Clifford, Hepzibah's love offers an only partial refuge. Both siblings seek solacing substitutes for this maternal love.

Other Hawthorne romances stress homoerotic as well as heterosexual longing: both women and men register Dimmesdale's and Hollingsworth's desirability. (Much the same was true of the strikingly handsome Hawthorne himself, as many commentators have noted.) Roger Chillingworth's obsession with the young minister climaxes in his strangely erotic relish at seeing the young man's body splayed out and his chest exposed, like a violated heroine in a bodice-ripper; we learn about Hollingsworth's beauty and desirability, which lie in his gender fluidity, from Coverdale's perspective. Clifford embodies the relentless Judge's monetary desire rather than his homoerotic interest. But Hawthorne gives the young Clifford's backstory an interesting detail. He had a close relationship with a solitary bachelor uncle, "a man living so much in the past, and so little in the present" that providing restitution to the Maules a century and a half later seems perfectly sensible (23). Suggestively described, the uncle has an "eccentric and melancholy turn of mind," his personality "secluded and antiquarian" (22, 23). Given the possibility that Hawthorne may have had an incestuous relationship with his maternal uncle Robert Manning, this avuncular bond is suggestive.⁵⁴ Clifford's entire relationship to both his own beauty and to beauty as a broader concept demands consideration here via the structural relationship between incest and narcissism that defines the novel's sexual logic. The precedents for this thematic include Ovid's *Metamorphoses* (the Narcissus and Myrrha myths) and, as I have suggested, Sin and Satan's relationship in *Paradise Lost*.⁵⁵ Also noted, the aged Clifford's ruined beauty evokes how Milton distinguishes the prefallen and fallen Satan, and Hepzibah recalls both Milton's Sin (the dragon-like woman) and Eve's encounter with her own image.

Exposed to the marketplace, Hepzibah suffers the ravages of pitiless public scrutiny; she overhears cruel banter about her scowl, and "it seemed to hold up her image, wholly relieved from the false light of her self-partialities, and so hideous that she dared not look at it" (48). Indeed, the inwardly kindhearted heroine succumbs to bitter feelings as she begins to suspect that customers come into the shop simply to satisfy "a wicked wish to stare at her," a bitterness that intensifies when an especially striking customer enters the shop: "a lady, in a delicate and costly summer garb, with a floating veil and gracefully swaying gown, and, altogether, an ethereal lightness" that leads the onlooker to inspect her feet to see if "she trod on the dust or floated on air" (54–55). The distinctions between the unattractive Hepzibah and this gossamer apparition reinforce the sense that

Nathaniel Hawthorne, The Greatest American Writer of Fiction, c. 1899. (Library of Congress)

surface realities carry more weight in a public world that prioritizes the visual sense, the subject's outward show.

Moreover, the episode conveys that Hepzibah feels specifically *gendered* shame and inadequacy. She seethes as she stares, her anger fueled, perhaps, by a homoerotic sense of the other woman's attractiveness, which flows from that lady's greater financial ease. Karen Lystra has discussed the commentary of an antebellum woman, Alice Baldwin, who "lamented her insignificance" in precisely these terms. "I would be someone if I had a chance," Baldwin wrote, "but with neither money influence or *beauty*—which is *every thing* in a woman what hope do I have?"[56] Scarcely indifferent to the marketplace's promised pleasure and opulence, Hepzibah longs for precisely these experiences. Though a seeming frump accustomed to meager means, Hepzibah fantasizes about lavish living, imagining the return of an uncle who sailed for India fifty years ago. In her Orientalist fantasy, he will employ her as "the comfort" for his advanced age and "adorn her with pearls, diamonds, and oriental shawls and turbans, and make her the ultimate heiress of his unreckonable riches" (64). Hawthorne exposes the marketplace's sexual politics, the ways in which persons achieve value through a carnal desirability that visual and public display establishes.

Lacking economic resources or youth, both siblings endure invisibility. In chapter 17, "The Flight of the Owls," in which, momentarily escaping the terrible house where Judge Pyncheon's freshly expired corpse lies heaped in a chair, Hepzibah and Clifford haphazardly enter the public world, their eccentric appearances do not attract as much attention as one might expect. What really attracts "notice" is the figure "of a young girl, who passed, at the same instant, and happened to raise her skirt a trifle too high above her ancles [sic]" (254). The elderly pair disappear in the inclement day's dismal atmosphere, "melt[ing] into that gray gloom" (254). They pose no challenge to the priorities of the sexual marketplace that emphasizes objectifying the female and the youthful body.[57] Hepzibah understands her status in American culture's visual regime. "Look at my face!" she commands Phoebe, giving her a glimpse of her physical future should the younger woman remain in the accursed gabled house (74). Hepzibah speaks from a Sin-like position that recognizes the harrowing disparity between her physical attributes and the beauties of America's anointed youth, resplendent in their loveliness like the prelapsarian Eve and Adam that wounded envious Satan with their beauty.

As if to restore some faith in beauty's restorative power, Hepzibah then shows her young cousin the Malbone miniature, asking Phoebe, "How do you like the face?" Phoebe responds, "It is handsome!—it is very beautiful!" (75). Phoebe corroborates the elderly woman's view of her brother's youthful beauty. Returning home after his thirty-year prison sentence, Clifford, as Phoebe's observant eye correctly deduces, once again wears "a damask dressing-gown" as he had in the miniature, but now he appears a "wasted, gray, and melancholy figure—a substantial emptiness, a material ghost" (105). Hawthorne thus stresses his character's spectacular decline.

Clifford's love of beauty, which would have been "his life" had he not been imprisoned, goes a long way toward making *The House of the Seven Gables* one of the antebellum period's major queer texts (108). "Insofar as modern homosexual identity gained public intelligibility as an inversion of Victorian gender roles," argues Christopher Castiglia, Hepzibah and Clifford, "refusing to hold to their 'proper' genders," are "arguably among American literature's first homosexual characters," and Clifford represents "a proto-Wildean aesthete."[58] Clifford is the homosexual male associated with a beautiful mother who was herself wounded in some way (the "beautiful infirmity" Hepzibah notes with tender fondness [60]); both have been "persecuted" (60). Moreover, natures such as his are always "selfish" (109), narcissistic. Clifford, unlike Hester and Hepzibah, cannot withstand a queer "battle with the world" (108). He is a "Sybarite" (108), a "person devoted to luxury or pleasure; an effeminate voluptuary or sensualist."[59] Clifford adheres to the cult of beauty that makes Hepzibah a pariah. That he cannot stand to look at her is his sister's "misfortune; not Clifford's fault" (109).

Thus, Hepzibah suffers. In a poignant scene, while her brother sleeps in a deep, soft, well-cushioned chair, she steals the chance to examine his visage, "more attentively than she had yet dared to do. Her heart melted in tears . . . she felt that there was no irreverence in gazing at his altered, aged, faded, ruined face. But, no sooner was she a little relieved, than her conscience smote her for gazing curiously at him, now that he was so changed" (113–14). She has longed for this opportunity and now dares to grasp it, oscillating between an assurance that her perusal contains no "irreverence" and a conscience-stricken sense that she has gazed too long. Her desire for her "woman-hearted brother" is indeed "unutterable," as Ripley sensitively described. Clifford cannot bear to look at her, yet she longs to look at him.

Their relationship exemplifies a study in thwarted and irreconcilable loves and the impasse between incest and narcissism.

SOCIAL ABJECTION AND COMPENSATORY PLEASURES

A chapter in *This Sex Which Is Not One* transcribes a seminar that took place with Luce Irigaray in March, 1975, in the Philosophy Department of the University of Toulouse. In response to a question about family relations, Irigaray responded, "As far as the family goes, my response will be simple and clear: the family has always been the privileged locus of woman's exploitation."[60] When next asked if the family could not also be the site of a man's alienation, Irigaray responded, "Of course, alienation always works both ways. But historically, appropriation isn't oriented in just any random direction. In the patriarchal family and society, man is the proprietor of woman and children. Not to recognize this is to deny all historical determinism." Irigaray disputes the possible objection that mothers wield power in patriarchy: "this power exists only 'within' a system organized by men." Irigaray notes that while men also suffer loss in a system organized around "phallocratic" power—chiefly, the man loses "the pleasure of his own body"—historically "it is the father-man who alienates the bodies, desires and work of woman and children by treating them as his own property."[61]

Hawthorne's representations of structures of familial and gendered power and their effects on women and certain kinds of males has a surprising correspondence with Irigaray's contentions. Hawthorne's novel insinuates that incestuous desire provides sexual possibilities for a character denied, by cultural and literary proprieties that extended well beyond the antebellum period, the right to desire. An elderly, impecunious spinster and therefore a social outsider, Hepzibah nevertheless maintains erotic agency through her inordinately intense feelings for Clifford. Hawthorne associates the queer Clifford with narcissism, specifically *a traumatic narcissism* in which the individual mourns a prior and lost state of beauty, much like Milton's Satan. This standard, alternately socially inflicted and self-imposed, holds the individual up to scrutiny in the unfavorable glare of an imagined, or at the very least idealized, prior state of perfection.[62] Sufficiently abstracted into love of Beauty, the Sybaritic Clifford's tastes, predilections, and sexual wants parallel Hepzibah's incestuous desire in that they do not reach a level of intensification that would result in explicit revelations. At the same time, the narrator takes great pains, as we have touched on, to account for the odd, because nontraditionally masculine, aspects of the Sybaritic sensibility.

Unlike the other male protagonists of Hawthorne's major romances, Clifford does not wield the patriarchal power that Luce Irigaray associates irreducibly with masculinity. Instead, he embodies that loss—the loss of "the pleasure of his own body"—that even those who enjoy masculinist power can experience, but crucially, he lacks their compensatory phallocratic authority. Clifford's tragedy, Hawthorne strongly suggests, is that he failed to experience sexual love due to his thirty years' imprisonment, which represents the ultimate privacy rights violation.[63] (This is not to suggest that he did not experience sexual abuse during this period.[64]) Hepzibah, who does not know what love "technically" means (as the narrator notes when he depicts her matutinal toilette [32]), parallels him. Like his sister, Clifford "had never quaffed the cup of passionate love" (141). Both spinster and queer male are virgins.

Hawthorne pointedly emphasizes how poignant Clifford's loss of (hetero)sexual love was; this loss manifests itself in textual incoherence. In the chapter "The Flight of the Owls," Hepzibah and Clifford begin a rail journey that lacks a clear destination. Stricken with melancholy panic, Hepzibah helplessly observes the manic Clifford, who, suddenly exhilarated, offers a stunning, rambling theory concerning human civilization to an older, impatient gentleman who eyes his interlocutor with increasing alarm: "all human progress is in a circle; or, to use a more accurate and beautiful figure, in an ascending spiral curve. While we fancy ourselves going straight forward ... we do actually return to something long ago tried and abandoned, but which we now find etherealized, refined, and perfected to its ideal" (59). After Clifford delivers this surprisingly yonic discourse, his aspect grows youthful, and his "countenance glowed" (60). As his visage becomes an age-defying, nearly "transparent mask," some "merry girls" scrutinize him and "said to themselves, perhaps, that ... this now decaying man must have stamped the impress of his features on many a woman's heart. But, alas, no woman's eye had seen his face, while it was beautiful!" (261). The movement from free indirect discourse, the narrator inhabiting the merry girls' possible thoughts, to his decisive statement that no woman had beheld the ruined man's once-beautiful face, bears closer inspection.

In the Centenary Edition's "Textual Notes" section, the editors indicate that this passage contains some grammatical problems and concede "that Hawthorne intended some meaning in mind that was not clearly expressed. It is certainly possible that he intended the reader to equate the woman's eye in line 4 that had not seen Clifford's beauty with the woman's heart in line 3 that had not had his features impressed on it (in other words, fallen in love with him) . . . Thus Hawthorne may be regretting that the eye of no woman *in love* had seen his face" when it was still beautiful (332–33; original emphasis). The editors note that, whether Hawthorne intended this or some other meaning, "the method of expression is far from precise" (333).

Given the generally Latinate precision of Hawthorne's prose style, this moment is especially striking. I would argue that this gap in clarity indicates that one cannot acknowledge either the real presence of "a woman in love" who *had* seen his beautiful face—Hepzibah—or Clifford's all-but-explicated indifference to female sexual attention. As Hawthorne's discussion concerning Clifford's disposition to the opposite sex—embodied by his pretty, appealing cousin Phoebe—clarifies, Clifford "was a man, it is true, and recognized her as a woman." He does not fail to note "every charm that appertained to her sex," "the ripeness of her lips," her virginally developed bosom (141). He appraises her as a gendered visual object, cataloguing her charms: "But, after all, it seemed rather a perception, or a sympathy, than a sentiment belonging to himself as an individual." He reads Phoebe "as he would a sweet and simple story" and listens to her as if she were a "verse of household poetry." "She was not an actual fact for him," but instead "the interpretation" of his own earthly losses that plays "warmly" on his mind, so much so that "this mere symbol or lifelike picture had almost the comfort of reality." "But," the narrator avers, "we strive in vain to put the idea into words" (142). The narrator has told us a great deal about Clifford's disposition, despite this customary demurral of authorial powers. Phoebe and femininity loom before Clifford as ideals. His attractive young cousin embodies plenitude and possibility, the life experiences that Clifford lacks due to his incarceration and perhaps his disposition. "She was not an actual fact for him": as I interpret this language, Phoebe and femininity represent desire and pleasure but are not the sources of such for Clifford. Her vitality signals what he has lost and longs for.

As the narrator exhorts, Clifford, "partly imbecile; a ruin, a failure, as almost everybody is," should enjoy his afternoons with his sister, Phoebe, the Daguerreotypist, and Uncle Venner, and experience them *as* happiness: "Why not? If not the thing itself, it is marvelously like it" (158). Phoebe and, by extension, womanliness appear to approximate carnal and emotional desirability without being, for Clifford, the thing—desire—itself. Or, put another way, he can intellectually and even sensually appreciate her appeal without feeling desire: she remains "a perception," an "interpretation." That is, while Hawthorne's Clifford *prefigures* the Freudian homosexual, he is not *definitively* homosexual; the author leaves his sexuality ambiguous. His appreciation for Phoebe represents an authentic desirous experience that remains nebulous. He aestheticizes her beauty rather than longing for consummation.

The House of the Seven Gables thematizes a concept that I call *compensatory approximation*. The narrator encourages us to appreciate experiences and persons that substitute for their more authentic versions, and this encouragement opens an important dimension of the novel that, I believe, clarifies its value as a queer text. In psychoanalytic terms, Heinz Kohut's work illuminates this concept. Kohut theorizes that defensive structures conceal narcissistic defects, while compensatory structures offer recompense rather than hiding them.[65] The novel's undesirables, particularly its brother-sister pair, discover how to live in a world that does not suspend or obscure their knowledge of profound loss but allows them to endure, and even ultimately to prosper, despite this loss.[66] To many readers' dissatisfaction, Hawthorne makes a zealous effort to provide compensation to the thwarted pair—they, along with Phoebe and Holgrave, who marry, and even old Uncle Venner, enjoy quantifiable fruits when they inherit all the dead Judge Pyncheon's wealth and land at novel's end. Though this material compensation (which we can identify as Hawthorne's capitulation to commercial tastes as well as a longing for atonement) may appear questionable, the novel explores much richer and more ambiguous terrain as it depicts sexually nonnormative characters' efforts to carve out an alternative social and, possibly, erotic space.

MASCULINIST VIOLENCE AND FEMALE INTRANSIGENCE

I turn now to a topic whose presence has subtly informed this reading: misogyny. Intertextual poetics and visual identity, seemingly discrete questions, intersect in the larger issue, one both material and allegorical, of women's relationship to vision. Hawthorne's reworking of Milton emerges from the authors' shared fascination with female visuality, which evokes the intricate history of social constructions of femininity and female sexuality. Visuality also signals the occluded yet palpable investments in women's sexuality that deeply interest male writers in the Western tradition, including Hawthorne and Milton.

Male aggression informs the narrative of *The House of the Seven Gables*. The colonial-era Colonel Pyncheon accuses Matthew Maule of being a witch so he can obtain the Waldo County land; in turn, Maule curses him indelibly. Jaffrey Pyncheon unceasingly intimidates and persecutes Clifford, and by extension Hepzibah, so that the judge can recover the deed and, hence, the Maules' land. However, a key scene depicting sexualized violence synthesizes Hawthorne's central concerns.

Holgrave tells Phoebe the story of Alice Pyncheon, a beautiful young woman educated in Europe by her aristocratic father, Gervayse Pyncheon, the duplicitous Colonel Pyncheon's grandson. In order to locate the deed to the Maule lands, Gervayse summons the services of the carpenter Matthew Maule, the grandson of the Maule hanged for witchcraft and who wields the same occult powers (198–99). Bristling with class-based and ancestral rage, Maule agrees to Gervayse's request, stipulating that he be allowed to use the "clear, crystal medium" of his daughter Alice's "pure and virgin intelligence" (200). And Gervayse agrees to Maule's request. The scene foregrounds the traffic in women (the woman as commodity of exchange between men). Moreover, Hawthorne demonstrates a striking awareness of male desirability and ties this awareness to a motif unusual during his period, the theme of a woman's sexually appraising gaze.

Combining a "certain gentle and cold stateliness" and a "womanly ... tenderness," Alice immediately observes the bristling Maule's sexual magnetism, which Hawthorne registers using telling, almost homoerotic details. Walter Benn Michaels argues that Alice "fancies herself immune to possession (in effect, to appropriation) simply because she feels no desire.... thinks of herself as an impregnable citadel..... she is free from what Hawthorne, in McCarthyesque fashion, calls 'treachery from within.'"[67] Yet the author's depiction of Alice's desiring gaze undercuts Michaels's reading: "As Alice came into the room, her eyes fell upon the carpenter, who was standing near its centre, clad in ... a jacket ... loose breeches, open at the knees, and with a long pocket for his rule, the end of which protruded" (201). "A glow of artistic approval" suffuses her expression; "she was struck with admiration—which she made no attempt to conceal—of the remarkable comeliness, strength, and energy of Maule's figure" (201). But her "admiring glance" does not receive a receptive response. Being a glance that "most other men, perhaps, would have cherished" as a sweet memory, it startlingly kindles a demonic anger in Maule: "Does the girl look at me as if I were a brute beast!" he thinks to himself, "setting his teeth" (201). Hawthorne uses this episode to dissect the sexual politics of the gaze, the prohibitions on the female gaze and the male subject's investment in maintaining visual dominance, which Alice's objectifying appraisal jeopardizes.

A key factor here is Alice's pride. She deems herself "conscious of a power—combined of beauty, high, unsullied purity, and the preservative force of womanhood." Moreover, she understands, "instinctively," that Maule's plan and personality menace her in their "sinister or evil potency" (203). Nevertheless, she participates in this "contest," which pits "woman's might against man's might; a match not often equal, on the part of a woman" (203). Hawthorne portrays her as a narcissistic woman well aware of her strengths. This dimension of Alice's character links her to the narcissistic Eve, similarly male-dominated and subversive.

Seeking vengeance for Alice's haughty, sexually speculative look, Maule seizes his opportunity. Though he initially planned only to mesmerize Alice, Maule turns her into a zombie-like servant, making her laugh and dance inappropriately and humiliatingly, taunting her father for his complicity regarding her fate. But when he forces her out, barely clad, to attend his new bride on their wintry wedding night, Alice catches a fatal cold, leaving her persecutor shattered, knowing that he has destroyed a woman's life. While Hawthorne does not idealize Alice—she is no Phoebe—and makes her somewhat complicit with her fate, on balance he uses this episode to explore Alice's desire, which extends beyond her appraisal of Maule and includes her narcissistic self-fascination. She feels a sexual charge when looking at Matthew with his erect, phallic ruler, but she seems as titillated by her own power to look. Alice Pyncheon's story clearly allegorizes the Pyncheon and Maule family struggles. But its depiction of a specifically sexualized violence that makes the traffic in women the contest of male competitive relations is not limited to female sexual exploitation and abuse; Hawthorne also critiques male sexual anxiety and the class-based ramifications of that anxiety.⁶⁸ Alice denudes Maule with the phallic force of her transgressive gaze, and he essentially rapes and kills her in retaliation.

Alice's story allegorizes a key feminist dimension of Hawthorne's work, chiefly the prohibited female gaze and affiliated desire that link Alice and Hepzibah over time.⁶⁹ The elderly woman stares longingly and transgressively at her sleeping brother: Hepzibah can, like Alice, look at the male, but with potentially dire results. *Paradise Lost* uses Eve's nativity account to establish a powerful precedent for prohibiting both the female gaze and narcissistic desire, which has queer implications. Eve recounts her own birth and her assimilation into normative sexuality (4:460–76). Created from Adam's rib, Eve must relinquish her original desire and display only properly marital and heterosexual desire that, first, God and, second, Adam stipulate. Where does Eve's desire originate? Given the scene's prescriptive heterosexual dynamics, which the citation of the Narcissus myth as cautionary tale exemplifies, the episode clearly aims to correct her misdirected desire (a narcissistic one for self or a homoerotic one for another woman, if we recall that she does not initially recognize the pleasing creature reflected in the water as herself). Eve's poignant line "what could I do, / But follow strait, invisibly thus led?" (4.475–76) speaks volumes about female experience and conscription into the normative sexual and gendered social order.

While many commentators have discussed this episode from feminist, psychoanalytic, and queer perspectives, Hawthorne's intertextual reworking of Milton lays emphasis on a particular point.⁷⁰ In both authors' works, the woman's subjectivity and her desire are inextricable, perhaps indistinguishable, from her right to *look*, at the self in Eve's case, at the other in Hepzibah's. Narcissism, according to classical psychoanalysis, is a pathological desire that emerges in its later, secondary form as an ingenious alternative route to desire. In this regard, it gives crucial opportunities to both the homosexual male and the narcissistic woman. Freud describes both homosexual male and heterosexual female sexuality as narcissistic.⁷¹ Despite numerous ensuing controversies, several scholars have noted a surprising feminist usefulness in Freud's theoretical narcissistic woman, who can wield something like phallic agency by manipulating her narcissistic allure and her physical appeal. Through such efforts, the narcissistic woman can, in Kaja Silverman's words, "protest her forced identification with lack," subverting a culture devoted to standards of "absolute" feminine beauty.⁷²

Both Eve, who "pined with vain desire" (*PL,* 4.466), and Alice Pyncheon suffer the punitive ban on the erotic female gaze. Hepzibah's visage evinces her suffering; the involuntary scowl figures both her own inaccessible desire and her implausibility as a desirable object. Eve's encounter with her own reflection also bears incestuous overtones: the image that entrances her, her own image, could just as easily belong to a twin, another sibling, or a mother. (Indeed, the second–century AD traveler Pausanias offered his own version of the myth: Narcissus had a twin sister who died and whose image he reverences in his own reflection in the pool. As Jaś Elsner observes, Pausanias substitutes incest for homosexual panic, yet "this transgression is itself subsidiary to the fundamental taboo underlying all versions of the myth," which is autoeroticism.[73]) Milton revises the Ovidian Narcissus myth to reproduce its complex gender and sexual dynamics, transmuting Ovid's Echo, who can only helplessly repeat her beloved Narcissus's words, into the female Narcissus, Eve. Hawthorne's work explores gendered loss across time, the prohibitions on subjectivity and desire that affect, in his narratives, female and queer subjects most directly. Recalling the argument made in the introduction, we can further theorize that Hawthorne takes an Echo-like position, contemplating the Narcissus of his intertextual objects.

The novel's infamous happy ending notwithstanding, awareness of its outcast subjects' fragile hold on reality and claims to social power make *The House of the Seven Gables* both affectively resonant and politically useful. The novel's value resides in its acute analyses: of the gendered marketplace that isolates sexual desirability and normativity as prized commodities, and of the delimited possibilities afforded both female and queer desire. As with Ovid and Milton, sexuality in Hawthorne's work, permeated with an awareness that the sexual and gendered subject is endlessly violable, encodes the struggles for personal and social agency.

3

"TO VEIL FULL PURPOSE"

The Blithedale Romance *and Shakespeare*

DESPITE SEVERAL YEARS OF INTEREST in the transatlantic dimensions of American romanticism, very little work has been done on the overlaps between Hawthorne's work and Shakespeare's.[1] The esteemed Hawthorne critic Michael Colacurcio identifies Shakespeare as a predictable "literary" source for Hawthorne's work, conventional and comforting rather than more challengingly and properly "historical."[2] Presumably, then, the Hawthorne-Shakespeare connection is a scholarly interest so obvious as to have become exhausted. Yet a search for analysis of the topic yields surprisingly scant results. Hawthorne's reworking of Shakespeare in *The Blithedale Romance* (1852) inspired the most scholarly interest in the 1970s, which saw the publication of John O. Rees's "Shakespeare in *The Blithedale Romance*," Howard D. Pearce's "Hawthorne's Old Moodie: *The Blithedale Romance* and *Measure for Measure*" in 1973, and William E. Grant's "Hawthorne's *Hamlet:* The Archetypal Structure of *The Blithedale Romance*" in 1977. Beyond that, Ffrangcon Lewis published an essay in a 1992 issue of the *Journal of American Studies* that references Shakespearean aspects of the novel's female-centered themes.[3] And Joel Pfister provides a helpful analysis of *Blithedale*'s elaboration of an "Ophelia complex."[4]

Indeed, *Blithedale* teems with Shakespearean motifs, given its clear overlaps with *Hamlet* (1609) but also *Pericles, Prince of Tyre* (1619, cowritten with George Wilkins), *Cymbeline* (1623), *Coriolanus* (believed to have been written between 1605 and 1608), and particularly, as I will discuss, *Much Ado about Nothing* (1598–99), *Measure for Measure* (1603–4), and *King Lear* (1605–6). Rees observes: "Shakespearean drama exerts several kinds of influence" in the novel. The "precise limits of this influence" cannot be fixed, nor can "its most conspicuous signs" be interpreted "with entire assurance." But the most crucial point is that Shakespeare's influence reveals Hawthorne's work as "a fiction of assimilation."[5] If echoes of Shakespeare resound, so too do those of Spenser and Milton. Hawthorne's sustained engagement with English literary tradition complements the Hellenism that marks his work and Melville's. To focus on either Shakespeare's or Milton's influence is a partial approach to larger intertextual questions. Nevertheless, *Blithedale* crystallizes the Shakespearean aspects of Hawthorne's art, especially the concerns with women's sexuality and constricted social position within patriarchy that preoccupy both authors.

This chapter focuses on *Blithedale*'s reworking of *Much Ado about Nothing*, especially, as well as *Measure for Measure* and *King Lear*. While Pearce's 1973 essay compares *Blithedale* and *Measure for Measure*, this chapter is the first comparative analysis, to my knowledge, of *Blithedale*, *Much Ado*, and *Lear*. However distinctly, these works foreground awareness of misogyny and its pernicious effects. While some have read *Lear* as itself misogynistic, and while both Hawthorne and Shakespeare continue to generate controversies over their female depictions, I argue that these works critique male fantasies of femininity and their inevitable misogyny. In the context of the "power of women" trope that dates back at least to medieval literature—the belief that women embody sin and pose a threat to men, who are easily susceptible to feminine charms—Shakespeare offers resistant portraits of female intransigence. Hawthorne's reworking of Shakespeare emphasizes this intransigence.

The figure of the veiled woman unites *Much Ado*, *Measure for Measure*, *Blithedale*, and the concerns of this chapter. First, I discuss *Much Ado* and the meanings of the veil. Next, I focus on Shakespeare's treatment of female characters generally and in relation to Hawthorne's. From there, I discuss *Lear*'s overlaps with *Blithedale*, particularly themes of the female will, the suspect father, and a figure I call the patriarchal daughter. Lastly, in the second section on the veil, I discuss *Measure for Measure* and its significance for Hawthorne's depiction of a female character who self-veils.

THE VEIL AND THE POWER OF WOMEN

The chief link between *Much Ado* and *Blithedale* is the figure of the veiled woman. The veiled woman has a long-standing provenance. In the biblical context equally relevant to Shakespeare and Hawthorne, veiled women recur. At the sight of Isaac approaching her caravan, Rebekah swiftly veils her face (Genesis 24:64–65). Tamar, impersonating a prostitute to seduce Judah, dons a veil (Genesis 38:14–15). A famous instance of the veil relates to Moses, who covers his face after having received the Law the second time: "And the children of Israel saw the face of Moses, that the skin of Moses' face shone: and Moses put the vail upon his face again, until he went in to speak with him" (Exodus 34:35). Given that Hawthorne also envisions the veiled male—the titular figure of his indelible tale "The Minister's Black Veil" (1832)—his veil motif suggests a continuum of gender anxieties.

Lina Perkins Wilder notes a contemporary intertext for Shakespeare's veiled women. Lucina, the aspect of the Renaissance tripartite Diana associated with childbirth, is depicted as veiled in Vincenzo Cartari's *Le imagini degli Dei Antichi* (Richard Linche did the English translation, called *The Fountain of Ancient Fiction,* published in 1599). Veils function doubly as markers of feminine purity—signaling postnatal churching ceremonies—and as indicators of prostitution, associations stemming from the Judah-Tamar story.[6] Diana was a crucial figure for Hawthorne as well as Shakespeare.

The novel's pervasive veil imagery, associated with Zenobia's young half-sister, the seamstress Priscilla, signals its Orientalist origins.[7] Reflecting robust renewed scholarly interest in the veil's Orientalist meanings, Ali Behdad writes regarding the figure of the traveler, "The Oriental veil does not annul the subject's desire; rather, it arouses his scopic urge to overcome the barrier." In Lacanian terms, the Oriental woman's veil "conveys a kind of lack, the absence or concealment of the object that arouses his desire for unity with the Other; as Lacan has shown, desire is a *défense,* meaning both 'defense' and prohibition." The veil's "concealment of the body multiplies the signifiers of desire."[8] Studying veil imagery in Shakespeare, Brinda Charry observes:

> While the semantics of the veil vary with historical context, and issues surrounding it in our own time clearly cannot be imposed on the early modern era, a study of European representations of veiled Muslim women, then, will

perhaps help comprehend the ways in which the female body and its attire have always been a site of social regulation and have also played a role in the construction of cultural difference. The veil has complex symbolic meaning in discourses of cultural alterity and is a metaphor for the complexities of representation itself: the "other" is always the veiled figure, mysterious and unknown, and travelogues and ethnographies concern themselves with "unveiling" or "dis-covering" him/her. The veil signifies the persisting boundary between "us" and "them."[9]

Hawthorne's figure of the Veiled Lady, the mysterious entity performed by Priscilla, combines Eastern and Western contexts in the male subject's fantasies of veiled femininity.

The veiled woman's ambiguous as well as wholly negative associations correspond to the long-standing "Power of Women" topos of the Middle Ages. The topos's premise holds that even the best of men—Jason, Hercules, Aristotle; Samson, David, Solomon—fall helplessly prey to the irresistible seductive wiles of women. Women are the agents of love's destructive forces on men: "Eve's deception of Adam, Delilah's betrayal of Samson, and Solomon's wives' seduction of the old king into worshipping false gods" are three examples among many. The Power of Women topos was weaponized, used to terrify men and women into adopting "an ascetic morality based on fear of and hostility toward the body and toward the female sex with which the body was closely identified."[10] These pernicious notions endure as justifications for misogyny and animate misogynistic tirades such as King Lear's rebuke of his daughters and the reformer Hollingsworth's screed against women's rights in *Blithedale*.

Just as crucial to the figure of the veiled woman is the moment of unveiling, a revelation of her essential, corrupting duplicity. Melinda Gough, in an excellent discussion, outlines the genealogy of this trope in Renaissance texts:

> Scholars have long identified Ludovico Ariosto's famous tale of Ariodante and Ginevra [in *Orlando Furioso*] as the primary source for Edmund Spenser's Phedon-Claribell episode in book 2 of *The Faerie Queene*. They also typically cite Spenser's and Ariosto's versions of the story among probable subtexts for the Hero-Claudio plot in William Shakespeare's *Much Ado*

about Nothing.... [These texts share not only] the familiar motif of a beautiful woman falsely exposed as a whore but another juxtaposed with it in both Ariosto and Spenser and appropriated, in turn, by English antitheatricalists: the beautiful enchantress exposed as a whorish hag.[11]

A prime example of the latter, the enchantress Circe in *The Odyssey* turns the wayward hero Odysseus's men into pigs. Hawthorne reworked this episode in "Circe's Palace," one of his children's literature Greek myth-retellings in *Tanglewood Tales* (1853). Circe leads an entire "power of women" tradition, as Milton's references to her myth in his depiction of Eve adumbrate.

In an important *Blithedale* chapter, "The Masqueraders," first-person narrator Miles Coverdale uneasily returns to the utopian community he left earlier in the novel. He discovers its members in costume, reveling in the woods at night. Someone masquerades as "the goddess Diana, with the crescent on her head, and attended by our big lazy dog, in lack of any fleeter hound," evoking the myth of Diana and Actaeon. (The hunter Actaeon foolishly spies on the goddess when naked and bathing. She punishes the hunter by turning him into a stag hunted and killed by his own hounds. This story is told in Ovid's *Metamorphoses* [book 3: 165–252].) Hawthorne's ironic evocation of the goddess of chastity in a novel obsessively fixated on the question of female virginity parallels *Much Ado*. Shakespeare's frequent references to Diana—who appears in a vision to the titular hero of *Pericles*—include the moment in *Much Ado* when Claudio, about to marry the virtuous Hero but deceived by the villain Don John into believing her unchaste, bitterly likens her to "Dian in her orb'" (4.1.57). He then condemns the young woman as "more intemperate in your blood / Than Venus, or those pamper'd animals / That rage in savage sensuality" (4.1.60–61).[12]

"The Masqueraders" chapter directly references Milton's masque *Comus,* which contains a striking image of the veiled woman:

Come, let us our rights begin,
'Tis only day-light that makes sin,
Which these dun shades will ne'er report.
Hail, Goddess of nocturnal sport,
Dark-veil'd Cotytto! t'whom the secret flame
Of midnight torches burns; mysterious dame,

That ne'er art call'd, but when the dragon woom
Of Stygian darkness spetts her thickest gloom,
And makes one blot of all the air. (*Comus,* 125–33)

"During Comus's initial appearance as the forest enchanter-seducer," J. Karl Franson writes, "he calls upon his retinue, partially transformed into beasts, to join him in a libidinous ceremony." Cotytto is the "Thracian goddess of licentiousness, worshipped only on the darkest (or Stygian) nights"; Milton's "invocation to 'Dark-veil'd Cotytto'" is the "primary source for the darkly draped female" in William Blake's illustration of the poem, shown "riding through a treetop gloom that obscures sky, stars, and moon."[13] Though Hawthorne makes only a passing reference to *Comus, Blithedale*'s pervasive themes evoke the masque's central drama, the suspenseful encounter between Comus, the son of Circe and Bacchus and a predatory seducer of women, and the virtuous and chaste Lady he entraps. The villainous mesmerist Westervelt's commercial and possibly sexual exploitation of the young and vulnerable Priscilla evokes Comus's sexual predations and the endangerment of the Lady.

HAWTHORNE AND SHAKESPEARE

Hawthorne's knowledge of and commitment to Shakespeare are well documented. F. O. Matthiessen makes this connection paramount in his chapter on Hawthorne in *American Renaissance.* In his recent book on Hawthorne and the British Romantic Elizabeth Inchbald, Ben P. Robertson amply documents Hawthorne's knowledge and uses of Shakespeare, including Hawthorne's familiarity with Inchbald's collection of Shakespeare's plays. While I have not found specific evidence that Hawthorne read *Much Ado about Nothing,* or that he deliberately envisioned *Blithedale* as a reworking of this play, the play was collected in Inchbald's series and performed in Boston in 1828 and 1846.[14]

Several thematic and narrative overlaps exist between both works. The tart interactions between Coverdale and the theatrical, witty Zenobia in *Blithedale* echo the "merry war" (1.1.58) between Shakespeare's bantering, bickering, and eventually married pair Beatrice and Benedick (perhaps former lovers). One of the most famous bachelors in American fiction,

Coverdale recalls Benedick, who rails against marriage, but also his friend Don Pedro, Prince of Aragon, who remains a confirmed bachelor at play's end. The now, finally, marriage-bound Benedick remarks, "Prince, thou art sad—get thee a wife, get thee a wife!" (5.4.120). Zenobia, an actress and raconteur and local celebrity who reads Shakespeare to her fellow community members, resembles Beatrice in her fiery, retaliatory wit and penchant (an inconsistent one) for pointing out men's flaws to men. Strong parallels exist between the young women Hero, who is Beatrice's cousin, and Hawthorne's Priscilla, who is Zenobia's half-sister: questions of marriageability, virginity, desirability to the opposite sex, and male attitudes toward these questions. Hero, her waiting woman Margaret, and Hero's cousin Beatrice appear masked near the close of the play; throughout *Blithedale*, the mysterious public sensation the Veiled Lady, a shrouded woman said to be in touch with the spirits, makes several appearances; the novel's later action reveals Priscilla as this occult entity. Someone who causes harm for its own sake, the villainous Don John, Don Pedro's illegitimate brother, prefigures both Old Moodie, whose sadistic whims regarding his daughters, the half-sisters Zenobia and Priscilla, drive the plot, and the sinister mesmerist Westervelt, the impresario who controls and exhibits the Veiled Lady and, it is strongly implied, was once Zenobia's husband.

Shakespeare's Don John convinces Claudio, a lord of Florence and Don Pedro's friend, that Hero, whom Claudio falls in love with on sight, is nothing more than "a contaminated stale" (2.2.23), or whore, after arrangements are made for Claudio and Hero's marriage. A succinct example of what Gayle Rubin terms "the traffic in women,"[15] Hero is offered to Claudio as a marriage prospect through male homosocial negotiations. During a masquerade ball, the masked Don Pedro woos Hero on behalf of his love-smitten friend Claudio, an episode that Don John, in a preliminary attempt to undermine Claudio in order to wound Don Pedro, uses to convince Claudio that his seemingly loyal friend is stealing his love; Don Pedro must convince Claudio otherwise. With Claudio now set to marry Hero, Don John puts his full diabolical scheme into motion. He convinces Don Pedro and Claudio that, from their perspective on the ground, they are peering upwards at Hero in her chamber window being courted by Borachio, one of Don John's companions. (The woman above is actually Margaret, duped into impersonating Hero). Don Pedro vows to join Claudio in denouncing his fiancée publicly: "And as I wooed for thee to obtain her, I will / join with thee to disgrace her" (3.3.114–15). Making a grotesque mockery of the ceremony, Claudio calls Hero a whore at their wedding, intending to unmask her and echoing similar moments in Ariosto and Spenser.

Though depicted as doting, Hero's father, Leonato, demonstrates a capacity for violence with his own apoplectic rebuke of his daughter. The officiating Friar and Beatrice intervene, the first suggesting that some deception is responsible for the men's belief in Hero's wantonness, the second standing fiercely by her cousin and her honor. Eventually, a plan to settle the matter of Hero's innocence is established, a deception to shatter deception. Hero's death is announced while she goes into hiding. Don John's villainy finally exposed, Claudio begs Leonato for forgiveness, and the older man asks Claudio to atone by marrying his niece instead (the plan being to reunite Hero and Claudio): "And since you could not be my son-in-law, / Be yet my nephew. My brother hath a daughter, / Almost the copy of my child that's dead" (5.1.278–79).

At the second wedding scene, Beatrice, Hero, and her waiting-gentlewomen Margaret and Ursula emerge masked; her disguise removed, Hero stands before the thunderstruck Claudio, who can hardly believe that he beholds his beloved returned to him.

> *Claudio:* Another Hero!
> *Hero:* Nothing certainer.
> One Hero died defiled, but I do live,
> And surely as I live, I am a maid.
> *Prince:* The former Hero! Hero that is dead!
> *Leonato:* She died, my lord, but whiles her slander lived. (5.4.63–68)

"The Hero-Claudio story evidently appealed to the Renaissance consciousness," given that "seventeen variants of the legend have been traced in the period. Males no doubt saw in it an image of silent, submissive womanhood; females an image of women's sufferings," writes John Cox in his introductory essay to the *Shakespeare in Production* volume of the play.[16] Nevertheless, ambivalence informs the marital resolution that classifies this work as a comedy. Lina Perkins Wilder notes, "The veil represents both privacy and knowledge denied.... The masked women in the final scene" evoke male fantasies of women as unreadable, "deceptive surfaces," while also cuing the audience to remember the crimes against Hero, though "obliquely."[17] Margaret and Ursula remain "masked and undomesticated, emblems of the opacity and potential unruliness of women."[18] Shakespeare acknowledges the lack of resolution within the scene, which seemingly signals closure.

"Although *Much Ado* is certainly a comedy, it displays the usual Shakespearean dark underside with considerable prominence: physical and emotional violence between men, and between men and women," observes Thomas J. Scheff. Even "in comedy, Shakespeare intimates a deadlock in the relationship between men and women. . . . we may see that the feud between Beatrice and Benedick is kin not only to the comedic treatments of this theme, as in the verbal battles between Rosaline and Biron and the physical fights between Katherina and Petruchio. It is also related to his tragic lovers."[19] Considerable levels of disturbance, ambiguity, and ambivalence characterize this play. Shakespeare's comedy, by the very nature of its form, however, ultimately transmutes trauma into triumph. Hawthorne inverts the process, turning sexual comedy into gendered tragedy; he reworks *Much Ado* to emphasize an ineluctable progression toward, or devolution into, trauma. Or, to put it another way, he heightens the lingering unease that inheres even in the seemingly happy, romantic resolution of Shakespeare's comedy.

Much Ado, Comus, Paradise Lost, and *Blithedale* all link the question of female sexuality to morality. Feminist activist though she is, Zenobia is consistently presented as a sexual enigma and therefore threat. This is not to suggest that Zenobia is presented unsympathetically—far from it. Nevertheless, Coverdale's insistent speculations about her virginity or lack thereof, the likelihood that she has been previously married, color his interactions with her. In chapter 6, "Coverdale's Sick-Chamber," he speculates at length about Zenobia's sexuality in a passage that both foregrounds his misogyny and his uncanny, though not exculpatory, awareness of it as such:

> Her unconstrained and inevitable manifestation, I said often to myself, was that of a woman to whom wedlock had thrown wide the gates of mystery. Yet sometimes I strove to be ashamed of these conjectures. I acknowledged it as a masculine grossness—a sin of wicked interpretation, of which man is often guilty towards the other sex—thus to mistake the sweet, liberal, but womanly frankness of a noble and generous disposition. Still, it was of no avail to reason with myself nor to upbraid myself. Pertinaciously the

thought, "Zenobia is a wife; Zenobia has lived and loved! There is no folded petal, no latent dewdrop, in this perfectly developed rose!"—irresistibly that thought drove out all other conclusions, as often as my mind reverted to the subject. (47)

Beatrice is cajoled by those around her into revealing her love for Benedick, as he is in turn cajoled regarding Beatrice. In contrast, Zenobia receives very little support—except, perhaps, from Coverdale—in her romantic pursuit of the charismatic, intense, but stony and unyielding Hollingsworth. Which is to say, the romantic comedy does not come to fruition, and Zenobia's ardent desire meets an obliterating refusal. Hollingsworth rejects the passionate Zenobia in favor of the pallid (though surprisingly steely) Priscilla.

The masked women at the end of *Much Ado* represent both the comeliness of women and their essential mystery, if we understand femininity in its conventional, indeed mythic terms. Their function is not to absolve the crimes committed against a specific woman, but instead to purify the disordered atmosphere created in the community by Don John's actions and their toxic aftermath and Claudio and Don Pedro's susceptibility to his falsehoods. The procession of masked women participates in a ritual designed to restore the victimized woman's good name as virgin. At the same time, we remember Perkins Wilder's observation that the function of this ritual is to remind us, however obliquely, of the crimes against Hero. Rather than embodying a kind of achieved social equilibrium or some measure of détente between the sexes—and again, Shakespeare makes the tenuous and contingent nature of such evident—the Veiled Lady signals the perpetuation of women as embodiments of male fantasy who reconcile warring elements of conventional notions of femininity. Speaking of veiled women, Elizabeth Cady Stanton (1815–1902), an abolitionist feminist and one of the organizers of the first Woman's Rights Convention in America, held in Seneca Falls, New York, in 1848, wrote in *The Woman's Bible* (published in 1895 and 1898) in response to religious edicts that women should be veiled: "It is certainly high time that women in a Republic should rebel against a custom based on the supposition of their heaven-ordained subjection. Jesus is always represented as having long, curling hair, and so is the Trinity. Imagine a painting of these Gods all with clipped hair. Flowing robes and beautiful hair add greatly to the beauty and dignity of their pictures."²⁰ That Hawthorne sympathized with such views comes through clearly in *The Scarlet Letter,* the sensual gush of raven hair when Hester Prynne unloosens her bonneted locks before Arthur Dimmesdale in the forest.

The Veiled Lady exquisitely signifies the subjection Stanton agitates against. The figure is volatile, however, in that it embodies equally held beliefs in women's inherent chastity and sexlessness—supported by the theories of sexuality promulgated by phrenologists and other antebellum medical practitioners, the basis for the antebellum Cult of True Womanhood—and penchant for licentiousness.²¹ Little wonder then that Hawthorne's initially comic notes turn to tragic ones. If at the very least Hero's honor is restored and the false accusations against her refuted, Priscilla's rescue by Hollingsworth from Westervelt's clutches, and her continued servitude as the Veiled Lady, produces a far more ambivalent outcome.

Priscilla's sexual integrity is maintained at considerable difficulty given her status as a seamstress, a figure associated with prostitution in the antebellum period (as Allan Lefcowitz and Barbara Lefcowitz elucidate in their article "Some Rents in the Veil"), and her compulsory performance as the Veiled Lady, making her an object of not only public fascination but also corporeal pliancy to male spectators. Though Westervelt boasts of the impregnable force field her shrouded nature lends the Veiled Lady, his showy efforts to demonstrate this impregnability push the idea to its offensive, misogynistic breaking point by subjecting the imperiled woman to public male abuse. During the Veiled Lady's final appearance, Westervelt instructs the lyceum's male spectators to storm the stage and bellow into her ear, which deafening assault, it is claimed by the mesmerist, will be unheard by the medium. It's possible that Priscilla really does not hear these thunderous verbal assaults; possible, too, that she does not smell the men's breath or feel the tactile spray of it on her face; yet it is highly unlikely to be the case that the misogynistically used object Priscilla is as insensate as her odious handler avers.

Hollingsworth dramatically comes to the rescue, taking to the stage and telling Priscilla to come to him instead. Yet his actions hardly signify a restoration of female integrity given the manipulative cunning that characterizes Hollingsworth's own exploitation of the women of Blithedale. To fund his grand plan for prison reform, Hollingsworth first obscurely woos Zenobia, whose wealth draws him in; but when Old Moodie disinherits

Zenobia for having failed to demonstrate appropriately sisterly affection toward Priscilla and makes the younger woman the rich one, Hollingsworth shifts his romantic interest to Priscilla, whom he marries, shattering Zenobia in the process. These actions confirm Hollingsworth's role as, in Nina Baym's indelible description, "the spirit of authoritarian domination."[22] The intense and protective love that Beatrice feels instinctively and consistently for Hero does not inform the relations between women in Hawthorne's novel; Zenobia remains essentially if resignedly antagonistic toward her half-sister, a prime example of what Helena Michie describes as "sororophobia," an enmity between women successfully engineered by the estranged sisters' perfidious father, despite his frequent demands that Zenobia show Priscilla love. What Hawthorne unmasks or unveils is a culture of misogyny where woman's identity remains forever shrouded by male fantasy.

SHAKESPEARE'S FEMININITY

Before turning to a comparative discussion of *Blithedale* and *King Lear*, I want to address, through the perspectives of feminist Shakespeare scholarship, themes of misogynous violence and the female will. Juliet Fleming addresses Shakespeare's apparently uncanny understanding of women and femininity as a cultural myth whose sturdy provenance dates to Margaret Cavendish's claim in her 1664 *Sociable Letters* that he was able to "Metamorphose from a Man to a Woman."

> To those women who have loved him, Shakespeare's great gift has usually been said to be his ability to draw women "from life" ... Such critics have tended to stress the strengths rather than the weaknesses of Shakespeare's women ... If Shakespeare's heroines appear to be idealized, that is because women's nature—the nature she will be free to express only once she has been liberated from the distorting influence of her current constraints—*is* ideal. It is in this sense that Shakespeare can be said to understand the women of the future while ... the women of the future will be able to recognize themselves in Shakespeare's heroines.[23]

If we should be skeptical of claims, however controversial, that writers like Shakespeare and Hawthorne who demonstrate an acute sensitivity toward their female characters are somehow privy to special knowledge about women, we can nevertheless establish that their value lies in their abilities to discern, call attention to, and at times critique the feminine ideal, a binding multifaceted mythology of women as archetypal. It is precisely this mythic ideal nature of women that emerges in heightened form in the procession of masked and veiled women at *Much Ado*'s climax and that beckons *Blithedale*'s ravening male spectators. Indexing feminine myths, the veil signals the idea that woman is fundamentally enigmatic: hidden, shrouded, unattainable, unknowable, her unknowability a lure that erotically bedevils and compels men. This misogynous fantasy, its simultaneous allure and power to estrange, lies at the heart of the cultural myth of women as timeless, universal, infinite.

For a comic work, *Much Ado* derives its power from a barely suppressed level of misogynistic violence. This violence, argues Mihoko Suzuki, lies not in actual murders of wives by their husbands but "a symbolic murder of a young woman by her betrothed," an act supported by both "illegitimate and marginal" and "highest-ranking members of the social order," Hero's father Leonato included. In this realm, those who want to disrupt the workings of the social order can readily avail themselves of the "universal anxiety concerning women's sexuality as an index of her agency and potential unruliness."[24] Suzuki argues that the "negative and disquieting associations" in *Much Ado*'s sources "and in literary tradition itself—from classical antiquity to Elizabethan England" indicate "the overdetermined construction of Hero as a duplicitous and sexually experienced woman. Literary tradition here stands for the cultural context in which Shakespeare is writing."[25] Hawthorne, an American romantic emulating and collaborating with his precursor, finding his image within this intertextual mirror, inherits Shakespeare's problematic and daring reinterpretation of traditional views of women; moreover, Hawthorne inherits Milton's revisions of the Shakespearean model. "Dark-veil'd Cotytto" rises up from the Stygian depths of misogynistic myth, the image of illicit female sexuality portrayed as monstrous and all-consuming. Tearing away the hag's seemingly beautiful visage, shining a light on the seemingly virtuous woman's sexual transgressions, and similar efforts to expose the female sexual monster fail at eradicating her threat, which looms over narrative. Zenobia evokes Milton's fearsome Cotytto in her air of mystery and in Coverdale's constant speculations about her scandalous promiscuity. The queenliness of Zenobia, named for the defeated third-century Queen of Palmyra, lends her an authority and magnitude that darkly reinforces her associations with the sinister goddess of sex without constraint. Though unmarried and possibly having once had a sexual relationship with Benedick, Beatrice never bears the mark of sexual shame that her cousin Hero must so prominently wear. In Hawthorne, sexual crime chiefly stains the Beatrice-like Zenobia, leaving his Hero-like Priscilla suspect yet unblemished.

In her often startling study of the radical conventionality of women in Shakespeare's plays, Kathryn Schwarz notes the prevalence of "feminine subjects [who] defend the standards by which they are defined, and contractual systems [that] excise valueless men."[26] Early modern misogyny is a discourse that "asserts the power to determine *what* women mean," and is also driven by the question of "*how* they mean, and with how they signify their capacity to intend." The "edict to discipline and define" undergirds this discourse's authority, but its "narratives trace feminine meaning as a purpose in a process, which precedes and shapes the disciplinary mandate itself." The urgent need to disavow while responding to "the active work of the feminine will" mutates into unruly fusions, "clichés of nature and essence" combined with "conjectures about strategic self-invention."[27] Schwarz's argument leads us to consider the possibilities afforded to female characters seeking autonomy in Shakespeare, Milton, and Hawthorne— how far do these possibilities go, and do female characters justify the misogynistic status quo? Antebellum works as varied as Margaret Fuller's magisterial feminist study *Woman in the Nineteenth Century* (1845); Poe's tale "Ligeia" (1838), whose titular heroine avails herself of "the will" to conquer death; and Harriet Jacobs's *Incidents in the Life of a Slave Girl* (1861) and its intransigent heroine, Linda Brent, provocatively foreground woman's will as a formidable and disruptive dimension of femininity. Hawthorne complicates the question throughout his work, with surprisingly resistant feminine portrayals such as Hepzibah's defiance against Jaffrey Pyncheon. *Blithedale* explores a range of female manifestations of the will and of conformity to male rule.

Much Ado foregrounds the frightening potentialities of female will when Beatrice demands that Benedick, if he truly loves her, must "kill Claudio" (4.1.288) after he has slandered and rejected Hero at the would-be wedding.[28] Beatrice clearly expresses her own rage at misogynistic men in this moment, made salient by her subsequent language: "O, God that I /

were a man! I would eat his heart in the market place" (4.1.315).[29] Indeed, Beatrice's anger kindles into misandrist contempt: likening Claudio to the cloying "Count Comfit," she fulminates, "O, that I were a man for his sake! Or / that I had any friend would be a man for my sake! / But manhood is melted into curtsies, valour into compliment, and men are only turned into tongue / and trim ones, too" (4.1.315–18).[30] Though initially expressing skepticism and surprise at Beatrice's enflamed request, Benedick agrees to challenge Claudio for having "wronged Hero" (4.1.326). Given *Much Ado*'s precarious tension between elements that challenge gender conventions and those that uphold them, and given that Benedick's role as "the witty misogynist" is to express "traditional patriarchal ideology," it is striking that Benedick's own position as a traditional male so hangs in the balance.[31] While one shares Beatrice's anger toward the misogynistic males who have wronged Hero, her contempt for "Count Comfit" and his melting ilk bespeaks a disdain for male effeminacy, for men who take little or no action. Benedick will fall into the same disesteem should he fail to kill Claudio.[32]

Blithedale reanimates these tensions, putting a man of inaction at its center, oscillating between the self-hating silence of a wronged woman when she hears misogynistic abuse (Zenobia in the chapter "Eliot's Pulpit") and her fiery explosion of condemning words when her betrayer shows his manipulative hand (Zenobia in the chapter "The Three Together"). "But how is it with you?" Zenobia blisteringly questions Hollingsworth. "Are you a man? No; but a monster! A cold, heartless, self-beginning and self-ending piece of mechanism!" (218) Beatrice sees Claudio as a slight, cloying confection, his inadequacy only adding to her rage that he wields so much power over her cousin's fate; Zenobia sees Hollingsworth, who casts her aside when her financial fortunes go awry, as a cold, unfeeling machine, her final verdict infused with the agony of spurned affections.

PATERNAL NARCISSISM, TRAGIC DAUGHTERS: LEAR IN BLITHEDALE

That considerable overlaps between *Much Ado* and *King Lear* exist have been established. Claire McEachern's notable 1988 article "Fathering Herself" locates these overlaps in Shakespeare's revisioning of his sources and specifically in his complex rendering of fathers—Leonato, Lear—and paternal desire. Drawing on feminist and psychoanalytic readings of *Lear*, I want to think through Hawthorne's reworking of *Lear* in his depiction of father-daughter relationships in *Blithedale*. While the novel oscillates between several key plot points—the possibilities of reform, the meanings of community, the varieties of sexual desire, femininity as spectacle, ruined relations between men and women, between men, between women—its center is, arguably, the relationship between an elderly man and his female offspring.

Lear was a crucial Shakespeare intertext for both Hawthorne and, as we discuss in the next chapter, Melville: "In addition to reading Shakespeare's drama, Hawthorne attended dramatic performances of the plays when the opportunity arose. In a letter to his mother on 6 March 1821, at the early age of sixteen, Hawthorne mentions having seen a performance of *King Lear*, starring Edmund Kean, which 'was enough to have drawn tears from millstones' and which made him almost lose himself in his own contemplations about the play."[33]

Lear's plot is well known. The old king Lear, at the start of the play, demands expressions of profuse love from his three daughters, in birth order Goneril, Regan, and Cordelia. Goneril and Regan falsely and prodigiously flatter Lear to gain possession of his kingdom; Cordelia, the third and youngest, refuses to acquiesce to Lear's demands; rather than fawning over him, she responds succinctly, "I love your Majesty / According to my bond; no more nor less" (1.1.94–95). Lear, apoplectic at her parsimonious answer, banishes Cordelia. Her two older sisters, once in control of Lear's kingdom, strip him of all rights and cast him out. Over the course of his madness-laden exile, Lear develops some sense of his having wronged Cordelia.

Hawthorne substitutes Moodie, an old man of great financial means (acquired, squandered, regained) for Lear, giving him two highly contrastive daughters, the magnetic Zenobia and, unbeknownst to her, a half-sister in the younger Priscilla. Moodie, behind the scenes, observes Zenobia's attitude toward Priscilla, vowing to disinherit her should she fail to treat Priscilla lovingly, a rigged game considering that Zenobia remains unaware of her lineage until too late. Hawthorne emphasizes the old man's unredeemable egotism, the vengeful exertion of his idiosyncratic and obscure will as he ensnares his daughters in a plot he devises, whereas Shakespeare moves toward Lear's redemption when he finally reunites with the banished

Cordelia, whose forgiveness frees him from damnation even though the play ends tragically with both their deaths.[34] The chief distinction between *Lear* and *Blithedale* is the thematization of forgiveness in the former (critics disagree about whether forgiveness is an accurate description for Cordelia's actions), and the near absence of this theme in the latter, or, more properly put, the possibility of forgiveness in *Lear* and its much narrower possibilities in *Blithedale*. I will return to this point.

Both *Lear* and *Blithedale* foreground patriarchal fascination with and dread of female will even as they depict the disastrous consequences of male caprice. In both works an aged man who wields power puts women to the test, their emotions, decisions, and desires his crucible. The fascination with women's unpredictable natures; the construction of women's natures *as* unpredictable, volatile, unclassifiable, mercurial; the very idea of a scenario meant to test women: all signal patriarchal attempts to control and condition femininity. Kathryn Schwarz's analysis of *King Lear*'s female depictions illuminates misogyny's central role: "Misogyny, in early modern contexts, often manifests a concern that women interact too closely with men, and in *Lear* this appears as hyperbolic dread."[35] In their ardent zeal to separate themselves from women, "men make all feminine will equally dangerous, and the constancy of Cordelia becomes as deadly as the violent caprice of Regan and Goneril."[36] Schwarz continues: "When the misogynist repudiation of women succeeds, it connects subjects across ethical, emotional, and aesthetic boundaries, opposing transactional feminine volition to the stasis of masculine detachment."[37] *Lear*'s representation of femininity does not uniformly and starkly oppose a good femininity (Cordelia) against a bad one (Goneril and Regan); rather, it examines the effects of the varieties of female will—which makes will *visible,* as opposed to its invisible and, at least ostensibly, smooth operations in patriarchy—on male-centered social relations.

Moodie's manipulation of his daughters foregrounds male fantasies of women's willfulness while revealing an even deeper kinship between *Lear* and *Blithedale,* their critique of the family that breeds estrangement rather than kinship. Bennett Simon, in his brilliant *Tragic Drama and the Family,* establishes nonrecognition of kin as one of *Lear*'s central themes, informing the play's thematization of female sexuality as monstrous. Nonrecognition of kin "powerfully illuminates what it means to recognize. Recognition of the other implies acknowledgement of a balance between autonomy and dependency; acknowledgement of the power, but also the limits, of the bond between father and daughter," as Cordelia's expression of love "according to my bond; no more nor less" (1.1.94–95) evinces.[38]

Nonrecognition of kin centrally informs *The Blithedale Romance*. Zenobia's inability to recognize Priscilla as her half-sister leads her into a realm of sustained ignorance about her own origins and especially about her father. It is strongly suggested that Zenobia was once married to the villainous mesmerist Westervelt, who presents Priscilla to the public as the sideshow attraction the Veiled Lady. That Zenobia abets Westervelt's exploitation of Priscilla lends nonrecognition of kin an acute horror. Moodie obsessively schemes to witness the recognition scene between Zenobia and Priscilla—the older sister recognizing her younger one *as* a sister—yet this scene never occurs, only its feeble substitute. In the last encounter between the women, the defeated Zenobia acknowledges Priscilla as kin but, given her impending marriage to the man Zenobia loves, more importantly as victor. Moodie's disinheritance of Zenobia effects a legal and emotional act of nonrecognition, a willed obliteration of knowledge of the other. The heartrending scene of recognition and forgiveness between Lear and Cordelia near the end of the tragedy both heals and overwhelms, providing succor if not resolution. Hawthorne not only withholds but renders unthinkable any such healing recognition. Daughters remain maddeningly disconnected from their fathers, fathers from their daughters, sisters from their sisters.

Hawthorne's revision of *Lear* in *Blithedale*, then, preserves and jettisons certain aspects of the plot. Preserved: a vain and foolish old man demands an unreasonable display of fealty from his daughters and wreaks havoc on his progeny. Jettisoned: the idea of three sisters of the same parentage; the idea that the loyal Cordelia-like daughter is the truly virtuous one. Zenobia resembles Goneril and Regan in being vivid, larger than life and passionate and in wielding power through paternal resources. Priscilla resembles Cordelia in being comparatively restrained and in her estrangement from her sibling. Moodie's dangerous game, lurking in the shadows to observe his daughters' interactions and monitor the levels of intimacy between them, echoes Lear's plot-driving demand that each of his three daughters profess their laudatory love for him. Hawthorne crucially reworks this plot. Women's affectional ties and struggles provide the fodder for Moodie's agonized and sinister fantasies. Hawthorne transforms the elderly king's demands for declarations of love from his daughters into Moodie's obsession with witnessing an act of sororal intimacy between the wealthy, captivating daughter he barely knows and the daughter of his "shame." Moodie substitutes the impoverished, drab Priscilla for himself, a murky strategy for satisfaction and recognition.

Zenobia has lived opulently, raised by her prosperous bachelor uncle without ever knowing her parents or that she has a half-sister. Moodie lost his wealth and stature through serious criminal acts (most likely forgery), his first wife, Zenobia's noble and virtuous mother, dying in the scandal's wake. Once a free man, Moodie lives life impecuniously and marries again, this time "a forlorn, meek-spirited, feeble, young woman" (185) whom their daughter Priscilla resembles. Moodie has inherited the funds of his dead brother (who may have acquired the disgraced Moodie's funds when he was imprisoned), leaving him once again a wealthy man, however shabbily attired. Unbeknownst to Zenobia, Moodie is not only her father but also holds her financial fate in his hands. When Coverdale first journeys to Blithedale, Moodie has already started weaving his eccentric but unyielding plot to confirm Zenobia's love for Priscilla. This act of recognition never occurs, and Moodie disinherits Zenobia, giving his regained wealth to Priscilla.

Both Shakespeare and Hawthorne place continuous emphasis on the father's whims, vainglory, and the genuine violence that undergirds their deceptively whimsical (Lear) or slight (Moodie) surface. In devising a contest between daughters who, in the old man's eyes, represent distinct phases of his life, Moodie pits his former prosperity against his present shame. As he baldly puts it, "in Zenobia, I live again!" (192). Laying out his backstory for Coverdale in a later scene set in a tavern, Moodie, calling his former self Fauntleroy, ruminates:

> I am unchanged,—the same man as of yore!" said he. "True, my brother's wealth—he dying intestate—is legally my own. I know it; yet of my own choice, I live a beggar, and go meanly clad, and hide myself behind a forgotten ignominy. Looks this like ostentation? Ah! but in Zenobia I live again! Beholding her, so beautiful,—so fit to be adorned with all imaginable splendor of outward state,—the cursed vanity, which, half a lifetime since, dropt off like tatters of once gaudy apparel from my debased and ruined person, is all renewed for her sake. Were I to reappear, my shame would go

with me from darkness into daylight. Zenobia has the splendor, and not the shame. Let the world admire her, and be dazzled by her, the brilliant child of my prosperity! It is Fauntleroy that still shines through her!

But he adds a note of frightening caution: "My poor Priscilla! And am I just to her, in surrendering all to this beautiful Zenobia? Priscilla! I love her best,—I love her only!—but with shame, not pride. So dim, so pallid, so shrinking,—the daughter of my long calamity! Wealth were but a mockery in Priscilla's hands. What is its use, except to fling a golden radiance around those who grasp it? Yet let Zenobia take heed! Priscilla shall have no wrong!" (192–93). Zenobia's beauty mirrors Moodie's narcissistic self-fascination with his vaunted earlier self; her wealth functions similarly. Yet that her stature remains entirely contingent on his whims clarifies her function as the embodiment of his fluctuating fantasies. It's almost as if he wishes to transfuse the pallid Priscilla with glamorous Zenobia's lifeblood, saturated with his former richness. Devastatingly, he reveals to Coverdale that he does not love Zenobia, that he loves Priscilla "only." However shame-laden his love, his younger daughter can claim it as a commodity unavailable to Zenobia, who is rejected—unloved—by her father and by the man she loves. Indeed, Priscilla is loved several times over, by her father, Hollingsworth, and, in the seemingly shocking last-line reveal, Coverdale himself. It's almost as if Cordelia rather than Lear were given the three expressions of profuse love without excessive and duplicitous flattery needing to buttress it. (That having been said, each of Priscilla's lovers can be considered suspect along with their love.)

Moodie clearly views Zenobia as a collection of surfaces, components ripe for fetishization. Having summoned her to his abode while keeping his paternal identity a secret, he examines her corporeal form with the aid of a lamp. Her diamonds emit their own glittering light in his dismal chamber. "It was the splendor of those jewels on her neck, like lamps that burn before some fair temple, and the jewelled [sic] flower in her hair, more than the murky yellow light, that helped him to see her beauty" (191). And beholding her beauty he grows flushed with pride: "his own figure, in spite of his mean habiliments, assumed an air of state and grandeur" (191–92). Tellingly, this perusal of Zenobia's body and beauty—only this—allows Zenobia provisional access to her finances. Moodie concludes: "Keep your wealth. You are right worthy of it. . . . Keep all your wealth, but with only this one condition. Be kind—be no less kind than sisters are—to my poor Priscilla!" (192).

Zenobia's role meshes with Goneril's and Regan's, yet, interacting with Moodie for the first and only time in the novel, she hardly takes a serpent-toothed stance. Summoned by him to his hovel, she initially seems taken aback, asking him if he requires charity and, matter-of-factly, why he needs her aid, which she views as his "privilege" to receive given his "age and poverty" (191). After Moodie tells her that she can keep her wealth, but with one condition, Zenobia does not avariciously and cunningly ask what this condition is. Instead, her immediate response is to be "moved with pity" as she beholds "an old man beside himself" (192). She follows up her pitying response with an offer of genuine aid: "'Have you none to care for you?' asked she. 'No daughter?—no kind-hearted neighbor? . . . Tell me, once again, can I do nothing for you?'" (192). This moment reveals Zenobia's generous and compassionate nature, given that she still has no inkling of Moodie's relation to her or control over her finances.[39]

Hawthorne offers in muted and pointedly diminished form the indelible moment in *Lear* when the outcast, suffering, maddened king experiences compassion from the daughter he banished. As she tenderly comforts him, the returned Cordelia pityingly marvels, "Was this a face / To be opposed against the warring winds? / To stand against the deep dread-bolted thunder?" (4.7.31). Lear, disoriented and fragile, responds, "I am mightily abused. I should e'en die with pity, / To see another thus" (4.7.53). However muddled his thoughts, Lear can look upon his own condition from a perspective of detachment, look upon his own abjection. In this manner, he inhabits Cordelia's experience of pity, which is to say, he empathizes with her pain at looking at his pitiful, wounded, discarded condition. In contrast, Moodie can only look on Zenobia as the embodiment of his narcissistic fantasies and therefore cannot apprehend his daughter's true character, reflected in her offer of help to an enigmatic stranger. He sees only her use value. Ostensibly, his imposed condition—"Be kind—be no less kind than sisters are—to my poor Priscilla!" (192)—bespeaks a love-thy-neighbor philosophy, but Moodie's nature defies such a reading. His directive can be translated as follows: "Keep your wealth so that you can be the living embodiment of the status I once enjoyed, but forever humble yourself to your impecunious sister so that your subservience to me never loses its urgency."

Claire McEachern observes in her essay "Fathering Herself" that patriarchy, far from being monolithic and monolingual, is "founded in ideological contradictions, inconsistencies, and incongruities."[40] McEachern establishes that Shakespeare's reworking of his sources—the way he reads his culture—provides the basis of her feminist interpretation of "Renaissance patriarchy through the study of fathers and daughters, using both Shakespeare's literary fathers and those fathers and daughters that he presents in his plays."[41] Her analysis intersects with the concerns of this book. "In revising his sources," she writes, "he recasts and demystifies the role of the father, and, mimicking the action he represents, Shakespeare, in the rebellious but also revisionary act of rewriting, questions the power of fathers, a power that demands replication for the perpetuation of the patriarchal system."[42] In works such as *Much Ado* and *Lear,* Shakespeare "confounds the relationship between social and psychological realities, moving beyond the economic or civil rhetoric to expose [patriarchy's] potentially destructive emotional logic."[43] Considering his revision in *Much Ado* of the source material in Bandello's story of *Timbreo and Fenicia,* McEachern argues that in "Shakespeare's version, the social status and concerns of father and suitor no longer completely dictate their behaviors or define their roles" because now Leonato and Claudio share a similarly high social status: "Thus economic considerations do not explain [Leonato's] rejection of Hero."[44] His rejection of Hero, a genre-defying moment of ugliness in a comic work, transparently reveals an effort to "regain his social power among men."[45] Shakespeare nevertheless reveals patriarchy's "radical investment in the affective order of the family" in Leonato's love for his daughter despite his gendered biases.[46] A confrontation with Hero's sexuality forces Leonato "to recognize his daughter's identity as separate from his own."[47] Of Hero's simulated death, McEachern observes: "Only the fictional death of her offending flesh will allow Hero to escape . . . In order for the play to conclude in marriage, Leonato must become a father again in a less possessive way."[48] Similarly, Lear's desire to possess the entirety of his daughters' love, which so bewilders and vexes Cordelia, leading her to ask Lear why his daughters should even bother to marry when their father demands so much devotion, must undergo a crucial revision over the course of the play.[49] Lear's "perversion of the dowry ceremony reveals his desire to prevent its consummation"; the "relationship under negotiation here is not between two men but between father and daughter," as Lear expresses a wish to "secure a pledge of love that . . . would make [Cordelia's] marriage impossible."⁵⁰

Also discussing Shakespeare and his revision of source materials, Meredith Skura in her 2008 article "Dragon Fathers and Unnatural Children" notes that "balancing a father's story with a child's, Shakespeare's play remains closer to the original plot of *King Leir* (c. 159?), his primary source, than we have realized." While the original play shows us Cordelia's life in France after Lear banishes her, and Shakespeare "crowds Cordelia out of the main plot," "he maintains *Leir's* balance" by keeping the focus on two main plots, Lear's life and death and the travails of the outcast Edgar. "What Shakespeare does change," however, "is the moral imbalance in Leir's presentation of father and child. In the old play, it is clear that Leir is wrong and Cordella is right. . . . Shakespeare's dual plots suggest instead that father and child are both sinned against and sinning. . . . Generations always threaten to eat each other like creatures of the deep. . . . Parents harm their children," intentionally or otherwise.⁵¹ Still, Shakespeare's Lear is self-protectively self-deluded. He "sees himself as 'more sinned against than sinning' (3.2.60). Except for fleeting, if poignant, moments, he never recognizes or changes his desire to possess Cordelia all for himself. He first strides onstage announcing a 'darker purpose' (1.1.38) and may never realize how dark his purpose is, how much he wants to swallow his children whole and make them messes."⁵²

Hawthorne pointedly reworks *Lear* and its themes in his portrait of a selfishly motivated paterfamilias's interaction with his distinctly drawn daughters. Ultimately, Hawthorne imagines a far less redemptive story than did Shakespeare, however circumscribed a redemption he offers in his ineluctably tragic play. Lear's ability to reconnect with Cordelia returns some forfeited portion of his humanity. Moodie can make no such claim. Lear reclaims his heroism when he kills Cordelia's assassin; and his humanity, when he operatically mourns murdered Cordelia. Moodie plays a decisive role in Zenobia's suicide by disinheriting her, leaving her impoverished and ensuring that she is no longer desirable to Hollingsworth. At Zenobia's burial, Moodie is not even mentioned by name: "Nearest the dead walked an old man in deep mourning, his face mostly concealed in a white handkerchief, and with Priscilla leaning on his arm" (239). That Moodie can only namelessly attend Zenobia's funeral and never finds redemption indicates that Hawthorne saw him as unworthy of tragic grandeur, in sharp contrast to Lear and to Melville's Lear-like Ahab. Old Moodie's tragedy constitutes a small-bore dissolution.

Hawthorne repeatedly depicts older male figures ambivalently. A recurring motif is older male predation on younger males as well as women. (Similar patterns of intergenerational male violence characterize Melville's fiction.) Striking examples include the Satanic old man with a serpent-like walking stick in the tale "Young Goodman Brown," who slyly observes, intimidates, and ensnares the titular protagonist; the sinister voyeur and scientist Rappaccini, who ensures the poisoned fate of the young male who has fallen in love with the scientist's fatal daughter; and the wizened manipulator Chillingworth in *The Scarlet Letter*, who moves in with the young, guilt-ridden adulterer Minister Dimmesdale. Tales such as "Roger Malvin's Burial" and "My Kinsman, Major Molineaux" realistically depict oedipal strife and its narcissistic dimensions. The older male / younger male conflict figures a consistent crisis in self-image located in the American historical past and allegorizes antebellum gender anxieties.[53]

Then there are the misogynistic oppressors whose sense of women's inferiority and imposition of masculine will make them villainous, such as Jaffrey Pyncheon and Hollingsworth. If Moodie represents fatherhood as both petty and sinister, grasping and destructive, Hollingsworth, going beyond Moodie's view of women as entities designed to fulfil men's fantasies of personal grandeur, makes explicit his belief that a woman belongs solely at "man's side," her "office" that of "Sympathizer, the unreserved, unquestioning Believer; the Recognition, withheld in every other manner, but given, in pity, through woman's heart, lest man should utterly lose faith in himself; the Echo of God's own voice, pronouncing—'It is well done!'" (122). Hollingsworth echoes Lear's infamous misogyny, centered in a view of women's sexuality as infernal: "Down from the waist they are / centaurs though women all above. But to the girdle do / the Gods inherit, beneath is all the fiend's: there's hell, / there's darkness, there is the sulphurous pit, burning, / scalding, stench, corruption!" (4.6.121–25). Lear's horrifying denunciation of women's animalistic physical and sexual attributes transmute into Hollingsworth's view of women as the second sex, man's helpmeet only. A woman who tries to be anything else is a "monster," as Hollingsworth puts it, "an almost impossible and hitherto imaginary monster—without man, as her acknowledged principal!" (122–23). Monstrosity is a common theme.

Lear's explicitly anti-woman statements find another unsettling complement in Coverdale's endless speculations about Zenobia as a feral creature whose sexuality has run amok. *Lear*'s unleashed fantasies of unlicensed female power, both political and sexual, find a balm in the equally fervent fantasy of woman as Redeemer, Cordelia's ultimate role. Similarly, in *Blithedale*, Hollingsworth holds his views of women as viragos and Redeemers side by side, Coverdale hoards nuggets of misogynistic, salacious fantasy while nursing a sense of himself as sympathizer to women, and Moodie derives newfound pleasure in regained stature by conscripting his daughters as psychic helpmeets.[54] Lear directs some of his most abusive language about women to Goneril, his eldest daughter. Calling her "detested kite," a kite being a bird of prey, Lear curses Goneril, asking Nature to "dry up in her the organs of increase" (1.4.254, 1.4.271). Moodie's vindictive attitude toward Zenobia echoes Lear. Lear wishes the inability to bear children on his eldest, whereas Moodie renders his impecunious and, not for the first time, an orphan.

Between *Lear* and *Blithedale*, complementary fantasies of women as pernicious or redemptive take active life. Perhaps the most acute link between these works is the theme of the motherless daughter. Both works strongly imply that without a mother's care a daughter is unmoored. And unmoored because cast adrift in the seething waters of the father's misogyny. Janet Adelman's well-known study *Suffocating Mothers: Fantasies of Maternal Origin in Shakespeare's Plays* pays close attention to the surprising yet pervasive theme of motherlessness in *Lear,* surprising because of the literal absence of mothers in the play: "Lear's confrontation with his daughters ... repeatedly leads him back to the mother ostensibly occluded by the play: in recognizing his daughters as part of himself he will be led to recognize not only his terrifying dependence on female forces outside himself but also an equally terrifying femaleness within himself—a femaleness that he will come to call 'mother' (2.4.56)."[55] A watered-down Lear, devoid of grandiosity and poetry, Moodie identifies with his daughters but without insight, seeing and using them as props for his feeble, rage-filled psyche. Moodie experiences no shock of recognition, at least insofar as explicit depiction goes. Indeed, in his final appearance Moodie passes across the page unnamed, only implicitly present at his elder daughter's funeral: "Nearest the dead walked an old man in deep mourning, his face mostly concealed in a white handkerchief, and with Priscilla leaning on his arm" (239). If a state of "deep mourning" encloses Moodie, perhaps he feels some measure of guilt and culpability for Zenobia's death; after all, it was his decision to cut her off financially that catalyzed the destruction of her hopes. Nothing in Hawthorne's depiction of Moodie approaches the sublime sorrow of Lear's final tableau of grief, the old wounded king entering the stage carrying his dead beloved Cordelia in his arms—and this is precisely the point. Moodie merits no tragic elevation. Instead, we feel deepest sorrow for Zenobia, pushed to the point where suicide felt inevitable.

THE VEIL AND INTERTEXTUALITY

When writing *Blithedale*, Hawthorne clearly had concerns directly related to his social moment and to his personal experiences with reform—his stint at Brook Farm, the real-life utopian community he joined and withdrew from—and used the novel to address these concerns.[56] But Hawthorne was not writing solely or chiefly for the purposes of capturing the zeitgeist. He was joining, once again, ongoing debates dating back to Genesis over questions of female sexual autonomy, original sin, and women's corrupting carnality. A deep misogyny intersecting with a protofeminist sympathy inextricably informs this tradition, stemming from translations of Ovid to Spenser, Shakespeare, Milton, the English Romantics, and nineteenth-century romantic and realist authors. Dispensing with notions advanced by phrenologists and other upholders of the Cult of True Womanhood that women were sexless and passionless, Hawthorne envisions—not for the first time—a strong female character who ardently, romantically, and sexually desires a man.[57] Along with Coverdale's voyeuristic appetite, Zenobia's passion for Hollingsworth drives the narrative.

Two of the best-known contemporary studies of *Blithedale* focus on the figure of the veiled woman: Richard Brodhead's "Veiled Ladies: Toward a History of Antebellum Entertainment," a chapter in his book *Cultures of Letters* (1993); and Russ Castronovo's "That Half-Living Corpse," a chapter in his book *Necro Citizenship* (2001). Both chapters teach us a great deal about antebellum contexts for Hawthorne's figure of the veiled woman. Brodhead offers a particularly suggestive treatment of Hawthorne's Veiled Lady as "the personification of woman domestically defined [who] is in no sense domestic. Produced as a creature of physical invisibility, the Veiled

Lady nevertheless leads a life of pure exhibitionism."[58] Neither treatment, however, mentions the Shakespearean intertext for Hawthorne's work, or indeed any other literary and nonmaterialist intertext. Instead, each chapter focuses on Hawthorne's work as symptomatic, situated within the author's material and cultural contexts and as such reflective of the social ills of his time.

"The Veiled Lady sits on the stage," argues Russ Castronovo in *Necro Citizenship*, "as the disembodiment of history, placid and unmoving, her wispy transparency the very stuff of an ideology that mystifies hierarchical social structures by turning to the spiritual."[59] It is true that Hawthorne makes Priscilla as the Veiled Lady the relentlessly exploited pawn of a mesmerist. But as Westervelt's supposed seer, Priscilla exerts powers that elicit scant depiction. Priscilla's vaunted mesmeric arts, given how little we see them in action, arguably constitute a red herring. For Castronovo, though, mesmerism is central, not only to Hawthorne's era but to this novel. Mesmerism's claims on the spiritual realm's accessibility indicate "an occult sphere of citizenship that popularized the suspension of historical awareness."[60] The novel tells "an important story about the death of political life."[61] Moreover, "clairvoyance and somnambulism model citizenship." Eschewing a "historical narrative of Jacksonian activism," mesmerism's "psychosocial discourse of passivity and abstraction" produce an overall "political passivity."[62] Castronovo offers his version of a familiar argument in Hawthorne criticism that associates not just the author's work but the author himself with passivity and political inaction.[63] Variations on the theme recur: "Priscilla's rigid, unresponsive body ... her public performance as a corpse dramatizes citizenship as an act of political necrophilia."[64]

Castronovo's claim that the Veiled Lady suspends history loses persuasive urgency when we consider the novel (or long romance) in terms of influence and intertextuality. For the Veiled Lady signals precisely the historical awareness that Castronovo insists she suspends when we consider her symbolic value as sign of literary tradition's consistent, recurring image of femininity as ominously unknowable, hidden—in a word, veiled. And because Hawthorne incorporates the Shakespearean image of the veiled woman in his critique of tradition's prevailing myths of femininity (as do Shakespeare and Milton), his work foregrounds rather than suspends critical historical awareness.[65]

In 1973, Howard D. Pearce presciently brought *Blithedale* into dialogue with Shakespeare's *Measure for Measure* (1604),[66] a work teeming with overlaps for Hawthorne's sexual and gender themes.[67] In this "problem play," set in Catholic Vienna, the Duke makes Angelo his deputy in the Duke's absence. In this role, Angelo, crusading against prostitution, among other signs of moral decline, gives Claudio a death sentence for fornication. When Claudio's sister Isabella, in training to be a nun, appeals to Claudio and asks him to spare her brother's life, Angelo offers to comply on the condition that Isabella have sex with him. Desperate to save her brother while preserving her sexual honor, Isabella joins in with a plot—devised by the mysterious Duke, in disguise as a friar—to force Angelo finally to marry the woman, Mariana, whose sexual reputation he has sullied. (He rescinded his plan to marry her once her dowry was lost at sea.) Rocco Coronato outlines the play's veil motif, including the moment when "Mariana veils her face (*MM* 5.1.168)."[68] Linking this veil imagery to the myth of Perseus and Medusa retold by Ovid, he calls Isabella "an eloquent Medusa that points back the mirror to Angelo."[69]

In their first scene together, the corrupt Angelo informs Isabella:

> Thus wisdom wishes to appear most bright
> When it doth tax itself; as these black masks
> Proclaim an enshield beauty ten times louder
> Than beauty could, display'd. But mark me;
> To be received plain, I'll speak more gross:
> Your brother is to die. (2.4.78–83)

Andrew Gurr argues that at this point Isabella wears "the Tudor gentlewoman's familiar outdoor wear, a black velvet mask."[70] Precisely the mask that hides her visage amplifies Isabella's "enshield[ed] beauty" in Angelo's eyes. The pious Isabella has no sexual interest in him whatsoever, but he takes her masked or veiled appearance as a dramatic expression of the beauty that enflames his desire. And his declaration of her beauty's palpable impact on him occurs immediately before he plainly, brutally informs her that her brother will die. Both her discernable beauty and Claudio's fate are hard facts. Shakespeare makes use of the masked or veiled woman to allegorize truth. When Isabella and Mariana appear together in the final act to ensure that Angelo will marry the wronged Mariana, they are masked; the removal of their masks, their "uncasing," symbolically signifies the revelation of their identities and the truths they expose.⁷¹

Marjorie Garber notes that this play teems with "stripping and unmasking" moments, and especially in the long last scene in act 5, which depicts the Duke disguised as a friar, Mariana veiled, and Claudio "muffled." In act 4, Isabella laments to Mariana about their ornate scheme, devised by the disguised Duke, to expose Angelo's corruption while getting him to do the right thing and marry Mariana at last: "To speak so indirectly I am loath—/ I would say the truth, but to accuse him so, / That is your part—yet I am advised to do it, / He says, to veil full purpose" (4.6.1–4). Garber adds:

> The idea of seeing indirectly in a fallen world so as to be able to glimpse the truth more clearly has its own biblical precedent, notably in Corinthians: "For now we see through a glass, darkly; but then face to face" (1 Corinthians 13:12). This is the same book of the Bible in which Saint Paul offers his influential views on virginity and marriage ... the mode of the final revelations *is* revelation, and its poetic equivalent, romance. The appearance of Mariana, as a mystery woman swathed in veils, translates the dramatic action into a different key.⁷²

The veiled Mariana "can be said to represent the mystery of woman."⁷³ Her unveiling exposes men's crimes.

Teresa Heffernan, in her study of veiled women in representation from the eighteenth century to present, notes that the "European enlightenment's desire to 'unveil' women in the name of 'truth' was not limited to Muslim women." Regarding a speech by Charles Pinot Duclos, a fellow of the Royal Society in 1764 who remarked that men pursue women in search of "Truth" and therefore "seek to strip them of everything that we think hides Truth," Heffernen observes: "Woman, like the 'emasculated' Orient, is first constructed as mysterious and irrational; stripped, pursued, conquered, she is then encouraged to surrender to the force of masculine reason." Heffernen cites Peter Brooks on Duclos's speech: "We have only to think of representations in painting and sculpture to acknowledge that Truth, in our culture, is indeed a woman. She may be naked, or she may be veiled, in which case the veils must be stripped, in a gesture which is repeated in countless symbolizations of discovery ... In a patriarchal culture, uncovering the woman's body is a gesture of revealing what stands for ultimate mystery."[74] Hawthorne's Veiled Lady references the veiled women in Shakespeare's works who embody ambivalence. The sign of femininity, the veiled woman forecloses knowledge about the person behind the veil. The woman's unknowability lends itself to misogynistic male myths about femininity but can also provide the unco-opted space for personal identity.

Echoing the black veils worn by women in *Measure for Measure,* Hawthorne imagines Zenobia as a retributive force. She declares to Coverdale, "'I intend to become a Catholic, for the sake of going into a nunnery. When you next hear of Zenobia, her face will be behind the black-veil; so look your last at it now—for all is over! Once more, farewell!' She withdrew her hand, yet left a lingering pressure, which I felt long afterwards" (227–28). Defeated and despairing after Hollingsworth's rejection, Zenobia now contemplates taking the veil and getting herself to a nunnery, like an Ophelia who does so volitionally. Nancy Sweet reads this moment as reflective of the importance of Roman Catholicism to the novel.[75] Zenobia's proleptic image of self-veiling, of a black veil that hides a face, is also importantly a Shakespearean intertext, recalling not only Hamlet's violent advice to Ophelia "get thee to a nunnery—why wouldst thou be a breeder of / sinners?" (*Hamlet,* 3.1.119–20) but also the heroines' pointed wearing of veils to expose male perfidy in *Measure for Measure*. As Andrew Gurr observes of *Measure for Measure,* "In the final Act Mariana, standing in the public street with Isabella for her encounter with the returned Duke, wears the standard lady's black velvet mask to conceal her identity from Angelo."[76] Zenobia intends not only to conceal but to obliterate her black-veiled identity.

Hawthorne reworks the Medusa myth in his tale "The Gorgon's Head," one of the Greek myths he reimagined for children in *A Wonder-Book for Girls and Boys* (1851). Zenobia's narrative of Theodore and the Veiled Lady includes a Medusa motif, the possibility that if he lifts the veil he will discover the fearsome Gorgon's face (110). Seemingly unmasked and symbolically decapitated by Hollingsworth, Zenobia reshields herself, defying the Power of Women myth. In a novel rife with Medusa references, Zenobia is an eloquent Medusa who points the mirror back at the vain and murderous Perseus in her life.[77] That her suicide is imminent cannot be overlooked. Zenobia's arc inverts Isabella's: she begins as a nun-in-training and by the end of the play has been offered a proposal of marriage by the Duke, paralleling the securing of Mariana's marriage to Angelo. Zenobia contemplates getting herself to a nunnery before taking her own life, which signifies both decisions as successive movements towards self-oblivion as a form of female protest.

"There is all a woman in your little compass," Zenobia marvels at the half-sister she underestimated and still calls "my poor sister" (220). In their final encounter at the scene of her devastation, Zenobia watches Hollingsworth depart with Priscilla, whom he declares he loves. For all the worshipful regard she has heaped on the older woman, Priscilla faces little difficulty in accepting the suspect ardor of the man Zenobia loves. Frail and vulnerable though she seems, Priscilla defies expectations. Of all the characters in *Blithedale*, she is the most mysterious, the least classifiable, the most resistant. Unveiled, she reveals still little. Her most notable characteristics are her ardently demonstrative and needful affection toward Zenobia, her "reverence" for Hollingsworth, and her curt, almost acid indifference to Coverdale. Nevertheless, Hawthorne does give us, in the narrator's final encounter with Priscilla, a subtle clue about her personality that references the veil imagery associated with her but reorients this imagery to amplify certain qualities.

Several years after Zenobia's suicide and the collapse of Blithedale, Coverdale, brimming with spite, visits the married couple Hollingsworth and Priscilla. He sees a visible change in the once mighty Hollingsworth, who clings to Priscilla as he unsteadily walks. Coverdale drives in the spiteful nail, asking Hollingsworth, "how many criminals have you reformed?" Hollingsworth responds, "I have been busy with a single murderer!" that is, himself. (Pearce describes vengeful Coverdale here as a "Fury" [14].) This surprising and wracked admission has a profound effect on Coverdale: "the tears gushed into my eyes, and I forgave him" (243).

Of interest, however, is Priscilla's affect when Coverdale greets her and the feeble husband in her care: "As they approached me, I observed in Hollingsworth's face a depressed and melancholy look, that seemed habitual; the powerfully built man showed a self-distrustful weakness, and a childlike or childish tendency to press close, and closer still, to the side of the slender woman whose arm was within his. In Priscilla's manner there was a protective and watchful quality, as if she felt herself the guardian of her companion; but, likewise, a deep, submissive, unquestioning reverence, and also *a veiled happiness* in her fair and quiet countenance" (242; emphasis added). While there are many ways of interpreting Priscilla generally and specifically at this moment, Hawthorne, or the narrator, emphasizes that Priscilla is happy and keeps this pleasure private, "veiled." One might think that having lost a beloved sister with whom she never developed a longed-for intimacy and caring for an ailing, guilt-plagued husband might have worn Priscilla down, but none of this seems to be the case. Instead, Priscilla maintains a composure, an equilibrium borne of contentment. Hawthorne suggests Priscilla has always been veiled, that the veil, symbol of Westervelt's—and, alas, Zenobia's—grotesque exploitation of her also connotes an irreducibly personal element in Priscilla's enigmatic character. One might say that, in an interesting variation on Isabella, Priscilla "veils full purpose." The ambivalence of the veil—echoes of Shakespeare—lies in its ability to signify the monstrous oppression of women and the unyielding autonomy of women at once.

4

SURVIVORS AND STEPMOTHERS
Moby-Dick *and* King Lear

HERMAN MELVILLE WROTE TO EVERT DUYCKINCK on February 24, 1849, "Dolt and ass that I am I have lived more than 29 years, & until a few days ago, never made close acquaintance with the divine William. Ah, he's full of sermons-on-the-mount, and gentle, aye, almost as Jesus." The occasion for Melville's ecstatic, epiphanic rediscovery of Shakespeare was the 1837 American edition of the Hilliard, Gray, and Company's *Dramatic Works of William Shakespeare* seven-volume set, in which Melville marked thirty-one plays (the markings available for perusal in *Melville's Marginalia Online*). Melville found this edition, which had a copious apparatus—contextual and textual notes, as well as Dr. Johnson's glosses (with which Melville engaged)—eye-opening in many ways.[1] Every previous edition assaulted him with "vile small print unendurable to my eyes," but he "exults" over this "glorious" larger-print edition, "page after page."[2]

One might say that Melville's richly productive encounter with Shakespeare was overdetermined. Jonathan Arac notes, "During the romantic period the most consequential writers of the various Western national cultures found Shakespeare an indispensable means of defining their own innovations."[3] Arac summarizes Shakespeare's impact on Melville:

> In the midst of writing *Moby-Dick*, Melville registered a double encounter with literary greatness which, scholars have argued, caused him to reconceive

his work in progress at a higher level of ambition and complexity. He had been passionately reading in a recently acquired edition of Shakespeare (now in Harvard's Houghton Library), which had print large enough for his bad eyes. The fruits of this reading mark his letters and found their first printed form in "Hawthorne and His Mosses" (1850), a review essay on Nathaniel Hawthorne, to whom *Moby-Dick* was dedicated when it appeared in 1851.... Through Shakespeare, Melville feels his own powers.[4]

Melville's Marginalia Online, a digital archive of books Melville owned, borrowed, and consulted, allows readers to search these volumes for Melville's notes, several of them newly recovered through digital technology:[5] "Computational approaches to Melville's marginalia allow readers to calculate word counts and frequencies, word variety, topic clusterings, and sentiment associations. Complemented with informed acts of careful reading and source elucidation, these text analyses reveal Melville constructing new paths in his own writing from his experiences of reading Shakespeare."[6] Ohge and Olsen-Smith make the case that "using distant reading strategies with the marginalia, in their own right and in the service of close reading, we arrive more informed than ever at the 'very axis' of their genius."[7]

The sheer variety of Melville's applications of Shakespearean precedents demands a discrete study. Melville engaged widely with the full range of Shakespeare's work, a total immersion indicated by the nearly seven hundred instances of marginalia across all seven volumes of the Hilliard, Gray, and Company edition. Digital analysis of Melville's marginalia has also revealed a more extensive engagement with comedies and histories than with the tragedies. As Olsen-Smith and Ohge showed in their 2018 article, there is much potential in examining Melville's allusions to the comedies and other, lesser-known plays like *Henry VIII.* Also, while central to his thinking, Shakespeare was far from the only writer influencing Melville. Robin Grey has extensively studied connections between Melville and Milton and several other British precursors. Melville interprets Shakespeare, Milton, and Sir Thomas Browne as authors, Grey says, "who dared to question the very moral, natural, and theological paradigms that structured their worlds."[8]

While mindful of these concerns, I focus here (with the intention of breaking new ground in oft-trodden territory) on a connection long noted by critics, Melville's self-conscious reworking, in *Moby-Dick; or, The Whale*

(1851), of Shakespeare's tragedy *King Lear* (1605–6). It is safe to say that in this work widely acknowledged as his masterpiece, Melville "feels his own powers." In *Call Me Ishmael,* Charles Olson argued that Melville's immersion in Shakespeare led him to produce a radically distinct second draft, the novel we know today. "*Moby-Dick* was two books written between February 1850 and August 1851," Olson notes, adding provocatively, "The first book did not contain Ahab. It may not, except incidentally, have contained *Moby-Dick*." He continues: "It was *Lear* that had the deep creative impact. In *Moby-Dick* the use is pervasive. That its use is also the most implicit of any play serves merely to enforce a law of the imagination, for what has stirred Melville's own most is heaved out, like Cordelia's heart, with most tardiness."[9] Julian Markels's book *Melville and the Politics of Identity* extensively corroborates Olson's point. *Lear* reshapes Melville's "millennialist preoccupation with Shakespeare as a prototype for the American writer and imparts a local habitation and a 'visable truth' to the universal themes Melville finds in Shakespeare. . . . Melville worships Shakespeare's courage and capacity to recognize the finality of an intolerant universe."[10] In "Hawthorne and His Mosses," Melville—in the midst of some more combative words about the Bard's stronghold on American literary consciousness—uses Lear as a central example of Shakespeare's peculiar genius: "Tormented into desperation, Lear the frantic King tears off the mask, and speaks the sane madness of vital truth." Melville, scorning those who mindlessly reverence the Bard ("the blind, unbridled admiration that has been heaped upon . . . the least part of him"), continues, "Truth is forced to fly like a scared white doe in the woodlands; and only by cunning glimpses will she reveal herself, as in Shakespeare and other masters of the great Art of Telling the Truth,—even though it be covertly, and by snatches."[11]

Our knowledge of "Melville's markings in Shakespeare's plays," as Markels titled his book's foundational essay, has been clarified through digital archival research, a statistical analytical tool to which Markels did not have access. Though using different methodological means, Ohge and Olsen-Smith concurred with these earlier critics, and Ohge later glossed: "It is difficult to imagine Ahab's character coming into being with such force—and nuance—if Melville had not studied Shakespeare's plays."[12]

Two themes reveal, as Olson put it, the simultaneously "implicit" and "pervasive" presence of *Lear* in *Moby-Dick:* survival and femininity, the first of which concerns the analogous roles of Ishmael and Edgar, the legitimate son and heir of the Earl of Gloucester, a nobleman loyal to King Lear. The implicit relation between Ishmael and Edgar is their shared status as survivors and symbolic orphans. Thinking of Edgar and Ishmael as *queer* survivors, wayward sons cut off from the father's economic, social, and personal power, dovetails with current concerns in both queer theory and Shakespeare studies. Tricked by Edmund, who convinces him that Gloucester believes Edgar to be part of an assassination plot against him, Edgar flees the kingdom, disguising himself as a "Bedlam beggar" and calling himself "Poor Tom" and spends much of the play in this disguise and state of estrangement. Although Edgar's half-brother Edmund, Gloucester's illegitimate son and a Machiavellian schemer who successfully plots to oust Edgar from the kingdom, typically steals the focus from his more upstanding sibling, it is Edgar, a character much debated by critics, who fascinates in his weirdness and shifting role.

The ultimate survivor, Ishmael famously quotes Job in the epilogue: "And I only am escaped alone to tell thee" (Job 1.14–19). After a two-day eternity of floating on the sea after the destruction of the *Pequod*, Ishmael is rescued by the "devious-cruising Rachel, that in her retracing search after her missing children, only found another orphan" (573). William V. Spanos describes Ishmael as "a nameless orphan, a centerless self in a Fatherless and decentered world."[13] I concur with Spanos regarding the stepson-orphan Ishmael but disagree with his reading of the *Pequod* world as "Fatherless," given Ahab's overwhelming authority to rule his men. Commanding us to call him Ishmael, *Moby-Dick*'s narrator raises the possibility that his identity is a mask, his "biblical/Puritan name" a convenience of the moment. Ishmael's penchant for highlighting his own fictionality, and the use of similar metatextual resonances "demystify the mystique of authorship" while deepening the orphan theme.[14] The forms of disguise—Edgar's performance as Poor Tom, including bodily transformation (besmearing his body with dirt, wearing ragged clothes), and Ishmael's rhetorical masquerades—signify defenses against and expressions of outcast status. If Edgar inexorably moves toward the reclamation of his identity and the right to rule, his passage to restoration is a fraught one, tinged throughout with melancholy. Ishmael inexorably moves toward the status of survivor, a passage that signals the obliteration of all of those around him, including his friend Queequeg. To be a survivor is to lose everyone else.

Second, the vexed issue of *Moby-Dick*'s treatment of the feminine is

"Edgar (from 'Twelve Characters from Shakespeare')," John Hamilton Mortimer, 1775. Etching. (Metropolitan Museum of Art, Rogers Fund, 1968)

less explicit yet also highly significant and, as does Melville's 1852 novel *Pierre* (especially in its echoes of *Hamlet*), indexes intertextual concerns. *Pierre* offers remarkable portraits of femininity, especially that of Pierre Glendinning's half-sister Isabel Banford (if she is indeed that) and her highly involved backstory and subsequent entanglement with Pierre's life, to say nothing of Pierre's formidable mother, Mary. In *Moby-Dick,* Ishmael's stepmother appears in chapter 4, "The Counterpane," where Ishmael and Queequeg share the titular blanket, and then reappears in a late chapter that answers and extends the implications of this one, chapter 132, "The Symphony," where Melville makes reference to "the step-mother world." *Moby-Dick*'s stepmother, the nonbiological mother with the power to reject, abandon, and replenish the subject, a figure of rejection and abandonment, echoes the themes of motherlessness and misogyny in *Lear*.[15]

SURVIVOR: EDGAR

Lear and *Moby-Dick* foreground the idea of patriarchal authority and depict its undoing. In the case of Edgar, whom primogeniture should have safeguarded, his beggar-exile status as Poor Tom mirrors that of the outcast, vulnerable Lear and the blinded, wandering Gloucester. Similarly, Ishmael wanders the world of the unhinged father, the messianic madman Ahab. Cut off not only from family but also his own identity, Edgar nevertheless develops a new relationship with Gloucester after he has been horribly blinded by Regan and Cornwall. Looking after his blinded, bereft old father, Edgar nevertheless does not reveal his actual identity to Gloucester until late in the play, a revelation that occurs offstage along with Gloucester's death. Edgar in effect becomes Gloucester's, and perhaps Lear's, adopted child. Ishmael neither dons a disguise nor stands to inherit a kingdom. Yet Ishmael is also cut off from family—he gives no indication of present-day contact with any relation—an orphan status literalized in the epilogue. As Eyal Peretz puts it in *Literature, Disaster, and the Enigma of Power*, Ishmael's naming of himself as such "indicates an abandonment by the authority of the father and an exilic, homeless existence in the lawless desert."[16] The only familial detail Ishmael gives us is the reference to his stepmother. Ishmael's stepchild status parallels the themes of bastardy (Edmund) and child adoption (Edgar) in *Lear*. Both Ishmael and Edgar have, as Raymond Hughes describes the latter, the power to "endure."[17]

Survival provides a conceptual intersection between queer theory and Shakespeare scholarship. A special issue of *Shakespeare Quarterly* edited by Jonathan Gil Harris is organized around the theme "Surviving Hamlet."[18] Lee Edelman's characteristically dense essay in this issue, "Against Survival: Queerness in a Time That's Out of Joint," later a chapter in his *Bad Education: Why Queer Theory Teaches Us Nothing* (2023), focuses on *Hamlet* and responds to numerous Derrida commentaries beginning with his observations about *Hamlet*, inheritance, and "patrimonial filiation" in *Ghostly Demarcations: A Symposium on Jacques Derrida's "Specters of Marx."*[19] Edelman's *No Future: Queer Theory and the Death Drive* (2004) argues that given the social and cultural demands for reproductive futurity embodied by the figure of the Child, and given society's wide-ranging associations of queerness with death, the properly queer response to such associations is to embody the death-drive, offering to the social order a countermirror of nullity and death. Edelman holds the line of his ongoing argument in "Against Survival." Ingeniously seizing on *Hamlet*'s most famous line, he observes that "To be, or not to be" (3.1.58ff) "carries an explicit negativity that Hamlet and the play both seek to expel."[20] Edelman explains, "negativity, like the queer, is intolerable. . . . To be queer, in fact, is not to be, except insofar as queerness serves as the name for the thing that is not, for the limit point of ontology, for the constitutive exclusion that registers the no, the not, the negation of being." Because it opposes normativity, "queerness confounds the notion of being as being at one with oneself." Queerness is the "zero, the nothing, that invariably structures the logic of being but remains at once intolerable to and inconceivable within it."[21] Given queerness's political value as this limit point, it must oppose regimes of survival.

Anyone familiar with Edelman's work will not be surprised by his argument's conclusion: "*Hamlet* must sublimate the impossible Thing ... so long as we bestow ... on its always ungraspable queerness ... the marketable value of a domesticated and domesticating good, of a faith in the power of literature to make us better, more fully human."[22] Something that *Hamlet* "does not and cannot teach, and what we can never know" is how to remain "in the place of the zero; how to allow for *not* saying 'yes' to the imperative of life."[23] Edelman's argument dovetails with the current emphasis in queer theory and feminism on the possibilities of failure rather than resilience.[24] (Edelman's refusal, a consistent one since *No Future,* to write in favor of any prescriptive application of queer energies is quite distinct from critical efforts of the present to correct the failures, lapses, and limitations of the historical past. What I resist in Edelman is that he leaves the queer subject no recourse except a willingly embraced self-annihilation. The only agency left available to the queer subject is the willingness to embrace such a position. The question of "how to allow for *not* saying 'yes' to the imperative of life" seems to me a much less urgent one than the question of how to make one's life meaningful in a culture that renders queer life, nonwhite life, and nonwhite male life, meaningless.)

Simon Palfrey, in his bracing *Poor Tom,* talks of Tom's crucial "shattering," one that is "necessary for his becoming." Tom's shattering is "his own particular radiance or radiation": "No arrival, no survival without the shatter."[25] Palfrey's observations have relevance for a queer reading. One immediately thinks of Leo Bersani's famous theory of self-shattering as a crucial component of gay male sexuality. Bersani refers to the radical willingness of the submissive partner in gay male sex to submit to the annihilation of his identity (an argument as vexing as it is fascinating).[26] Palfrey refers to the shattering (Edgar's being deceived into exile) that gives life to Tom. Given that Edgar is effectively killed off early in the play and reborn, his role illuminates as it is illuminated by the play's recurring motif of dead children, culminating in the image of Cordelia predeceasing her father. The horror of this image, Palfrey writes, is "immanent throughout—the horror of wasted life, of being born to die, of never really getting to live." And it is this world that "discharges Tom—the retched-up wretch . . . the undead child, clamoring in the in between spaces; the prevented child, spending curses upon the living; the returned child, dizzily spinning in sin; and the dying child, because all are alone, and none can be protected, and parents are helpless beneath the skies." Tom embodies these motley offspring, "and none of them close enough to comfort."[27]

Yet Edgar-as-Tom does offer his father Gloucester some comfort. In a much-debated scene, Edgar appears to assist in the blinded Gloucester's suicide, leading his father to what he believes is a precipitous cliff-top in Dover and allowing him to jump, only for Gloucester to discover that, having fallen a short distance, he is unharmed and very much still alive. Shedding light on his enigmatic motivations, Edgar says in an aside, "Why I do trifle thus with his despair / Is done to cure it" (4.16.32–33). Some critics, however, interpret Edgar's actions as entirely self-serving, in keeping with a general contemporary trend to read Edgar negatively. If, as Janet Adelman observes, "the absolute goodness and nobility of Edgar . . . has been assumed in much of the criticism of the twentieth century," more recent criticism tends to emphasize his suspect qualities.[28] Vividly typifying this attitude, Richard McCoy questions Edgar's behavior during Gloucester's would-be suicide, especially given that Edgar denies his father knowledge of Edgar's identity until so late in the play.[29] In a similar vein, Frederic B. Tromly writes in *Fathers and Sons in Shakespeare*, "If Edgar is delivering therapy, it seems to be aimed more at his own fears of cosmic meaninglessness than at his father's desire to commit suicide . . . [which] suggests that Edgar is performing a buried but more efficacious exorcism on himself."[30] Edgar's actions have also been interpreted as cruel.[31] But if we take him at his word, he is trying to help his father by staging a situation designed to yield a cathartic release of emotion. Gloucester and even Lear can be helped, assisted to change for the better; Ahab, despite acutely vulnerable moments, remains unreachable and unshakable.

Millicent Bell observes that *King Lear* focuses not only on "altered roles of parent and child" but also "on the general changeableness of social relations." The self "is a condition readily altered."[32] Perhaps for this reason, Edgar wages "a certain warfare of denial" that determines his refusal to disclose his identity to his father, even when he leads the suicidal, blind old man to the cliff-top. In allowing Gloucester to believe that he has jumped to his death, Edgar behaves in a manner "both kind and cruel."[33] Likening Edgar's Poor Tom performance to Hamlet's feigned madness, Bell notes, "Edgar's disguise and apparent madness are theatrical . . . his impersonations and simulated state of possession . . . a reminder of how alienable—rather than the reverse—is the core of self we call character."[34] Poor Tom is a "Bedlam beggar," "a byword for fraud" and a "disguise of a disguise," Shakespeare's anticipatory "postmodernist suggestion that there may be no irreducible residuum of identity."[35] Bell declares, however, that whether Edgar is "fraud or actor, victim of possession or authentic madman," he becomes Lear's "most absolute companion at the height of his suffering," like the dispossessed king "reduced to bare, forked animal."[36] Edgar "emerges, in the Folio text, as the chief survivor and the successor to Lear's battered crown." When, "both naked and shivering," they embrace on the storm-pounded heath, a connection that "represents their realized likeness and union," they share one another's ordeal "more completely than anyone else in the play."[37] This relationship and that between Lear and his fool reverberate in the bond between Ahab and his close companion Pip, the Black cabin boy associated with Connecticut and Alabama. Pip falls into the sea and emerges mad from the experience but also becomes a visionary, his dreamlike speech reminiscent of Poor Tom's. Melville bifurcates Edgar's role in the characters of Pip and Ishmael, all of whom share the status of survivor, though Pip only provisionally. Pip has emerged as the cynosure of contemporary reworkings of Melville's novel emphasizing race, sexuality, and queerness, a dazzling response that reanimates questions of influence and demands a discrete treatment.[38]

Emily Sun, in her book *Succeeding King Lear*, observes that "Edgar figures in the play . . . doubly as spectator and actor," but that what "distinguishes Edgar is how he maintains more than the other characters a strict separation between being a spectator and being an actor" (64). His "disguises . . . sustain a more fundamental opposition for him between acting and viewing." The naïve early Edgar falls prey, as does his father, to Edmund's plot: "It is only after being deceived and banished from the kingdom that Edgar begins to inhabit the world critically, to question rather than readily accept appearances, and himself to manipulate them" (65). His newly critical perspective informs his "distinctly theatrical relationship to the kingdom." What is more, "Edgar views the kingdom spectatorially as a stage that awaits his return and vindication, a stage on which he may at last heroically reappear as actor to purge and be purged of 'false opinion'" (65). The self-consciousness of Edgar's role—his cunning performance as Poor Tom—anticipates that of Ishmael, whose "prophetic self-consciousness emerges in direct address"[39] and who creates through allusion a "literary" world, "the product of Ishmael, who, like Shakespeare, is an actor turned dramatist."[40] While one could easily say the same of Edmund, whose soliloquies enact what Harold Bloom calls a modernity-making "self-overhearing," Edgar learns to observe himself from the outside in, becoming aware of himself enough to say, famously, "Edgar I nothing am" (2.3.21).[41] Edmund's treachery shakes self-consciousness into Edgar. Aware of himself, Edgar can discard himself, viewing identity as adaptable, a series of performable roles.

For critics such as Richard McCoy, Edgar's language betrays his suspect nature: his "predilection for smug sententiousness constitutes one of his most questionable characteristics."[42] We are denied the scene where Gloucester realizes that the Bedlam beggar who has kindly tended him is actually his son, whom he regrets having wronged and now has the chance to honor. When, near the end of the play, Edgar reports of his father's offstage death, his "claim that his father's heart 'burst smilingly'" when he finally learns that Tom is Edgar "slightly coys," says McCoy. Edgar's language amounts to "pretty artifice . . . [it] diminishes his father's final moment of suffering and anagnorisis with his characteristic smiling spin."[43] But this is not all, McCoy insists. Edgar's demeanor when he confronts his villainous half-brother Edmund near the end of the play only worsens matters: "The last act brings the death of his father and the defeat of Lear, but Edgar is unbowed. Putting aside the rags of Poor Tom, he marches forth in the armor of a knight whose 'name is lost' (5.3.120) to challenge his wicked stepbrother to formal combat." (I am not sure why McCoy refers to Edmund as stepbrother since he and Edgar are related.) Edgar bestows glory on himself by fighting Edmund, who is left mortally wounded. For McCoy, Edgar thereby distracts us from the real suffering of Lear and Cordelia, whom Edmund has killed from afar by issuing orders for her death. Then, "after defeating his villainous brother, Edgar magnanimously proposes to 'exchange charity' (5.3.165) and discloses his identity. His account of their father's blinding is remarkably harsh, combining smug sanctimony with misogynistic insult to his brother's bastard origins."[44]

The misogyny in Edgar's description of his brother's begetting is indeed unmistakable:

> The Gods are just, and of our pleasant vices
> Make instruments to plague us;
> The dark and vicious place where thee he got
> Cost him his eyes. (5.3.169–71)

Edgar's misogyny is a trait he shares with other characters, Lear especially. Interestingly, Edgar provides a darker, harsher version of his father's own ribald misogyny in the first act. Discussing Edmund with Kent, Gloucester remarks that he has so long "blushed to acknowledge him that now I / am brazed to't" (1.1.9–10). In response, Kent remarks that he cannot "conceive" what Gloucester is saying, to which Gloucester jovially responds, "this young fellow's mother could" (1.1.11–12). Though Edmund is a "knave [who] came somewhat saucily to the world / before he was sent for, yet his mother was fair, there was / good sport at his making" (1.1.20–22). Gloucester's crude remarks regarding Edmund's mother, described as dispensable plaything, indicate his dark side. Edgar's misogynistic description of Edmund's origins reduces the mother to mere vessel, an interior, a "dark and vicious place" devoid of corporeal associations, taking his father's ribaldry as occasion for venom.

There is no way to defend Edgar's speech here except to say that he is chiefly castigating the enemy that shattered his life, betrayed his brotherly trust, and implicitly robbed their father of his eyes. Though Nahum Tate's now-infamous revised 1681 version of *King Lear*—with a happy ending in which Edgar and Cordelia climactically marry and Lear regains his kingdom—establishes Edgar as heterosexual hero, Shakespeare does not in any way do so. (Shakespeare's original version was not performed on the stage again until, due to nineteenth-century demand for it, William Charles Macready's production of it 1838.[45]) Shakespeare's Edgar remains unattached to any woman or heterosexual romance. His speech attacking Edmund's origins, however misogynistic, bespeaks an estrangement from the opposite sex, viewed as alien, other. In stark contrast, the evil but charismatic Edmund manages to seduce both Goneril and Regan, who vie to possess his oft-noted desirable body. In equally stark contrast, Tom earlier described himself as a heterosexual lout, "one that slept in the / contriving of lust and waked to do it ... and, in woman, out-paramoured the Turk" (3.4.87–90). This mendacious self-description by Tom, who does not exist, contrasts acutely with Edgar's chasteness. Further, this speech anticipates his later calumniation of Edmund's origins: Tom describes himself as having "served the lust / of my mistress' heart" and having done "the act of darkness with / her" (3.4.84–86). He is a Joseph who indulges the sexual demands of Potiphar's wife. Heterosexual sex can only be described as an "act of darkness," being born of woman as emergence from a "dark and vicious place." Tom gives this account of himself shortly after he has presented himself to Lear as a naked wretch exposed to the elements, leading Lear famously to describe Tom as an exemplum of "unaccommodated man," "a poor, / bare, forked animal" (3.4.105–6). Edgar concocts in Tom a persona that roguishly ravishes women, his sexual vim in striking opposition to the "presented nakedness" (2.2.182) that strikes Lear as utterly abject. If Edgar imagines in Poor Tom the Bedlam Beggar a being as utterly unlike himself as possible, his unlikeness includes a capacity for heterosexual desire.

Edgar's fascination lies in his refusal to be erased even as he is forced into exilic nonlife. His put-on Poor Tom performance is an example of queer resilience, a refusal to be defeated by the forces conspiring to obliterate him, and a determination to keep going, living, even under abject circumstances, and indeed, making use of these dire circumstances as cover for growth and goad to ingenuity. Edgar gives comfort to the father who betrayed him and the symbolic father whose abjection surpasses his own. This is to say that even within his victimization, Edgar does not lose the ability to empathize, nor the ability to connect with and lend aid to others. As discussed, not everyone agrees with such a reading of Edgar. And Edgar vexes efforts to champion him. But I believe that his final words, also those of the play, bespeak the heart of a wounded character who has learned from his wounding:

> The weight of this sad time we must obey.
> Speak what we feel, not what we ought to say.
> The oldest hath borne most; we that are young
> Shall never see so much, nor live so long. (5.3.320)

Edgar has learned to trust his emotions and to let their authenticity guide him. This is an especially significant speech, given the readings of anti-Edgar critics who find his words redolent of a smug and manipulative character. Edgar understands that his own suffering pales in comparison to that of his father and Lear, and that the sublimity of their suffering exceeds anything he can experience (at least, he hopes this is the case). Rather than indulging in generational elitism that inherently privileges the younger generation's greater insights and aplomb, he recognizes that he and those who "are young" will—most likely—not have to go through the kind of traumatic upheaval that mark Lear's and Gloucester's final days. To clarify, I am not championing Edgar as a transhistorical model of youthful humility in the face of the patriarchs, who must be reverenced or else. Rather, I am pointing to the significance of this speech at this point in the play and in the context of Edgar's relationships with fallen fathers. Edgar's last words are an act of empathetic generosity, his survival an act of memory-keeping and recognition rather than of keeping score.

SURVIVOR: ISHMAEL

Moby-Dick is a tale told by a survivor, a retrospective narrative act. For all its dynamism of portraiture, the novel makes vivid and lifelike a series of persons long since annihilated. Only the narrator, Ishmael, has survived to tell the tale of Captain Ahab's disastrous quest to destroy the titular white whale. Melville thematizes survival through references to the biblical figures of Job, the survivor of persecutory trials; Jonah, who survives engulfment by a whale; the Rachel of Jeremiah 31:15, the symbolic mother of the Jews inconsolably lamenting the loss of her children; and the ultimate biblical survivor, Ishmael, cast out along with his mother, Hagar, into the desert by Abraham at his wife Sarah's behest.

If Melville revises the relationship that Edgar-Tom maintains with Gloucester and Lear in his depiction of Ishmael's relationship to Ahab, the young man's interactions with the fatherly figure are more diffuse than Edgar's with his father and the deposed king. Ishmael maintains a discrete distance from Ahab throughout the novel, even given his uncanny insights into Ahab's mind and his unfathomable access to private conversations Ahab conducts with other crewmembers. Ishmael and Ahab do not interact; no dialogue between them exists, a remarkable silence substituting for revealing interaction. The narrator can get close to Ahab only by "orally sculpting him ... he not only does not come near his captain; Ahab never even sees him."[46] Ishmael presents Ahab as icon, charting his ascent into dark Satanic antihero and cataloguing his numerous flights of rhetorical grandeur. He documents Ahab's interactions with Pip, who plays the wise fool to the mad kingly captain, but Ishmael never joins this duo to form a ragtag community that parallels the wayward band of Lear, Gloucester, the Fool, and Edgar in *Lear*. Keeping Ishmael at a significant interpersonal distance from the captain while making him, rhetorically and narratively, Ahab's bosom companion emerges as one of Melville's chief fictive strategies.[47] Yet chapter 41 begins with lines that clarify Ishmael's allegiance to and identification with the fallen father: "I, Ishmael, was one of that crew; my shouts had gone up with the rest; my oath had been welded with theirs; and stronger I shouted, and more did I hammer and clinch my oath, because of the dread in my soul. A wild, mystical, sympathetical feeling was in me; Ahab's quenchless feud seemed mine" (179). In *Exiled Royalties*, Robert Milder reminds us that however "diabolized Ahab may become ... it is important to remember that Ishmael's early allusions associate him with heroes and redeemers (Christ, Prometheus, Perseus) and establish his revenge as a collective one drawing upon 'the sum of all the general rage and hate felt by his whole race from Adam down' (184)."[48]

The falsely accused and outcast Edgar's performance as the Bedlam beggar Poor Tom finds it foundation in stylized and self-consciously poetic language ("Who gives anything to Poor Tom? / ... Tom's a-cold" [3.4.50–57]). Pip most closely echoes Tom's art language, his dialogue with Ahab "among the most self-consciously literary in the novel."[49] The aristocratic Edgar performs a class masquerade by impersonating a Bedlam beggar (who themselves impersonated the mad) by physical and verbal disguise: "My face I'll grime with filth," Edgar-Tom declares, and, noting the "roaring voices" of these outcast performers (2.2.180–85), announces "Edgar I nothing am" (2.2.192). Melville's characterization of Ishmael throbs with the class tensions that echo Shakespeare's depiction of Edgar as the slumming son of a nobleman. In "Kings and Commoners in *Moby-Dick*," Larry Reynolds incisively challenges earlier readings of Ishmael as an inveterately democratic narrator, "the commonest of commoners" who emerges by novel's end as the apotheosis of "the rise of the common man."[50] Reynolds counters, "while many of narrator Ishmael's attitudes are thoroughly democratic, the matter and manner of his narrative itself contain an elitist and antidemocratic bias that ultimately places him closer in attitude and outlook to Ahab than to any member of the crew."[51] Reynolds continues, "Although Ishmael as common sailor participates in the democratic society of the forecastle, as narrator, he is more closely allied with the uncommon individual occupying the quarterdeck ... [Ishmael] ironically undercuts his idealization of democracy by presenting the crew as the knights, squires, and commoners of a feudal hierarchy" while extolling Ahab's greatness, which "ultimately lies in grief."[52]

In preserving Ahab as king, Ishmael fulfills his Edgar-like role, not only by acknowledging Ahab as the presiding ruler of the *Pequod* but also by preserving the impasse between Lear and Edgar in Shakespeare's tragedy. As Simon Palfrey notes in his superb *Poor Tom,* Simone Weil observed that *Lear* foregrounds a truth that no one has the capacity or the willingness to recognize as such, "the bitterness of possessing the truth and having won at the price of nameless degradation, the power to utter it and then being listened to by nobody."[53] (Weil expressed these views in a 1943 letter to her parents.) Palfrey names, beyond even Lear and the Fool, Edgar-in-Tom and Tom-as-Tom as the chief embodiment of Weil's "nameless degradation," which involves a profound sense of not being heard or recognized. Offering someone recognition is to hear and to listen to them. Palfrey writes,

> Lear moves toward something like this when he addresses the naked beggar [Tom] in the storm. His famous recognition—"Is man no more than this?"—is undoubtedly crucial to Weil's immersion in the play, as it is to Shakespeare's purposes for the alarming figure of Tom. But still Lear doesn't quite get there—or if he does we do not witness it. The king never responds to Tom's answers (if indeed Tom gives any). After Lear's first searing recognition, distraction takes over, and the beggar is distanced, sentimentally instrumentalized; Tom morphs in the king's mind into a comical Socrates, addressed as "learned Theban," "good Athenian," and "Noble Philosopher," only without the dialogue that should follow.[54]

The impasse between Edgar and Lear finds a complement in Ishmael's relationship with driven, eloquent, myopic Ahab, who fails to recognize Ishmael in even the delimited ways that Lear can recognize the abject Edgar.

For if Lear cannot recognize Edgar (as Gloucester also cannot), Lear can recognize something of Edgar's abject status within Poor Tom's condition. When Edgar–Poor Tom presents himself to Lear as a naked wretch exposed to the elements, Lear famously describes him as an exemplum of "unaccommodated man," "a poor, / bare, forked animal" (3.4.105–6). In contrast, Ishmael remains unknown to Ahab, like the crew at large, whose right to existence remains, in Lear-like fashion, only slenderly known by Ahab.

THE FATES' LIEUTENANT

Most of the readings of Melville's reworkings of *Lear* in *Moby-Dick* focus on the relationship between Lear and Pip, Pip being linked to both Lear's Fool and Poor Tom. Indeed, most readings of Melville's reworkings of *Lear* in *Moby-Dick* focus on male characters and what we might call male-oriented themes—the burdens of kingship, masculinity versus nature, the agon of Melville's attempt to match Shakespeare's literary potency. Leland S. Person observes that *Moby-Dick* both "apotheosizes and critiques nineteenth-century models of manhood—aggressive, competitive, self-centered, phallocentric. It also explores alternative constructs, especially in the marriage between Ishmael and Queequeg."[55] The understanding that *Moby-Dick* is a novel about and for men stems from the long-standing view that the novel has no women in it or that it has nothing *for* women. Rita Bode has helpfully outlined and analyzed the numerous instances in which femininity is referenced in a novel presumed to be, in Richard Brodhead's words, "so outrageously masculine that we scarcely allow ourselves to do justice to the full scope of its masculinism."[56] Her essay focuses on the references to mothers, both human and nonhuman, and on the theme of the lost mother. Scholars such as Grace Farrell have discussed this theme in terms of Poe's *Narrative of Arthur Gordon Pym* (1838), his one novel, also a sea fiction. Bode draws attention to Melville's singular masculinization of the sea, typically depicted as feminine, as in Whitman's description in "Out of the Cradle Endlessly Rocking" of the "savage old mother incessantly crying."[57] Bode argues, however, that the "dominance of *Moby-Dick*'s masculine images is deceptive, for a pattern of transformations emerges in which the masculine gives way to suggestions of the maternal."[58]

Moby-Dick and *Lear* share a powerful theme: motherlessness. By motherlessness, I refer to the literal absence of mothers and to the artistic decision on the part of playwright and romancer to eschew the mother. *Lear* both is and is not a female-centered work, having dazzlingly memorable female characters, on the one hand, and focusing on its males, Lear most acutely, on the other hand. *Lear*'s explicitly misogynistic rhetoric deepens its repression of the maternal, but as Janet Adelman argues in *Suffocating Mothers,* the maternal nevertheless informs the play's key themes and conflicts. *Moby-Dick* similarly evokes femininity and the maternal even though, in his choice of subject matter and the workings of the plot, Melville chose to eschew the tragedy's central female characters and female-centered concerns. The novel provides a crucial opportunity to think through the politics of influence and intertextuality from feminist and queer perspectives, given, on the one hand, its exploration of queer male survival and, on the other hand, its emblematic difficulties in representing femininity in works that grapple with precursor texts themselves mired in difficulties of female representation.

Adelman notes key differences between Shakespeare's tragedy and its source material, *The True Chronicle Historie of King Leir,* which opens with the king's grief over the death of his wife and that his daughters have been left maternally bereft. In contrast, the Lear of Shakespeare's tragedy "has no wife, his daughters no mother . . . Queen Lear goes unmentioned [save for the moments when Lear references her to question his paternity] . . . But Lear's confrontation with his daughters . . . repeatedly leads him back to the mother ostensibly occluded by the play: in recognizing his daughters as part of himself he will be led to recognize not only his terrifying dependence on female forces outside himself but also an equally terrifying femaleness within himself—a femaleness that he will come to call 'mother.'"[59] Though *King Lear* seems to be a motherless text, the maternal nevertheless informs the play's major themes and conflicts. Much of "the play's power comes from its landscape of maternal deprivation or worse, from the vulnerability and rage that is the consequence of this confrontation and the intensity and fragility of the hope for a saving maternal presence that can undo pain."[60] *Moby-Dick* similarly evokes femininity and the maternal even though, in his choice of subject matter and the workings of the plot, Melville chose to eschew the tragedy's central female characters and female-centered concerns. Seemingly devoid of the feminine, *Moby-Dick* is fueled by the energies of a repressed female presence.

In chapter 4, "The Counterpane," Ishmael recalls an incident in which a maternal presence neither saves nor undoes pain, but instead inflicts it. Scampering about and attempting to climb inside a chimney, the child Ishmael incurs his stepmother's punitive wrath. She sends him to bed without supper. Although the stepmother signifies a maternal presence, this presence conveys the theme of maternal deprivation Adelman locates in *Lear*. Oddly, Ishmael's recollection occurs while experiencing Queequeg's surprisingly familiar "bridegroom clasp" in their room at the Spouter-Inn (26) While a certain amount of discomfort and embarrassment colors this episode where a male stranger made doubly strange by his exotic appearance holds the narrator close, it is one marked by Ishmael's growing sense of curiosity about his new friend, whose toilette he studiously observes and whose "civility and consideration" he praises (27). This chapter is a prelude, then, to the two men's pleasurable physical intimacy as they keep each other warm in chapters 10 and 11. In contrast, Ishmael's childhood memory is a potentially traumatic flashback marked by an inscrutable yet telling further episode in which, banished in his room for sixteen hours, he wakes up from a nightmare to feel a "supernatural hand" that seems "placed" in his own (26). Ishmael describes, I argue, a desire for a maternal comfort and loving gesture that is, first, answered nightmarishly in the phantom hand that clasps his own and, second, is given the beginnings of an answer in Queequeg's bridegroom clasp. Inevitably, we think ahead to the ecstatic moment in chapter 94, "A Squeeze of the Hand," of collective male sperm-squeezing that emblematizes same-sex camaraderie. This rapturous moment has its origins in a ghostly and ominous childhood episode over which hovers the mother or the mother's frightening doppelgänger, and in the experience of being clasped in close quarters by another man. To ignore the implications of the step-maternal, as even some very acute readers of Melville have done, is to leave the scene of male-male intimacy only partially understood.[61]

If Ishmael is an Edgar cast out not through the machinations of a duplicitous half-sibling but from a set of circumstances beyond our knowing, who reverences the fallen father Ahab as Edgar does Lear, the step-maternal familial background Ishmael provides is a brief but telling indication that he has suffered an estrangement prior to the "damp, drizzly November in my soul" that provokes his wandering quest. The homoerotic affection and attention he receives from Queequeg, framed in marital terms, also substitutes for the maternal love Ishmael was denied. Queequeg offers this to Ishmael. Pip does the same for Ahab, who claims to know his "fiery father," but "my sweet mother, I know not. Oh cruel! what hast thou done with her?" (508). Pip offers Ahab, who ultimately rejects the gesture, the gifts of the "compassionate feminine."[62] Leslie Fiedler, in his characteristically pathologizing yet suggestive manner, identified this pattern in nineteenth-century American literature as the image of the "white man, wounded by the evil woman who would have separated the two good companions and feels no love, only a lust that does not even demand to know the name of the phallus-bearer who satisfies it, ends up lying in the arms of the colored man, who sings to him like a mother to a child; and still together, more than ever together, they are borne off to jail."[63] Well beyond Fiedler's reading, there is a legitimate critique that nonwhite male characters, far from volitionally offering maternal love to white protagonists, do so because this emotional labor is one of their compulsory burdens. I contend that the scenes of interracial same-sex intimacy cannot be reduced to the phobic, pathological, or racist.[64] The intimacy between Ishmael and Queequeg and Ahab and Pip has a plangency that resists that reduction. Samuel Otter's finding in *Melville's Anatomies* poignantly summarizes what is at stake here: "In *Moby-Dick,* there is no easy identification with others. It is a difficult thing to see oneself in another's skin, especially if that skin has been marked as radically different or inferior."[65] William Ellery Sedgwick, often prone to point out perceived failures of fully realized human portraiture in Melville, locates in the Ishmael-Queequeg relationship a humanity that gives Melville access to the full range of emotions in *King Lear.*[66]

Much like the titular protagonist's mother in Melville's next novel, *Pierre,* the stepmother in *Moby-Dick* connotes censure, not affection; stringency, not love. For these reasons, it is significant that when the stepmother returns, she does so in a reversal of these earlier affective terms. In chapter 132, "The Symphony," Melville foregrounds a conversation between Ahab and Starbuck where Starbuck comes extremely close, or so it would appear, to persuading driven Ahab that he must abandon his suicidal mission to hunt down and kill the White Whale:

> Slowly crossing the deck from the scuttle, Ahab leaned over the side, and watched how his shadow in the water sank and sank to his gaze, the more and the more that he strove to pierce the profundity. But the lovely aromas in that enchanted air did at last seem to dispel, for a moment, the cankerous thing in his soul. That glad, happy air, that winsome sky, did at last stroke and caress him; the step-mother world, so long cruel—forbidding—now threw affectionate arms round his stubborn neck, and did seem to joyously sob over him, as if over one, that however wilful and erring, she could yet find it in her heart to save and to bless. From beneath his slouched hat Ahab dropped a tear into the sea; nor did all the pacific contain such wealth as that one wee drop. (543)

Occupying the place of the cruel stepmother of myth and fairy tale, Lear's daughters Goneril and Regan inflict violence, emotionally on Lear, physically on Gloucester, whose eyes are plucked out at Goneril's suggestion (3.7.6), while stagings frequently depict Regan plucking out at least one of his eyes. When Lear finally rejoins Cordelia, whom he banished for failing sufficiently to shower him with encomiums at the start of the play, he finds a healing balm in her acceptance and love. Cordelia shatters the stepmother world of Goneril and Regan. Interestingly, in Ahab's fantasy, the stepmother is not replaced by the loving mother but instead herself transforms into one: "long cruel—forbidding," she now wraps "affectionate arms round his stubborn neck, and did seem to joyously sob over him, as if over one, that however wilful and erring, she could yet find it in her heart to save and to bless." Indeed, the stepmother now becomes an entire "world" embracing the wayward male subject. If only in fantasy, Ahab experiences what Ishmael, who appeals to his stepmother for leniency but gets punishment instead, longs for, the change in attitude that results in a loving gesture. The comparisons so often made between Ahab and Lear now seem especially apt, as woman's love frees the vainglorious and oppressive tyrant from his own self-annihilating and destructive qualities, if only for a moment. Just as Cordelia in her reappearance at the end of *Lear* tacitly and redemptively forgives her misguided and injurious father, the figural stepmother who appears near the end of *Moby-Dick* offers newfound love to the wayward subject. In *Powers of Horror* (1982), Julia Kristeva famously theorized abjection in terms of the subject's relationship with the maternal body. Subjectivity depends on the ability to transcend the maternal realm.

Associated with the preoedipal mother, abject materials—things that have been expulsed from the body and provoke disgust, like spit, vomit, feces, and related excrescences, such as the skin that forms over milk—must be repudiated by the subject for maturation to occur. Consequently, the widely developing subfield of abjection theory has tended to focus on the subject's flight from the maternal. Works such as *Moby-Dick* and *Lear*, however, make palpable an equally potent desire to return to the mother.

Melville's thematization of the stepmother world extends to the entirety of *Moby-Dick*, which teems with references to maternal and other kinds of feminine figures, often rendered with palpable ambivalence. Ishmael offers, early on, a portrait of himself in thrall to a powerful female authority figure, his stepmother. Toward the end of the novel, Ahab reveals that he is equally in thrall to powerful female entities. In chapter 134, "The Chase—Second Day," Ahab confesses to Starbuck that he has "felt strangely moved to thee," indicating that Starbuck's efforts to persuade him to give up his obsessive quest have made an impact. But Ahab emphasizes that their conversations as well as his quest are preordained: "This whole act's immutably decreed. 'Twas rehearsed by thee and me a billion years before this ocean rolled." Then Ahab calls someone—Starbuck or himself—"Fool!" before he declares, "I am the Fates' lieutenant; I act under orders" (561).

Christopher Sten observes that Ahab's language of fate indicates "the advanced state of his *amor fati*, the failed hero's fatal love of fate that masks his yearning to be free of all personal accountability for his actions."[67] Specifically, however, it is to the Fates, rather than fate, that Ahab relinquishes agency. The novel consistently distinguishes "fate" from the Fates even if both often have the same function.[68] Sten's interpretation is more aptly suited to Ahab's line in the chapter "The Symphony": "By heaven, man, we are turned round and round in this world, like yonder windlass, and Fate is the handspike" (545). I concur with William Spanos that the issue of fate in the novel is "more ambiguous" than it seems, and my effort to register this ambiguity is to think about the Fates as specifically gendered entities distinct from a generalized fate adumbrated by the prognostications of doom uttered early on by Elijah and Father Mapple.[69]

The Fates, the Greek Moirai and the Roman Parcae, three mythic and supremely powerful goddesses that were said to frighten even Zeus, are comprised of Clotho (in Greek, the "spinster" or "spinner" of destiny), Lachesis (in Greek the "disposer of lots"), and Atropos (in Greek the "inexorable, inflexible" one, i.e., death). Clotho spins the web, Lachesis measures it, Atropos cuts it.[70] In "The Theme of the Three Caskets," Freud interprets Lear's three daughters as versions of the Fates. Freud, beginning with *The Merchant of Venice* and concluding with *Lear,* argues that the male subject's determination to avoid death inspires the fantasy that he can choose an option other than death. The recurring figure of three women is a tripartite female goddess, the mother, wife, and the mother-death who waits for and finally claims the subject. (Lear believes that he carries the dead Cordelia in his arms, but Freud contends that it is really Cordelia who carries him into death.)

Melville does not, in his rendering of *Lear's* themes, include his own versions of Lear's daughters, a female triad that recalls the Fates and echoes another crucial Shakespearean intertext for *Moby-Dick, Macbeth,* and the Three Weird Sisters who prognosticate the titular protagonist's rise and fall (like *Lear,* it dates to 1605–6). Ahab presents himself as a Lear figure, bound to the vagaries of female power ("the Fates' lieutenant"). Indeed, the Fool's censure of Lear for having "mad'st thy / daughters thy mothers," leaving the humiliated and infantile king to "play bo-peep" (1.4.171), haunts Ahab's sense of himself as in thrall to female authority. Though contemporary feminist reinterpretations of Regan and Goneril make a case for their complexity, Melville's marginalia indicates that he conventionally viewed Regan and Goneril as corrupt and cruel villains. Regan refers to Gloucester as "ingrateful fox, 'tis he" (3.7.27) before she and Cornwall torture their victim, a sadistic scene culminating in the plucking out of both his eyes. Melville pencil-underlined her comment and, using double cross-checks for emphasis, sardonically annotated, "Here's a touch Shakespearean— *Regan* talks of *ingratitude!*"[71] In his last published novel in his lifetime, *The Confidence-Man* (1857), Melville gives the name Goneril to the termagant wife of John Ringman, the version of the confidence man with the long weed on his hat, emphasizing her masculine toughness. (Lacking all maternal qualities, she abuses their young daughter, leading Ringman to take the child away from her mother. Goneril sues, bankrupts, and destroys the reputation of her husband before dying herself.)

Both Melville and Hawthorne were struck by an artistic rendering of the Fates that affected Emerson enough that he hung it above the mantle in his book-strewn study, where it was seen by Margaret Fuller (a firm believer in the Fates), among others.[72] Though writing after the composition of

Moby-Dick, Melville observed in his journals on Friday, March 27, 1857, that "The 3 Fates of M. Angelo," which he saw when revisiting the Pitti Palace, was a painting with an "Admirable Expression." A striking painting whose significance was no doubt enlarged by its attribution to the legendary Michelangelo, *The Three Fates* (c. 1550) is now believed to be the work of Francesco Salviati. Melville's appreciation of it influences our interpretation of the Fates' significance to *Moby-Dick.* What makes the painting's expression "Admirable" in Melville's eyes is "the way one Fate looks at other—Shall I?—The expectancy of the 3rd" (*Journals,* 115–16). The reading I have been pursuing here, the comparative consideration of the outcast, orphaned, Edgar-like Ishmael and the repressed yet manifest presence of femininity in *Moby-Dick,* can be summarized as this affecting gesture, the way one Fate looks at another. The queer and feminist valences of the novel intersect in the image of a powerful female presence that rises unbidden, perhaps in defiance, of an attempt to suppress her (if we consider Melville's eschewal of the strong female presences in *Lear* as suppression). Just as same-sex desire was suppressed in Melville's time and at times in his work yet miraculously manifests itself, so too does the presence of the feminine transcend its silencing confines.

Prior to the appearance of the mourning and salvific maternal figure of the *Rachel,* the ship that saves the orphan sole survivor Ishmael at novel's end, a related female force holds the *Pequod* in its grip. In chapter 135, "The Chase—Third Day," the surviving but soon-to-expire sailors in consternation search for sight of the ship: "Soon they through dim, bewildering mediums saw her sidelong fading phantom, as in the gaseous Fata Morgana" (409). Fata Morgana is the Italian name given to the sorceress of Arthurian legend Morgan le Fay.[73] Thomas Malory's famous *Le Morte d'Arthur,* among other works, establishes her as Arthur's half-sister. By mentioning Fata Morgana, Melville refers to the castle-like mirages on the sea that confuse the sailors beholding the "gaseous" entity's "dim, bewildering mediums." If the Moirai control destiny, Morgan le Fay obscures vision and confuses sense, a fitting emblem of the destruction of the *Pequod* and all but one of its crew, caused by a misguided man's inability to see clearly, himself least of all, a destruction that figures the harrowing powerlessness of this crew however "outrageously masculine," exposing the myth of male power precisely as such.

Coleridge, in his famous lectures on Shakespeare (also developed through marginalia), has occasion to mention the concept of the Fata Morgana: "In the plays of Shakespeare, every man sees himself, without knowing that he sees himself as in the phenomena of nature, in the mist of the mountain, the traveller beholds his own figure, but the glory round the head distinguishes from a mere vulgar copy.... Or as the Fata Morgana at Messina, in which all forms, at determined distances, are presented in an invisible mist, dressed in all the gorgeous colors of prismatic imagination and with magic harmony uniting them and producing a beautiful whole in the mind of the spectator."[74] Melville, an American Romantic, echoes his British counterpart in finding in Shakespeare a Fata Morgana of like unlikeness, a precursor in whose image Melville "beholds his own figure."

5

"FALTERING IN THE FIGHT"
Pierre *and* Hamlet

ARGUABLY HIS MOST INFLUENTIAL LITERARY READING, Freud interpreted Sophocles's tragedy *Oedipus Tyrannus* as an allegory for childhood psychosexual development. The inescapability of killing one's father and marrying one's mother in the Sophoclean tragedy becomes for Freudian theory the impossible and nullifying desire, however unconscious, to do both. Our properly socialized subjectivities emerge when we substitute exogamy for endogamy and, crucially, identify with rather than war against the father, identification also eliminating the unwanted presence of homoerotic desire for the same-sex parent, a process that Judith Butler calls "the melancholia of gender identification."[1] Shakespeare's tragedy *Hamlet* runs a close second as a foundational psychoanalytic myth. Hamlet's uncle Claudius murders his brother, the King of Denmark and Hamlet's father. Claudius then becomes the King and proceeds to marry Gertrude, his brother's wife and Hamlet's mother. The young prince Hamlet is at university in Wittenberg when these events occur. When he returns, the Ghost of his dead father appears before him and impels Hamlet to avenge the dead King's murder:

> O, horrible! O, horrible! Most horrible!
> If thou has nature in thee, bear it not.

>   Let not the royal bed of Denmark be
>   a couch for luxury and damned incest. (1.5.80–83)²

Hamlet does revenge his father, but in a wayward, hesitating fashion that, in the end, leaves dead not only Claudius but also the hero's girlfriend, Ophelia; her father Polonius; her brother Laertes; two duplicitous school friends, Rosencrantz and Guildenstern; and Gertrude.

In classical psychoanalysis, Hamlet's protracted attempt to kill his uncle, and horror at what he perceives as his mother's unlicensed sexuality, adulterous and incestuous at once, is a reworking of Oedipus's patricidal crime and incestuous union with his mother. As Freud writes in *The Interpretation of Dreams*, the differences between *Hamlet* and Sophocles's tragedy are as significant as the similarities: while the later play has "roots in the same soil," "the changed treatment of the same material reveals the whole difference in the mental life of these two widely separated epochs of civilization: the secular advance of repression in the emotional life of mankind." Freud reads

"Ophelia / after R. Regrove, R.A," c. 1880–1900. (Library of Congress)

Oedipus as a dreamlike manifestation of the oedipal child's "wishful phantasy" to murder the father and sexually possess the mother. But in *Hamlet*, this phantasy remains repressed: "we only learn of its existence from its inhibiting consequences."³ A signal indication of the differences between these works is that, unlike Oedipus when he encounters Laius (unbeknownst to Oedipus, his father), Hamlet has a hard time killing Claudius: "Hamlet is able to do anything—except take vengeance on the man who did away with his father and took the father's place with his mother, the man who shows him the repressed wishes of his own childhood realized." *Hamlet* represents the increasingly balked state of civilized man, unable to act on his unconscious wishes, mired in repression and ensuing neurosis.⁴

Sophocles's play haunts *Hamlet*, even though Shakespeare was unaware of its existence.⁵ John Hollander's concept of intertextual echoes—the uncanniness of influence, the relationship between unlike works and authors, the elusive yet palpable presence of one work in another—finds a fitting embodiment in the relationship between Sophocles and Shakespeare. Even if, in its strictly Sophoclean form, the myth did not directly influence Shakespeare himself, it is also true that Oedipus lives on in the "secondary" tradition of classical Roman literature that was Shakespeare's chief literary influence. The Roman tragedian Seneca wrote a reimagined version of *Oedipus* that was performed on the Elizabethan stage, and it most likely influenced Shakespeare's work, as Seneca did generally.⁶ Ovid, another important Renaissance influence, includes the Oedipus myth in his epic poem *The Metamorphoses* (presenting Oedipus as the killer of the Sphinx rather than as the emblematic representation of the Oedipus complex; Ovid does not explore the relationships between Oedipus and his parents). The mythic Oedipus intersected with Shakespeare's work long before psychoanalysis made those connections, using them to fashion mythologies of its own.⁷

Jonathan Arac notes, "During the romantic period the most consequential writers of the various Western national cultures found Shakespeare an indispensable means of defining their own innovations."⁸ As we have established, Herman Melville's work reflects the centrality of Shakespeare's influence, rivaled only by Milton's, for American Romanticism. Melville's novel *Pierre; or, The Ambiguities*, published in 1852, has been discussed in terms of its intertextual relationship with *Hamlet*. My discussion proceeds from this basis but, unlike other treatments, focuses on the issue of sexuality. Both works thematize a profound male heterosexual ambivalence that, while treated distinctly, links their respective protagonists, who share a problematic relationship with their mothers. In this regard, *Pierre* seems less like a radical break from *Moby-Dick* than a continuing exploration of its themes of the motherless male outcast. *Pierre*'s strong incestuous overtones, echoing *Hamlet*'s, synthesizes the centrality of incest discourse in nineteenth-century America.[9] As we discussed in chapter 1, incest provided Romantic writers with a capacious metaphor for the artist's relationship to the world, their own creativity, and sexuality. In *Pierre,* the Shakespearean incest theme centered in the mother-son relationship is expanded to include the titular protagonist's improbable, increasingly intense relationship to a woman who identifies herself as his half-sister, Isabel Banford. Incest complexly provides the logic of human relationships generally here, as Cindy Weinstein has argued, linking Pierre's relationships not only with his mother and Isabel but also with his deceased father, claimed by Isabel to be her father as well. Hawthorne's influence, specifically *The House of the Seven Gables,* hovers over this work. Just as Hawthorne reworks Milton to consider themes of male-female relationships and homosexual identity, so too does Melville rework Shakespeare in *Pierre,* having discovered the Elizabethan dramatist somewhat tardily in the late 1840s and avidly making up for lost time. Before turning to *Pierre,* I discuss the themes of incest and sexual revulsion in *Hamlet* that Melville extends. This chapter returns to Milton and women's relationship to authorship, the image, and intertextuality, Eve's account of her nativity once again a crucial intertext.

HAMLET, INCEST, AND THE ENDLESS PRIMAL SCENE

The visitation from the ghost of his father returns Hamlet to the primal scene, Freud's concept of parental sexual intercourse witnessed by the child. Old Hamlet's spectral narrative depicts this scene, however, as a homoerotically charged murder of not only one man by another but also one brother by another. Reenactments of the primal scene recur throughout the play, a Russian-doll series of embedded performances, prior acts reproduced in new forms, plays within plays. Much of the tragedy's misery and cruelty, as well as its vital, nasty wit, stem from the nausea Hamlet experiences at this forced act of sexual remembering and witnessing.

Hamlet finds ever more inventive ways to restage the scene of parental sexual union, a scenario stretched out to encompass the fullest emotional range from murderous violence to heartrending grief. Though contemporary source materials such as Thomas Kyd's *The Spanish Tragedy*, written sometime during the 1580s, remain unacknowledged, *Hamlet* foregrounds its intertextual aspects, including the reworking of material in Seneca and Virgil. Shakespeare underscores the moment in *The Aeneid*, a work that defines intertextuality, when Pyrrhus kills the elderly Trojan king, Priam, a nod to Christopher Marlowe and Thomas Nashe's version of the sack of Troy in their play, *Dido, Queen of Carthage*. Pyrrhus is the son of Achilles, the reluctant demigod Greek hero of *The Iliad*. Avenging his slain father on Priam, Pyrrhus's murderlust, graphically conveyed in the speech that Hamlet remembers and recites for the Players in act 2, one of whom then continues the speech Hamlet recited, clearly echoes Hamlet's revenge plot. (Achilles's Trojan rival Hector kills Patroclus, Achilles's friend and lover, and so Achilles kills Hector. Priam is Hector's father and also father to Paris, whose affair with the married Helen of Troy instigates the Trojan War. Though presented as a beautiful fop of sorts, Paris kills the seemingly unconquerable killing machine Achilles in battle, a scene depicted in the lost ancient Greek epic the *Little Iliad*.)

Inexpressibly bereaved, displaying a grief intense enough to move the gods to tears, Shakespeare's "mobled [muffled or disguised] queen" Hecuba recalls Ovid's wildly lamenting Hecuba in book 13 of *The Metamorphoses*. Shakespeare's Hecuba witnesses her husband Priam's murder by Pyrrhus, who, after a long and eerie pause, repeatedly impales, with a volcanic fury, the old man with his sword (2.2.464). Sadism suffuses Pyrrhus's destruction of the old man: he makes of his act of murder a "malicious sport." Shakespeare recreates the primal scene, but in radically reimagined form: now the son impales the father figure as the wife-mother, in anguish, witnesses this violent penetration. Shakespeare offers a counterbalance to the violent and vengeful lamenting Hecuba of Ovid and in contrast to Virgil establishes Hecuba as witness to the scene of oedipal violence.[10] Shakespeare emphasizes Hecuba's role as wife rather than mother, reinforcing the ideas of Hecuba's connection to a man, and Hecuba and Priam as the primal parental couple.

Sequence is key to *Hamlet*'s emotional logic. Before the ghost of Hamlet's father has even appeared to him and conscripted his son into a revenge plot, Hamlet already expresses contemptuous feelings towards his uncle and his mother. He seems particularly incensed by his mother's apparent lack of tact and decorum in having married her dead husband's brother, famously observing of his mother's inconstancy, "frailty, thy name is woman" (1.2.146). When his father died, his mother initially behaved "like Niobe, all tears," but this outward grief has quickly ceded to sexual desire for Claudius. "O God," Hamlet laments, "a beast that wants discourse of reason / Would have mourned longer" (1.2.150–51). Her son wonders what she sees in Claudius, a man who resembles her late husband as little as Hamlet estimates he himself does Hercules (1.2.154). In Ovid, a woman transforms into a beast because her grief reaches a cataclysmic fever pitch; in *Hamlet*, a woman who cannot grieve is less than a beast.

The sense of Claudius as an inadequate substitute for his father deepens in the significant scene "in his mother's closet" between Hamlet and Gertrude. Holding up two images before her eyes, one of his father, the other of Claudius, the "counterfeit presentment of two brothers," Hamlet explicitly commands that she look at them; and implicitly, that she draw the same conclusions that he does.[11]

> See what grace was seated on this brow;
> Hyperion's curls, the front of Jove himself;
> An eye like Mars, to threaten and command,
> A station like the herald Mercury
> New lighted on a heaven-kissing hill—
> A combination and a form indeed
> Where every god did seem to set his seal
> To give the world assurance of a man.
> This was your husband. (3.4.56–65)

In comparison, Claudius is a "mildewed ear" (3.4.62), which fuses images of blighted corn, Pharoah's dream from the Joseph story (Genesis 41:5–7), and Claudius's fratricidal method.

Hamlet's reverent love for his father deepens into homoerotic ardor, as suggested by the first item in the loving blazon of his father's attributes, "Hyperion's curls." This phrase deepens an earlier reference within the sustained motif of Claudius as a poor imitation of his brother: "So excellent a king," Hamlet says of his father, "that was to this / Hyperion to a satyr"

(1.2.139–40), Hyperion being in Greek mythology one of the Titans who overthrew their devouring father, Cronos. *Pierre* echoes this homoerotic oedipal connection. Claudius's fratricide figures the male ear as an orifice penetrated by another man. He signifies a defeated and corrupted masculinity in contrast to the strong male body of his brother, the King. A mere mildewed ear, Claudius is outmatched even in his decay by his brother, whose body underwent a spectacular disintegration when Claudius poured poison into his ear.

Hamlet himself fails to uphold male rectitude. As if to suggest that Hamlet's homoerotic regard for him threatens to make his son less of a man, the Ghost appears one last time in the closet scene, warning Hamlet, violently berating his mother, to "leave her to heaven" (1.5.86). Before the Ghost reveals the details of his murder and impels Hamlet to revenge, Hamlet already pines for the release of deliquescence: "O, that this too too sallied flesh would melt, / Thaw, and resolve itself into a dew, / Or that the Everlasting had not fixed / His canon 'gainst self slaughter" (1.2.129–32). (Scholars have long argued over whether "sallied," used in the first and second quartos, should be emended to "solid," given in the folio, or "sullied."[12]) Hamlet tellingly links his fantasy of physical transformation from a hard and sturdy body (masculinity, in essential terms) to a soft and liquid one (femininity, in essential terms) with suicide, violently described as "self-slaughter." Such imagery runs rampant in *Pierre*.

Anticipated in Hamlet's moody dissatisfaction when he returns home and his contempt for his mother's marriage to his uncle, with the Ghost's appearance, oedipal conflict becomes the prevailing structure of Hamlet's life. Now, Hamlet must literally invade the marital bed, tearing it asunder; now, he must kill the father and claim his mother for himself. That Claudius is the substitute for his father allows Hamlet to have the Oedipus complex without guilt—he can kill the father's image rather than the father, kill this image because it so poorly reproduces the father. It is a crucial detail that Hamlet reveals his fixation upon the marital couple and their unseemly union before the Ghost appears to him: the Ghost speaks to Hamlet from the basis of Hamlet's own desires to return to the scene of parental sexuality. His attitudes towards Gertrude and Claudius exude horror at the sight of this couple's union even in a public setting, to say nothing of a more intimate one.

One of the many overlaps between Freud's and Shakespeare's conclusions is the issue of temporality, figured as intrinsic to scenes of the sexual.[13] In his case study *From the History of an Infantile Neurosis* (1918), better known as *The Wolf-Man,* Freud associates deferred action—*Nachträglichkeit*—with the effects of the primal scene on the young Sergei Pankejeff (the Wolf-Man). Analogously, *Hamlet*'s most vexed issue is the protracted and delayed action of its hero's revenge. The dreamlike temporal distortions in *Hamlet* and in Freud's case study challenge normative sexuality's linear logic. If sex is a linear narrative that begins with an act of parental sexual intercourse that we witness and then serves as a model for normative sexuality, both *Hamlet* and *The Wolf-Man* forestall, even thwart, this narrative. Hamlet's frustrating inaction can be interpreted as an ingenious response to being thrown back into the marital bed; his stagings of theatrical performances that evoke the primal scene both mock and defend against adult sexuality. Reinterpreting Shakespeare, Milton in *Paradise Lost* has Satan gaping at the prelapsarian splendor of Adam and Eve, and Melville in *Pierre* makes central the irresolvable conflict in its hero's response to the image of parental sexuality.

Hamlet's understanding of Claudius as "more than kin, less than kind" and his nausea over his mother's second marriage alert us to his disposition toward family: a sense of their overbearing intimacy and potential for cruelty (1.2.65). Yet this disposition includes a fixation on his biological parents' sexual relationship, his mother's sexuality, and his father's sexual magnetism. Implicitly, Hamlet idealizes parental sexuality as wholesome and satisfying, everything that Gertrude's and Claudius's could never be. Yet Hamlet's sexual disgust, noted by critics from Freud and Ernest Jones forward, especially vivid in his interactions with Ophelia, exceeds the parameters of his justifiable anger. More likely is it that Hamlet displaces his disgust at the thought of marital sexual intimacy onto the "shadow couple," in Raymond Bellour's phrase, Gertrude and Claudius, who both fail to live up to his idealized standards.[14] Hamlet's revulsion from sexuality, in its intensity, suggests underlying grief and anger.

As in the psychoanalytic account of childhood psychosexual development, Hamlet moves from the primal scene to the Oedipus complex. Now, it is not the father but the uncle that the son wishes to kill, allowing the father to remain idealized. Hamlet has a hard time killing Claudius, Freud conjectures, because Claudius was able to fulfill Hamlet's murderous and incestuous fantasies. Without disputing Freud, I propose a different motivation. The Ghost awakens Hamlet's ambivalent feelings about his parents' sexual union, suggesting that his Oedipus complex remains unresolved. The welter of homoerotic idealization for his father, hatred towards his uncle, and desire for his mother reveals a great deal about the protagonist. Hamlet centers his rage at Gertrude's incestuous desires, yet *he,* rather than his mother, is biologically connected to Claudius.

Writing of the recreated scene of Old Hamlet's murder, Julia Reinhard Lupton and Kenneth Reinhard argue that the play "consolidates Oedipal crime across the figure of the demanding Woman," noting that while Gertrude is "decisively included in the biblical allegory, she is nonetheless excluded from the fratricidal scene that the passage strives to narrate, a scene in which only the two men appear as actors." (Presaging Milton's dramatic uses of biblical iconography, Shakespeare sets Claudius's murder of Old Hamlet in a garden where a serpent roams.) They conjecture that

> it is as if Oedipal violence between men can only occur in relation to a woman—not, however, the passive object of male exchange at the heart of Oedipal and mimetic desire, but a figure of woman whose demands unnaturally exceed the domestic parameters of need. According to the Ghost, Gertrude is voraciously sexual even to the point of coprophagy, desperately filling up the remainder between need and demand with the rank leftovers of marriage: "So lust, though to a radiant angel link'd, / Will sate itself in a celestial bed / And prey on garbage" (1.2.55–57).[15]

Gertrude, figured as a ravenous, unseemly Eve-figure, is indeed excluded from the fratricidal scene. Yet on another level she is always already present within it. The murder of virtuous Abel by his brother Cain, who, unlike Abel, fails to sacrifice in a way pleasing to God, informs the scene of Old Hamlet's murder at Claudius's poisoning hand. Yet this scene and the biblical intertext of Cain and Abel are themselves subsumed by the primal narrative of Eve's fall at the serpent's temptations, Adam's fall by Eve's hand, and the married pair's joint fall into sexual shame.[16] The male-male scene of violence is secondary to, a revision of, the scene of male-female violence, betrayal, and erotic mystery. Moreover, a long-standing tradition equates Eve with the serpent.[17]

The Ghost's fevered narrative of his murder at his brother's hands returns Hamlet to the primal scene, reimagined as a circuit of male relations. Claudius's murder of his brother parodies marriage and marital sexuality. Like the folkloric virginal, submissive bride, Old Hamlet lies ready and waiting for Claudius, who penetrates him. Instead of filling up the body of this submissive partner with procreative fluids, Claudius fills his brother up with the poisons that corrupt and destroy his body. This homoerotic copy or double of heterosexuality—to evoke the language of Judith Butler's early work—complements the Gertrude-Claudius relationship, pervasively described as rank and unnatural. The criminality of a perverse sexual union threatens to make all sexual unions perversely criminal, a theme that recurs in Milton, Hawthorne, Freud, and Melville.[18]

Hamlet accuses Gertrude in the closet scene of living "in the rank sweat of an enseamed bed, / Stewed in curruption, honeying and making love / Over the nasty sty—," words that Gertrude experiences as precisely the daggers Hamlet vowed to speak to her (though not to drive into her flesh) (3.4.90–95). Yet Hamlet seems to regard heterosexual relations this way generally. His taunting rebuke of Ophelia, his horror at the very idea of heterosexuality, suggests this. His meandering manner, frustrating the revenge plot, also frustrates the gendered demands of normative masculinity. One moment comes close to explicating this idea. As Hamlet bids Claudius goodbye, he oddly says, "Farewell, dear mother." Claudius corrects him, responding, "Thy loving father, Hamlet." To which Hamlet responds: "My mother. Father and mother is man and wife, man and / wife is one flesh. So, my mother. Come, for England" (4.3.45–50). Here, Hamlet, evoking the biblical language of male-female oneness, articulates the logic of institutionalized heterosexuality. Moreover, he conveys an understanding that the woman carries the ideological weight of this biblical mythology, must outwardly bear the sign of her union to her father-husband. The figure Mother rests on either side of the line about the one-flesh bond between father and mother, man and wife. Mother contains within her the ideology of both parenthood (father and mother) and marriage (man and wife). Hamlet's discussion of these points suggests his awareness of the overarching narrative of heterosexual and parental relations that exceeds his specific familial conflicts. If one could argue that what Hamlet undertakes is the impossible task of restoring his parents to their rightful prelapsarian unified state, he stands before such a state in an attitude of mystification.[19]

One of Hamlet's ingenious maneuvers is to force Claudius to relive his homoerotic fratricide. Ophelia's brother, Laertes, dying of the poison meant for Hamlet, unites with his would-be brother-in-law against the corrupt father. "The treacherous instrument is in thy hand," he tells Hamlet, "Unbated and envenomed." Swinging finally into climactic action, Hamlet forces Claudius to drink from his weapon: "Drink off this potion. Is thy union here? / Follow my mother" (5.3.295–306). Just as Claudius symbolically raped Old Hamlet by pouring poison into his ear, Hamlet now forces Claudius to drink from his weapon, which is "unbated," not blunted but engorged with poison. In this dizzying play of gendered metaphors, Hamlet exchanges his phallic poisoned sword for the yonic cup from which his mother drank, forcing Claudius to drink himself to death; the lips of his mother's vaginal cup bring death once they touch Claudius's own. In the end, the question Hamlet poses to Claudius seems truly to be in earnest: "Is thy union here?" Sex cannot, finally, be distinguished from murder.

Dying into freedom, as Harold Bloom evocatively puts it, Hamlet finds a way to resolve his conflicts over his own wayward masculinity and his attitudes towards parental heterosexuality by destroying nearly all the participants in this sexual pageant.[20] But his beloved friend Horatio survives, the witness to this endless scene of sexual crime. That the loving friend, who regards Hamlet as a "sweet prince," remains standing is a suggestive touch. Crucially, Horatio survives. He lives to take over Hamlet's witnessing role and preserve his friend's memory and valiant struggle. These ardent testimonials to male friendship and queer survival will be savagely overturned elements of Melville's revision. Melville can imagine the survivor and ardent male ties in *Moby-Dick*, but not in *Pierre*.

PIERRE AND THE LAW OF THE MOTHER

Moby-Dick had not done well, partly due to the disastrous first publication of the novel in England that failed to include the final chapter revealing Ishmael's survival. *Pierre* was an outright disaster, sparking the New York *Day Book*'s infamous headline, "HERMAN MELVILLE CRAZY," on September 8, 1852.[21] Melville parodied the sentimental novel and Gothic fiction in this tale of a once-prosperous young man's descent into madness when he meets a woman who claims to be his half-sister.

Nineteen years old and handsome in the manner of Billy Budd, Pierre Glendinning, named after his father, enjoys an idyllic, unassuming life in Saddle Meadows (upstate New York). His relations with his mother, Mary, are affectionate and flirtatious; even in the relatively tranquil earlier chapters, the son and mother's tensely cheerful interactions verge on the incestuous, with Pierre calling his attractive mother "Sister Mary," she calling him "Brother." Soon, Pierre is to marry the appealing, blonde Lucy Tartan, who emerges from the tradition of the romance, a union of which his controlling mother approves.[22] But when Pierre meets the enigmatic, dark-haired young woman Isabel Banford, haunted and haunting, he becomes entranced by her story and her. Isabel claims that she and Pierre share a father; her mother was a European refugee (and, it is insinuated, a victim of the French Terror). Isabel's remarkable dreamlike, sustained narrative of her life before she met Pierre is one of the novel's high points. Drawn to Isabel in a manner that nearly explicates the palpable but unspoken incest theme, Pierre decides on a radical plan to solve the dilemma Isabel endures and poses. He breaks off his engagement to Lucy and marries Isabel, the marriage ostensibly a platonic one. Melville's depiction of Isabel evokes the Victorian femme fatale, whose appearance radically alters the male protagonist's life when he becomes hopelessly infatuated with her. Isabel, however, is a deeply melancholy siren who seems to be lured by her own death song. She is associated with music; her emblem, the guitar that speaks for her ("Now listen to the guitar; and the guitar shall sing to thee the sequel of my story; for not in words can it be spoken. So listen to the guitar" [126]).[23] Determined to give her half of their father's money, Pierre must then contend with his mother, Mary, furious over Isabel's presence, Pierre's acceptance of her, and the broken engagement to Lucy. Pierre and Isabel, joined by a socially ostracized young woman named Delly Ulver, the disgraced victim of a rake, move to New York City, where Pierre's cousin, Glendinning Stanley, instead of helping, rejects and shuns him. Glen's behavior stuns and wounds Pierre, because he and his cousin were once extremely close in youth, but it is in keeping with Melville's consistent depiction of male relations as fractious, prone to betrayal. When Mary dies, she vindictively leaves all her money and property to Glen, who further vanquishes Pierre's legacy by becoming engaged to Lucy Tartan. Lucy, however, remains tethered to Pierre and, in a surprising move, joins him and the other women at the Church of the Apostles. Literally barring her passage, Glen and Frederic,

Lucy's elder brother, try to prevent Lucy from entering Pierre's abode, violently tussling with him. Finally, overcome by financial difficulties and his failure as a writer, Pierre murders Glen, shooting him in the street, and (like Bartleby in Melville's most famous short story) is sent to the prison known as The Tombs. When Isabel and Lucy visit him there, Lucy hears Isabel referring to Pierre as her brother and dies of shock. Pierre drinks from the vial of poison that hangs from Isabel's neck. When Frederic bursts into the prison cell in search of Lucy, he discovers her corpse as well as Pierre's and expresses penitent regret, recalling fond times when they were younger. Rebuking Frederic, Isabel then drinks from the same poison vial and dies: "her whole form sloped sideways, and she fell upon Pierre's heart, and her long hair ran over him, and arbored him in ebon vines" (362).

While there is an almost inexhaustible amount of material to explore in *Pierre,* in terms of its revision of *Hamlet,* I will focus on three major dynamics: Melville's depiction of femininity, especially Mary and her role in the central mother-son relationship, contrasted with Pierre's idealized father; the incest theme, which ultimately unites Pierre and Hamlet in a shared refusal of normative heterosexual desire; and the use of the Enceladus myth, which effectively links Shakespeare's and Melville's protagonists as defeated would-be giants.

Pierre's mother represents one of the most formidable female characters in nineteenth-century American fiction. With Shakespearean notes very self-consciously echoing throughout his language, Pierre contemplates his relationship with Mary, as well as his own fate:

> She loveth me, ay;—but why? Had I been cast in a cripple's mold, how then? Now, do I remember that in her most caressing love, there ever gleamed some scaly, glittering folds of pride. Me she loveth with pride's love; in me she thinks she seeth her own curled and haughty beauty; before my glass she stands,—pride's priestess—and to her mirrored image, not to me, she offers up her offerings of kisses. Oh,'small thanks I owe thee, Favorable Goddess, that didst clothe this form with all the beauty of a man, that so thou mightest hide from me all the truth of a man. Now I see that in his beauty a man is snared, and made stone-blind, as the worm within its silk. (90)

Pierre's own thoughts, this passage offers an analysis of woman's desire for power and the role that male beauty plays in women's efforts to achieve and exert power. Most tellingly of all, it represents a male's fantasy of these female fantasies, Pierre's as well as Melville's. The question of Melville's treatment of femininity generally is a vexed one; Pierre contains his most extensive exploration of femininity even if one thoroughly mediated through male eyes.[24]

As Pierre contemplates his mother's desires, he catalogues the varieties of narcissism. Mary Glendinning does not see Pierre; rather, she sees herself, "her own curled and haughty beauty" in the "glass" Pierre's image provides. Of course, Pierre's fantasy of maternal narcissism, while it may accurately interpret the psychosexual foundations of Mary's image-based preoccupations, reveals his own investments in his beautiful manly form. Pierre expresses the deep fear of effeminacy—historically associated with Shakespeare's Hamlet—that courses through Victorian American culture. In his contemptuous address to the "Favorable Goddess" who adorned him in beauty, thereby keeping him blind to the "truth," gendered as "the truth of a man," Pierre rebukes the sexual female gaze that renders him feminized as its object. This theme is an intertextual echo of Matthew Maule's rage at Alice Pyncheon's approving sexual appraisal of him in *The House of the Seven Gables,* a text Melville knew well. Melville likens Mary in her pride to a snake or a dragon adorned with "scaly, glittering folds," an intertextual echo of Milton's fallen trio Satan, Sin, and Eve and their shared and distinct serpentlike qualities (and another link to Hawthorne's novel). But the self-pitying Pierre imagines himself, encased and entrapped within his beauty, as "the worm within its silk," blind and ensnared (90). The image of Pierre as worm, while it follows and corresponds to the image of Mary as a slithering snake, also establishes the male artist as defenseless, stalked by his predatory mother. Moreover, it renders her phallic, he soft, malleable, viscous. Demanding a reading from a disability studies perspective, Pierre imagines himself as "a cripple" and the regard, or lack thereof, his mother would have had for him had he been cast in such a "mold." The imagery of the crippled male dovetails with the most stunning set-piece in the novel, Pierre's dream of the defeated but intransigent giant Enceladus.

Buried within this passage, too deeply buried perhaps, is something of a feminist interpretation of Mary's determination to achieve agency and derive some satisfaction from the beauty of her son. What is particularly interesting here, then, is Melville's reversal of the historical pattern of women existing as mirrors that reflect male beauty and power back to men.

The power and the pleasure that males gain from self-reflection depend, writes Judith Butler, on the role that women, as girls or mothers, play in male narcissism, reflecting back to the man his own self-image of dominance and authority.[25] While Pierre upholds the tradition of seeing his own masculine stature reflected in his mother's hungry eyes, the passage allows us to imagine the possibilities of a female desire for self-reflection and the male as reflective surface. *Pierre* reminds us that Melville's work complicates the normative structures of gender, sexuality, and desire in multivalent and still-challenging ways. His analysis of women's sexual desire continues along these lines in his late poems "After the Pleasure Party" and "Timoleon," both printed in the 1891 collection, *Timoleon, Etc.* That same year, in which the author died, *Billy Budd* was written and left uncompleted in Melville's writing desk drawer, confirming that male homoerotic and homosocial tensions continued to arrest and perplex Melville's attentions up until his final literary efforts.

In the closet scene, often performed as if an explicit rendering of mother-son incest, Hamlet tells Gertrude, increasingly frantic in the face of her son's volatility, "Come, come, and sit you down; you shall not budge; / You go not till I set you up a glass / Where you may see the inmost part of you" (3.4.18–20). Hamlet wants to force Gertrude to confront her "inmost part," a conscription into self-recognition, as if visible perusal will produce interior reckoning. Adding the considerable arsenal of misogynistic associations between vain woman and mirrors and other reflective surfaces to his assault against his mother's character, Hamlet imposes the long-standing cultural narrative of Narcissistic Woman on her. Pierre follows suit. Melville reveals his hero's interiority through free indirect discourse, giving us access to his private thoughts in all their contours. While, from dialogue alone, we have considerable evidence of Mary's questionable character, our immersion in Pierre's private musings gains us a sense, *his* sense, of his mother's self-love and frustrated desires for power and the son's instrumental and frustrating role in these tangled aspirations. If Pierre does not treat Mary with the relentless rhetorical (and possibly physical) violence that informs Hamlet's treatment of his mother, he nevertheless maintains a sense of maternal authority as a rule to be opposed and overturned while idealizing the dead father. Melville's depiction of Mary as, arguably, the chief villain in the novel, certainly as the most powerful persona, accords with psychoanalytic theory's "law of the mother," which Juliet Mitchell describes as the ban against parthenogenesis.²⁶ Mary wields an authority that she believes to be absolute, and Pierre's defiance of her shatters this fantasy. Her comeuppance is a necessary component in Pierre's fierce scheme to reorder the world and to remake his own identity. In effect, he refashions himself as parentless, ultimately rejecting Mary as she rejected him yet also destroying the "chair portrait" of his father that Mary repudiated but he reverenced, the visible emblem of his idealized love for his father.

Dating from the late eighteenth century, a cultural investment in the face as the visible manifestation of truth and authenticity has been a preoccupation of American life, as Christopher Lukasik has shown.²⁷ As we discussed in the previous chapter, the face was part of a network of visual signifiers connoting, at once, identity and nonidentity in Melville and Hawthorne's work: faces, veils, masks all distinctly metaphorize the external manifestation and impenetrable mystery of the self. Isabel's maddening, mesmerizing face metonymizes her, goading Pierre to seek her out after he glimpses it.

Visual representation, ekphrastically rendered on the page, intersects with and extends this signifying network: portraits, paintings, wooden figureheads, and marble statues connote a similar duality between the lifelike and the intangibly, distantly aesthetic. In *The House of the Seven Gables,* the imposing portrait of Colonel Pyncheon, which he stipulated could never be removed, exerts male authoritarian rule on Hepzibah's house in lieu of him; the daguerreotypist Holgrave's portrait of Judge Pyncheon appears to materialize the enduring presence of this Pyncheon ancestor's suspect character; the Malbone miniature portrait of Clifford memorializes his lost youthful beauty.²⁸ These distinct portraits constitute a history of masculine styles; they also reflect discomfort with and defiance of gender role norms. Melville evokes a similar oppositional history here. The official portrait of Pierre Glendinning Senior, approved by Mary, contrasts starkly with the chair portrait of the hero's father as a young man, painted in secret by his cousin, Ralph Winwood, and a record, in the view of Pierre's spinster aunt Dorothea, of his father's affair with a young French woman. According to her, Cousin Ralph intended to capture Pierre Senior's pining desire for this woman in portrait form. Mary extols the paunchy middle-aged official portrait of her husband that hangs in the drawing room, but she loathes the chair portrait, which she claims in no way resembles Pierre's father. The strong implication is that Mary knows the truth of her husband's youthful affair and that of Isabel's existence as well, hence her ire at the chair portrait.

The contrast between the official drawing room and the repudiated chair portrait has attracted considerable scholarly attention over the years, including James Creech's extensive analysis of the queer implications of this contrast. These analyses have not frequently included a consideration of Melville's intertextual uses of Shakespeare and *Hamlet*'s relevance to the paternal portraits' significance.[29] In *Closet Writing / Gay Reading,* Creech offers an intensive account of the "winking" rhetoric whereby Melville conveyed a coded but excavatable queer sensibility. My argument here focuses on a dimension of the work that is not Creech's focus, Melville's intertextual relationship with Shakespeare, though I share Creech's premise that *Pierre* is a richly and disturbingly significant homoerotic text.

As Creech observes, "the bourgeois, heterosexual paterfamilias, flower of homosocial culture, is represented by a large oil painting which hangs prominently over the mantlepiece in the drawing room." In sharp contrast to this depiction is the "small oil of Pierre senior as a young bachelor," which Mary detests but Pierre reverences. He keeps it in "a small chamber next to his bedroom. Melville consistently terms this space a 'closet.' A closet in this nineteenth-century usage was not the small wardrobe that it is today, but rather a more intimate chamber than the adjoining bedroom." Creech reminds us that autobiographical links between Melville and his protagonist include the fact that these paintings "correspond point for point with extant portraits of Melville's father Allan who died when Herman was twelve years old," a most tragic end mired in bankruptcy and madness for a once larger-than-life father.[30]

In terms of *Hamlet*'s relevance to the paternal portraits' significance, Nancy Fredricks incisively observes in *Melville's Art of Democracy* that

> for Hamlet and Pierre, the crisis of representation centers primarily around the world of the father and the patriarchal social structure that seeks to perpetuate itself through words and images. Both texts focus on imagery of portraiture as both heroes probe beneath the deceptive surfaces of appearance. Hamlet asks Laertes, "was your father dear to you? Or are you like the painting of a sorrow, A face without a heart" (4.7.106). Pierre reads his copy of *Hamlet,* "The time is out of joint, / Oh cursed spite, / That ever I was born

to set it right" (235). Melville appears to be drawing on imagery of framing in *Hamlet* to denote Pierre's crisis of representation. The two portraits that Hamlet holds up to the "seeming virtuous queen" of his "Hyperion" father and "Satyr" uncle (3.4), illustrate for Hamlet a political and moral disjuncture. Pierre uncovers a similar disjuncture, but Melville avoids the melodramatic personifications of good and evil [by locating Hyperion and Satyr in one man, his own father].[31]

Given the sustained theme of incest in the novel, *Pierre* does not content itself to focus on one kind of incest but on its varieties. Pierre's relationships with Mary and with his half-sister Isabel (if she really is his blood relation, which he comes to doubt) are shocking enough in their openly erotic character, but Melville adds to this Pierre's homoerotic desire for his handsome young father as captured in the chair portrait, and for his cousin Glen. Indeed, the chapter on Pierre and Glen's relationship, "The Cousins," is the most thorough analysis of homoerotic male relations in antebellum American literature. It implies that Glen's rejection of Pierre has a basis in their sexual relationship as adolescents, one that must be repudiated in adulthood. Hamlet's fraught relationship with other men dominates the play: his egregious murder of Ophelia's father, Polonius, takes the contempt he has for the dithering old man to a grotesquely excessive level; his acid attitude to her brother, Laertes, as he grieves over his sister's corpse in the grave outrageously ignores his culpability in Ophelia's death and the fact that he actually murdered Laertes's father; and if Rosencrantz and Guildenstern, his friends from university, betray him, Hamlet nevertheless seems to delight in vengefully securing their deaths. This leaves Claudius, certainly worthy of Hamlet's ire, but also unworthy of the intensity of Hamlet's disgust. In other words, had King Hamlet simply died and Claudius replaced him in terms of both crown and marriage bed, it is likely that his angry nephew would feel much the same animus toward him, minus the urgency of the revenge plot.

THE MEANINGS OF INCEST

In chapter 2, we established the central significance of incest to Romantic writing, especially as a metaphor of artistic self-love. Incest was also a central theme in Gothic fiction, including the work of Horace Walpole, whose genre-defining novel *The Castle of Otranto* and play *The Mysterious Mother*, the protagonist of which agonizes over an act of incest with his mother, Melville admired.[32] The fine critic George E. Haggerty notes that *The Mysterious Mother* "creates the spectacle of horror" around the image of the married couple. "In the figure of incest," Walpole dramatizes "the horror of the marriage bond." Much the same can be said of *Pierre*, which dovetails with Haggerty's argument that a specifically abject masculinity presented as spectacle recurs in the Gothic tradition.[33]

"*Hamlet*, as well as serving Goethe for the bildungsroman, was the primary earlier literary point of reference (along with *Paradise Lost*) for Horace Walpole and Anne Radcliffe as they founded the mode of Gothic prose fiction," notes Jonathan Arac. Shakespeare's play provided "the great model in earlier English literature for the haunting ancestral presences, the ghosts, that define the ambience of the gothic, even when displaced from a fully spectral figure into the discomforting vivacity of a portrait."[34] *Hamlet* provides a foundation for *Pierre's* foregrounding not only of the paternal image but of the paternal *as* image. Most relevantly, it establishes the horror of incest as a screen for its hero's fantasies of and revulsion against adult genitality. Analogously, Pierre, while in seeming thrall to an inescapable incestuous passion, takes a course of action that ensures his sexual inviolability.[35] It cannot be overlooked that Pierre devises his outlandish plan to marry Isabel, to transform himself into one half of the shadow couple, just when he is about to embark on a legal, socially affirmed marriage to Lucy Tartan. While some have argued the opposite, there is no indication in the novel that Pierre and Isabel, however erotically charged their relationship, actually have sexual relations.[36]

In Haggerty's view, Walpole uses incest to oppose the normative sexual order, the cynosure of which is the heterosexual couple; Melville follows suit. *Pierre* is, without question, its author's most explicit and sustained heterosexual narrative. While true of *Typee* and *Mardi*, *Pierre* feverishly eroticizes femininity. If Isabel recalls the Victorian figure of the femme fatale, Lucy Tartan embodies her foil the *femme fragile*, who models delicacy and innocence and always verges on being deathly ill; Lucy and Isabel typify the Victorian tendency toward female doubles.[37] Isabel has a backstory brimming with dire specificities, but that always remains deliberately obscure, an index of femininity's symbolic associations with the enigmatic and unknowable. Wendy Stallard Flory, in an important reading that I both concur with and dissent from, likens Isabel to Romantic poetry's mythic images of woman as muse, imagination, and symbol of artistic creativity. Clear parallels exist between Isabel and Coleridge's "damsel with a dulcimer" in his fragment-poem "Kubla Khan": "In a vision once I saw: / It was an Abyssinian maid / And on her dulcimer she played, / Singing of Mount Abora." Like this dreamlike female figure, Isabel is associated with a musical instrument, her guitar, and can be said to evoke in Pierre a similar state of exaltation and dread. Nothing about Isabel connotes a realistic attempt at portraying a female character; in this regard, she strongly recalls Poe's own dark-haired muse-siren, Ligeia, who has a similarly galvanizing and destructive effect on a suspect male protagonist.

I regard *Pierre* as a radical novel on two crucial levels: Melville's at times excruciating, often daring manipulations of language, typified by his transformation of one kind of word to another, such as verbs into adverbs (Pierre contemplates Isabel's journey across the sea in her mother's secret tow: "she had probably first unconsciously and *smuggledly* crossed it hidden beneath her sorrowing mother's heart" [137]) and his sustained immersion in heightened rhetorical registers; and his refusal of traditional codes of masculinity in Pierre's refusal of them. But the novel's depiction of Isabel as unreadable, unknowable, "mysterious"—literally noted in the song that emanates from Isabel's guitar, fervently uttering the words "Mystery of Isabel!" and "Isabel and Mystery!" (126)—can only be described as a highly traditional interpretation of women and femininity, anticipating Freud's infamous description of femininity as "the dark continent." A hazy, muffled, blurry presence, Isabel enters the narrative as a decorporealized figure: a mesmerizing face, a series of incantatory utterances. Her ghostly quality throughout, with the exception of her humanly jealous rivalry with Lucy Tartan, makes it possible to imagine that Isabel is an object of desire without that desire necessarily translating into sexual consummation.

Incest functions as a screen for sexual as well as social relations in *Pierre*. Its tantalizing/horrifying possibility allegorizes the longing and the antipathy that defines the novel's major relationships. Given incest's long-standing metaphorical uses as coded homosexuality, male/female incest here also stands in for same-sex desire. Registered with thoroughgoing dread in *Hamlet,* incestuous sexuality signifies more complicatedly in *Pierre,* suggesting at once utopian oneness transcending difference, and the dread of intimacy. *Pierre* foregrounds the sense that all sexuality is incestuous.³⁸ Family members—his mother, cousin, possible half-sister—constitute the hero's major relationships, all of which are erotically tinged; while his relationship with Lucy is a nonbiological tie, she effectively becomes a family member by joining his small sorority at the Church of the Apostles.

In *Hamlet,* the question of Gertrude and Claudius's shared perfidy sparks the hero's revulsion and rage, suggestive of his attitude toward sexuality generally. The famous play-within-the-play scene, relevant in many ways for *Pierre,* collapses adultery, incest, and homoeroticism, as evinced by the prosy stage directions:

> Enter a KING and a QUEEN [very lovingly]; the QUEEN embracing him and he her. [She kneels, and makes show of protestation unto him.] He takes her up, and declines his head upon her neck. He lies him down upon a bank of flowers: she, seeing him asleep, leaves him. Anon comes in another man, takes off his crown, kisses it, and pours poison in the sleeper's ears, and leaves him. The QUEEN returns; finds the KING dead, makes passionate action. The POISONER with some three or four come in again, seem to condole with her. The dead body is carried away. The POISONER woos the Queen with gifts; she seems harsh awhile, but in the end accepts love. (3.2.120)

A scene that Claudius and Gertrude must witness, it serves as a grotesque mirror for the crime undergirding their noxious union. But it is a mirror for Hamlet as well; tellingly, it is the vulnerable, wronged Ophelia—in every respect Hamlet's chief victim, unconscionably abused by him even as he has felt himself abused—whom he sits beside during this mock performance. Just as Gertrude fails to honor Old Hamlet's memory in Hamlet's eyes, so too does Hamlet fail to honor his past intimacy with Ophelia, which the play suggests was sexually tinged.³⁹ The play-within-the-play's action rebukes Hamlet no less than the criminal adulterers he wishes to shame and expose.

Melville stunningly reworks this Shakespearean tableau. Pierre's marriage to Isabel reconceives marriage as parodic assault on compulsory sexual norms. A transgressive and volatile union, Pierre and Isabel's marriage threatens to bring ruins as yet unimagined. Even the disgraced Delly Ulver, wronged and rejected, fears that their marriage will result in her greater perdition: "If I stay, then—for stay I must—and they be not married,—then pity, pity, pity, pity, pity!" (321). Isabel's hostility toward Lucy when she joins them insinuates Isabel's more-than-sisterly tie with Pierre (especially since Isabel feels protective toward rather than competitive with the non-rival Delly). This theme of sororophobia, to use Helena Michie's term, is one indication among many that, far from signifying a utopian alternative to institutionalized heterosexual marriage, the sham marriage between Pierre and Isabel creates as many social divides as it transcends.

Pierre's fantasy of male heroism—that he can somehow single-handedly rescue not only Isabel and Delly but also Lucy—results ultimately in the deaths of Isabel and Lucy as well as himself. (It is not clear what fate befalls Delly, left alone in their quarters at the Apostles, but that it is a less grim one is unlikely.) Melville here offers his own version of Hamlet's questionable behavior toward his mother and dishonorable treatment of Ophelia, while combining Hamlet's bifurcated attitudes toward male relationships; Pierre's friendship-turned-enmity with Glen combines a Horatio-like love with a Laertes-like poisonous rivalry. The collapse of male friendship and love into murderous hate further signifies a dark side to Pierre's attempts to break free of social strictures. This is not to suggest that Pierre's utopian impulses are themselves wrong. Rather, Melville cannot imagine a utopian effort at transcendent unities, heterosexual or homosexual, that escapes wreck and ruin. Pierre is earnest but also vaingloriously rash and foolish, ensuring the destruction of those he vows to protect and rendering the vulnerable even more vulnerable with him than without him. *Pierre* transforms *Hamlet*'s elaborate climax involving poisoned lances and cups and a mass death scene into the prison cell's barren, desolate tableau, in which the bodies of dead women festoon dead Pierre.

FALLEN GIANTS

Pierre explicitly mentions incest six times; five of those times occur in the paragraph on the fallen giant from Greek mythology Enceladus. The sixth mention of the term *incest* comes later, in book 26, during a discussion of the portrait of Beatrice Cenci, at the time attributed to Guido Reni.[40]

Of its many significant dimensions, *Pierre*'s reference to Enceladus intriguingly nods to *Hamlet*'s implicit reference. Grief-stricken over her suicide by drowning and furious at the priest who balks at giving her a proper funeral service for this reason, Laertes leaps into Ophelia's grave. He then frames himself as a giant of grief by evoking the giants who battled the Olympians:

> Now pile your dust upon the quick and dead,
> Till of this flat a mountain you have made,
> To o'ertop old Pelion, or the skyish head
> Of blue Olympus. (*Hamlet*, 5.1.241–44)

The war between the Giants and the gods was retold by Ovid in the first book of *The Metamorphoses,* which Shakespeare could have read in the original and in the translation of Arthur Golding.[41] In order to reach heaven, the Giants piled mountains atop one another, heaping Ossa and Olympus on Pelion, or Pelion and Ossa on Olympus, hence the proverbial phrase "to pile Pelion on Ossa," meaning to make a bad situation worse. Not to be outdone, Hamlet provocatively taunts Laertes, extending his rival's allusion and associating himself with the Giants:

> Dost thou come here to whine?
> To outface me with leaping in her grave?
> Be buried quick with her, and so will I:
> And, if thou prate of mountains, let them throw
> Millions of acres on us, till our ground,
> Singeing his pate against the burning zone,
> Make Ossa like a wart! (5.1.269–72)

(Though one chafes against Hamlet's mockery of Laertes's brotherly grief, and how unsatisfactory he must find Hamlet's "travesty of an apology," that Laertes himself only feigns reconciliation "in the lead up to their fencing match" will allow Laertes to match "dissimulation with dissimulation."[42]) J. Anthony Burton notes that *Hamlet*'s several references to the Giants' rebellion inform the play's power dynamics. The Elizabethan audience would have understood that the Giants "were the polar opposites of the divine Olympians. Variously described as impious, foolhardy, impetuous, treasonous, indiscreet, inglorious, beastlike, dangerous, vile, and tyrannous, their cause was always reprehensible."[43] So neither Laertes nor Hamlet cover themselves in glory when likening their affect or cause to that of the Giants.

As he tries and disastrously fails to become a writer, Pierre's mythological avatars emerge as Hamlet, Dante, and the Giant Enceladus, mistakenly identified as a Titan here, which underscores the frequent interchangeability of the two in the myth's reception. Nancy Fredricks observes, "Like Hamlet, who evokes the myth of Enceladus when he becomes disgusted by Laertes' feeble attempts to 'outface' him at the grave of Ophelia, Pierre, in launching his attack on the world of seeming, imagines himself the Titan, Enceladus, the offspring of the incestuous marriage of two worlds, heaven and earth, forever beaten down by the Olympians who bury him alive."[44] In an ekphrastic tour de force, Melville reads the sculptor Gaspard Marsy's work *The Enceladus Fountain,* sculpted in lead between 1675 and 1677 and prominently displayed in the Groves of Versailles, as an allegorical figure for the artist defying his oppressors, intransigent in the face of certain defeat: shorn of limbs, he turns "his vast trunk into a battering-ram."[45] Even vanquished, the Titan, as Melville classifies him, transforms his very dismembered body into a weapon against his enemies. Pierre, having a dream that could be called a nightmare, cries out the Titan's name in his sleep. "Enceladus! it is Enceladus!" And the Titan faces him, though from that moment Pierre "saw Enceladus no more; but on the Titan's armless trunk, his own duplicate face and features magnifiedly gleamed upon him with prophetic discomfiture and woe"; the "ideal horror" of his dream transmutes into "all his actual grief" (346).

Interestingly, Melville provides the giant's backstory after this oneiric vision:

> Old Titan's self was the son of incestuous Cœlus and Terra, the son of incestuous Heaven and Earth. And Titan married his mother Terra, another and accumulatively incestuous match. And thereof Enceladus was one issue. So Enceladus was both the son and grandson of an incest; and even thus, there had been born from the organic blended heavenliness and earthliness of Pierre, another mixed, uncertain, heaven-aspiring, but still not wholly earth-emancipated mood; which again, by its terrestrial taint held down to its terrestrial mother, generated there the present doubly incestuous Enceladus within him; so that the present mood of Pierre—that reckless sky-assaulting mood of his, was nevertheless on one side the grandson of the sky. For it is according to eternal fitness, that the precipitated Titan should still seek to regain his paternal birthright even by fierce escalade. Wherefore whoso

storms the sky gives best proof he came from thither! But whatso crawls contented in the moat before that crystal fort, shows it was born within that slime, and there forever will abide. (347)

Pierre aligns himself with Enceladus and with the likewise "mixed, uncertain, heaven-aspiring, but still not wholly earth-emancipated" Hamlet. Though not incestuous himself, Enceladus is the progeny of incestuous unions across generations. If all sexuality is incestuous, as the novel appears to claim, Enceladus models this idea.

In *Hamlet in His Modern Guises,* Alexander Welsh discusses Enceladus's context within *Pierre*'s incest plot. Pierre's "dare to free himself and Isabel to incestuous desire, or to commit incest if he should so please, has more probably to do with the impossible quest for originality and Promethean heroics. Pierre asks to make love to his own devoted mirror image and dreams of being the titan Enceladus, 'the present doubly incestuous Enceladus within him.' Once it becomes clear that Pierre is also a writer, the act of tearing works of Dante and Shakespeare to shreds can be seen as indicative of similar strivings."[46]

I do not see Melville as tearing his literary precursors to shreds but rather as reimagining and extending their ideas for his own purposes. He sparks off the Enceladus-related allusions and energies of *Hamlet* to envision a wayward contemporary version of Shakespeare's protagonist, one less counseled and guided and even more unmoored, whose revenge plan stumbles entirely because so diffuse and inscrutable.

LIKENESS VISIBLE

In his essay "On Love," Percy Bysshe Shelley writes, "Thou demandest what is Love. It is that powerful attraction towards all we conceive, or fear, or hope beyond ourselves when we find within our own thoughts the chasm of an insufficient void and seek to awaken in all things that are, a community with what we experience within ourselves . . . If . . . we feel, we would that another's nerves should vibrate to our own, that the beams of their eyes should kindle at once and mix and melt into our own . . . This is Love."[47] When we desire, we desire self-likeness. This potentially radical idea gets much less radical when it reifies misogynistic constructions of femininity as reflective surfaces for male self-likeness. Anne K. Mellor critiques "On Love" as reflective of the narcissistic sensibility that she calls "masculine Romanticism." She identifies the "fundamental desire of the romantic lover" as the effort "to find in female form a mirror image of himself," what Shelley calls in "On Love" the "anti-type."[48] In response to Mellor, Steven Bruhm writes that he has no wish "to deny that such Romantic narcissism effaces and destroys the represented woman"; nevertheless, he points out that the view of narcissism as pathological imposes an anachronistic paradigm on Romanticism and its uses of the Ovidian Narcissus myth: "Romantic male authors purposely exploited the implications of looking at—and looking into—oneself," which has relevance for "the dangerous and volatile field of same-sex relations within the homosocial spectrum."[49]

Melville upholds narcissistic desire's centrality to Romantic writing, in part by explicitly naming Narcissus in his work, which he does in *Moby-Dick*. Yet throughout *Pierre*, it is primarily the female characters who see *their* likeness in the male. Mary, if Pierre's interpretation of his mother's desire holds true, sees in him her own idealized likeness as well as her gender-based loss of opportunities. Pierre's aunt Dorothea fetishizes the chair portrait that she brings to Pierre's attention, seeing in it the image of her brother that she prefers to the one Mary commissioned. Yet Dorothea verges on seeing *herself* in the portrait, as she suggests when explaining to the child Pierre her role in the portrait's creation: "My child, it was I that chose the stuff for that neckcloth; yes, and hemmed it for him, and worked P. G. in one corner; but that aint in the picture. It is an excellent likeness, my child, neckcloth and all; as he looked at that time. Why, little Pierre, sometimes I sit here all alone by myself, gazing, and gazing, and gazing at that face, till I begin to think your father is looking at me, and smiling at me, and nodding at me, and saying—Dorothea! Dorothea!" (79). The face connotes, at once, identity and nonidentity in Melville's (and Hawthorne's) work. Isabel's maddening, mesmerizing face metonymizes her, goading Pierre to seek her once he glimpses it. Isabel's own relationship to her face is a highly vexed one. In a passage that intertextually echoes Milton's Narcissus-like Eve and her narration of her nativity in book 4 of *Paradise Lost*, Isabel recalls having stared at her reflection in a smooth lake when she was a girl. She then sees that reflected image of herself in the face of the man who speaks the word "Father" to her and that she comes to believe *is* her father (124). Isabel cannot claim even Eve's limited visual and psychological autonomy when in Milton's poem she gazes into the lake and sees her own, desirable reflection. When Isabel sees her reflection, it leads to paternal facial recognition, a stunningly concise statement about the patriarchal subsumption of the female gaze. When Pierre brings Isabel and Lucy into an art gallery and they discover a portrait of a man that recalls the image of Pierre's father, titled "No. 99. A stranger's head, by an unknown hand," Isabel exclaims. "'My God! see! see!' cried Isabel, under strong excitement, 'only my mirror has ever shown me that look before! See! see!'" (349–50). Eugenia C. DeLamotte has noted the recurring significance of ancestral portraits in the Gothic, usually for the purpose of authenticating a family's rightful heirs. But throughout *Pierre,* Melville links "the quest for knowledge with the quest to express knowledge in art." Enceladus captures this idea, as a figure of the writer reaching for heaven "but trapped in the 'imprisoning earth.'" The art gallery holds "the walls of the world" amply filled with paintings, but these paintings are failures, miserably empty. The desire to know and the desire to express knowledge through art fail at once; seeing the portrait of the stranger's head by an unknown hand leads Pierre to question Isabel's blood relation to him and whether art matters at all.[50] As Wyn Kelley observes, Enceladus, "the product and victim of monstrously bad parenting," figures Pierre's domestic difficulties. "Heroically resisting his progenitors' destructive family patterns in a spirit no less resistant than that of such female rebels as Fanny Fern's Ruth Hall or E.D.E.N. Southworth's Capitola," Pierre adopts a "reckless sky-assaulting mood" (347). Like these female protagonists, Pierre tries to "escape the sins of his demonic fathers and grandfathers by resisting male authority . . . [and establishing] a nonpatriarchal household."[51]

If Enceladus provides the ur-image of the castrated artist, this artist is buried in the earth, immobile, immured along with his defiance. As Isabel's self-apprehension-as-paternal-image allegorizes, femininity is frozen in the image; Isabel can only recognize herself in the image of the male, unable to move beyond this spectatorial position even if knowledge of her own situation and desires emerges from it. Hamlet's forcing Gertrude to stare at the two different portraits, one of his father and the other of his hated uncle, provides an especially sadistic intertext in light of this Melvillean theorization of women's relationship to the image. In forcing Gertrude to acknowledge the inadequacy of the one and the "Hyperion"-like superiority of the other, Hamlet entombs his mother in a conceptualization of the gaze that always already leads to the recognition of male superiority. Melville takes this idea further and challenges it, but only to a certain extent. Pierre's ruminations on Mary's experience when seeing herself reflected in her comely young son's form offer fascinating insights into male psychology, mother-son relationships, and the narcissistic self-regard that links Pierre to his mother. Yet the passage where Pierre contemplates his mother's fixation on him is a phobic one, evoking Mary's icy character but also rebuking the autonomous and forthright woman's desire. Isabel's apprehension of being reflected in the image of her ostensible father and in the "stranger's head" portrait leads to her further entrapment in the idealized male image. It also loosens Pierre's faith that they are related and deepens his suicidal futility, which includes an increasing belief in the impossibility of both knowledge and art.[52]

Pierre ruminates on his relationship to his precursor: "Hamlet taunted him with faltering in the fight. Now he began to curse anew his fate, for now he began to see that after all he had been finely juggling with himself, and postponing with himself, and in meditative sentimentalities wasting the moments consecrated to instant action" (170). *Hamlet* taunts both Pierre and Melville, and in tribute to this prior text, Melville envisions a hero forever "faltering in the fight." Pierre's ceaseless faltering grimly revises *Hamlet:* Hamlet's qualified triumph at the play's climax, compared to Pierre's nihilistic achievement, seems comparatively optimistic. Melville concludes with faltering, his hero's Pyrrhic victory a testament to Melville's own intransigence in the face of literary giants.

6

"A JEWISH ASPECT"
The Marble Faun *and* The Merchant of Venice

HARDLY THE ONLY EXAMPLE of her controversial tweets, the famous fictionist and critic Joyce Carol Oates started a 2017 Twitter thread thusly: "'Othello' is a great enough work of dramatic art that, if the racial element were entirely removed, the play would still be a profound accomplishment. That Othello is a 'Moor' could be made—almost—irrelevant. (Disagree?)."[1] The negative response was swift and copious. Summarizing it, Princess Weekes of the online publication *The Mary Sue* responded,

> If you took race out of Othello, it would just be like a non-supernatural Macbeth or Hamlet or Julius Caesar. Race is interwoven into Othello's sense of identity and removing that would make the character utterly dull, because let's be real the reason we remember Othello isn't because of the main character, it is because of Iago. Iago is the character everyone wants to really play. He has all the best lines and he is the most well-defined. Othello is still a great character because of his nobility, but it is nobility in the face of discrimination. If it was not for his race and the insight the play gives into the thoughts around non-white people at the time, the character of Othello would be very uninteresting. (December 27, 2017, 2:14 p.m.)[2]

One would want to nuance Weekes's commentary, given that it threatens to suggest Othello is only interesting because of his race. But I still take her point: to excise the play's racial themes is to excise the play.

The moribund status of the question of literary influence in Americanist literary criticism stems, it would appear, from a sense that to discuss such topics is to instantiate, perpetuate, a white-male-author canonical ideal and standard. This may be true. As I have attempted to demonstrate in this book, it is also to do other things. In terms of the authors under discussion here, it is to work through our understanding of a particular preoccupation, within the development of American literary consciousness, with questions of foundational British elements, embodied powerfully though not exclusively by Shakespeare and Milton. Just as pressingly, a preoccupation with the feminine, with female subjectivity, agency, or lack thereof, on the part of male writers working through the precedents set by previous male writers, animates and motivates scenes of influence.

The question of literary influence intersects with the antebellum era's central social problems ("hard facts," as Phil Fisher called them): racism, ranging from negative attitudes towards Native Americans and Africans; religious prejudice toward those of non-Protestant faiths, such as Jews and Catholics; homophobia, in response to the incipient presence of homosexuality, gaining definition as a "type" and a subjectivity over the course of the century, an outgrowth of the hostility and ambivalence toward sexual deviance and, indeed, sexuality generally; misogyny, organized around the Cult of True Womanhood and its mythologies of essential female passivity, passionlessness, sexlessness, and inferiority; and "masculinity" as a coherent standard, an image to be achieved, maintained, and fulfilled. That is, *pace* Oates, one cannot get away from hard facts when studying a great work; indeed, to do so diminishes the work.

Hawthorne embeds his attitudes towards Jewishness in the design of *The Marble Faun; or, the Romance of Monte Beni* (1859), the last of his novels to be published in his lifetime. *The Marble Faun* clearly contains negative depictions of Judaism yet also displays something approaching sympathy towards the history of Jewish oppression. Certainly, it is a work that recognizes the centrality of Judaism to Western culture even within its most avowedly classical and Christian cultural underpinnings.[3] Set in the artist communities of 1850s Rome, it has two heroes and two heroines who represent distinct gendered and ethnic types: the mysterious Miriam

Schaefer, of a number of possible racial descents, but also clearly a representation of "the Jewess," and Donatello, the primitive twenty-year-old Italian whose appearance recalls the titular classical faun and who turns out to be the Count of Monte Beni, his lineage traced back to Etrurian Tuscany; on the white Protestant side, the American sculptor Kenyon and the "New England girl," Hilda, a copyist of the Old Masters. The darkest character of all is the Model, who stalks Miriam after she encounters him in the Catacombs of Saint Calixtus.

The Marble Faun recalls *The Last of the Mohicans*'s psychosexual exploration of racial prejudice and women's struggles for autonomy and self-recognition. Bringing this study full circle, Shakespeare's comedy *The Merchant of Venice* once again provides a foundational intertext. Cooper's Magua evokes Shylock in the fiery indignation that leads him to seek revenge against white Christian male power, while Cora Munro's unflinching response to Magua's demands for vengeance echoes Portia's resolve in the trial scene where she cautions the vengeance-seeking Shylock to stand down. Shylock's famous speech establishes the humanity that, as a Jew, he has been denied by Christians:

> I am a Jew. Hath not a Jew eyes? hath not a Jew
> Hands, organs, dimensions, senses, affections, passions?
> Fed with the same food, hurt with the same weapons,
> subject to the same diseases, healed by the same means,
> warmed and cooled by the same winter and summer as
> a Christian is? If you prick us, do we not bleed? If you
> tickle us do we not laugh? If you poison us do we not die?
> And if you wrong us shall we not revenge? (3.1.53–60)

In a pivotal scene in *The Marble Faun,* Miriam begs her friend Hilda, an unyieldingly moralistic "daughter of the Puritans," for compassion, which Hilda rebuffs. Miriam's response to Hilda evokes Shylock's language. As Miriam puts it, "I am a woman ... endowed with the same truth of nature, the same warmth of heart, the same genuine and earnest love, which you have always known in me. . . . Have I deceived you? Then cast me off! Have I wronged you personally? Then forgive me, if you can!" But if she has "deeply sinned" "against God and man," she asks Hilda to "be more my friend than ever, for I need you more!" (208).[4] Though we eventually learn that Miriam has Jewish blood from the maternal line, the novel has long hinted, as Sacvan Bercovitch established in a 1969 essay "Miriam as Shylock," that she is Jewish: "We should recall, first, that he dwells upon Miriam's Jewish background. He gives her a Jewish pseudonym (p. 486), stresses the fact of her Jewish blood (p. 486), details the Hebraic subject-matter of her paintings (pp. 60–67), and models her Semitic features (p. 38) on those of 'a beautiful Jewish lady' he had 'admired' in London."[5] When Miriam evokes Shylock's famous speech, she does so from a position of Jewish identity, but primarily as a *woman*, "endowed" with the gifts of the feminine, "truth of nature, warmth of heart, genuine and earnest love." Hawthorne converts Shylock's speech about the humanity of Jews into a specific credo about one's woman's humanity. These and other moments in Hawthorne's reworking of *The Merchant of Venice* emphasize the gender of Jewishness.

The issue of gender emerges as a powerful, wide-ranging lens to reexamine the novel: its treatment of Judaism and antisemitism, to begin with, but also anti-Catholic feeling, as relevant here as the issue of antisemitism; the legacy of classicism as it informs the transatlantic tensions Hawthorne foregrounds in this novel about the American confrontation with European history; and the ways in which normative constructions of male and female roles as well as racial prejudices determine and are thwarted by art and aesthetics.

The trajectory of this chapter is as follows: we analyze Hawthorne's account of his dinner at the home of the Lord Mayor of London, David Salomons, where the author met the "beautiful Jewish lady," Salomons's sister-in-law. Hawthorne's admiring comments about female Jewish beauty and disparaging comments about male Jews synthesize crucial and consistent aspects of his depictions of gender identity and sexual difference, his bifurcation of "ugly" men and darkly beautiful women elsewhere. The Jewish man and woman synthesize his positions towards gender identity—they are not simply "the Jews of Jews," but also representatives of maleness and femaleness.

Contextualizing Hawthorne's depictions of Jewish masculinity and femininity does not exculpate his antisemitism, nor, indeed, his racism. It does allow us to develop a richer understanding of what the figure of the Jew meant to him. Such an analysis promises to yield insights not only into Hawthorne's work—valuable enough, given its importance—but also into mid-Victorian thought about these matters. Toward this end, I discuss nineteenth-century antisemitism generally, focusing on its gendered aspects. I then offer a reading of Miriam Schaefer and the Model as closeted Jewish characters. These considerations lead me to an analysis of Hawthorne's reworking of *The Merchant of Venice,* an undiscussed topic save for Bercovitch's article. Focusing on two central themes—conversion and revenge—we can trace the intertextual connections between both texts and consider Hawthorne's depiction of Jewish characters in light of Shakespeare's precedent.

BEHOLDING JEWISHNESS

On Sunday, April 13, 1856, Hawthorne attended a banquet in London at the Mansion House, to which he was invited by David Salomons, the Lord Mayor of London. Salomons was honoring Hawthorne in his capacity as US consul in Liverpool, a position awarded him in 1853 by United States President Franklin Pierce, the author's best friend since their student days at Bowdoin College and whose campaign biography Hawthorne wrote. The consulship was an extremely important one at the time given Liverpool's centrality in transatlantic trade and commerce between England and the United States. (The position no longer exists.)

Hawthorne may or may not have been aware that Salomons was a pioneering activist for Jewish rights in the simultaneously tolerant and antisemitic Victorian England.[6] The author's account in *The English Notebooks* of the Salomons dinner explicitly reveals his deep-seated antisemitism and his intense fascination with the figure of the Jewess. From the description he provides, Hawthorne and David Salomons did not develop a rapport. "He said little to me," Hawthorne notes, "except that I must hold myself in readiness to respond to a toast which he meant to give; and though I hinted that I would much rather be spared, he showed no signs of mercy" (21:480). Hawthorne also observed that his lordship "is a tall, hard-looking, white-headed old Jew, of plain deportment, but rather hearty than otherwise in his address." Hawthorne deemed Salomons's wife "a short and ugly old Jewess" (21:479).

In the opening scene of *The Scarlet Letter,* Hawthorne moves from depicting the hard-bitten Puritan women scornfully gawking at Hester

Prynne to languorously sensual descriptions of her. In a similar movement, Hawthorne transitions from his harsh description of Salomons's wife to a much more rapturous one of Salomons's sister-in-law, Emma Abigail Montefiore Salomons, sitting "nearly opposite me, across the table." His descriptions of her and her husband Philip Salomons need to be quoted at length, and within the one continuous paragraph in which they appear:

> She was, I suppose, dark and yet not dark, but rather seemed to be of pure white marble, yet not white; but the purest and finest complexion (without a shade of color in it, yet anything but sallow or sickly) that I ever beheld. Her hair was a wonderful deep, raven black, black as night, black as death; *not* raven black, for that has a shiny gloss, and her's [*sic*] had not; but it was hair never to be painted, nor described—wonderful hair, Jewish hair. Her nose had a beautiful outline, though I could see that it was Jewish too; and that, and all her features, were so fine that sculpture seemed a despicable art beside her; and certainly my pen is good for nothing. If any likeness of her could be given, it must be by sculpture, not painting. She was slender, and youthful, but yet had a stately and cold, though soft and womanly grace; and, looking at her, I saw what were the wives of the old patriarchs, in their maiden or early married days—what Rachel was, when Jacob wooed her seven years, and seven more—what Judith was; for, womanly as she looked, I doubt not she could have slain a man, in a good cause—what Bathsheba was; only she seemed to have no sin in her—perhaps what Eve was, though one could hardly think her weak enough to eat the apple. I never should have thought of touching her, nor desired to touch her; for, whether owing to distinctness of race, my sense that she was a Jewess, or whatever else, I felt a sort of repugnance, simultaneously with my perception that she was an admirable creature. But, at the right hand of this miraculous Jewess, there sat the very Jew of Jews; the distilled essence of all the Jews that have been born since Jacob's time; he was Judas Iscariot; he was the Wandering Jew; he was the worst, and at the same time, the truest type of his race, and contained within himself, I have no doubt, every old prophet and every old clothesman, that ever the tribes produced; and he must have been circumcised as much as ten times over. I never beheld anything so ugly and disagreeable, and preposterous, and laughable, as the outline of his profile; it was so hideously Jewish, and so cruel, and so keen; and he had such an immense beard that you could

see no trace of a mouth, until he opened it to speak, or to eat his dinner,—
and then, indeed, you were aware of a cave, in this density of beard. And yet
his manners and aspect, in spite of all, were those of a man of the world, and
a gentleman. Well; it is as hard to give an idea of this ugly Jew, as of the beautiful Jewess. He was the Lord Mayor's brother, and an elderly man, though
he looked in his prime, with his wig and dyed beard; and Rachel, or Judith,
or whatever her name be, was his wife! I rejoiced exceedingly in this Shylock,
this Iscariot; for the sight of him justified me in the repugnance I have always
felt towards his race. (21:481–82).

Any admirer of Hawthorne will be despondent to learn of the depths of his prejudice.[7] It behooves us, however, to dwell at length upon the *complexity* of prejudice—to think about the character, the nuances and the idiosyncrasies, and, in particular, the gendered dynamics of Hawthorne's antisemitism. His depiction of Emma Abigail Montefiore Salomons is enraptured, admiring, erotically charged, and in many ways no less alarming than his explicitly negative portrait of her husband, relying on the same essentialisms. Why do so many qualities about the Jewish woman strike Hawthorne as aesthetically and sensually pleasurable, even as he registers the inescapable "repugnance" he feels towards her, while his aversion towards the Jewish man is so unalloyed?

Hawthorne's encounter with Mrs. Salomons not only provides a striking template for *The Marble Faun*'s Miriam Schaefer, whose mysterious past swirls around the enigmatic question of her racial and ethnic identity, but also establishes a retrocontinuity between this real-life woman and the fictional ones that preceded her. While it is commonly accepted that Hawthorne's major female characters evoke the dark lady archetype, that they evoke the Jewess of Hawthorne's 1856 description is perhaps more to the point.[8] Raven-haired, passionate, darkly mysterious, extremely intelligent, Hawthorne's great heroines Hester Prynne, Zenobia, and Miriam all share Mrs. Salomons's uncanny ability to provoke male feelings of desire and alienation, attraction and "repugnance." Despite offering numerous erotically charged and admiring descriptions of Zenobia's sensual beauty and wit in *The Blithedale Romance,* Coverdale reassures the reader as well as himself that all these thoughts are "purely speculative; for I should not, under any circumstances, have fallen in love with Zenobia" (48). What lies behind this insistence that an erotic and emotional connection will not be pursued, under any circumstances, with a woman who clearly arouses the narrator's desire for both? And why would the Jewess, encountered after such a depiction, emerge as the living quintessence of the fictional dynamics? The intersection between racist and antisemitic attitudes must also be noted. *The Marble Faun* offers tantalizing hearsay about Miriam early on: "It was said that Miriam was the daughter and heiress of a great Jewish banker," suggested by "a certain rich Oriental character in her face," and also that "she was the offspring of a Southern American planter, who had given her an elaborate education and endowed her with his wealth; but the one burning drop of African blood in her veins" filled her with a "sense of ignominy" intense enough to impel her to flee the United States (22–23). Miriam recalls the mixed-race Cora Munro and her personally discomfiting "rich blood."

If Hawthorne's antisemitic accounts of the Salomons echo in *The Marble Faun*'s themes of desire and repugnance, these themes undergo a thorough analysis within the novel. Hawthorne used fiction as an occasion to work through his personal prejudices while also voicing them. The gendered imbalance in Hawthorne's phobic disposition towards the Jew—the bifurcation of the figure of the Jew into the beautiful, if also disturbing, Jewess and the wholly displeasing Jewish male—requires further unpacking. His presumably heterosexual orientation is an inadequate explanation for why he could find beauty in the Jewish woman while finding none in the man. Even more so than that of Herman Melville, who has generally inspired more consideration as a queer author, Hawthorne's work teems with descriptions of male beauty. Far from being incapable of finding beauty in other men, Hawthorne does so repeatedly in his gallery of males who possess "significant personal beauty" (Fanshawe, Robin Molineaux, David Swan, Giovanni Guasconti, Feathertop [at least provisionally], Dimmesdale, the young Clifford Pyncheon, Coverdale, Westervelt [at least until he opens his mouth], Donatello, and, most interestingly, the mixed-race Septimius Felton). For Hawthorne, beauty in males proceeds from a Hellenic basis, as most of his attractive males are cast in a Greco-Roman mode.[9] These males are almost always young, morally callow, and regarded skeptically. Hawthorne's Hellenic aesthetic is marked by a critical disposition towards the males who embody its heightened form.

"A DAUGHTER TO HIS BLOOD"

That Hawthorne likens Philip Salomons to Shylock and Judas Iscariot, the apostle who betrays Christ, among other Jewish archetypes contextualizes his antisemitism within recurring negative images of Jewishness, some stemming from Shakespeare's play. The Model, Miriam's nemesis, most clearly evokes Shylock understood as an antisemitic portrayal, particularly the description of Miriam's stalker as "Demon." That said, Shylock's reception history, oscillating between views of him as either a villain or a clown, underwent considerable permutations in the antebellum era, which added the view of him as an emblem of wronged and suffering humanity. Writing in 1850, George Henry Lewes, a dramatic critic now best known for his relationship with the eminent Victorian writer George Eliot (a writer influenced by and who may have influenced Hawthorne), observes, "Nothing can, I think, be clearer than the malignity of Shakespeare's Jew . . ." Yet he proceeds to say that "if Shylock be not represented as having the feelings of our kind, *The Merchant of Venice* becomes a brutal melodrama, not a great tragedy." Shylock's daughter Jessica and his fondness for her centrally illuminate his humanity. Jessica elopes with the Christian Lorenzo and converts to Christianity, acts which yield a "tenfold bitterness" in her father. If Shylock is presented as "a savage, blood-thirsty wretch, the whole moral is lost; if his fierceness is natural to him, and not brought out by the wrongs of the Christians, all the noble philosophy of the piece is destroyed," the key to Shylock's humanity lying in his "fatherly affection."[10]

Lancelet Giobbe, the "Clown," who is first employed by Shylock and then by Antonio, addresses Jessica as "most beautiful pagan, most sweet Jew! If a Christian do not play the / knave and get thee, I am much deceived" (2.3.10–14). He describes her thusly after she gives him a letter for Lorenzo, her Christian lover. Jessica then laments, "Alack, what heinous sin is it in me / To be ashamed to be my father's child! / But though I am a daughter to his blood, I am not to his manners" (2.3.15–20). Temperamentally, the tough Miriam is as distinct as possible from the more ingenue-like Jessica. Yet she and Jessica share a revulsion at being linked with the Jewish male.

Recent treatments of the Shylock legacy contextualize it within a much larger, long-standing tradition of a central relationship between a Jewish father and his daughter, especially Efraim Sicher's 2017 study *The Jew's Daughter: A Cultural History of a Conversion Narrative*. Shylock and

Jessica fit into this pattern as a central example, but only one of many. Other famous examples can be found in Marlowe's play *The Jew of Malta*, Walter Scott's novel *Ivanhoe*, and Eliot's novel *Daniel Deronda*. Scott's seminal *Ivanhoe* and its Beautiful Jewess archetype in the character of Rebecca, closely aligned with her father, with whom she flees to Granada to avoid persecution in England, clearly influences Hawthorne as it did Cooper. Sicher points out that a theme of motherlessness informs the Jewish father-daughter trope, in keeping with the pervasive motif of motherlessness—maternal deprivation—in the works we have discussed. Another characteristic aspect of this narrative is the daughter's conversion to Christianity, much to the aggrieved Jewish father's chagrin. Heather S. Nathans, in her sweeping study of Jewish representation throughout theater history, notes, Shakespeare's Jessica "was the best-known and most frequently performed Jewess in American playhouses. . . . [She] presents a quintessentially feminine and domestic character, much more so than the aggressive Portia." For centuries, Jessica's conversion to Christianity modeled the proper solution for the wayward Jewess, conscripted into a redemptive change of religious identity.[11] For critics such as Janet Adelman, however, Jessica, though a convert, faces the same level of harrowing vulnerability as does her father, and the play's anxiety about the negotiation of her uncertain and threatening status is palpable.[12] Hawthorne's reworking of these interlocking themes preserves antisemitic elements in Shylock's reception history while also idealizing the Jewess and her conversion. Yet by making his Shylock figure the Model, like Miriam the subject of a conversion narrative, and by exposing the conversion itself as the site of trauma, Hawthorne daringly sheds light on the antisemitic pressures catalyzing conversion. When the Model and Miriam, as they frequently do, confront one another, it is as if they are participating in a sequel to *The Merchant of Venice* where the debilitated Shylock, converted against his will, confronts his apostate daughter, an encounter fueled by the menace, betrayal, and deep ambivalence reflected in the violated characters' myriad impasses and curious intimacies.

The chief evidence we have of Hawthorne's knowledge of *The Merchant of Venice* contains a telling reference to Jessica. Horatio Bridge, Hawthorne's loyal and loving friend since his Bowdoin College days, recounts a moment that occurred between them when they were undergraduates, walking along the Androscoggin River: "I remember that, on a moonlit evening, Hawthorne and I were leaning over the railing of the bridge just below the falls, listening to the falling water, and enjoying the beauties of the scene, when I recited some passages from the colloquy between Lorenzo and Jessica in 'The Merchant of Venice.' Then Hawthorne, in his deep, musical tones, responded with the following verses," which the author had written before college.[13] It would appear that Bridge provides his friend's verse from memory, one of many indications of the ardent love that led him anonymously to fund the publication of Hawthorne's first collection of stories, *Twice-Told Tales*. At this time, Jessica and Lorenzo's banter would have been considered seductive love talk, as opposed to contemporary understandings of Lorenzo as a smooth operator wooing Jessica in order to access her father's ducats. Bridge recites this love talk to his friend on a moonlit evening. I propose that Bridge was expressing his homoerotic regard for his friend, whose beauty he extols in the memoir, through the expressive medium of a positive Shakespeare romance, positive because Jessica ostensibly transcends her troublesome Judaism through it.[14] Years later, Hawthorne would preserve the scene of homoerotic intimacy in several aspects of *The Marble Faun*, most notably Kenyon's extended and very interpersonal stay with the guilt-ridden, fallen Donatello, after his murder of the Model. But Hawthorne no longer views Jessica's conversion positively, if he did at the time of Bridge's declamation. For Hawthorne, ahead of his time, conversion was clearly an enforced and altering transformation (to evoke his original title for the novel used in England), a punitive strike against one's deepest character, a mark that wounds indelibly.

THE GENDER OF ANTISEMITISM

Hawthorne's beautiful males correspond to the Greco-Roman ideal of symmetrical, lithe, and abstracted beauty embodied by the Vatican sculpture the *Apollo Belvedere*, a central figure and point of celebration for the eighteenth-century German art historian Johann Joachim Winckelmann (1717–68). His writings on classical aesthetics inspired the nineteenth-century craze for the Grand Tour, an improving journey throughout the great cultural centers of Europe, focusing on the classical past. Hawthorne read Winckelmann's *The History of Ancient Art* (1764) shortly after having completed *The Scarlet Letter*,[15] and he applied the German art critic's theories to his own experience of European art in the late 1850s. Hawthorne's immersion (along with his wife, Sophia, a visual artist, and his family) in the European art world produced a rich series of commentaries on European culture and aesthetics, recorded in *The French and Italian Notebooks* and *The Marble Faun,* which drew heavily on them. Winckelmann, as has been frequently discussed, was a pioneer in the popularization of Hellenism and the development of a transatlantic homoerotic Hellenic aesthetic.[16] Hellenic images in antebellum literature and the other arts, sculpture especially, bore the dangerous attractions of the homoerotic. *The Marble Faun* opens with a stunning ekphrastic description of the titular figure that both coyly and teasingly hints at the faun's pansexual threateningness as well as charm. Hawthorne presents the Hellenic aesthetic as foundational on the level of *species* as well as culture, the faun being a more innocent prototype of humanity. *The Marble Faun*'s clash of cultures and histories, its strategically staged oppositions between peoples (pagans, different kinds of Christians, Jews, Africans, "Orientals") and temporalities (ancient times and the contemporary world) revolve around the faun, who represents racial, species, and sexual ambiguity, while being utterly nonambiguous as the embodiment of the classical world, understood as the foundation of Western culture.

Hawthorne establishes the classical model as standard in his descriptions of male beauty and describes males who deviate from the model as ugly. One possible inspiration for Miriam Schaefer was a real-life person who shares her last name, the French schoolteacher "Monsieur Schaeffer" with whom Hawthorne and his dear friend Horatio Bridge enjoyed a sunny bachelors' holiday in Augusta, Maine, in the summer of 1837. Schaeffer was at the time a boarder in Bridge's house. Schaeffer, writes Hawthorne, does not seem much older than twenty-one, "a diminutive figure, with eyes askew, and otherwise of ungainly physiognomy," ill-dressed, to boot, lacking in "French coxcombry" though not in the "monkey-aspect inseparable from a little Frenchman" (32–33). Hawthorne notes that his "insignificant personal appearance stands in the way of his success," and that young Schaeffer, who must teach French to unreceptive American youth, is quite bitter. Schaeffer's last name suggests a possible German or Austrian Jewish ancestry. Anna Brickhouse has theorized that, while the Frenchman whom Hawthorne met in Maine may seem an unlikely real-life father for the fictional Miriam Schaefer, who is said to be of possible partial African descent, "Hawthorne's observation of a portrait of the Empress Josephine" as it hangs on the wall of an inn located in a French-settled area of the

Maine countryside "underscores the intimate, even familial, relation to the slaveholding francophone sites of the Americas" such as Martinique, birthplace and home of Napoleon Bonaparte's future wife, Josephine, the daughter of a wealthy Creole planter.[17] It is a surprise that Brickhouse's excellent reading of these possible overlaps, that the Frenchman Schaeffer could well have fathered a daughter with African blood in her veins, does not include a consideration of the relevance of M. Schaeffer to the possible Jewish or Black ancestry of Miriam Schaefer.

As Brenda Wineapple writes, "Monsieur Schaeffer, observed Hawthorne with some surprise, 'has never yet sinned with woman.' (Had Hawthorne? The "yet" sounds as though he had.)"[18] This entire homosocial episode of the bachelors' summer suggests a casual ability to discuss sexual matters, at least among men, as well as Hawthorne's sense of Schaeffer's differentness, even as Hawthorne described himself as "a queer character in my way." Schaeffer gave Hawthorne the French name, Aubépine, that he would go on to use as an alter ego in his letters as well as in the playful preface to his tale "Rappaccini's Daughter" (1844). The French schoolteacher's significance to Hawthorne's views of himself as an artist and normative masculinity become clear. Schaeffer, a tutor to poorly educated American children (in his frustrations within this position, the Frenchman recalls the sour-tempered pedagogue Ichabod Crane) and a man who is still himself a child in sexual terms, at least insofar as Hawthorne perceives him, embodies several competing aspects: insight into the worlds of knowledge and art, on the one hand, and an essential befuddlement before the enigmas of sexuality, women, and male identity, on the other hand. In this respect, he has something in common with the emasculated Philip Salomons, circumcised ten times over (in a description that also, to be sure, suggests its opposite, a massive phallic power that cannot be diminished however many assaults it undergoes). The sexually innocent, untried, unmanly, ugly Frenchman and old, emasculated, ugly Jewish man share a sexual diminishment that corresponds to their physical unattractiveness.

While Schaeffer may or may not have been Jewish, he shared with several non-Jewish males who defied the Hellenic model of male beauty—registered in Hawthorne as "well-shaped," proportionate features and limbs—the same aesthetic opprobrium that Philip Salomons incurred. In his September 1, 1842, journal entry, Hawthorne described the Concord naturalist Henry David Thoreau this way: "He is as ugly as sin, long-nosed, queer-mouthed, and with uncouth and somewhat rustic, although courteous manners." Hawthorne liked Thoreau much more than he did Ralph Waldo Emerson, with whom Hawthorne maintained a mutually chilly relation. Probably for this reason, he found Thoreau's ugliness "honest and agreeable," noting that it actually suited this singular, solitary man better "much better than beauty" (8:353–54). In the 1860s, when Hawthorne met President Abraham Lincoln, he observed that the president was just "about the homeliest man I ever saw, yet by no means repulsive or disagreeable" and made note of Lincoln's "lengthy awkwardness," "the uncouthness of his movement," and his "shabby slippers" (23:412). Yet he also noted the President's commendable qualities. For men he liked and admired, Hawthorne added positive views of their character or manner that ameliorated their physical ugliness. This kind of qualification appended at or near the end of an unflattering physical description informs Hawthorne's portrait of Philip Salomons: "And yet his manners and aspect, in spite of all, were those of a man of the world, and a gentleman."

As is well known, Hawthorne himself was considered a very handsome, indeed, a beautiful man in life, as exemplified by the legend of an old gypsy woman stopping the young Hawthorne in the forest to ask whether he were "a man or an angel," for seldom was a man so beautiful.[19] His aesthetic assessment of other males preceded from a narcissistic basis—a man who did not reflect Hawthorne's own beauty back to him was deemed "ugly as sin." Hawthorne's model of male beauty was his friend Pierce. Harry Truman considered Pierce the best-looking of all US presidents. Noting that Hawthorne would probably have agreed, Leland S. Person summarizes Hawthorne's appreciation of Pierce's physical appeal in his campaign biography of Pierce:

> he paints a complex portrait that recalls some of his own ambiguously gendered male characters. "The old people of his neighborhood give a very delightful picture of Franklin at this early age," he observes. "They describe him as a beautiful boy, with blue eyes, light curling hair, and a sweet expression of face." Based on his first-hand observations of Pierce at Bowdoin, Hawthorne catalogs his friend's virtues: his "sweetness of disposition," his "cordial sympathy," his "delicate texture of sentiment" and "generous and affectionate nature," his "soft" manners (23:279). He had "the boy and man in him," Hawthorne concludes, "vivacious, mirthful, slender, of a

fair complexion, with light hair that had a curl in it: his bright and cheerful aspect made a kind of sunshine, both as regarded its radiance and its warmth; insomuch that no shyness of disposition, in his associates, could well resist its influence." (23:280)

As Person observes, "this youthful Pierce seems cross-gendered or effeminate—a gentle man indeed."[20] That so many males Hawthorne knew personally repeatedly struck him as unattractive in specific ways informs our understanding of his horror at the Jewish male. In Hawthorne's view, Jewish males are like most men, only more so, men like Pierce very much the exception.

Hawthorne's depiction of Jewish masculinity derives from the figure of the Wandering Jew that was so central to nineteenth-century constructions of the Jewish male, as we discuss below. The Jewish male occupied an emphatic place in Hawthorne's *general* understanding of male ugliness. The valences among Hawthorne's descriptions of Schaeffer, Thoreau, Salomons, and Lincoln exceed the category of the Jew while also together creating a particular model of "ugly" masculinity: ill-proportioned of both face and form, indeed, audacious in its unself-conscious display of its own asymmetrical "queerness." "The Jewish stereotype fulfilled a position of alterity necessary to naturalize the Aryan, heterosexual male," Dennis Denisoff observes of the late Victorian era and George Du Maurier's 1894 novel *Trilby*.[21] Caricatures of the Jewish man as dark and oily, with black, beady eyes and pointed beards, "were common in late-Victorian England," Denisoff writes, "where an assumed physical difference between Jews and gentiles made the Jewish man a surrogate for all men considered to be threateningly abnormal."[22] Hawthorne's portrait of Philip Salomons dovetails with Dickens's depiction of Fagin in *Oliver Twist* (1838) and Melville's odious Jewish pawnbroker in *Redburn* (1849), indicating that antisemitic imagery proliferated at mid century as well.

Scholars such as Sander L. Gilman, Ann Pellegrini, Daniel Boyarian, and George L. Mosse, to name only a few, have powerfully analyzed these caricatures. Nineteenth-century North America and Europe extolled the healthy body while heaping opprobrium on onanism, or masturbation, as the most grievous failure to regulate one's health properly. Mosse discusses the ideal of beauty concomitant with these medical regimes in the context of nineteenth-century Germany:

The ideal of beauty so important in the construction of modern masculinity was reversed. Jews, for example, were regarded by many as the inverse of Germans in every respect and were sometimes reviled as subhuman..... [But] the subhuman had to be concretized, to be made familiar if it was to pose a believable threat. Jews and the other outsiders were stereotyped as evil kinds of men but nevertheless still recognizable as men even if they reversed traditional values..... the Jewish body was thought to be different from that of normal men, as Sander Gilman has explained so well, and that difference was made manifest through precisely those parts of the body that command most attention: nose, feet, neck, and coloration.[23]

Mosse explains that the "so-called Jewish nose, bent at the top, jutting hawklike from the face," already existed as a sixteenth-century caricature, but became an indelible "so-called Jewish trademark" only by the mid-eighteenth century. While Winckelmann, whose aesthetic theories proved so influential to modern conceptions of beauty from the late eighteenth century forward, had not explicitly condemned the Jewish nose—he condemned, instead, the "squashed nose usually attributable to blacks"—it become the negative contrast to the beautiful, straight Greek nose Winckelmann had celebrated. Moreover, the Jewish nose embodied every negative Jewish stereotype, chiefly untrustworthiness and immorality.[24] Mosse eloquently describes the ways in which pernicious applications of the Winckelmannian model oppressed all those who fell outside its delimited constraints, not only Jews but also the emergent figure of the homosexual, whose emergence in the latter nineteenth century was facilitated by the Winckelmann cult and transatlantic Hellenism, popularized by Winckelmann-inspired homophile authors such as Walter Pater and Oscar Wilde.

THE WANDERING JEW AND THE JEWESS

The Wandering Jew, newly popularized by English gothicists and Romantics, keenly combined cultural fantasies of the Jewish male in the nineteenth century. Hawthorne's depiction of the Model in *The Marble Faun* evokes this mythic figure, perhaps inspired by contemporaneous depictions such as Eugène Sue's novel *Juif errant* (*The Wandering Jew*) in 1844, Gustave

Doré's designs (twelve wood-cut engravings) in 1856, and Grenier's poem on the subject "La mort du Juif errant," or "The Death of the Wandering Jew" (1857), most likely inspired by Doré's designs. Hawthorne's depiction of the Model in *The Marble Faun* evokes one of the variations of the Wandering Jew.[25] Joseph Gaer's psychological study establishes two basic themes in the Wandering Jew legend: "the curse of abnormal longevity, and the conviction that for him who is so cursed *it had been good for that man if he had not been born;* and the other is the problem of guilt and absolution—the road of penance a man must travel to reach redemption."[26] Adolph L. Leschnitzer argues that the everlasting Jew who mocked Christ on his way to the crucifixion and was cursed by him to wander the earth until Christ's return dates back to medieval legend. An ironic version of this legend also exists, "a man who never settles down, a figure of a restlessly roving person."[27] The sinister aspect of the figure derives from his life-in-deathness, a defiance of the natural order. Jewishness is abnormal, Jewry a "living corpse, a specter. It has survived the great peoples of ancient history and reaches into our time, a mystery, an enigma. Jewry lives on and on, although it has lived up to its destiny, has accomplished its task."[28] In his essay "The Wandering Jew as Sacred Executioner," Hyam Maccoby describes this figure's nineteenth-century negative cast: "the possibility of regeneration for the Jews through repentance, found in the positive version, was ruled out completely by the racialist doctrine" that emerged in this century. Maccoby continues, "The Wandering Jew was a wanderer in the sense that he had no human attachment to any human group, but was the common enemy and scourge of mankind ... The detailed picture of the Jew was built up from medieval sources: the blood-sucking usurer, the murderer of children, the enemy of chastity, the poisoner of wells, the fiend in barely human shape." But, as Maccoby explains, racialist nineteenth-century antisemitism departed from "its Christian origins in providing no safeguard or loophole for Jewish survival." Whereas the hope for the millennial conversion of the Jews preserved their culture even in the times of their greatest peril in earlier eras, the nineteenth century produced a modern form of antisemitism in which the worst aspects of its life within Christianity persisted "without any of its restraints."[29] Hawthorne's description of Philip Salomons portrays the Jewish man as the toxic "distilled essence" of his culture. But the Wandering Jew in *The Marble Faun* and Hawthorne's tales "A Virtuoso's Collection" (1842) and "Ethan Brand" (1852) is an ambivalent figure, a

Christian fantasy of Jewishness as remote, lost, perpetually wandering, but also seeking eventual redemption. In his last major work, the unfinished and in his lifetime unpublished *Septimius Felton,* Hawthorne returned to the idea of a man who could not die, reworked here as a quest for immortal life. The Wandering Jew allowed Hawthorne to expand his gothic Romantic aesthetic. The Model in *The Marble Faun* is thoroughly in the gothic mode, evoking fear and horror and sadistically controlling Miriam. Though intimately involved along with Miriam in an infamous scandal that Kenyon describes, in his "postscript" dialogue with narrator, as "one of the dreadful and mysterious events that have occurred within the present century," the mysterious Model somehow manages to become the subject of Miriam's painterly art, posing for Miriam after Miriam encounters the Model again in the Catacombs of Saint Callixtus (4:467). Just as he poses for her, she will pose for him—in several striking scenes, Miriam kneels before the Model, signaling penitence or "thralldom," a gesture at once suggestive of the Catholic confessional and gothic sadomasochism.

While consistently described as Miriam's "Demon," a ceaseless stalker and a loathsome and frightening specter, the Model may be as wronged and sympathetic as he is odious (paralleling the vengeful but cuckolded Chillingworth). The first version of a possible backstory for the enigmatic Miriam includes the details "that Miriam was the daughter and heiress of a great Jewish banker, (an idea perhaps suggested by a certain rich Oriental character in her face,) and had fled from her paternal home to escape a union with a cousin, the heir of another of that golden brotherhood; the object being, to retain their vast accumulation of wealth within the family" (22–23). In her excellent essay on the novel, "Hawthorne and Judaism," Elissa Greenwald considers the Model's relationship to Miriam, arguing that through it Hawthorne worked through personal anxieties over incest, possibly within his deeply intimate relationship to his own sisters. (In this, Greenwald joins in with critics such as Edward Haviland Miller and Gloria Erlich.) Whether or not one finds this aspect of her reading credible, Greenwald's problematization of the Model is highly interesting.

> The model's role remains ambiguous. He is certainly someone from Miriam's past—perhaps the rejected cousin. The plot configuration implies he may be the incestuous father, for Donatello kills him with Miriam's implicit consent in the echo of the [Beatrice] Cenci story.... If the model is Miriam's father,

his final conversion to Christianity (to become a monk) would be particularly anti-Semitic.... When Miriam says to the model, "I have known you to pray, in times past," she may be referring to the Jewish religion. The model's anxiety about prayer may be guilt at his attempt to conceal himself as a Christian: "In this man's memory, there was something that made it awful for him to think of prayer."³⁰

If we consider, along the lines of Greenwald's argument as well as Augustus M. Kolich's in his essay "Miriam and the Conversion of the Jews," that both the Model and Miriam are converted Jews, a more sympathetic reading of the Model emerges, complementing the more sympathetic treatment given to Miriam. Given that the Model, in death, is revealed to have been, in life, the Capuchin monk Brother Antonio, his conversion was not only a personal matter but also one that involved a powerful participation in and public performance of his new faith. If both the Model and Miriam are Jewish converts, they are both victims at war with their culture as much as they are with each other, and their mutual enmity is certainly informed by, though also certainly not explained away by, their shared experience of antisemitic oppression.

As Kolich points out, antisemitism heavily infused the atmosphere in 1850s Rome, in which Jews were ghettoized and denied several basic rights (he cites an infamous incident in which a Jewish boy, who had been "baptized" by a governess when he was an infant, was forcibly removed from his family by the Catholic Church and raised by the Pope). Miriam and the Model are representative of two antithetical yet linked figures, the Suffering Jew, a figure prominent in anti-Catholic Protestant reform literature, and the Secret Jew, "a threat to unwary Protestants who allow themselves to become enmeshed in [their] desperate plight," as embodied by Miriam's wrenching predicaments. Both figures, if read in this light, emerge as crucial to a far more sensitive and thoughtful understanding, as well as political critique, of the antisemitism rife within the Rome of Hawthorne's direct experience in the late 1850s as well as in Victorian England, where the situation for Jews was considerably better, in social terms, but no less complicated, conversion of the Jews being the goal of even the most ardently sympathetic and tolerant Christian advocacy groups. As Nadia Valman illuminates in her important study *The Jewess in Nineteenth-Century British Literary Culture,* a number of groups fought for improved conditions and social acceptance for the Jews of Victorian England. The majority of these groups, led by Protestant Christian women's groups, focused on the figure of the Jewish woman, oppressed by her apparently masculinist religion, and, even as they advocated tolerance, worked towards the conversion of the Jews as their ultimate goal. In this respect, *The Marble Faun* is thoroughly in keeping with broadly liberal cultural attitudes in Victorian England, synthesized in Eliot's great *Daniel Deronda,* where Hawthorne spent several significant years. Whereas Eliot strives for evenhandedness in her depictions of all her Jewish characters, Hawthorne maintains a sympathetic though necessarily guarded relationship to the Jewish woman while treating the Jewish male with opprobrium.

"In nineteenth-century England," Michael Ragussis writes, "the clearest sign of the ideology of Jewish conversion was its institutionalization in such well-known societies as the London Society for Promoting Christianity amongst the Jews (founded in 1809) and the British Society for the Propagation of the Bible among the Jews (founded in 1842)."[31] Similar campaigns and groups sought the same goals in the United States, such as, as Louis Harap notes, the Female Society of Boston and Vicinity for Promoting Christianity among Jews (founded in 1816, it survived until 1843) and the American Society for Meliorating the Condition of the Jews, "'melioration' meaning the acceptance of Jesus as Savior." This important group numbered John Quincy Adams and De Witt Clinton amongst its supporters and was led by the converted German Jew Joseph S. C. Frey. This society survived until 1870.[32] If Hawthorne wrote *The Marble Faun* within the context of a millennial transatlantic quest to restore Jewish people to the Christian faith, and if, as we have seen, he shared with many of his culture the same "repugnance" towards this people, what is remarkable about his 1860 novel is the degree to which it renders the idea of conversion from one religious faith to another traumatically violent.

The Marble Faun makes the unusual decision of staging its climactic moment in the middle of the narrative. Donatello, often linked to the animal world, likened not only to the faun but also to an increasingly vicious dog, kills the Model by flinging him off the Tarpeian Rock, employing the same methods of retribution for criminal activity that the classical Romans did. He does so, by every account, at Miriam's silent yet implacable behest: a glance from Miriam, her Medusan glare, impels Donatello to fling the Model over the cliff. This act of murder becomes the oozing, unstanchable wound of the text, refusing to heal or be closed up. Menacing and loathsome though the Model, variously described as the Spectre of the Catacombs, the Shadow, and the Demon, is, the Model nevertheless does not deserve this treatment—does not deserve to be murdered. Hawthorne would appear to be suggesting that the fear of otherness, however calamitously difficult one's apprehension of this otherness may be, does not justify violence.

Indeed, this is, in my view, what this novel chiefly explores—the place of otherness in the social order. The killing of the Model is an act that places prejudice outside the law, that turns prejudice into the ultimate and least defensible crime, murder. Hawthorne would appear to be suggesting that, however simultaneously fascinated and repulsed one is by the other in whatever form, the other has a distinctive subjectivity that must be allowed an autonomous existence that one has no right to stamp out. While a great deal of commentary on the novel has focused on the Miltonic theme of the felix culpa, or Fortunate Fall—the Christian interpretation of the Genesis myth of Adam and Eve's fall as an ultimately salutary experience because it leads them to greater penitence and devotion to God, greater awareness of the magnitude of their sin and desire to be sinless—Hawthorne may actually be, for all of his own career-long protestations against such readings of his art, much more directly and immediately concerned with the sociocultural milieu that he experienced in Rome, informed by his prior experience in England.[33] Hawthorne may be addressing the antisemitism he not only witnessed firsthand but understood on an intimate personal level—the desire to destroy the maddening specter of the other becomes, in his novel, an actual crime that must be punished. Hawthorne critiques, in the end, the entire culture of suffering and secrecy that antisemitism produces—the forced conversions that lead to internecine hatred between Miriam and the Model, and the atmosphere of mistrust and violence that leads to Donatello's hatred-fueled murder of the Model. In his fiction, at least, Hawthorne thought through the implications of the hatred he himself could only give full vent to in his private prose.

CONVERSION HYSTERIAS

The Marble Faun is principally concerned with the emotional and psychological effects of religious conversion, an overarching theme that organizes all the competing concerns of the novel, the "gender of Jewishness" perhaps chief amongst them. Hawthorne depicts Miriam and the Model, reimagined versions of Philip Salomons and his wife, as, implicitly, converted Jews, and the novel should be understood as a treatment of the effects of religious conversion. Hilda's much-discussed flirtation—if this word can be used for so austere a character—with Catholicism complements the theme of Jewish conversion to Catholicism embodied by the relationship between Miriam and the Model.

In chapter 3, "Subterranean Reminiscences," the various rumors Miriam's mysterious identity has inspired, presented with Hawthorne's customarily ambiguous style, together add up to a portrait of her as a kind of key to all mythologies of the exotic feminine:

> It was said, for example, that Miriam was the daughter and heiress of a great Jewish banker, (an idea perhaps suggested by a certain rich Oriental character in her face,) and had fled from her paternal home to escape a union with a cousin, the heir of another of that golden brotherhood; the object being, to retain their vast accumulation of wealth within the family. Another story hinted, that she was a German princess, whom, for reasons of state, it was proposed to give in marriage either to a decrepit sovereign, or a prince still in his cradle. According to a third statement, she was the offspring of a Southern American planter, who had given her an elaborate education and endowed her with his wealth; but the one burning drop of African blood in her veins so affected her with a sense of ignominy, that she relinquished all, and fled her country. By still another account she was the lady of an English nobleman; and, out of mere love and honor of art, had thrown aside the splendor of her rank, and come to seek a subsistence by her pencil in a Roman studio. (22–23)

The third chapter's list of Miriam's possible identities does not end there; it includes the detail that she may be the daughter of a great "merchant or financier" (23). By Miriam's own account to Kenyon of her parentage in chapter 47, "The Peasant and Contadina," she describes

> herself as springing from English parentage, on the mother's side, but with a vein, likewise, of Jewish blood; yet connected, through her father, with one of those few princely families of southern Italy, which still retain a great

wealth and influence. And she revealed a name, at which her auditor started, and grew pale; for it was one that, only a few years before, had been familiar to the world, in connection with a mysterious and terrible event. (429–30)

The parental source of her Jewishness remains controversial to critics. Kolich, for instance, argues that the above paragraph makes it clear that Miriam's Judaism stems from her paternal line. Greenwald does not explore this issue beyond saying that the account Miriam gives may represent Hawthorne's own fantasy of Emma Salomons's ancestry and Miriam's own English mother, though Greenwald does not specify if this fantasy "meliorates" or confirms that Miriam's mother was Jewish. Harap identifies her as the daughter of a Jewish Englishwoman, and it seems clear to me, from the grammar and syntax, that Hawthorne is suggesting the Jewishness in Miriam stems from her mother. The information about her maternal ancestry comes before the semicolon and therefore seems all of a piece: Miriam's mother is English, but with a "vein" of Jewish blood; the next cluster of information comes after the semicolon, and it delineates her paternal ancestry, that her father is Italian and from a family with a "princely" amount of "wealth and influence."

If we see a secret Jewishness as part of the bond that inextricably links Miriam to the Model, we are left to speculate—no surprise in a novel that relentlessly forces us to speculate, being especially reticent about imparting any direct information about these characters in particular—about what, exactly, impelled them to convert to Catholicism and about the degree to which their secret Jewishness is allegorized by, caught up within, or otherwise expressed through the maddening haze of the "secret" scandal that inextricably binds Miriam to the Model. If he is the cousin whom she was being forced to marry and whom she fled in order to escape this marriage, he is not just a stalker but a would-be suitor, someone who cannot accept the loss of a promised bride. If this is the case, why does Hawthorne go out of his way to infer that some terrible crime took place, one that implicates both Miriam and the Model, almost as if they both had participated in it and were fleeing its consequences? That having been said, it also infers that the crime is a scandal that implicated Miriam but of which she was actually innocent. In any event, Hawthorne takes great pains to suggest that some terrible, binding, unspeakable knowledge makes Miriam's connection to the Model indissoluble.

One of the most significant terms that Hawthorne employs to characterize Miriam's relationship to the model is "thralldom." Rachel Blau Duplessis, in a study of this theme in the poet H. D.'s work, writes that female thralldom, on a romantic and spiritual level, is a common feature of literary plots because they so frequently rely upon conventions of "love and marriage, quest and vocation, hero and heroine":

> Romantic thralldom is an all-encompassing, totally defining love between unequals. The lover has the power of conferring self-love and purpose upon the loved one. Such love is possessive, and while those enthralled feels it completes and even transforms them, they are also enslaved. The eroticism of romantic love, born of this unequal relationship between the sexes, may depend for its satisfaction upon dominance and submission.... Viewed from a critical, feminist perspective, the sense of completion or transformation that often accompanies thralldom in love has the high price of obliteration and paralysis, for the entranced self is entirely defined by another. I do not need to emphasize that this kind of love is socially learned and that it is central to our culture.[34]

Hawthorne was a feminist malgré lui. His thematization of thralldom, unexplored in treatments of this novel, makes *The Marble Faun* an important text for feminist interpretation as well as for the other issues we have raised in this chapter. In terms of the latter, to what extent does the "conversion" plot intersect with the theme of thralldom?

The control that the Model wields over Miriam "was such as beasts and reptiles of subtle and evil nature sometimes exercise upon their victims." The narrator marvels at "the hopelessness with which—being naturally of so courageous a spirit—she resigned herself to the thralldom in which he held her," a thralldom he describes as an "iron chain ... round her feminine waist" that "must have been forged in some such unhallowed furnace as is only kindled by evil passions and fed by evil deeds" (93). Several more references to thralldom lead to the moment in which Kenyon observes Miriam, having washed her hands in a fountain (images of once cleansing, and then polluted, fountains abound in this work), glancing up at the Model, which leads Kenyon to imagine that "Miriam was kneeling to this dark follower, there, in the world's face!" (108). If his suspicions are accurate, Kenyon thinks to himself, "what a terrible thralldom did it suggest!" (108).

The Marble Faun is hardly the first Hawthorne work to thematize one person's psychological and even bodily enslavement to another, a theme that would have been, of course, deeply fraught in this era of slavery and of debates over it leading to impending war. The odious and enigmatic Westervelt wields a strange power over vivid Zenobia and her wan half-sister Priscilla in *The Blithedale Romance,* for example. In these novels, the precise nature of the woman's relationship to the man who holds her in bondage is left unclear, indeed is quite deliberately rendered enigmatic, but is strongly inferred to be sexual in nature. Both the narrator and Kenyon are prone to equally evaluative and moralistic pronouncements. In the face of their mutual judgment, even a character as fiery and independent as Miriam is rendered vulnerable and left adrift. Many different cultural contexts inform Hawthorne's depiction of female sexual thralldom, such as the antebellum practice of mesmerism and the looming reality of slavery.[35] The author takes great pains to suggest Miriam's actual "innocence" of the crime, and equally great pains to infer the unspeakable sexual characteristics of the crime or scandal that indissolubly links her to the Model. Miriam's thralldom, in all its multifaceted complexity, plays a crucial role in Hawthorne's exploration of the gender of Jewishness and of his own antisemitism, couched in largely misandrist terms though not exclusively in these, since misogyny is not absent in his more rapt appreciation of the Jewess's beauty as well as her particular social and gendered predicament.

In an essay on the Victorian Gothic, Alison Milbank argues that "in Dickens's later fiction, the weight shifts away from social regeneration achieved through the release of the woman from confinement, to the thralldom of individual men to Gothic fictions," such as Pip's to Miss Havisham in *Great Expectations*.[36] For Hawthorne, however, quite the reverse is the case—he moves from a depiction of neurotic young sexual criminal Minister Dimmesdale's enthrallment to Chillingworth, to his increasingly common figuring of female enthrallment to a man: Alice Pyncheon to Matthew Maule in *The House of the Seven Gables,* the Zenobia-Priscilla-Westervelt relationship in *The Blithedale Romance,* Miriam and the Model here. Much as Freud will also theorize some decades later, Hawthorne adduces that thralldom inheres in the relationship between men and women when this relationship is tied to marriage, as Miriam's relationship to the Model suggests.

If, as I have been suggesting, the problem of Jewishness for Hawthorne is that it seems to distill the essence of the genders, generally, so that his confrontation with Jewishness is also one with all of his conflictual feelings towards other men and towards women, it makes a certain, phobic sense that he would regard the Miriam-Model relationship as, at once, indicative of negative patterns within male-female relationships and exemplary of the Jewess's relationship to the Jewish male. As converted Jews, each enacting a quite complex performance of Christian faith, the Monk especially, Miriam and the Model literally dance around each other, each the other's partner in a sustained masquerade that any admission of sympathy threatens irreparably to disrupt. Part of the perverse play in their relationship lies in the Model's very acquisition of that name—how could this man who inspires so much dread in Miriam have also been her artistic subject as she sketched? What kinds of sadomasochistic energies must have inevitably informed an artist-subject relationship that Hawthorne barely sketches out?

Here lies the depth in Hawthorne's depiction of their relationship: each the other's secret sharer, they can share nothing but their own inadmissible shame; each the other's judge, trial, and jury, they make their own law, even if they sentence each other to an apparently endless retribution. Hawthorne is saying something interesting here, in my view, about not only the nature of prejudice but also one of the strategies some have employed to either elude or deflect it: passing. Passing as Christian, Miriam and the Model sustain each other in their shared self-alienation, yet such is the nature of this bond of abnegation that neither can provide comfort nor intimacy nor refuge to the other. Presumably, as a Capuchin monk, Brother Antonio, or the Model, would feel a sense of community and kinship with his fellow monks; otherwise, it is inconceivable that he would devote so much time to hounding Miriam. The novel suggests that he feels no such fraternal kinship. The perpetual bewilderment she triggers in others suggests that Miriam, forever a mystery of her own creation, feels a similar lack of community. The experience of prejudice—the strategies that the objects of social scorn employ—leaves one lonely, but more importantly, does not promote intimacy between those who suffer from prejudice.

Hawthorne, in this regard, would appear to come to the same conclusions that Nella Larsen does in *Passing* (1929), where the Black women and childhood friends Irene and Clare both pass, though in different ways, yet can never achieve anything like emotional intimacy (much less the physical intimacy that the narrator suggests they also conflictually crave). Miriam's thralldom to the Model, sexually charged though it is, ultimately emerges as a substitute for intimacy that also indicates an intense, inescapable kinship with their own repudiated identity. Mutually accusatory, Miriam and the Model are mirror images of a self-hating and secret identity maintaining itself in a phobic world. Miriam's desire to break free of the Model would appear to be motivated by her desire to break free of her own memory of her renounced Jewishness, making her a contemporary version of Shylock's daughter Jessica. And yet, her almost irresistible pull towards him also suggests the opposite. It is telling that it is only towards the end of the novel, and after the Model has been murdered before her eyes—as a result of her eyes—that Miriam can discuss her own ancestry and reveal her partial Jewishness to Kenyon. It is as if the Model were the threat of the spilling of this secret as well as the secret itself, holding both in a precarious balance that gives way after his death, which releases Miriam from her enthrallment, not only to him but also to the burden of her unclaimable past.

Overall, this is a novel that explores the experience of a lack of intimacy, in a broader way than the specific issue of Jewishness, but one intensified by it. When Miriam visits Kenyon in his studio, her heart heavy with the burdens of her past and her predicament over the model, Hawthorne exquisitely stages a scene of modern, urban alienation and anomie through which he reworks in fiction his recorded real-life encounter with the Jewess. These two intelligent and sensitive people cannot forge a connection; indeed, Kenyon in particular cannot overcome a certain trepidation over Miriam's character—is it his inescapable repugnance towards her? His moralizing authority comes to seem not a reaction to but a defense against her enigmatic threat. Miriam seems unable to find intimacy with anyone. Hilda rejects her after witnessing the Model's murder, and no genuine scene of rapprochement occurs between the women, locked within what Helena Michie has called "sororophobia," a disruption in bonds between women, alleviated only by the pity that Hilda (somewhat) develops after her brush with the Catholic confessional.[37] Miriam has little use for Donatello until he kills the Model, and while their bond grows strong afterwards, it is one steeped in mutual guilt and recrimination, and moreover has an expiration date: Donatello must go to prison to pay for his crime. Miriam's relationship with Donatello rehearses the one that she maintained with the Model, another bond forged in secret sin and guilt, albeit without the deeper bond of a repudiated religious and cultural kinship. Indeed, the theme of passing continues to inform the Miriam and Donatello relationship, as suggested by their masquerade during the carnival as peasant and *contadina,* much to bewildered Kenyon's frustration.

Though a full discussion of this topic exceeds the scope of this chapter, what would appear to organize this culture of failed intimacy and also empathy is the Protestantism represented by Kenyon, especially, and also by Hilda. The larger theme of conversion exceeds the theme of Jewishness, in that Hilda's threatening attraction to Catholicism—depicted with full Calvinist whore-of-Babylon opprobrium by Kenyon—threatens to make her a convert as well, an apostate to Protestant morality and authoritarian order. Catholicism emerges as an increasingly viable alternative to Kenyon's Protestant rigidity, a faith that can negotiate the discordances in and withstand the messiness and murk of the conflicts among Miriam, the Model, and Donatello—the sheer bewilderment of human motives and actions embodied in the welter of their desires. Jewishness implicitly emerges as another, though less viable, alternative.

In a brilliant reading of the novel, Emily Miller Budick argues along these lines regarding the final appearance of Miriam, seen as a "female penitent" kneeling beneath the "Eye," or open dome, of the Pantheon by Kenyon and Hilda (459). So posed, Miriam suggests that "the wandering Jewess and the lapsed Roman Catholic" Donatello may be less lost than the seemingly anointed Protestant pair walking off into the marital sunshine. Miriam extends her hands before the pair, in "a gesture of benediction"; but these hands "repel" even as they "blessed the pair" (461).[38] Kenyon and Hilda, for all their anguished moralizing, ultimately cannot pierce the mystery that binds together their friends and the Model. Protestantism emerges, writes Budick, as "no more forgiving than its Jewish and Roman Catholic predecessors. If anything it is only more ignorant in its sternness, more in flight from the realties of human being that both Roman Catholicism and Judaism are at least willing to acknowledge."[39]

In this regard, it is significant, I think, that Hilda and Kenyon stand before the tomb of Raphael and that Miriam kneels beneath the Eye of the Pantheon.[40] Miriam does not kneel before a Catholic saint, nor before the tomb of an artist who represents Italy itself and Renaissance humanism. Hilda and Kenyon's posed position before the tomb of Raphael, one of the Old Masters she reverences, confirms them as votaries of the world of art, in a pagan temple to all the classical gods that has been transformed into a site of Catholic worship. (Looming above the tomb of Raphael is a sculpture of the Madonna and child by Lorenzetto, which was there long before Hawthorne would have seen the tomb in the late 1850s.) All three artists are linked to the pagan and Catholic worlds of great art, with Kenyon and Hilda representing a dominant, overmastering Protestantism. But in standing beneath the Eye, Miriam occupies a more ambiguous, less definable position, one that could be pagan or Catholic, or the transcendence of any religious affiliation.

Disquietingly, Miriam's rejection of the same culture that rejects her, those hands that repel as well as bless the Protestant pair Kenyon and Hilda, suggests an internalization of the "repugnance" that this culture, insofar as Hawthorne's personal views gave it voice, feels towards her as a Jewish person, even as the gesture also conveys defiance against this repugnance and all its implications. The world of art, metonymized by the spirit of the dead Raphael, is only another chimerical refuge from the realities of prejudice animated by competing fears and desires. Harrowingly, the gesture that repels and blesses at once reveals far more about Miriam's own self-regard than it does about her disposition to the normative culture that estranges her—about her own internalized sense of herself as belonging nowhere, or only belonging anywhere provisionally.

A great deal more needs to be said about the role aesthetics plays in the novel. Hilda and Kenyon's proximity to Raphael and his disciple suggests a devotion—as well as submission—to the world of art, beauty, and tradition. But Miriam's defiant separation from this world, her final guise as veiled penitent, reminiscent of Zenobia taking the "black-veil," suggests that the racially or ethnically marked female subject must find an alternative path that allows her to transcend the confines of prejudice and of cultural and religious affiliations—or subservience to them. Of course, such an escape from these affiliations carries with it the very great and very real threat of loss, a self-erasure, especially for the artist aligned with tradition. Hence the searing pain of conversions, thematized on so many levels, in the novel. A powerful theme runs throughout Hawthorne's work, informing works beyond *The Marble Faun* but culminating in this supremely important novel. Subjects internalize, make a part of their very own psychic framework, the prejudices, phobias, and opprobrium that attends to their identities, especially if these identities are minoritized. Miriam's internalized antisemitism—for that, in the end, is the great theme of this novel, certainly of Hawthorne's characterization of Miriam and also the Model, whose other identity as a Capuchin monk embodies the thematic of self-erasure—echoes Hester Prynne's internalized misogyny in *The Scarlet Letter*, written roughly a decade before *The Marble Faun*.[41]

It should be noted that Hawthorne fascinatingly reworks a key episode in the campaign of the American writer Delia Bacon to expose Shakespeare as an imposter, not the true author of his plays. Hawthorne attempted to aid her cause in his role as US Consul in Liverpool, even though he did not agree with her theories. Bacon's visit to Shakespeare's tomb, which Hawthorne describes at length in a retrospective account of his experiences with Bacon in London, provides a suggestive and eerie foundation for Miriam's vigil before another great artist's tomb. Published in the January 1863 issue of *The Atlantic*, Hawthorne's essay "Recollections of a Gifted Woman," one of his most dazzling pieces of writing (an elaboration of passages from his account of his time in England in *Our Old Home*), includes a lengthy retelling of Bacon's effort to prove her theory—that Francis Bacon (no relation), Walter Raleigh, and other eminent minds rallied together to produce Shakespeare's plays. As Bacon put it in her *Philosophy of the Plays of Shakspere Unfolded*, Francis Bacon specialized in a style that he called "the enigmatical," and he tells us that this style conveys "the *secrets* of knowledge [that] are reserved for *selected auditors*," "a new method" whereby "knowledges are to be delivered as a thread to be spun on."[42] What looks to us like Shakespeare's body of work is actually this new method in disguised form.

Delia Bacon believed that Francis Bacon's writings, properly decoded by her, led her to a stone adjacent to Shakespeare's tomb, beneath which were documents proving the truth of her conspiracy theory. Having conspired to visit the tomb, she intended to access the materials beneath the stone. After a crisis of conviction, Bacon decided not to disturb the tomb site—to leave the stone unturned.[43] While more elaboration is needed, clearly Hawthorne, who heard this story in 1856, the year before he began writing *The Marble Faun*, had it in mind as he imagined Miriam's vigil before another great artist's tomb. Bacon visited a tomb in order to debunk an artist's stature; Miriam does not take a position beside Raphael's tomb in order to align herself with his stature but instead maintains a self-conscious distance from it.

SHAKESPEARE, SHYLOCK, AND CONVERSION

Having examined Hawthorne's mingling of antisemitism and Jewish sympathy, we are led back to *The Merchant of Venice* and Shakespeare as intertext. What most powerfully links both works is the treatment of conversion as trauma. James Shapiro aptly describes *Merchant* as "so unsettling a comedy," in that it "produces the fantasy ending in which the circumcising Jew is metamorphosed through conversion into a gentle Christian." Shylock and Antonio—through a "circumcision of the heart and a baptism that figuratively uncircumcises," respectively—each seeks to convert his "adversary into his own kind."[44] Reflecting this idea, Hawthorne fuses Antonio and Shylock in the Model, whose assumed identity is revealed to be that of the Capuchin monk Brother Antonio, as if Shylock, forced to convert, took on his hated adversary's identity.

In a superb essay, "We All Expect a Gentle Answer, Jew: *The Merchant of Venice* and the Psychotheology of Conversion," Heather Hirschfeld outlines the play's treatment of Shylock as someone who must ineluctably yield to Christian will through conversion, the play thematizing what Hirschfeld terms "an increasingly compulsive interest in Shylock's conversion."[45] If the conversion of Jews has been an "object for hundreds of years of intense theoretical and practical interest," it has been intertwined with paranoid fantasies of secret Jewish commitment to Judaism beneath the convert's veneer. In psychoanalytic terms, the play foregrounds "a desire to see Shylock convert and the desire to see him not convert," an agonizing impasse that finds a complement in several aspects of *The Marble Faun,* chiefly the secret relationship between Miriam and the Model forever verging on explication. Using Eric Santer's term "psychotheology" and Jeremy Cohen's "the hermeneutical Jew," Hirschfeld theorizes Shylock, in light of soteriological programs of Shakespeare's cultural and theological moment, as a fantasy of the "Jew as a model of potential election or reprobation, a figure against which the Christian could actively assess himself and his own promise of redemption."[46] Though expelled from England in 1290, Jews held a role in the Christian imagination, and in Shylock Shakespeare dramatizes "the Venetians' effort to maintain Shylock" in "the moment of conversion," "to preserve him in his role on the verge of a predetermined salvation or damnation that remains unknown to them."[47] Shylock, however, in Kenneth Gross's reading, though spitefully mirroring the antisemitic attitudes of the Venetians, "makes the face of Jewish malice more unsettling than they thought they knew or could have imagined. He is a mask formed from both inside and outside, at once shield and punishment, wound and weapon."[48]

The Model's function in *The Marble Faun* is to catalyze Christian redemptive feeling, to inspire self-reflection and moral self-reckoning, and to establish stark differences between the saved and the unsavable. He is a stranger within intimate relations, Judaism, and Christianity at once. In this regard, he extends themes inherent in Shakespeare's play. Janet Adelman puts the matter with characteristic incisiveness: "*Merchant* simultaneously gestures toward and defends against" the knowledge that "the Jew is not the stranger outside Christianity but the original stranger within it."[49] Yet another "stranger maiden" like the mixed-race Cora Munro, Miriam poses alienating, frightening, yet galvanizing challenges, to herself as well as to the others, in that she blends qualities of her friendship circle with the outsider, intrusive, predatory threat of the Model. Indeed, as Bercovitch pointed out, Miriam is Shylock. That the Model himself, like Miriam but more so, chiefly models the seeming solution—conversion—to the problem posed to normative Christian society, the unconverted and unconvertible Jew, evinces the novel's dialogue with the precursor text's themes and enduringly irresolvable dilemmas.

A JEWISH ASPECT

A description of a beautiful woman in *The Marble Faun* is often said to be of Miriam. But that's actually not quite right—it's a description of Miriam's self-portrait. Visiting the artist in her studio, the pining Donatello performs a dance that enlivens the gloomy space, for which Miriam rewards him with a rare glimpse of her painting, which tellingly has its back to the spectator. Reversed, the picture reveals the image of a woman "such as one sees only two or three, if even so many times, in all a lifetime; so beautiful, that she seemed to get into your consciousness and memory" (47):

> She was very youthful, and had what was usually thought to be a Jewish aspect; a complexion in which there was no roseate bloom, yet neither was it pale; dark eyes, into which you might look as deeply as your glance would go, and still be conscious of a depth that you had not sounded, though it lay

open to the day. She had black, abundant hair, with none of the vulgar glossiness of other women's sable locks; if she were really of Jewish blood, then this was Jewish hair, and a dark glory such as crowns no Christian maiden's head. Gazing at this portrait, you saw what Rachel might have been, when Jacob deemed her worth the wooing seven years, and seven more; or perchance she might ripen to be what Judith was, when she vanquished Holofernes with her beauty, and slew him for too much adoring it. (48)

Hawthorne clearly reworks the passage from his notebooks where he described Emma Abigail Montefiore Salomons.

Throughout the present study, we have encountered moments when a female character encounters her own image, one that is at times submerged within the male, patriarchal one. Here, Donatello is asked to look at a representation of Miriam that Miriam has created, "owns." Reflective of her tough-mindedness, Miriam takes possession of the female image and specifically of her own. This moment stands out, since it contrasts with a moment in the novel that specifically denies Miriam access to the image while also being an intertextual passage.[50] If this depicted woman is "really of Jewish blood, then this was Jewish hair, and a dark glory such as crowns no Christian maiden's head" (48). In such stark contrast to the physicalities of Shylock and the Model, this positive image of Jewish femininity and female beauty reflects not only the male gaze—the narrator, Donatello's, the author's—but also the female gaze, the female subject's self-understanding and self-representation. If a wounded, compromised narcissism, evocative of the mythic figure that gives the concept its name, characterizes antebellum femininities in the main, we can also acknowledge that Miriam—and the Jewess she represents—defies these strictures by laying claim to the image and its "Jewish aspect."

EPILOGUE

DOUGLASS AND INFLUENCE

HAD THIS BOOK FOCUSED on any one of the authors principally discussed, very little beyond brief acknowledgment of their whiteness, maleness, presumptive heterosexuality, and so forth would likely have been expected. Hypercanonicity—the focus on a single, galvanizing author who becomes a category of thought unto themselves, such as Joyce, Proust, and Herman Melville, as the ever-proliferating scholarship focused on him attests—would hold sway.[1] When the focus is on a group of authors who share the same identifying social, cultural, and ethnic characteristics, the critic would appear to be making a statement of sorts, probably an evaluation of their merits. I cannot dissemble; it's true that I think that all these authors reward study. That said, the value of including questions of influence and intertextuality when studying nineteenth-century writing clearly extends beyond them. My effort has been to undermine the presumption that studies of influence and white male authors simply reinforce preexisting standards of literary merit and topics that support those standards. At the very least, I have hoped to demonstrate that if we want to theorize about such authors' attitudes toward race, sex, and gender, considering the tradition is far from irrelevant; it's necessary. Considering tradition and influence reawakens these unawake Adonises.

I argued in the introduction that influence is not enmity—not an agon, a competitive intergenerational, oedipal struggle. Rather, it is about contemplation and collaboration and lingering. I draw on Freud's ideas about narcissism and melancholia as alternatives to the Bloomian agon's oedipal cast. To forecast future study and to test my theory anew, I want to turn to Frederick Douglass and his romance *The Heroic Slave* (1853), based on the *Creole* Mutiny. Of Douglass's voluminous output, this text is his only work of fiction, and one of the first works of Black American fiction. It demands consideration alongside the other works we have discussed given that it is "part of an American canon that was profoundly shaped by the historical fiction of Walter Scott, James Fenimore Cooper, Catharine Maria Sedgwick, Nathaniel Hawthorne, and many others."[2] Scholars have pointed out overlaps between this work and Melville texts such as *Moby-Dick* as well.[3]

The Heroic Slave showcases this study's concerns: using English tradition, exemplified by Shakespeare, Milton, and the King James Bible, as basis for new rhetorical modes; as immediately recognizable intertext; as primary model of eloquence; as a means of working through anxieties centered in gender, sexuality, and race.

SHAKESPEAREAN RESONANCES

Given the particularly intensive archive of Frederick Douglass's "extraordinarily subtle and far-reaching use of the works of William Shakespeare, with which Douglass repeatedly sought to engage and transform the thoughts and feelings of his white audience," in the words of Douglas Anderson, it behooves us to linger on this intertextual relation that, as with authors such as Melville and Emily Dickinson, has inspired new attention.[4]

Douglass referenced Shakespeare, his literary touchstone, throughout his numerous lectures, speeches, and essays spanning decades.

> References to Shakespeare's work first begin appearing in Douglass's speeches shortly after his visit to Stratford-on-Avon in February 1847. In late 1850 and 1851, as the controversy over sectional compromise intensified and the Fugitive Slave Act became law, Douglass responded with increasingly dramatic appeals to the texts of *Hamlet, Julius Caesar, Richard III,* and *Henry VIII*. In a speech in Boston on February 8, 1855, the year that he published *My Bondage and My Freedom,* Douglass memorably identified the

plight of the slave with Lear's bitter exposure: "Thou think'st 'tis much that this contentious storm / Invades us to the skin. So 'tis to thee, / But where the greater malady is fixed / The lesser is scarce felt" (4.4.6–9).[5]

Sandra Gustafson's essay "Eloquent Shakespeare" in the reader *Shakespearean Educations* considers Douglass's references to Shakespeare in his famous 1852 antislavery speech "What to the Slave Is the Fourth of July?" She writes, "His choice of passages from *Julius Caesar* and *Macbeth* . . . reinforces the 'scorching irony' that he identified as his central and necessary trope" for a nation whose foundation in liberty was wholly incommensurate with its continued support of slavery.[6] Daniel Webster, sorely disappointing his Northern supporters, abandoned his earlier abolitionist positions with support for the infamous Fugitive Slave Act of 1850. Both Webster and Douglass cited *Julius Caesar*. Based on her study of elocution manuals such as the legendary *The Columbian Orator*—Caleb Bingham's collection, first published in 1797, of political essays, poems, and dialogues—Gustafson notes that "modern republicans such as Webster identified with Brutus and Cassius, who murdered Caesar in an effort to preserve the Republic." Douglass, who read *The Columbian Orator* avidly, quoted the lines of Caesar's friend Mark Anthony, who gives a speech in the play in the wake of the leader's murder that grows increasingly hostile to his executioners after an initial conciliatory tone. Douglass quotes Anthony's funeral oration: "The evil that men do, lives after them, / The good is oft interred with their bones" (3.2.76).[7]

Douglass's citation of *Macbeth* in "Fourth of July" was a similarly pointed critique of Webster, referencing Webster's widely disseminated and anthologized 1830 "Second Reply" to South Carolina senator Robert Hayne: "In the Senate debate, Webster cleverly used an inept reference by Hayne to a passage in *Macbeth* to establish his interpretive [as well as moral] authority." But Douglass, referencing Macbeth's words to Macduff when the truth of his caesarean birth and therefore his threat to Macbeth are revealed, "argued that those who espoused a proslavery reading of the Constitution likened its authors to the deceptive witches" whose words impelled Macbeth to a fiendish and futile violence that resembled the slavocracy's own. Douglass further implied a link between the unstable, self-defeating Macbeth and those determined to interpret the Constitution as a proslavery text. Douglass deeply opposed and fought against this interpretation, arguing that the Constitution took an antislavery position, as evinced by George Washington's "deathbed abolition of his slaves."[8]

The study of antebellum authors' intertextual engagements with literary precursors generally focuses on these authors' transformations of the precursors' language, themes, characters, sensibility, and so forth. Julie Maxwell and Kate Rumbold, introducing the critical reader *Shakespeare and Quotation,* distinguish quotation from allusion, which might also seem to distinguish Douglass's use of Shakespeare from that of his literary contemporaries.[9] On the face of it, Douglass typically uses direct quotation of Shakespeare texts. For critics such as Douglas Anderson, however, "a process of receptive transformation [took] place in which Douglass reproduced a new literary culture out of the materials of his own intellectual and physical experience."[10] Douglass does more than merely cite; he creates a narrative tableau that recalls key Shakespearean equivalents. A notable example is the echoes of the Falstaff–Prince Hal relationship in Douglass's famous depiction of his agonized relationship and decisive battle with the notorious "slave-breaker" Covey.[11] Similarly, "Othello is the dramatic figure with whom contemporary audiences, in their romantic racialism, were most likely to identify Douglass's own passionate force. With characteristic penetration, however, Douglass chooses to reproduce in subtly transposed form Othello's maddened jealousy in the figure of a slave mistress [Mrs. Hamilton], abusing her servants for the real or imagined infidelities of her white 'lord.'"[12]

In his essay "The Exorcism of *Macbeth:* Frederick Douglass's Appropriation of Shakespeare" in the critical reader *Weyward Macbeth,* John C. Briggs makes the case that Douglass's use of quotation demands analysis. Comparing his and John Greenleaf Whittier's citations of a Shakespeare line, Briggs notes, "Douglass, by contrast, quotes Shakespeare's line with an unalloyed aggressiveness."[13] Briggs notes, as does Gustafson, that Douglass made use of *Macbeth,* which, following the well-established nineteenth-century practice of never referring to this cursed work by name, he calls "The Scottish Play." Douglass cites *Macbeth* to ironize the zeal of disunionists such as his early sponsor, the radical abolitionist William Lloyd Garrison, with whom Douglass was initially allied but who became a political foe. Briggs argues that in the last act of this tragedy, "Macbeth, for all his crimes and perversity, reaches for liberty when he breaks from his submission to the witches, from the hopes and fears they toyed with and helped make monstrous in him."¹⁴ Briggs notes that "Douglass's affinity for Macbeth—most notably, for Macbeth in his final hours when he discovers his freedom facing death" is "arguably the most charged connection to the man he called 'the great poet.'" Briggs argues that Shakespeare allowed Douglass to "place Macbeth within the poet's broadly ameliorative understanding of the world."¹⁵

After his 1838 escape from slavery, Douglass became closely allied with Garrison. But the men's relationship deteriorated bitterly by the 1850s when Douglass countered Garrison's view of the American Constitution as inherently proslavery. In "The Constitution: Is It Pro-Slavery or Anti-Slavery? (1860)," the speech that Douglass delivered before the Scottish Anti-Slavery Society in Glasgow, Scotland, he made his oppositional view clear, rejecting the view of the Constitution as proslavery maintained by both Garrison and Chief Justice Taney in the *Dred Scott* case of 1857, which ruled that African Americans were not and never could be citizens of the United States. Discussing this speech, Jason de Stefano observes, "Douglass argued the illegality of slavery on the grounds that a formalist interpretation of the law's use of person to signify an object of rights and duties necessarily included African Americans; moreover, a literal reading of the Constitution proved its antislavery intent precisely because the words *slave* and *slavery* never appear in the document."¹⁶ "Douglass recognized in the nexus of legal interpretation and fiction a means of aesthetic self-making... So it's telling, on this score, that ... he turned to William Shakespeare" in order to articulate these ideas.

> After insisting on the intrinsic justice of literal language in the Glasgow debate, Douglass noted: "This is a sound legal rule. Shakespeare noticed it as an existing rule of law in his *Merchant of Venice:* 'a pound of flesh, but not one drop of blood'" ("C," 3:359). He had also cited Shakespeare as legal authority in 1857: "I will admit nothing in behalf of Slavery that is not plainly [put] down in the bill. 'This bond doth give thee here no drop of blood'" ("P," 3:153).71 In Douglass's constitutional exegesis, flesh becomes word as the formerly enslaved become part of "The People." The personhood of all Americans, including African Americans, is "nominated in the bond."¹⁷

As we have discussed, Portia's "clever turn of legal hermeneutics against Shylock," which Douglass paraphrases, haunts early American writing such as *The Last of the Mohicans* and informs contemporaneous works such as

The Marble Faun. Douglass might be said to make the most productive and resistant use of Portia's legal ingenuity.

As Coppélia Khan and Heather S. Nathans elucidate in their introduction to *Shakespearean Educations,* "Americans' growing affinity for Shakespeare during the nineteenth century can be explained by a kinship between the long-established role of oratory, in both schools and public life, and Shakespeare's fine declamatory speeches, with their piling up of parallel phrases and emotional climaxes. Walt Whitman recalls 'declaiming some stormy passage from Julius Caesar or Richard' as he rode down Broadway in an omnibus."[18] They argue that "Shakespeare's language, quite apart from his plays as aesthetic objects or theatrical performances, became an oral and aural means of training Americans to use their native language as an instrument of self-improvement and as cultural capital." Lectures given by a range of commentators on Shakespeare were rife, including Ralph Waldo Emerson, who included his lecture on Shakespeare in *Representative Men* in 1850.[19] Shakespeare was crucial to the antebellum education system, designed to "fit a male citizen to occupy his destined role in society—one that would be shaped by his race, gender, and class."[20]

Considering Douglass's use of Shakespeare as a whole, what emerges is a portrait of Douglass as an artist whose work strives, along with other antebellum artists making use of Shakespeare, to create a distinctively American idiom of eloquence, impact, and other hallmarks of rhetorical power. Despite influence's associations with the dead white male canon, it is difficult to imagine a moribund, stultifying relationship to English literary tradition when one contemplates Douglass's vigorous and various engagements with Shakespeare. To take one example, from *My Bondage and My Freedom* (1855), the second of his three autobiographies, Douglass makes use of the phrase "hooks of steel" (*Hamlet,* 1.3.62–63) to describe the close relationship he forms with two of his fellow slaves at Mr. Freeland's house, the brothers Henry and John Harris. After his contentious experience with Covey, Douglass was sent to Mr. Freeland, described as an enlightened enslaver. While Douglass had been fervently imagining escape from slavery on his own, his time with Henry and John kindled in him "a friendship as strong as one man can feel for another; for I could have died with and for them." The year that he has spent with Freeland and his newfound friends has "attached me, as with 'hooks of steel,' to my brother slaves."[21]

This phrase appears within the lines of advice Polonius gives to his son,

Laertes, Ophelia's brother, in act 1 before Laertes heads back to France, a speech containing the famous piece of advice, "Neither a borrower not a lender be" (1.3.74). Laertes's contentious relationship with Hamlet and involvement in the plot to assassinate him and Shakespeare's comic characterization of Polonius—a bumbling figure whose murder by Hamlet provokes much less outrage than one might expect—render this paternal advice ambiguous: "Thou friends thou hast, and their adoption tried / Grapple them unto thy soul with hoops [hooks] of steel, / But do not dull thy palm with entertainment / Of each new-hatched, unfledged courage" (1.3.61–64). Polonius's advice is to hold on to your tried-and-true friends and keep new ones, "unfledged courages," at bay, advice Douglass subverts.

Controversies exist over whether "hooks" or "hoops" was the original usage.[22] Douglass characteristically extracts *Hamlet*'s language in a way that denatures the text: giving no context for it and never naming the character who utters it or to whom this language is uttered. He makes the original text work for him by emphasizing his love for his fellow enslaved and formerly enslaved people, the newfound brotherhood that links him to Henry and John, no longer a resolute lone rebel but now part of a community longing for freedom and willing to die for it. He uses the Shakespearean intertext to convey what this new love achieves and imposes, not just on the spirit but also the body, as benevolent and brotherly "hooks of steel" that resist erosion and removal tether him to new brothers. The Shakespeare intertext allows Douglass the opportunity to register a haunting paradox—the desire to escape slavery is a heroically intransigent act of unhooking oneself, while the love that grows between slaves is a transcendent act of hooking oneself to another.

"BLACK, BUT COMELY": SHAKESPEARE, MILTON, AND *THE HEROIC SLAVE*

The narcissistic dimensions of influence: an unsettling preoccupation with an image, with finding one's image in that of the precursor. Like Milton's Narcissus-like Eve staring, mesmerized, at her reflection in a lake's smooth surface, the strong poet finds in the precursor a galvanizing likeness, a foundation for the expression of the self that transforms self into expression. When God and Adam both prohibit Eve from fixation on the image—the image of her nameless precursor, in which she discovers, learns that she has seen, her own—they effect a ban on melancholia, an unceasing mourning for a lost object. Influence can be theorized as both the narcissistic and melancholic brooding over the image of the Other in order to find the image of oneself.

Douglass's *The Heroic Slave* vibrates within these theoretical concepts and alongside its precursor texts, which are legion. I will focus on *Hamlet*, the King James Bible, and Milton's *Paradise Lost* and *Samson Agonistes*.

Douglass wrote a fictionalized version of the 1841 *Creole* Mutiny of enslaved people led by Madison Washington, the largest successful one in US history. Washington and his fellow slaves, 135 in number, took over the slave ship *Creole,* bound for New Orleans, and demanded passage to the Bahamas. The British soldiers in Nassau freed the slaves who were not involved in the mutiny; later, Washington and his fellow mutineers, jailed and put on trial, were also freed. In part one of the novella, set in Virginia, Mr. Listwell, a "northern traveller," overhears Madison Washington deliver a soliloquy lamenting his life under slavery. So taken is Listwell by Washington's eloquence that he decides then and there to become an abolitionist. Listwell and his wife later give Washington shelter in Ohio when he happens upon their home after having escaped from slavery.

As Julia Lee notes, "Madison Washington, the enslaved protagonist of his novella, *The Heroic Slave,* is figured as a Byronic hero, a latter-day Childe Harold disillusioned by the gap between his romantic ideals and the modern world."[23] Lee continues:

> If Washington is Byronic in his suffering, he is also Shakespearean. *The Heroic Slave* is self-consciously theatrical, with Washington performing dramatic soliloquies as Listwell "listens well" in the wings. In part I, Washington becomes a modern Hamlet, brooding over his plight. Weighing life against possible death, slavery against possible freedom, Washington channels Hamlet's internal torment in his "To be, or not to be" speech. The moment recalls the parallel moment in the *Narrative* where Douglass describes the paralyzing fear of slaves contemplating escape and cites a passage from the same soliloquy. In *The Heroic Slave,* Douglass expands upon this connection, transforming Washington into a kind of tragic hero, a princely figure of "Herculean strength" whose face is "black, but comely"—quoting from *Song of Solomon* (1:5).[24]

Portrait of Frederick Douglass from *Narrative of the Life of Frederick Douglass,* published 1845. (Library of Congress)

I argue that Douglass registered his own beauty and its solicitation of the gaze in describing Washington in this way. The phrase "black, but comely" is an archive of intertextuality and influence.

Douglass's relationship to the visual, both as constant camera subject and as a theorist of visuality and the emergent technologies of photography and the daguerreotype, the first publicly available photographic process, needs to be addressed, and many scholars have done so.[25] Douglass was, according to the editors of *Picturing Douglass,* the most photographed individual of the nineteenth century, and an extraordinary camera subject.

Laura Wexler focuses on "Douglass's ideas of photography by comparing his published lecture of 1861, 'Pictures and Progress,' with his major revision of that lecture believed to have taken place circa 1865, which still exists only in manuscript form and is undated. . . . Douglass is in conversation with Lincoln over the image of the black man and the image of the American Union."[26] "The lecture," she elaborates, "was about photography. Douglass was an enthusiast of the invention. Americans at the time generally understood photography to be a product of the union of science with nature. To Douglass, this new kind of picture promised to remedy what he saw as badly distorted visual representations of black people made by white artists."[27]

Julia Faisst discusses the white male gaze that frames the portrait of Madison Washington: "Listwell endows Washington's face with the quality of life-likeness that is so decisive for portrait photography. When his gaze reaches his 'eye, lit with emotion,' the daguerreotype completely comes to life. Mirroring the eloquence of his soliloquy with his sensual expression, Madison's face is described according to the conventions of the portrait genre." She continues, "The way it is cast, Washington's image verges on the artistic borderline of two genres of photography," the more positive "portrait" genre, and the more suspect "figure" one, "and on the sociological and historical borderline between slavery and freedom. *The Heroic Slave* provides an early premonition of the slave's future as a freeman in which he will ascend to the middle class, free to employ photographs for his own purposes. . . . Even more significantly, his overstepping the boundary of black and white will result in a more integral vision of a racially diverse American identity. While Washington becomes a free man, Listwell becomes an abolitionist. Both transcend their traditional places in society."[28]

Here is Douglass's description of Madison Washington, crucially seen through the eyes of an unseen observer who is both white and male:

> Madison was of manly form. Tall, symmetrical, round, and strong. In his movements he seemed to combine, with the strength of the lion, a lion's elasticity. His torn sleeves disclosed arms like polished iron. His face was "black, but comely." His eye, lit with emotion, kept guard under a brow as dark and as glossy as the raven's wing. His whole appearance betokened Herculean strength; yet there was nothing savage or forbidding in his aspect. A child might play in his arms, or dance on his shoulders. A giant's strength, but not a giant's heart was in him. His broad mouth and nose spoke only of good nature and kindness. But his voice, that unfailing index of the soul, though full and melodious, had that in it which could terrify as well as charm. He was just the man you would choose when hardships were to be endured, or danger to be encountered,—intelligent and brave. He had the head to conceive, and the hand to execute. In a word, he was one to be sought as a friend, but to be dreaded as an enemy.[29]

Contextualizing the description in terms of visual history and Douglass's theories of visuality and relationship to the photographic imagery is important work. My focus here, however, aims to shed light on the issue of literary influence, which is surprisingly underexamined in analyses of this key textual moment.

The genre of the romance makes permissible the description of male physical beauty, and we can see examples of such rhapsodic responses in the works of all the authors we have discussed. Nevertheless, the strictures placed on gendered performance in the post-Jacksonian antebellum era made appreciations of male beauty suspect. Douglass was contending with the constrictions placed on male identity generally, the incommensurate social demands that asked men to be contained and incendiary, at once both stoic and aggressive, and the imponderable burden of inhabiting a positive image of Blackness in an era that negated that possibility.[30] By characteristic intertextual means, Douglass found an apt and fluid register for his self-contemplation and effort to create a space for the celebration and appreciation of Black male beauty.

In her study *Transforming Scriptures: African American Women Writers and the Bible,* Katherine Clay Bassard observes of the phrase "black, but comely" that it "had a double resonance of racial and gendered meanings" for African American women: "Zilpha Elaw grasped the significance of the translation issue in the dedication to her 1846 edition of her spiritual autobiography, *Memoirs of the Life, Religious Experience, Ministerial Travels and Labours of Mrs. Zilpha Elaw, An American Female of Color*. . . . Elaw's subtle rewriting of Song of Songs 1:5 through her phrase 'comeliness with blackness' (my emphasis) overturns the racial pejorative of the original terms."[31] Bassard further observes that "the Shulamite's words—'black but comely'—figured in a range of nineteenth-century racial discourses, including African American women writers' appropriations of the Scriptures for their self-representations. Although the phrase is clearly gendered in the biblical passage, it was often used to describe African American men."[32]

"Who are the lovers of the Song of Songs?" writes the biblical scholar Cheryl J. Exum. "They are identified neither by name nor by association with any particular time or place. . . . The Song's lovers are archetypal lovers—composite figures, types of lovers rather than any specific lovers." Regarding the oscillation between female and male points of view in this dialogue between lovers, "only the woman is concerned with self-description. Is this particularly or necessarily a woman's concern; for example, in 1:5–6, where, by calling herself lovely, she raises the issue of her appearance and how others might perceive her, and 8:10, where she describes herself in the context of societal expectations?"[33] The complex gender politics evoked by Douglass's use of the female lover's self-description "black, but comely," and the fact that it became signification for specifically Black *male* beauty in the nineteenth century, demands a discrete treatment. The entire passage describing Washington's beauty flows from the gender ambiguities of the intertextual citation "black, but comely," emphasizing the gender fluidity and moral dichotomies of the hero.

The passage detailing Washington's beauty positions Douglass as a Narcissus contemplating his own fictive self-portrait within the image of the precursor (here a multivalent category combining historical personages and literary intertexts). As we have been theorizing, Eve's encounter with her image in the lake in Milton's epic both models and defines the moment of influence. Milton's Ovidian description of Narcissus-like Eve provides a template for authors' contemplation of the precursor for the discovery of their own image. Here, I want to underscore a direct intertextual link between this Miltonic episode and Douglass's ekphrastic delineation of Washington's beauty.

When Eve, mesmerized by the image of herself in the lake, runs away from the less entrancing Adam, he calls her back to him, crying, "Return, fair Eve!" (4.481). Regarding this moment, James Nohrnberg notes that Milton's prelapsarian Adam contrasts with "the biblical Adam," "who confers Eve's life-affirming personal name on her *after* the Fall":

> Milton's unique departure from the authoritative biblical sequence might endow Eve's name with an otherwise suppressed pre-history.... Nonetheless, the actual imperative, "*Return,* fair Eve," *does* have a prehistory, itself, in Song of Songs 6:13: "Return, return, O Shulamite, return, return, that we may look upon thee." This verse names the Song's otherwise anonymous female paramour uniquely. Solomon's bride is presumed innocent of a shady history making her a black but comely Near Eastern fertility goddess, even if she was once an earth-mother wed to Baal—for *Shulamite* may be Hebrew for "Shulmanitu," an epithet for the Near Eastern love goddess Ishtar.[34]

As Nohrnberg assesses, "in his allegedly rational plea that 'fair Eve' return to his side, Adam argues she owes it to him: namely, her life.—And also something of her personhood, given that she relents, or submits, upon being called by her personal name."[35]

Reginald A. Wilburn, in his superb chapter on Douglass and Milton, has established a strong intertextual link between the authors. In particular, Wilburn sheds light on Douglass's frequent evocations of Christ's harrowing of hell in book 6 of *Paradise Lost*. Bingham's compendium *The Columbian Orator*, a crucial influence on Douglass, quoted lines 824–93 from this book. "Douglass plays mischievously with the satanic epic," writes Wilburn. He "codes his [first] autobiography as a satanic narrative. Such a narrative empowers Douglass to preach a gospel of black revolt while, at the same time, underwriting both his self-made status and his literary manhood."[36]

Wilburn does not settle the question of whether Douglass read Milton's *Samson Agonistes,* a tragic closet drama published along with Milton's *Paradise Regained* in 1671, but does argue that he "indirectly voices *Samson Agonistes* as intertext." He helpfully cites Gregory Machacek's study *Milton and Homer* to theorize Douglass's relation to this Milton text and for insights germane to any study of influence: "Intertextuality of this type, as Machacek argues, 'designates not so much a study of the relations between texts as a study of the semantic and cultural presuppositions that lie between two texts and allow both of them to have the meaning that they do.'"[37]

Douglass's description of Madison Washington has a Miltonic quality especially pronounced in its appreciation for male beauty, as evinced by the poet's descriptions of Satan (whose fallenness contrasts sharply with his archangelic former glory), Adam, the archangel Raphael, and many other figures. Most relevantly, the biblical phrase "black, but comely" links *The Heroic Slave*'s love of male beauty with that foregrounded in *Samson Agonistes:* "The Bible makes no mention of Samson's comely looks. Milton's hero has 'comeliness of shape,' is 'gloriously rigg'd' and 'eminently adorned.' The poet is particularly captivated with the symbolism and the beauty of Samson's hair. . . . Milton adds humility and comeliness to superhuman might."[38]

Douglass shares Milton's penchant for imagining male heroism as erotically beautiful. We might postulate that tradition, far from prohibiting a melancholic brooding over self-image, in fact stimulates this brooding, offering it a securely established precedent. Here we have the moment of influence, encased in the sequence of the *Hamlet* passage, where Douglass cites the precursor and reworks the material, making one of Hamlet's soliloquies a model for Madison Washington's overheard lament, followed by the Miltonic passage where Washington's beauty is recorded. Douglass follows romanticism's practice of narcissistic self-contemplation within the image of the precursor and melancholic brooding over this image. That this generally cohesive method and series of effects occurs among authors as distinct in their identities and aims as Douglass and the other writers we have discussed evinces the capacious, puzzling allure of influence.

NOTES

INTRODUCTION

1. These British influences include Spenser, the King James Bible, Bunyan, Walter Scott's historical romances, the British Romantics, and of course Shakespeare and Milton. Robin Grey, in her 1997 study *The Complicity of Imagination*, studies the impact and influence of a range of seventeenth-century British authors on nineteenth-century American ones. Grey notes that "the American Puritan origin myth" laid out by Perry Miller in *The New England Mind* and extended by Sacvan Bercovitch in *The Puritan Origins of the American Self* accounts for the lack of attention paid to Anglo-American literary relations as central to the American Renaissance: "American Puritan covenant theology has [thus] been... credited (perhaps exaggeratedly so) as the dominant source of national mythology and, in turn, of national identity" (2). She accounts for the notable and distinctive "eclecticism and extravagance" of American Renaissance prose by highlighting its penchant for "seventeenth-century heterodoxies" (3). The American writers of this period "were quick to employ English texts that were associated with the discrediting of traditional authority" and were also likely to "revise texts considered 'conservative' in their own time—like the writings of Sir Thomas Browne or Izaak Walton—for ironic or unsettling purposes" (4). The writers, leading with their eclecticism, "often challenged the educated and cultured conservative hegemony." Grey, *Complicity of Imagination*, 2–4.
2. For discussions of the importance of non-Western works to the development of American Romanticism, see especially Arthur Versluis, *American Transcendentalism and Asian Religions*; Wai Chee Dimock, *Through Other Continents*; Arthur Christy, *The Orient in American Transcendentalism*; Paul Friedrich, *The Gita within Walden*; Sterling Stuckey, *African Culture and Melville's Art*; Geoffrey Sanborn, *Whipscars and Tattoos*.
3. In his famous book *American Renaissance*, F. O. Matthiessen controversially but enduringly established a US literary canon while devoting a great deal of attention to antebellum authors' reworkings of Shakespeare and Milton, among others. Matthiessen's analysis of Shakespeare's impact on Herman Melville, who began intensively reading Shakespeare in his entirety in 1849, is representative: "so far as we can trace the genesis of any creative process, we have an example here of

how Melville's own sense of life had been so profoundly stirred by Shakespeare's that he was subconsciously impelled to emulation. Without the precipitant of Shakespeare, *Moby-Dick* might have been a superior *White-Jacket*." I believe that Shakespeare's impact on Melville, and on the other writers under discussion here, was importantly galvanizing no matter how one chooses to interpret the precise nature of this impact. (Matthiessen describes this stimulating impact as "emulation," but competitiveness or a shrewd co-optation for American audiences are just as likely.) Regarding Milton, his "conception of the struggle between passion and reason remained an integral part of American ethics." Matthiessen, *American Renaissance*, 416, 103.

4. Glazener, "Print Culture as an Archive of Dissent," 330.
5. DiBattista, "Introduction. American Shakespeare," xix.
6. Taylor, *Reinventing Shakespeare*, 167.
7. Arac, *Impure Worlds*, 6.
8. Taylor, *Reinventing Shakespeare*, 204–5.
9. Ibid., 207.
10. Stevenson, "Milton and the Puritans," 4. See also Bercovitch, *The Puritan Origins of the American Self;* Colacurcio, *The Province of Piety: Moral History in Hawthorne's Early Tales* and *Hawthorne's Histories, Hawthorne's World: From Salem to Somewhere Else;* Donahue, *Hawthorne: Calvin's Ironic Stepchild*.
11. Fuller, *Art, Literature, and the Drama*, 48–9.
12. Van Anglen, *New England Milton*, 230. In terms of the nineteenth century, Van Anglen primarily focuses on the Transcendentalists Emerson and Thoreau. See also Sensabaugh, *Milton in Early America*.
13. Blake, *Marriage of Heaven and Hell*, 30. This work was composed between 1790 and 1793.
14. Critics have often emphasized British Romanticism's ardor for Milton, its tendency to enshrine him, and more recently critical attention has been paid to "Victorian Milton"; yet the similar, overlapping strain in American Romanticism receives less notice, an oversight this book redresses. For a recent discussion of Milton's centrality to British Romanticism, see Jonathon Shears, *The Romantic Legacy of Paradise Lost* (2009); see also Lisa Elaine Low and Anthony John Harding, *Milton, the Metaphysicals, and Romanticism* (1994). At the same time, Milton's centrality to all major American Romantics is not clear-cut; Gary Schmidgall, for example, has argued that he was not crucial to Walt Whitman's work. See Gary Schmidgall's chapter "Milton and Whitman" in his *Containing Multitudes* (2014), 63–109.
15. The epilogue explores Milton's influence on Frederick Douglass, extending the work of scholars such as Reginald Wilburn. I have written about Harriet Prescott Spofford's indelible "Circumstance," a short story published in the *Atlantic Monthly* in 1860, and its direct reference of *Paradise Lost*. See Greven, "Sex, the Body, and Health Reform." The last line of "Circumstance" lifts from Milton's epic about, among other things, the first human couple, Adam and Eve, and their

expulsion from the Garden: "For the rest,—the world was all before them, where to choose" (Spofford, 96). The lines in Milton read thusly: "The world was all before them, where to choose / Their place of rest, and Providence their guide: / They hand in hand, with wandering steps and slow, / Through Eden took their solitary way" (12.637-49).

16. Bewley, *Complex Fate*, 3.
17. In making Bewley and Matthiessen foundational, I am implicitly aligning myself with a gay male critical tradition of interpreting American letters. Matthiessen's homosexuality has been much discussed in the past few decades in terms of its relationship to his formation of an American literary canon. For a representative analysis, see the Matthiessen-focused fourth chapter of Randall Fuller's *Emerson's Ghosts*. In terms of Bewley, Al Alvarez provides a firsthand account of his being a gay man in a closeted era. Bewley was a protégé of the famous English critic F. R. Leavis, indeed "Leavis's most favoured disciple, a subtle critic and also a brave man because . . . he made no secret of his homosexuality at a time when homosexual activity, even between consenting adults, was a criminal offense." Alvarez, *Where Did It All Go Right?*, 181. For a related account of the same era, see Edmund White, *City Boy: My Life in New York during the 1960s and '70s* (2009). See also Chris Castiglia's discussion in *The Practices of Hope* (2017) of Bewley and the significance of his being a gay and English critic in the Cold War United States.
18. McGill, "Introduction," 2.
19. Weisbuch, *Atlantic Double-Cross*, xviii.
20. Blum, *Turns of Event*, 2.
21. Schmidgall, *Containing Multitudes*, xix.
22. Chamberlin Hellman, *Children*, 10-11.
23. Parvini, *Shakespeare's History Plays*, 216. It should be noted that Early Modern scholars have been questioning the stronghold of materialist history and expanding its paradigms to include a return to form, among other newly revitalized approaches. See, for example, *Rethinking Historicism from Shakespeare to Milton* (2012), edited by Ann Baynes Coiro and Thomas Fulton.
24. Humanism enters into a suspect complicity with its institutional enemies, because it fears the wrath of the rabble: "Aesthetic experience and aesthetic education provide the crucial mediation between the constraints demanded by the structuration of political power and the desires of individual subjects. The richest and most complex of those mediations are sedimented in the works of Shakespeare. By internalizing this experience, the individual subject can facilitate his or her own self-integration within an already given ensemble of social constraints." If Shakespeare supposedly gives us unparalleled access to insights about the human condition, "unless we already know what the human condition is, there is no way to ascertain whether or not Shakespeare is telling us the truth about it." Shakespeare was and remains the cynosure of "a very thoroughgoing form of ideological processing." Bristol, *Shakespeare's America*, 22-23.
25. Its author's ambivalence toward deconstruction and the Yale School

notwithstanding, Harold Bloom's *The Anxiety of Influence* heralded the 1980s' commitments to high theory and deconstructive approaches. The preface that Bloom wrote for the 1997 second edition scarcely repudiates the claim that topics like influence stem from elitist and racist attitudes: "Politicizing literary study has destroyed literary study, and may yet destroy learning itself... The common assumption of all Resenters is that state power is everything and individual subjectivity is nothing... Unable to be Nietzsche, who made them all belated, our Resenters do not wish merely to re-proclaim the Death of God, so they turn instead to proclaiming what can only be called the Death of Shakespeare." Bloom, *Anxiety of Influence,* xvi–xviii. Bloom's resenters consist of women and people of color; he refuses to engage with opposing views, maintaining an indifference to the legitimate concerns many have had with the Western canon and with Bloom's monolithic tome by that name. Nevertheless, Bloom's early work, including *A Map of Misreading* (1975), remains crucial to any study of influence, indispensably laying out the groundwork. While I neither support the later Bloom's dismissive and hostile stance against "the school of resentment" nor advocate a return to an unreconstructed humanism, I contend that his work need not be jettisoned if we read it reparatively.

26. Hollander, *Melodious Guile,* 165, 56.
27. In their introductory essay to "'Come Again?': New Approaches to Sexuality in Nineteenth-Century U.S. Literature," the 2009 special issue of *ESQ* that they edited, Christopher Castiglia and Christopher Looby foreground the question of literariness: "That so much of queer studies has grounded itself in literary research sometimes gives pause to scholars in other disciplines, who wonder about the status of literary evidence for these purposes. Here, in a special issue of an avowedly literary journal, we perhaps do not need to worry excessively about the value of our kind of intellectual work. But we might well take care, when doing literary criticism as a means of analyzing and historicizing sexuality, to be at least as vigilant as usual in our attention to questions of representation, aesthetic autonomy, or literariness—however one might wish to label the particular characteristics that distinguish our objects of inquiry, literary artifacts. And so we might propose a variation on Sedgwick's proposition, and say as well that an argument about modern Western sexuality that takes the form of literary criticism will be, not merely epistemologically compromised, but unpersuasive and shallow to the degree that it does not self-consciously reflect upon the literariness of its adduced evidence. [New paragraph] Literariness means different things to different people, but whatever a scholar takes it to mean, it ought to be brought into lively relationship with the positive claims that are being made about sexuality as such, the history of sexuality, the politics of sexuality, and so forth." Castiglia and Looby, eds., "'Come Again?': New Approaches," 200.

    In terms of the careful attention to literariness that Castiglia and Looby rightly encourage, one of the reasons why literature is an important as well as interesting record of historical experiences of these matters is that literature represents—at its best, which would certainly authentically describe all of the primary texts I discuss here—the efforts to make sense of a particular time and place and historical moment on the part of a thoughtful and creative and insightful mind. I am much less interested in the steady compilation of *modes* of literariness from particular periods substituting for interpretive engagement with the various ways in which literature can be meaningful.

28. Bersani, "Foreword," xvi.
29. Kristeva, "Word, Dialogue, and Novel," 66. Emphasis in original.
30. Roudiez, "Introduction," 15; cited in Garber, *Muses on Their Lunch Hour,* 35.
31. Riffaterre, "Intertextual Representation," 142.
32. Hutcheon, "Literary Borrowing," 231, 234. Though she mentions other essays by the French literary theorist Roland Barthes, Hutcheon is clearly riffing here on a piece she does not cite, his hugely influential 1967 essay "The Death of the Author" ("La mort de l'auteur"), collected in *Image, Music, Text* (1977).
33. Clayton and Rothstein continue: "Thus influence assigns to intertextuality, under the slave names 'context' and 'allusion,' to an accessory role in a scenario that features imperious, charismatic Major Works. For its part, once intertextuality has reassigned to the provinces influence's concern with an author's intentions and his or her consciousness of them, it organizes what is left, textual comparison, into a formalism idiom where 'society,' 'culture,' and 'history' share legibility with the verbal sequences that traditionally have been called 'texts' or 'works.'" Clayton and Rothstein, "Figures in the Corpus," 17.
34. Ibid., 23.
35. Hellman, *Children,* 10-12.
36. The critic playfully and productively advises us to catch "the 'flu.'" Garber, *Muses on Their Lunch Hour,* 57.
37. Allen, *Intertextuality,* 137.
38. Fry, *Theory of Literature,* 185. He refers to Eliot's famous essay "Tradition and the Individual Talent."
39. Juvan, *History and Poetics of Intertextuality,* 7.
40. McDonald, "Introduction," 8.
41. Ibid., 9.
42. Vol. 42, no. 1 (Spring 2016).
43. Ohi, *Dead Letters Sent,* 64.
44. Ibid., 1.
45. I theorize intertextual desire in relation to Tennessee Williams's uses of Melville in my chapter "'Nothing Could Stop It Now!': Tennessee Williams, *Suddenly Last Summer,* and the Intersections of Desire" in *The Cambridge Companion to Erotic Literature.* Certainly, Ohi's term *queer transmission* applies here.
46. I have been heartened to see contemporary theorists such as Grace Lavery finding renewed relevance in Freud, including a case for his notorious theory of penis envy. See her essay "Trans Realism, Psychoanalytic Practice, and the Rhetoric of Technique," *Critical Inquiry* 46, no. 4 (Summer 2020): 719-44.

47. In terms of dissent from Sedgwick's argument, see, for example, Morrison, *Explanation for Everything,* 143–45.
48. Sedgwick, "Paranoid Reading and Reparative Reading," 8. Sedgwick refers to Klein's *Envy and Gratitude* (1957).
49. All references to Milton's *Paradise Lost* in this book will be from the Longman edition.
50. Love, *Feeling Backward,* 55.
51. Conley, "'League with You I Seek,'" 13.
52. Bloom, *Anxiety of Influence,* 5.
53. Ibid., 7.
54. Ibid., 14–16.
55. Ibid., 43.
56. Ibid., 43.
57. As Michael Dirda puts it: "Years ago, the Yale critic Harold Bloom promulgated 'clinamen'—that is, 'the swerve,' a term derived from Lucretius's philosophical poem 'On the Nature of Things'—as central to his controversial theory of literary influence. Writers, Bloom speculated, swerve away from the dominion, the overpowering authority, of earlier masters to clear a poetic space for their own work. Since then, other literary theorists—many of them, as you would guess, French—have employed their own notions of 'clinamen.' So it seems odd that Stephen Greenblatt in 'The Swerve' never mentions this familiar Bloomian use of 'clinamen.' Perhaps Greenblatt, who attended Yale, is himself swerving away from an older anxiety-producing master." Dirda, "Review of *The Swerve.*"
58. Schmidgall, *Containing Multitudes,* xxii.
59. Ibid., xxii. Schmidgall quotes Bloom's *Anxiety of Influence* from the 1997 edition as well.
60. Roger Sale complains that Bloom's "great limitation" is that he "makes ours a history of Romanticism when ours has been, ever since 1742 and the descent of darkness, the age of the novel." Sale blames the preeminence of Wordsworth for this obfuscation. He associates poetry with belatedness but argues that, in contrast, "the novel was allowed to be invented and to grow into a major art form almost without its being noticed." While poetry endured as the standard, with critics coming only very lately to the novel as a legitimate art form, the novel enjoyed a century of maturation before "anyone wanted it to be a self-conscious 'artistic' affair." Sale, *Literary Inheritance,* 141. Sale's points are arguable, especially about the time frame of the novel's achievement of cultural legitimacy, but my focus here on the novel as form does reflect an endorsement of Sale's understanding of the novel's resistance to belatedness.
61. Fry, *Theory of Literature,* 184–86. He discusses the introduction to *The Anxiety of Influence,* "A Meditation on Priority."
62. Bloom, *Map of Misreading,* 37.
63. Ibid., 125.
64. Ibid., 35–36.

65. Smith, *Works*, vol. 2, 17–18.
66. Piracy was indeed a major dilemma, as evinced by the sheer number of works republished abroad with no compensation for authors, a common pitfall of an era before copyright laws.
67. Melville's "Hawthorne and His Mosses" will be discussed in chapter 5.
68. Robert Douglas-Fairhurst in his reading of influence in *Victorian Afterlives: The Shaping of Influence in Nineteenth-Century Literature* (2002) expands this to the fears that all writers have faced about this question since ancient times: "Writers have often expressed, with varying degrees of confidence, despair, and success, their wish to live through their works." Douglas-Fairhurst, *Victorian Afterlives*, 20.
69. Douglas-Fairhurst cites John Hollander's *Melodious Guile* to discuss the idea of influence as a chain rather than one-on-one agon, as Bloom would have it: "The metaphor stretches back further still to Plato's description of a 'long chain' of poetic inspiration in the *Ion*." In this complex discussion that commences with the critic distancing himself from Bloom's reading of Emerson (because Emerson sees influence as a widely stretching "chain" rather than a Bloomian "antagonism" between one writer and a precursor), Douglas-Fairhurst, noting that Hollander's model refers back to Shelley's defense of poetic influence as a chain, points out the chinks in Hollander's rhetorical armor: "if textual glossing is not limited to one voice answering one other voice, his account could not explain how influence had come to constitute a 'chain.'" Most intriguingly, Hollander's concept of "intertextual answers," which Douglas-Fairhurst calls a "theoretical hiccup," dovetails with Wai Chee Dimock's concept of literary deep time. Douglas-Fairhurst, *Victorian Afterlives*, 37–38; Hollander, *Melodious Guile*, 56.
70. In his essay "Mourning and Melancholia" (1917), Freud describes mourning as the "normal" fatiguing away of grief. In melancholia, however, mourning achieves a perverse state of longevity, becoming interminable. One of the effects of withdrawal from the object is the reincorporation of the libido associated with that object-desire back into the ego: "the free libido was not displaced on to another object; it was withdrawn into the ego," and thereby established "an identification of the ego with the abandoned object." Freud's language takes on a biblical tone: "Thus the shadow of the object fell upon the ego, and the latter could be judged by a special agency, as though it were an object, the forsaken object." Freud, "Mourning and Melancholia," SE 14:249.
71. In the Lacanian scenario, the subject is captivated by the image in the mirror, identifying with this specular self; this seductive counterpart seizes, possesses, the subject (captation). The split between an illusory wholeness and *le corps morcelé* (fragmented body or the body in pieces) informs narcissism, itself a metaphor for this split; the ego is part of the Imaginary order and depends upon a misrecognition of the self as the specular self. For Lacan, narcissism is pathological because it is a subjectivity based on a mirage. See Lacan, *Freud's Papers on Technique*, 142; Lacan, *Écrits*, 2–6. I discuss these ideas at length in *The Fragility of Manhood: Hawthorne, Freud, and The Politics of Gender*.

72. Jane Gallop writes, "According to [Jean-Michel] Palmier, 'what seems to be first... is the anguish of the *corps morcelé* [body in bits and pieces].'... The *corps morcelé* is a Lacanian term for a violently nontotalized body image, an image psychoanalysis finds accompanied by anxiety." Gallop, *Reading Lacan,* 79.
73. Patricia White, writing about Hitchcock's 1940 film *Rebecca,* based on Daphne du Maurier's bestselling 1938 novel, describes the heroine's failure at the masquerade ball: "I," as the unnamed heroine is called, "fails at the masquerade; she doesn't measure up to the Woman as image." White, *Rebecca,* 86.
74. Shoulson, "Embrace of the Fig Tree," 889.
75. McColley, *Milton's Eve,* 75.
76. See Silverman, *Threshold of the Visible World,* 33; Kofman, *The Enigma of Woman,* 52–57.
77. See Gallop, *Reading Lacan,* 85; Edelman, *Homographesis,* 102–5.
78. All quotations from *Moby-Dick* are from the Northwestern-Newberry edition of *Writings of Herman Melville* and will be noted parenthetically throughout the text.
79. Quotes from Ovid come from the *Classical Library* edition and are cited parenthetically. David Hopkins writes, "On 4 July 1717 Jacob Tonson the Elder issued Ovid's *Metamorphoses, in Fifteen Books, Translated by the Most Eminent Hands,* the first of the two luxuriously printed books of verse which were to mark the end of his publishing career. This handsome folio volume was a complete English translation of Ovid's greatest poem, in which sections or episodes of widely varying length were rendered into heroic couplets by eighteen separate translators.... The Tonson *Metamorphoses* was edited by the poet and physician Sir Samuel Garth, who contributed translations of the whole of Book XIV and part of Book XV and introduced the volume with a substantial Preface." See Hopkins, "Dryden and the Garth-Tonson *Metamorphoses,*" 64. Melville consulted the 1844 Harper and Bros. printing of the Garth-Tonson edition.
80. All quotations from *Pierre* are from the Northwestern-Newberry Edition and will be noted parenthetically in the main text.
81. Richmond-Garza, "Translation Is Blind," 284. Garza quotes from several Derrida pieces, such as *On Touching—Jean-Luc Nancy* (164).
82. Peretz, *Literature, Disaster, and the Enigma of Power,* 97.
83. Richmond-Garza, "Translation Is Blind," 293; Andreas-Salomé is quoted from Schultz, "In Defense of Narcissus," 185.

I. THE STRANGER MAIDEN

1. Smith, *Works,* vol. 2, 17–18.
2. All quotations from the works of Shakespeare will come from the Arden editions.
3. See Cooper and Beard, *Deerslayer,* 9. Geoffrey Rans discusses the presence of Homer in *The Last of the Mohicans.* See Rans, *Cooper's Leather-Stocking Novels,* 118, 127–30. As Rans notes, "the epic permeates the style of this novel—which

teems with literary echoes of all sorts, but most obviously of Homer, Milton, and Shakespeare—and is integral to the novel's tragic themes" (118). Rans, *Cooper's Leather-Stocking Novels*. For a superb analysis of Homeric themes in Mohicans, see John P. McWilliams's chapter "Red Achilles, Red Satan" in his book *The American Epic*, 123–57, especially his comparison of the "concluding scene of *The Last of the Mohicans*, surely the finest chapter of fiction an American had yet written," and book 24 of *The Iliad* (141).

4. Harriet Beecher Stowe's *Uncle Tom's Cabin* (1852) overlaps with *The Last of the Mohicans* in many ways, influence included, and refers to *Paradise Lost* and *Merchant of Venice*. Both Stowe and Cooper were writers whose careers and importance were rehabilitated by Jane Tompkins in her 1985 *Sensational Designs* (her two best chapters in this book, by far, are those on Cooper and Stowe). Tompkins restored the importance of Cooper's and Stowe's attempts to discuss the difficult, often unresolvable complexities of race in the American context.

5. For example, Geoffrey Sanborn's excellent essay "James Fenimore Cooper and the Invention of the Passing Novel," which focuses on Cooper's novel *The Headsman: The Abbaye des Vignerons* (1833), does not consider influence as a factor in Cooper's complex, challenged, and challenging explorations of race and interracial identity and desire. The same holds true for Betsy Erkkila's *Mixed Bloods and Other Crosses*, Harry J. Brown's *Injun Joe's Ghost*, Debra J. Rosenthal's *Race Mixture in Nineteenth-Century U.S. and Spanish American Fictions*, and other notable studies.

6. Cooper, *Notions of the Americans*, 132.

7. Ibid., 148–49.

8. Cooper, *Notions of the Americans*, 318.

9. I do mean arguably, since even as far back as 1980 Robert Milder was defending *The Last of the Mohicans*'s stature. I write in agreement with Milder's astute assessment that *Mohicans* is among Cooper's "most carefully patterned works" and that "its commitment to the problem of America is as full and intense as *The Prairie*'s." Milder, "*Last of the Mohicans*," 407.

10. The set that Cooper owned was *The Plays of William Shakespeare in Eight Volumes*, edited by George Steevens (London: F. C. and J. Rivington and Partners, 1811).

11. Susan Fenimore Cooper reported that her father "could seldom be induced to read more than a page or two of Milton, at a time; the great epic poet he considered too correctly cold and classical in spirit, for his theme; and this opinion continued unchanged through life. 'Shakespeare should have written *Paradise Lost*. What a poem he would have given to the world!' was a remark he repeatedly made." See S. Cooper, "Introduction," *Pages and Pictures*, 17.

12. Gates, "Cooper's Indebtedness to Shakespeare," 716.

13. Dekker, *Cooper the Novelist*, 123.

14. Ibid., 128.

15. Franklin, *New World of James Fenimore Cooper*, 247–48.

16. Cooper references *The Tempest* in the epigraph to chapter 14 in his 1838 novel

Homeward Bound. Allusions to *The Tempest* have been noted in *The Prairie* (1827) and especially *The Water-Witch* (1830). Edward Vandiver notes that "this play must have been almost constantly in Cooper's mind." Vandiver, "Cooper and Shakespeare," 117.

17. On this point, Octave Mannoni comes down very hard on Prospero: "There is no logic to this argument. Prospero could have removed Caliban to a safe distance or he could have continued to civilize and correct him. But the argument: you tried to violate Miranda, *therefore* [I will banish you] . . . is primarily a justification of hatred on grounds of sexual guilt, and it is at the root of colonial racism." Then again, Mannoni observes of Caliban that while not as submissive as Miranda, Ariel, and Defoe's Friday, and prone to "assert himself by opposing," Caliban is "mere bestiality" (108). Mannoni, *Prospero and Caliban*, 106–8.

18. Coleridge, *Lectures and Notes*, 277–78.

19. Miranda explains to Ferdinand that she would love to be his wife but would settle for being his maid. He responds, "My mistress, dearest, / And I thus humble ever," to which Miranda responds, "My husband, then?" Ferdinand confirms, "Ay, with a heart as willing / As bondage e'er of freedom" (3.1.84–90). Miranda's asking of such a question goads him into assenting, a subtle indication of her forcefulness, to which he acquiesces.

20. Showalter, *Sister's Choice*, 27.

21. Ibid., 28.

22. Alden T. Vaughan and Virginia Mason Vaughan parse this critical reassessment helpfully: "In the early 1990s . . . scholars began to reassess *The Tempest* in the context of European colonialism, with particular emphasis on Caliban's relationship with Prospero. Stephen J. Greenblatt, for example, placed Caliban's declaration, 'You taught me to language, and my profit on't / Is I know how to curse' (I.ii.366–67) in juxtaposition with Spanish conquistadors' mistaken assumption that American Indians had no language of their own. For many scholars writing in the 1990s, including American historians, Caliban seemed to be Shakespeare's representation of a Native American, akin to the Powhatans that British settlers confronted in Jamestown." Vaughan and Vaughan, *Shakespeare in America*, 148–49.

23. Takaki, *Different Mirror*, 50–51.

24. Vandiver, "Cooper and Shakespeare," 112.

25. Dekker, *Cooper the Novelist*, 123n5.

26. In the evocative film version of the play directed by Michael Radford and starring Al Pacino as Shylock (2004), it is very clear that Antonio (Jeremy Irons) is in love with the darkly, sensually handsome Bassanio (Joseph Fiennes). Pacino gives a devastating performance.

27. Stokes, "Shakespeare in Europe," 305.

28. Vaughan and Vaughan, *Shakespeare in America*, 100.

29. Quotations from Cooper's *The Last of the Mohicans: A Narrative of 1757* are cited parenthetically from the State University of New York Press 1983 edition.

30. As Cooper's description of Cora continues in ennobling fashion, "there was

neither coarseness nor want of shadowing in a countenance that was exquisitely regular, and dignified and surpassingly beautiful. She smiled, as if in pity at her own momentary forgetfulness, discovering by the act a row of teeth that would have shamed the purest ivory; when, replacing the veil, she bowed her face, and rode in silence, like one whose thoughts were abstracted from the scene around her" (19).

31. John McWilliams parses Cora's mixture of responses thusly: "Pity and fear are the emotions Aristotle claimed were created and purged in dramatic tragedy. Admiration or awe is the emotion that the hero of an epic poem evokes within its listeners or its readers. Because we rarely admire and fear those whom we also pity, only a convincingly deep character can evoke all three emotions." McWilliams, *The Last of the Mohicans*, 58–59.
32. Dekker, *Cooper the Novelist*, 68. More debatably, Dekker goes on to argue that "marriage between Uncas and Cora was inconceivable—not because of Cooper's 'horror of miscegenation,' but because they had nothing to draw or keep them together except sexual desire" (72).
33. David Gamut is described thusly: "His legs and thighs were thin nearly to emaciation, but of extraordinary length . . . The ill-assorted and injudicious attire of the individual only served to render his awkwardness more conspicuous" (16). Gamut's improbability as a character, a dreamy, possibly non compos mentis singer adrift in the woods, and his improbable physicality mirror one another.
34. Artese, "'You Shall Not Know,'" 328.
35. Kristal, "Circulation of Resentment," 237.
36. Greenslade, "Shakespeare and Politics," 230.
37. McWilliams, *Last of the Mohicans*, 54.
38. Artese, "'You Shall Not Know,'" 331–32.
39. Gross, *Shylock Is Shakespeare*, 35.
40. McWilliams, *Last of the Mohicans*, 59–60.
41. We recall that George Dekker notes of Cooper's Shakespearean sensibility, "If with one part of his being he reveled in the intricate dissemblings of Shakespeare's comedies—and Shakespeare was certainly the romancer who most influenced him—with another part who stood allied with Cordelia and Kent against a world of duplicity, error, and illusion." Dekker, *Cooper the Novelist*, 128.
42. Milder, "*Last of the Mohicans*," 412.
43. Dekker, *Cooper the Novelist*, 70.
44. Kesterson writes, "The pictures are remarkably close: Magua, impulsive yet also reflective, proud, nursing his wounded vanity, now alone with his mixed thoughts about his next move; and Satan, also both impetuous and contemplative, smarting from personal defeat, alone with his thoughts of the past, his punishment, and his sworn revenge and intended corruption of man. And the same doubt that besets Satan as he thinks about his mission ('Sometimes toward Eden which now in his view / Lay pleasant, his griev'd look he fixes sad . . .' PL, IV, 27–28) besets Magua. In Chapter XXXII when, because of Cora's refusal to marry him, he must

finally carry out his threat of killing her, he is seized by uncertainty: 'The form of the Huron trembled in every fiber, and he raised his arm on high, but dropped it again with a bewildered air, like one who doubted' [337]. Unlike the culmination of Satan's errand, Magua's is suddenly determined for him when an impatient fellow warrior impetuously stabs Cora; whereas Satan, of course, finally pushes doubt aside and perseveres in his plans. But up to that point, the feelings of the two figures are almost identical." Kesterson, "Milton's Satan," 140-41.

45. McWilliams, *Last of the Mohicans,* 62.
46. Ibid., 62.
47. Hammond, *Milton's Complex Words,* 328.
48. Yarnall, *Transformations of Circe,* 154.
49. Michael C. Schoenfeldt, "Gender and Conduct in *Paradise Lost,*" in *Sexuality and Gender in Early Modern Europe: Institutions, Texts, Images.* Ed. James Grantham Turner, 331.
50. Shoulson, "Embrace of the Fig Tree," 874.
51. Ibid., 886.
52. Dyer, "Irresolute Ravishers," 340. Dyer focuses on the ways that "historical novels from the Romantic period attempt to deal with the problems attendant on the chivalrous desire to defend women."
53. Walker, *Medusa's Mirrors,* 158-87.
54. Moore, "Two Faces of Eve," 6.
55. Ibid., 10. Moore further explains, "Ironically, Satan is, in a sense, right—what she needs to know to help her in her immediate predicament is the knowledge of good and evil: 'if what is evil / Be real, why not known, since easier shunn'd?' (698-99). She should automatically choose God, but without the experience of good and evil, how is one to know that God is good?"
56. Schoenfeldt, "Gender and Conduct," 330-31.
57. Armstrong and Tennenhouse, "Recalling Cora," 223-45. Addressing the critical tendency to focus on the issue of race during the funeral scenes for Cora and Uncas, where Natty Bumppo infamously counsels grieving Munro that his words of racial harmony in the afterlife would confuse the Delaware Indian mourners, the critics argue, "Such a reading quickly reverts to the problem of consanguinity at the cost of ignoring Cooper's elaborately wrought description, leaving us without a more convincing explanation than racism as the reason why he allows the romance between Cora and Uncas to surface only when both are dead. Rather than make Cora the reproductive mechanism of an interracial nation, the novel's conclusion enjoins us to think of the aesthetic politics of their mixed legacy" (239). Armstrong and Tennenhouse's intervention is particularly welcome in the light of ongoing readings of Cora as reflective of Cooper's racial and gendered conservatism at once.
58. Luciano argues that new modes of personalized and decorum-defying, extended grief in the nineteenth century simultaneously accommodated and resisted an emergent system of regulating and disciplining national forms of mourning.

Luciano devotes considerable attention to Cooper's characterization of Cora. While unpacking her ambitious and ominous reading would require a discrete treatment, I want to point out how closely it echoes contemporary reviewers' responses to Cora. Luciano affords Cora a peculiar agency, the power to ensure her own destruction as she unravels male composure: Cora is "made to bear the blame for her own eventual demise" given the problems in temporality and gender coding she consistently presents; "Cora displays an ability to influence the men attracted to her away from their initial convictions, suggesting that once exposed to her, these men no longer have 'but one mind,' as Magua insists a chief must (315)"; and so forth. Luciano, *Arranging Grief,* 97, 93.
59. Harding, "'Without Distinction,'" 36-40.
60. Sorisio, *Fleshing Out America,* 35.
61. See my chapter on the Leather-Stocking novels, "Disturbing the Sleep of Bachelors," in *Men Beyond Desire.*
62. Gardiner, review of *The Last of the Mohicans, North American Review* (July 1826), repr. in Dekker and McWilliams, *Critical Heritage,* 110.
63. Unsigned review, *New-York Review and Atheneum* (March 1826), 285-92, repr. In Dekker and McWilliams, *Critical Heritage,* 96.
64. Simms, *Charleston and Her Satirists,* lines 852-61.
65. Ibid., lines 886-90.
66. In rebuking Eve, Milton's Adam fails to take responsibility for his own actions; his plummet into rank misogyny reflects his own moral weakness and self-centeredness. At the same time, when Eve, in response to his tirade, begs him for forgiveness, he relents; his heart softens, and he feels pity for Eve, encouraging her to retain hope. He also expresses a desire to endure the full brunt of God's punishment, wishing that "on my head all might be visited, / Thy frailty and infirmer sex forgiven, / To me committed and by me exposed" (10.955-57).
67. R. W. B. Lewis, *American Adam,* 91. Original emphasis.
68. Baym, "Women of Cooper's Leatherstocking Tales," 702.
69. Ibid., 709.
70. Franklin, *Early Years,* 481-82. Franklin continues, "Cooper's bundling of black, white, and red in *The Last of the Mohicans* might well be seen as a daring attempt to recalibrate the working categories of current cultural discourse." Franklin argues that Cooper follows "an Indian lead" in exploring the historical reality of intermarriage among Black people and Native Americans (482).

2. INCEST AND INTERTEXTUALITY

1. See Greven, *Fragility of Manhood,* for a sustained analysis of this theme in Hawthorne's body of work.
2. Young, *Hawthorne's Secret,* 15. Young's primary focus in this book is the colonial-era incest trial involving Hawthorne's maternal Manning ancestors.

3. Miller, *Salem Is My Dwelling Place,* 55.
4. Wineapple, *Hawthorne,* 40.
5. Ibid., 23.
6. Ibid., 162.
7. Michael J. Colacurcio's book *The Province of Piety* exhaustively (and exhaustingly) traces the connections between Hawthorne's early work—the tales—and his readings in Puritan theology and New England history. Colacurcio's emphasis is single-minded, to say the least, staunchly maintaining the view that Hawthorne was a prominent early American historian, but *Piety* is nevertheless very valuable as a resource.
8. Kesselring, *Hawthorne's Reading,* 10-12.
9. Ibid., 13.
10. Woodberry, *Nathaniel Hawthorne,* 256.
11. For an extended discussion of Hawthorne's reworkings of Milton, see F. O. Matthiessen's *American Renaissance,* 305-13.
12. Matthiessen, *American Renaissance,* 312.
13. Lathrop, *Study of Hawthorne,* 36.
14. Una was born in 1844 and named after a character in *The Faerie Queene.* Julian was born in 1846, Rose in 1851.
15. Matthiessen, *American Renaissance,* 304.
16. For a discussion of the feminist and queer implications of literary influence in "Rappaccini's Daughter," see chapter 6 of Greven, *Fragility of Manhood,* 141-80. This chapter pays close attention to the reference to Vertumnus, god of seasons, and Ovid's story of this shape-shifting god and the human woman he strenuously woos, Pomona.
17. Eve thinks to herself:

> ... But to Adam in what sort
> Shall I appear? Shall I to him make known
> As yet my change, and give him to partake
> Full happiness with me, or rather not,
> But keeps the odds of knowledge in my power
> Without copartner? So to add what wants
> In female sex, the more to draw his love,
> And render me more equal, and perhaps,
> A thing not undesirable, sometime
> Superior; for inferior who is free?
> This may be well: but what if God have seen,
> And death ensue? Then I shall be no more,
> And Adam, wedded to another Eve,
> Shall live with her enjoying, I extinct;
> A death to think! Confirmed then I resolve,
> Adam shall share with me in bliss or woe:

> So dear I love him, that with him all deaths
> I could endure, without him live no life. (4.816-34)

18. All quotations from Hawthorne's works are taken from *The Centenary Edition of the Works of Nathaniel Hawthorne* (Columbus: Ohio State University Press, 1962).
19. To be sure, that Beatrice functions thus as an allegory is deeply disturbing. Hawthorne based the tale on a legend in the *Gesta Romanorum* of an assassination plot to kill Alexander the Great by tricking him into having sex with a poisoned woman. For more on this, see Bensick's *La Nouvelle Beatrice*, 109.
20. William H. Shurr notes, "Among the allusions that abound in the story are more or less explicit references to Dante, Genesis, Ecclesiastes, Samuel, the Song of Solomon, the Gospels, Revelations, Ovid, Edward Johnson's *The Wonder-Working Providence of Scion's Saviour, Faust*, Emerson's *Nature*, Hamlet's most famous soliloquy, Sir Thomas Browne, and possibly Jonathan Edwards." Shurr, *Rappaccini's Children*, 1.
21. See, for example, Thorslev, "Incest as Romantic Symbol"; Richardson, *Neural Sublime*, 97-115.
22. See, for example, Long Hoeveler, "Beatrice Cenci"; Miller, *Salem Is My Dwelling Place*.
23. Harkins, *Everybody's Family Romance*, 1. Harkins focuses on how the treatment of incest shifted, serving as a metaphorical figure of national unrest in early American literature and moving to a cultural and social reality beginning in the 1980s, when accounts of incest, which represented hidden, suppressed familial trauma, proliferated. Surprisingly, Harkins does not list *Gables* here.
24. Hurh, "Sound of Incest," 259-60.
25. Herman Melville, *The Writings of Herman Melville: Correspondence*, 14:184-87. The editor tentatively dates this letter to April 16, 1851.
26. Weinstein, *Family, Kinship, and Sympathy*, 176.
27. Ibid, 176.
28. Hemphill, *Siblings*, 150.
29. De Rocher, *Elizabeth Manning Hawthorne*, 25. De Rocher draws on Philip Young's *Hawthorne's Secret*.
30. Miller, *Salem Is My Dwelling Place*, 35, and see also 101, 116; Erlich, *Family Themes and Hawthorne's Fiction*, 90-99; Herbert, *Dearest Beloved*, 294-95n15; Young, *Hawthorne's Secret*, 89-147, and in particular 124-32; De Rocher, *Elizabeth Manning Hawthorne*, 25.
31. Paglia, *Sexual Personae*, 646.
32. See, for example, Grey, *Melville & Milton*; Schirmeister, *Consolations of Space*; Van Anglen, *New England Milton*. See also Wilburn's *Preaching the Gospel of Black Revolt* for its insights into uses of Milton by Black American authors over the centuries.
33. See, for example, Norberg, Olsen-Smith, and Marnon, "Newly Recovered Erased Annotations." A notable exception in the dearth of Hawthorne-related

commentary has been the work of Pam Schirmeister, who locates the early 1850s as the central period of Hawthorne's engagement with Milton as well as Spenser and Shakespeare.

34. Wittreich, *Why Milton Matters*, xxi.
35. Poe's magnificent tale "The Fall of the House of Usher," another work haunted by Milton and that in turn haunts Hawthorne's work, similarly thematizes such interconnections in its Romantic depiction of brother-sister incest that emphasizes states of physical ruin in contrast to prior states of physical beauty.
36. Shoaf, *Milton, Poet of Duality*, 86.
37. Kilgour, *Milton and the Metamorphosis of Ovid*, 198.
38. For a relevant queer discussion of Satan as a figure of "defiance and abjection," albeit in this regard as a symbol for high modernism, see Love, *Feeling Backward*, 55.
39. See Baym, "Heroine." This essay argues that Hawthorne's depiction of Hepzibah is feminist.
40. While the name Hepzibah sounds arcane and sexless to the modern ear, the original Biblical context from which the name derives is anything but, as limned in the King James Bible: "Thou shalt no more be termed Forsaken; neither shall thy land any more be termed Desolate: but thou shalt be called Hephzibah, and thy land Beulah: for the LORD delighteth in thee, and thy land shall be married. For as a young man marrieth a virgin, so shall thy sons marry thee: and as the bridegroom rejoiceth over the bride, so shall thy God rejoice over thee" (Isaiah 62:4, 5). Hephzibah is the name given to the wife of Hezekiah in the Second Book of Kings. The names associated with her "mix the metaphor between woman and land," according to the religious commentator Roger E. Van Harn (386). Given the critical understanding that the obsessive concern with property rights in this romance stems from homosocial male competitiveness—the battle between Colonel Pyncheon and the wizard Matthew Maule, who curses his accuser with the famous imprecation "God will give him blood to drink!" (2:8); the search for the deed that each side believes will give them legal rights to Waldo County in Maine—the likelihood that Hawthorne chose the name for his female protagonist for its linkages to the significance of land disrupts such a view. It is Hepzibah who may represent the female "oozy heart" (2:27) of the fraught, vexed thematic of land rights. Property, however, is not my focus in this chapter. Van Harn, *Lectionary Commentary*.
41. See, for example, Sobchack, *Carnal Thoughts*, 41.
42. Berger, *Ways of Seeing*, 51.
43. Ibid., 54.
44. Nina Baym makes this parallel in "The Heroine of *The House of the Seven Gables*," 609.
45. Doy, *Picturing the Self*, 52.
46. George Ripley's review of *The House of the Seven Gables* was originally published in *Harper's New Monthly Magazine* 2, no. 12 (May 1851): 855–56; and is collected in

Nathaniel Hawthorne: The Contemporary Reviews, edited by John L. Idol and Buford Jones. Ripley, who founded Brook Farm in West Roxbury, Massachusetts, the brief (1841-47) and unsuccessful attempt at founding a utopian community in which Hawthorne unhappily participated, lauded *The House of the Seven Gables*'s "exquisite beauty" (168).

47. VanDette, *Sibling Romance in American Fiction,* 5.
48. Clifford's manic joy over Judge Pyncheon's grisly death from seemingly natural yet suspect causes complicates the idea of his defenselessness.
49. Goddu, "Circulation of Women," 120-21.
50. Ibid., 125. Not all critics agree that the Hepzibah-Clifford relationship suggests incest. Nina Baym writes, "I believe that the very point of Hepzibah's devotion to her brother is the transcendence of mating: its focus on, literally, brotherly—or, better put, sisterly—love" (615). Baym, "Heroine," 615.
51. Freud, *Three Essays,* SE 7:145n1. Freud's theories of male homosexuality remain controversial.
52. Mitchell, *Siblings,* 59.
53. Ibid., 65.
54. For discussions of Hawthorne's relationship with Robert Manning, see Mellow, *Nathaniel Hawthorne in His Times,* 610-66; Wineapple, *Hawthorne,* 39-40.
55. For important related considerations of Ovid's and Milton's revisions of the Roman poet, see Kilgour, *Milton and the Metamorphosis of Ovid,* 186, 198, 214.
56. Lystra, *Searching the Heart,* 140, original emphases and punctuation.
57. Clearly, all of these matters were charged with horrific resonances in the slavery era—for example, the visual logic of the slave auction that displayed the sexualized bodies of the enslaved for mass consumption. See Collins, *Black Sexual Politics,* 55.
58. Castiglia, *Interior States,* 278; for a related discussion, see Kilcup, "'Ourself behind Ourself, Concealed.'"
59. *Oxford English Dictionary,* s.v. "Sybarite," accessed August 18, 2023, https://www.oed.com/search/dictionary/?scope=Entries&q=sybarite.
60. Irigaray, *This Sex Which Is Not One,* 142.
61. Ibid., 143.
62. "Hawthorne's work foregrounds what I call a traumatic narcissism, a simultaneous nostalgia for a lost period of perfection and a bitter recognition of the impossibility of returning to this vanished, mythic state. If the Freudian concept of repetition-compulsion has emerged as a key means of understanding the patterns of American masculinity from the early republic to the present, Hawthorne's thematic of traumatic narcissism is a key aspect of what is politically resistant in his treatment of masculinity. The desire to return—or to repeat—is met with a stringent, self-critical self-awareness. Hawthorne promotes neither narcissistic nor compulsive longings to return or to repeat; indeed, he critiques the motivations for either. At the same time, he treats these motivations with a certain degree of empathy." Greven, *Fragility of Manhood,* 30-31.

63. Milette Shamir has eloquently described privacy as central to romance. Shamir, *Inexpressible Privacy*, 149–51, 173.
64. Hawthorne's exquisite sense of the violability of all persons under human law, which Hepzibah and Clifford both "gnash" (*HSG*, 85) their teeth against, may or may not include an awareness of prison sodomy. For an excellent discussion of nineteenth-century understandings of prison sodomy, which in the few reported cases focused on the "boys [who were] prostituted to the lust of old convicts," see Freedman, *Redefining Rape*, 172.
65. See Kohut, *Restoration of the Self,* 4–15; Siegel, *Heinz Kohut and the Psychology of the Self,* 82.
66. For a related but also quite distinct discussion, see Castiglia, *Interior States,* 285. Although Castiglia's utopian reading concerning shame and Hawthorne contains considerable insight, it obscures the inexpressible anguish Hawthorne depicts as well as his characters' attempts to manage it.
67. Michaels, *Gold Standard,* 108.
68. See Rubin, "Traffic in Women," in particular 180–83; Sedgwick, *Between Men*, 25.
69. Hepzibah, who chronicles family histories, tells Phoebe "vaguely, and at great length," about Alice Pyncheon (*HSG*, 83). Significantly, Hepzibah mentions Alice before Holgrave does, recounting the young woman's sad demise and discussing her harpsichord, the melancholy strains of which haunt the Pyncheon home along with Alice's ghost. Hepzibah, when she was a girl, learned music but was not allowed to play Alice's harpsichord. Specifically, her father forbade her from doing so, and therefore she "could only play on [her] teacher's instrument" (*HSG*, 83). Given Isabel's associations with music in *Pierre,* especially her mysterious guitar, and these novels' overlapping incestuous and homoerotic themes, it is significant that Hepzibah is barred from touching Alice's musical instrument by paternal authority. Hepzibah's "vague" version of the tale echoes the plangent namelessness of homoerotic desire in the period.
70. See Froula, "When Eve Reads Milton"; Gallop, *Reading Lacan,* 85; Edelman, *Homographesis,* 101–6; Goldberg, *Seeds of Things,* 191, 202.
71. Freud, "On Narcissism."
72. Silverman, *Threshold of the Visible World,* 33.
73. Elsner, *Roman Eyes,* 151.

3. "TO VEIL FULL PURPOSE"

1. Even a 2017 issue of the *Nathaniel Hawthorne Review* on *Blithedale* and transatlanticism does not address Shakespeare's influence. See Demson and Pacheco, "Transatlanticism and *The Blithedale Romance.*"
2. Colacurcio avers that the focus on Puritan texts rather than more canonical literary texts as influences makes scholars anxious. He writes, "evidently our discomfort is most acute when a source or pretext turns out to be 'historical' rather than

'literary,' in the ordinary (but now embattled) sense of that word. Books which allude to Shakespeare or Milton may betray, thereby, their want of absolute originality, but clearly they have nothing to fear by way of generating reduction: the texts speak to each other, we tend to assume, and at a level of privilege so rare that no real violation can occur; and thus we spread out an order of literature that retains its purity, even if no individual literary text is ever completely 'originary.' But what if the pretext is not Milton but Cotton Mather, not Shakespeare but John Winthrop?" See Colacurcio, *Doctrine and Difference*, 206. With his usual force, Colacurcio makes a provocative point, but one might counter that (1) Americanist literary studies of the present are far likelier to examine interconnections between nineteenth-century American authors and their Puritan forebears than those with the canonical English literary tradition, and (2) Colacurcio's argument depends on a presumption that the study of Hawthorne and literary influence revolves around the obvious examples of Shakespeare and Milton, whereas an archival investigation reveals the surprising paucity of any such studies in the corpus of Hawthorne criticism.

3. Ronan Ludot-Vlasak has published a book on the reinvention of Shakespeare in antebellum literature, *La réinvention de Shakespeare sur la scène littéraire américaine-1798-1857 / The Reinvention of Shakespeare on the American Literary Scene (1798-1857)*.

4. Pfister provides a helpful reading in the section "The Death of Ophelia as the Birth of Medusa" in his study *The Production of Personal Life: Class, Gender, and the Psychological in Hawthorne's Fiction*, 87–103. Of most relevance to this discussion, Pfister demonstrates that Coverdale projects Ophelia-like qualities, which more properly define Priscilla, onto Zenobia (90).

5. Rees, "Shakespeare in *The Blithedale Romance*," 84.

6. Wilder, "Veiled Memory Traces," 244–45.

7. Luther S. Luedtke has established, in his *Nathaniel Hawthorne and the Romance of the Orient*, the crucial role that literary Orientalism had on Hawthorne's imagination, and travel literature as well. *Blithedale*'s first-person narrator Miles Coverdale was doubtlessly inspired by "a long caravan of real and legendary travelers from Sir John Mandeville to Lady Mary Wortley Montagu and The Howadji" who returned from "behind the veil of the East" to tell their tales (199). The nom de plume of *Blithedale*'s heroine Zenobia, an actress and feminist reformer, refers to "the Syrian queen who took the reigns [*sic*] of government into her own hands following the death of her husband Odenathus in A. D. 267 and determined to make Palmyra the mistress of the Roman Empire. Her occupation of Egypt and invasion of Asia Minor" was threatening enough to the Roman Empire for Aurelian to lay waste to the city of Palmyra. The image of the vanquished queen Zenobia, who "claimed descent from Cleopatra and the Macedonian kings of Egypt," being led back to Rome in chains proved an indelible one, evoked by Hawthorne when defeat crushes his heroine toward the end of the novel. William Ware's popular novel *Zenobia; or, the Fall of Palmyra*, which first appeared serially

in the *Knickerbocker* magazine in 1836-1837, no doubt influenced Hawthorne (208). Luedtke, *Romance of the Orient*.
8. Behdad, "Orientalist Desire," 28.
9. Charry, "'[T]he Beauteous Scarf,'" 113.
10. Smith, *Power of Women*, 20, 21, 24.
11. Gough, "'Her Filthy Feature Open Showne,'" 1.
12. The British Romantic Elizabeth Inchbald, whose 1808 edition of Shakespeare's plays was familiar to Hawthorne, makes these comments in her preface to *Much Ado:* "Claudio and Hero are said to be in love, but they say so little about it themselves, that no strong sympathy is created, either by their joys, or their sorrows, their expectations or disappointments;—though, such is the reverence for justice implanted in humankind, that every spectator feels a degree of delight in the final vindication of her innocence, and the confusion of her guilty accusers" (Inchbald, *British Theatre*, vol. 2, B2).
13. Franson, "Serpent-Driving Females."
14. Cox, *Much Ado*.
15. Rubin, "Traffic in Women," 157-210.
16. Cox, *Much Ado*, 6.
17. Wilder, "Veiled Memory Traces," 245.
18. Suzuki, "Gender," 134.
19. Scheff, "Gender Wars," 164.
20. Stanton, *The Woman's Bible*, 157-58.
21. For discussions of the ideology of the Cult of True Womanhood and white Northern middle-class antebellum femininity, see Welter, "The Cult of True Womanhood: 1820-1860"; Cott, *The Bonds of Womanhood* and her essay "Passionlessness"; Kraus, *A New Type of Womanhood;* Greven, *Gender Protest*. For a discussion of the ways that this ideal disenfranchised Black women, see Hazel Carby, *Reconstructing Womanhood*. For a discussion of nineteenth-century medical and health reformers' views of women's inherent licentiousness, see Greven, "Sex, the Body, and Health Reform."
22. Baym, "*Blithedale Romance*," 558.
23. Fleming, "Ladies' Shakespeare," 16.
24. Suzuki, "Gender," 130.
25. Ibid., 130.
26. Schwarz, *What You Will*, 13.
27. Ibid., 79.
28. John Cox notes that a "precarious balance between serious and comic" tones informs how most production of *Much Ado*'s handle the "kill Claudio" line. "Beatrice is taut with outrage at the atrocity suffered by Hero, yet the extravagance and surprise of her demand are potentially comic" (2). Cox, *Much Ado*.
29. Beatrice posed a problem to the nineteenth century, which generally idealized Shakespeare's portrayals of women while finding Beatrice "an embarrassment. She was an example of so much that the ideal nineteenth-century woman was

not: aggressive, insubordinate, verbal, sharp-tongued, scornful, bawdy, formidable." Victorian representations of Beatrice tended to "soften and refine" the role with an emphasis on "the character's capacity for feeling" (Cox 23, 35). Her Beatrice-like qualities make Zenobia's silence in the face of Hollingsworth's misogynistic tirade all the more striking, and informs her later, lengthy rebuke of him when he makes his rejection of her explicit. Cox, *Much Ado*.

30. The Arden edition's editor Claire McEachern parses "Count Comfit" as "Count Sweetmeat," "the sense of an insubstantial confection," implying that Beatrice finds "Claudio's loverly demeanor as cloying as Benedick once did."
31. Cox, *Much Ado*, 5.
32. For a discussion of Americanists' impugning of Hawthorne himself as a man of inaction in terms of both the political and personal, see Greven, "Masculinist Theory and Romantic Authorship," 971–87.
33. Hawthorne (15:136). See Robertson, *Inchbald*, 83.
34. Marguerite A. Tassi, in *Women and Revenge in Shakespeare*, emphasizes the significance of the theme of the female avenger in *Lear*: "In Cordelia lies the promise of a sanctified avenger." She adds, "Literary critics typically fail to see Goneril and Regan as dogged female avengers partly because Lear, if any character, articulates most vehemently the Senecan rhetoric of *furor* and vengefulness" (152). Tassi also disputes the idea of Cordelia as self-effacing; rather, her "actions, silence, and speech" are "self-defining," giving her the moral agency in her role as royal daughter to resist her "father's unjust demand to flatter him publicly" (154). Cordelia alone accords with Thomas Aquinas's stipulations for the "lawful or virtuous avenger" (165). Tassi, *Women and Revenge in Shakespeare*.
35. Schwarz, *What You Will*, 184.
36. Ibid., 185.
37. Ibid., 184. In *What You Will*, Schwarz admirably outlines misogyny's historical specificities and intricacies, emphasizing that women in Elizabethan England could use the very binding and restrictive logic of misogynistic gender roles to advance their own causes and senses of selfhood.
38. Simon, *Tragic Drama and the Family*, 105.
39. This is a prime example of the compassion that makes Zenobia so sympathetic a figure, as Elizabeth Dill persuasively demonstrates in her article "Angel of the House, Ghost of the Commune," which argues for the importance of reading Zenobia in terms of sentiment.
40. McEachern, "Fathering Herself," 271.
41. Ibid., 272.
42. Ibid., 272. Janet Adelman makes related points that will be addressed in chapter 4.
43. Ibid., 275.
44. Ibid., 276.
45. Ibid.
46. Ibid.

47. Ibid., 277.
48. Ibid., 278.
49. Given the critical importance of the role of incest in *The House of the Seven Gables* and *Pierre*, and in the Shakespearean and Miltonic sources they rework, we could productively consider the much-discussed role of incest in *Lear* and its impact on *Blithedale*. Maureen Quilligan, in her bracing study *Incest and Agency in Elizabeth's England*, discusses this thematic in *Lear* with particular insightfulness. Of special note, she argues that if we are to see Cordelia's invasion of Lear's homeland and her former one at the end of the play as an act of agency on Cordelia's part, "we must admit that her love aims at an incestuous end," i.e., her love for her father (235). While I do think that one could make a case for an incest theme in *Blithedale*, especially given Moodie's shadowy but likely participation in Priscilla's prostitution and in some ways his willingness to prostitute the beautiful Zenobia, I believe that this chapter's focuses on Hawthorne's reworking of Shakespeare's themes of misogyny and woman's veiled character, in all of the multivalent senses of veiled, place different emphases. Quilligan, *Incest and Agency*.
50. McEachern, "Fathering Herself," 284–85.
51. Skura, "Dragon Fathers and Unnatural Children," 121–22.
52. Ibid., 125.
53. For an analysis of the oedipal-narcissistic conflicts central to these tales, see Greven, *Fragility of Manhood*, 69–90.
54. Coverdale's indulgence in prurient fantasy about Zenobia's sexuality and his self-nurturing, self-protective tergiversations are on ample display in his bed-bound ruminations in chapter 6, "Coverdale's Sick-Chamber." He begins by speculating about "whether Zenobia had ever been married"; how "if the great event of a woman's existence had been consummated, the world knew nothing of it"; and "then, also, as anybody could observe, the freedom of her deportment ... was not exactly maidenlike." She was "a woman to whom wedlock had thrown wide the gates of mystery. Yet, sometimes, strove to be ashamed of these conjectures. I acknowledged it as a masculine grossness—a sin of wicked interpretation ... Still, it was of no avail to reason with myself ... 'Zenobia is a wife! Zenobia has lived, and loved! There is no folded petal, no latent dew-drop, in this perfectly developed rose!'" (46–47). Hawthorne offers a masterclass in self-aware misogyny here, a tour of a male mind seducing itself into frenzied contemplation of female sexual availability and possibility. For these reasons, it is dismaying to encounter David B. Diamond's consistent apologia for male characters such as Coverdale and Dimmesdale, even as Diamond sheds illuminating light on the sympathetically drawn poignancy of Hawthorne's female characters such as Zenobia. See Diamond, *Psychoanalytic Readings of Hawthorne's Romances*.
55. Adelman, *Suffocating Mothers*, 104.
56. Brook Farm, a utopian community pioneered by the Unitarian minister George Ripley and his wife Sophia, was established in West Roxbury, Massachusetts,

(near Boston) in 1841 and closed its ranks in 1847. Hawthorne was a founding member of the community but officially resigned himself from it in 1842.

57. See "Hester Is Burning: Desire and Gendered Grief in *The Scarlet Letter*" in Greven, *Gender Protest and Same-Sex Desire in Antebellum American Literature.*
58. Brodhead, "Veiled Ladies," 51.
59. Castronovo, *Necro Citizenship,* 121.
60. Ibid., 105.
61. Ibid., 106.
62. Ibid., 111.
63. I discuss this consistent critical framing of Hawthorne's seeming passivity and the inadequacy of his political thought in my essay "Masculinist Theory and Romantic Authorship, Or Hawthorne, Politics, Desire" (2008).
64. Castronovo, *Necro Citizenship,* 117.
65. From the rise of New Historicism in the late 1980s and to the contemporary pervasive emphasis on the historical and material conditions of literary production, often with a pronounced ideological bite to the analysis, Americanist literary criticism jettisons questions of aesthetics, beauty, and literary sensibility in favor of compiling the factual, locating a prized sense of certainty in the archive. To be clear, I am neither advocating a flight from the historical or the archival nor advocating less vigilance about the pernicious effects of many overarching ideological positions and their enforcement.
66. Pearce does not discuss the gender politics of the novel. Instead, he offers a myth-criticism approach typical of his era. He interprets Moodie as the "king-father retiring so that his surrogate may be tested" (15), and Hollingsworth, interestingly, as Oedipus, particularly "Oedipus at Colonnus," "sanctified, having absorbed Priscilla's goodness," and "an outcast and a dependent" (14). Pearce, "Hawthorne's Old Moodie," 11–15.
67. In light of the 2018 confirmation hearings for the Supreme Court nominee and later judge Brett Kavanaugh, the most discussed aspect of which was the testimony of Dr. Christine Blasey Ford that Kavanaugh had sexually assaulted her when they were teenagers, several commentators mentioned *Measure for Measure* as a relevant work.
68. Coronato, *Shakespeare, Caravaggio, and the Indistinct Regard,* 78.
69. Ibid., 81.
70. Gurr, "Hoods and Masks," 99.
71. Andrew Gurr observes, "In the final Act Mariana, standing in the public street with Isabella for her encounter with the returned Duke, wears the standard lady's black velvet mask to conceal her identity from Angelo" (100). The final scene of the play, which involves the Duke's proposals of marriage to Isabella, is marked by "a whole series of uncasings ... First Mariana uncases her face to show Angelo his mistake" (102). Then, "what Isabella wears for the final scene and its sequence of uncasings and for the Duke's final proposal of marriage to her is the visual crux

of the play. . . . Isabella must at the end receive the Duke's proposal of marriage in her colorful gentlewoman's dress and not, as so many productions have had it, in the humble dress of a votarist of St. Clare." Gurr, "Hoods and Masks," 103.
72. Garber, *Shakespeare After All,* 582.
73. Ibid., 583.
74. Heffernan, *Veiled Figures,* 41; Brooks quoted from *Body Works,* 12–13.
75. "The Blithedale characters are poised to embrace the very Catholic forms rejected by their Protestant-reformer forebears as the idolatry, superstition, and vanity of the 'Romish' church. We might even say that the Blithedale apostles are 'half' Catholic, a term Hawthorne used in 1859 to describe himself after his eighteen-month sojourn in France and Italy." Sweet, "'Man Needs It So,'" 200–201. For Sweet, the importance of this Catholicism theme, rendered by the Protestant Hawthorne conflictually but repeatedly, relates to "an underlying Calvinist understanding of the unmediated, solitary individual working out salvation alone" (210).
76. Gurr, "Hoods and Masks," 100.
77. For an elaboration on *Blithedale*'s Medusa motif, see Pfister, *Production of Personal Life,* 91–95. For a discussion of Hawthorne's uses of Medusa as a gendered symbol and overlaps with Freudian theory, see Greven, *Fragility of Manhood,* 141–79.

4. SURVIVORS AND STEPMOTHERS

1. My thanks to Christopher Ohge for this reminder.
2. Melville, *Correspondence,* 119. Quotes from Melville's *Correspondence* are from the Northwestern-Newberry edition, edited by Lynn Horth, vol. 14.
3. Arac, *Impure Worlds,* 6.
4. Ibid., 21–22.
5. Olsen-Smith, Norberg, and Marnon, *Melville's Marginalia Online.* https://melvillesmarginalia.org.
6. Ohge et al., "'At the Axis of Reality,'" 65.
7. Ohge, "Digital Text Analysis."
8. Grey, "Legacy of Britain," 253.
9. Olson, *Collected Prose,* 47.
10. Markels, *Melville and the Politics of Identity,* 39.
11. Melville, "Hawthorne and His Mosses," 244.
12. Ohge, "Digital Text Analysis."
13. Spanos, *Errant Art of Moby-Dick,* 167.
14. Ibid., 75.
15. Though I do not have the space to address these themes here, Hawthorne's work of the 1850s similarly incorporates themes from Shakespeare that inform his representation of women. Wyn Kelley has addressed the significance of the symbolic collaboration between Melville and Hawthorne in reference to the

"Agatha" letters Melville wrote to Hawthorne. Melville encouraged Hawthorne to write the real-life story of a woman whose bigamous husband left her stranded for seventeen continuous years and then for several years after that. Hawthorne declined and encouraged Melville to write the tale himself, which, according to Hershel Parker, he did in *The Isle of the Cross,* now lost. See Kelley, "Hawthorne and Melville in the Shoals." The Agatha collaboration, even if unrealized, attests to the preoccupation with the feminine, and especially with male treatment of women, usually quite negative, in American Romanticism.

16. Peretz, *Literature,* 43.
17. Hughes is one of the few critics to link Ishmael and Edgar. In a 1932 essay, "Melville and Shakespeare," he remarks, "Shakespeare's King Lear, being Lear and a tragic hero, must challenge and be broken by the forces of the universe. Edgar, on the other hand, whose perception of evil is as penetrating as Lear's, can endure. Edgar, like Ishmael in *Moby-Dick,* is a relativist in thought and action. He is not crushed when he discovers the lack of absolute justice, divine or human. He is able, in short, to make the best of a bad situation" (Hughes 466–67). Hughes goes on to compare Edgar favorably to Cordelia: "Unlike Cordelia, Edgar can produce illusion in his father and understands the inapplicability to human life of the absolute truth and justice Cordelia upholds. Edgar accepts human weakness and human interdependence." Hughes, "Melville and Shakespeare," 103–12.
18. Jonathan Harris opens his essay "Surviving Hamlet" thusly: "A specter is haunting *Hamlet* criticism. In recent years, scholars have become increasingly enthralled by Horatio. Of course, it's hard for academics not to see themselves reflected in him: 'Thou art a scholar—speak to it, Horatio,' Marcellus commands (1.1.40), and even though (or maybe because) Horatio's speech to the Ghost proves ineffective, many a Shakespearean who has endeavored to speak with the dead might hear herself hailed in Marcellus' remark. Yet I'd argue that the fascination with Horatio is not just because he is the *doppelgänger* of modern Shakespeareans. It's also because he seems to be the very opposite of the specter to whom he speaks: Horatio's special power, after all, is that he *survives.*" Harris, "Surviving Hamlet," 145–47.
19. Derrida, "Marx & Sons," 231.
20. Edelman, "Against Survival," 148.
21. Ibid., 149.
22. Ibid., 169.
23. Ibid.
24. I am thinking about studies such as Jack Halberstam's *The Queer Art of Failure* and Sara Ahmed's discussion in chapter 9, "Lesbian Feminism," in her *Living a Feminist Life,* in which Ahmed argues against resilience. There are alternative ways of considering survival and resilience from a queer perspective. In *Black Queer Ethics, Family, and Philosophical Imagination,* Thelathia Nikki Young stirringly argues for "black queer survival" as "brilliantly resistant and creatively resilient": "Our survival, and continued pursuit of survival strategies, resists the potential

dehumanizing death that the normative schema serves to our bodies and selves" (139).

Most germane to this chapter on Melville, Benjamin Bateman, writing in *The Modernist Art of Queer Survival* about Henry James, Oscar Wilde, E. M. Forster, and Willa Cather, seizes on survival as a distinctively queer mode: "Queer survival, for these authors... means not the extension of an individual life into the future but the distension of life, and feelings of aliveness, across personal, species, imperial, and generational boundaries." Reconceptualizing survival in this manner, Bateman also reconceptualizes the individual, which "loses its status as the privileged locus of drama, animation, intention, and uniqueness" while not disappearing altogether. The individual now "expands by losing and lives by dying. If what appears is a fragile vision of a collective and interanimate survival, then what disappears is the certainty of individual distinctness and possession, and the desirability of placing national, racial, sexual, and creaturely limits on what counts as (my and our) life" (4). Bateman continues, "Queer survival for this modernist ensemble is not only the survival of explicitly queer persons, ideas, and sensibilities. It is also a queer approach to survival in which weakness, frangibility, uncertainty, dispossession, senescence, indistinction, and even morbidity play a vital role" (5). Using Cather's famous story "Paul's Case," in which the protagonist, all but explicitly named homosexual, commits suicide at the end, Bateman writes that his "split and splintered body literalizes the dissipation for which he dies." He thereby emerges as a fitting model for Bateman's study, the characteristic embodiment of "an imaginative defense of dissipation's spreading pleasures and encompassing ethical possibilities" (5-6). Any reader familiar with the way that Americanists focusing on the nineteenth century approach historical queer issues will find this argument unsurprising, given the consistent emphases on challenging cultural norms and commonplaces in any shared understandings of gender and sexuality, eschewing traditional valuation, and championing marginalized modes such as "dissipation" here. Bateman demonstrates that critics of Modernism share these nineteenth-century Americanist perspectives. (Given Bateman's ensemble of four of the most forceful literary artists of Modernism from the fin de siècle to the early twentieth century, it is somewhat dismaying to encounter a valuation of them that places the passionate attempt to create art of lasting significance that characterized them all second to their availability for readings of a reappropriated dissipation.) Bateman, *Modernist Art of Queer Survival*.

25. Palfrey, *Poor Tom*, 96-97.
26. Bersani's theory of "self-shattering jouissance" is outlined in his 1995 study *Homos* (94-95). Using Jean Genet's novel *Pompes funèbres* (*Funeral Rites*, 1948) as a template, Bersani develops a theory of queer antirelationality in opposition to demands for "healthy," affirming forms of sexuality, always already understood as heterosexual. This argument is commonly referred to as the antisocial thesis. Bersani argues that gay and queer fantasy manifests an identification

with oppressive straight culture, as evinced by the gay male sexual ardor for fascist and other kinds of authoritarian masculinities. Taking Bersani's paradigms even further, Lee Edelman's *No Future* (2004) argues that the social and cultural demands of heterosexist society are organized around reproductive futurity, embodied by "the figure of the Child," who must be protected at all costs (11). Bersani, *Homos*.

27. Palfrey, *Poor Tom,* 97–98.
28. Janet Adelman, introduction to *Twentieth Century Interpretations of* King Lear (Englewood Cliffs, NJ, 1978), 8; Adelman quoted by McCoy, "'Look Upon Me, Sir,'" 47.
29. McCoy, "'Look Upon Me, Sir,'" 47.
30. Tromly, *Fathers and Sons in Shakespeare,* 203. Tromly refers to Edgar's description of a "fiend," one his father is now rid of (4.6.69–74): "The most obvious interpretation of these lines is the one Edgar provides: Gloucester's supposed fall represents a symbolic death in which his evil spirit is finally exorcised" (203). As Tromly observes, there are undeniable parallels between "Edgar's deception of the physically blind Gloucester" and, in the second act, "Edmund's deception of the spiritually blind Gloucester" (202). Edgar does eventually reveal himself to his father, as Edgar explains in the final scene (5.3.205–19) in what Tromly calls "an ornate speech," but this recognition scene occurs offstage, and its consequences "are ironic," given that the reconciliation between Edgar and his father "precipitates Gloucester's death from cardiac arrest."
31. R. A. Foakes in his introduction to the Arden edition of *King Lear* notes: "Some have seen here another act of gratuitous cruelty, as Edgar plays a rather unpleasant trick on his father ... Critics, directors and actors ... disagree as to whether this episode is tragic, grotesque, absurd or even farcical ... Many find especially troublesome in this scene the question why Edgar does not reveal himself to a father whom he has heard say, 'O dear son Edgar, / The food of thy abused father's wrath, / Might I but live to see thee in my touch, / I'd say I had eyes again'" (Foakes 62–63; the quoted lines are 4.1.23–26).
32. Bell, *Hawthorne's View of the Artist,* 145.
33. Ibid., 145.
34. Ibid., 150.
35. Ibid., 151.
36. Ibid., 152.
37. Ibid., 152.
38. Namwali Serpell's second novel, *The Furrows: An Elegy,* indirectly references Pip. The book's first-person narrator, Cassandra, known as Cee, recounts a harrowing tale, one that reverberates and takes new shape throughout the novel. The twelve-year-old Cee and her younger brother, Wayne, go the beach one day, wading into the water to swim as usual. But suddenly Wayne, on Cee's shoulders, disappears into the sea. Serpell has mentioned Melville as an intertext for her novel *The Old Drift* (2019). *The Furrows*'s image of a Black male child lost in

unfathomable watery depths who continues to haunt, to saturate, the present, seems to me an extraordinary meditation on the meanings of Melville's depiction of Pip as an inadvertent visionary after his near drowning. Her brilliant, dreamlike, disturbing novel joins the dazzling array of contemporary responses to Melville's novel highlighting its resonances for critical race and queer theory. For example, the artist Ellen Gallagher's painting *Bird in Hand* (2006) directly riffs on *Moby-Dick,* fusing Captain Ahab, the tap-dancing star Peg Leg Bates, and "the untold stories of those thrown overboard on slave ships from Cape Verde, where the artist's paternal family hail from." See Skye Sherwin, "Ellen Gallagher's *Bird in Hand:* Slave Ships and Sunken Treasure," *The Guardian,* April 19, 2019. The artist Wu Tsang produced two highly touted 2022 works, a silent, feature-length film adaptation, *Moby Dick; or, The Whale,* and a digital film focusing on undersea life, *Of Whales.* Wu Tsang's *Moby Dick; or, The Whale* depicts Ishmael and Queequeg as lovers.

39. Reno, *Ishmael Alone Survived,* 62.
40. Dryden, *Form of American Romance,* 88.
41. In one of the most penetrating points he makes in *The Western Canon,* Harold Bloom, characteristically reading Freud through Shakespeare, observes, "When [Shakespeare's] characters change, or will themselves to change on self-overhearing, they prophesy the psychoanalytic situation in which patients are compelled to overhear themselves in the context of their transferences to their analysts" (365). Self-overhearing Shakespearean characters like Edmund rarely heed their own insights into their potential for destructiveness.
42. McCoy, "'Look Upon Me, Sir,'" 47.
43. Ibid., 47, 49.
44. Ibid., 48.
45. Emily Mullin's essay "Macready's Triumph: The Restoration of *King Lear* to the British Stage" argues for the crucial historical importance of Macready's production. She writes, "On the evening of January 25, 1838, at the Covent Garden Theatre in London, the curtain opened on the first performance of *King Lear* to restore Shakespeare's original story to the stage. For the first time in over 150 years, under the influence of the tragedian and manager William Charles Macready, the play ended tragically, included Shakespeare's Fool, and refrained from interjecting a romance between Cordelia and Edgar. This performance represents an essential moment in the study of Shakespearean criticism and understanding: until 1838 it was believed that Lear could not be represented onstage, that 'classical' performances in general were unprofitable, and that the story of Lear, in particular, was distasteful to the public." Mullin, "Macready's Triumph," 2.
46. Stein, *Pusher and the Sufferer,* 12.
47. Glauco Cambon observes, "it should be possible to accept Ishmael as a persona of Melville, invisibly present through his narration when he ceases to be directly present in it; and that this persona, even as he ceases to have objective existence,

has dramatic existence as actor-spectator of a half-remembered, half-conjured action." Cambon, "Ishamel," 523.
48. Milder, *Exiled Royalties,* 77.
49. Stein, *Pusher and the Sufferer,* 12.
50. Reynolds, "Kings and Commoners," 56. Reynolds takes issue with Ray B. Browne's argument in *Melville's Drive to Humanism:* "Ishmael, the commonest of the commoners, has been apotheosized as a symbol of the rise of the common man" (56). He also challenges F. O. Matthiessen in *American Renaissance,* specifically his argument that in contrast to Ishmael, Ahab is a "fearful symbol of the self-enclosed individualism that, carried to its furthest extreme, brings disaster both upon itself and upon the group of which it is a part" (459). Reynolds argues that in echoing Matthiessen here, critics like Browne and Milton R. Sterne along with Matthiessen oversimplify the "complex sociopolitical views represented by" Ishmael and Ahab (102-3).
51. Reynolds continues: "Ishmael's high regard for the idea of man and his sympathy for the lowly and oppressed are opposed and balanced by a dislike for the mass of mankind and an admiration for the noble few, among whom he includes himself and his captain. Like Emerson who admitted, 'I like man, but not men,' Ishmael acknowledges the paradox in his own thinking when he says, 'take high abstracted man alone; and he seems a wonder, a grandeur, and a woe. But . . . take mankind in mass, and for the most part, they seem a mob of unnecessary duplicates.'" Reynolds, "Kings and Commoners," 102; last quoted passage from *MD,* 466.
52. Here is Reynolds's language in full: "Although Ishmael as common sailor participates in the democratic society of the forecastle, as narrator, he is more closely allied with the uncommon individual occupying the quarterdeck. While he perceives and abhors Ahab's ruthless manipulation and sacrifice of others, he also sees and admires his 'globular brain' and 'ponderous heart' (p. 71) and the heroic suffering and courage they inspire. Ishmael's admiration for Ahab's greatness, a greatness that ultimately lies in grief, is often explicit as when he explains that 'great hearts sometimes condense to one deep pang, the sum total of those shallow pains kindly diffused through feebler men's whole lives. And so, such hearts, though summary in each one suffering; still, if the gods decree it, in their life-time aggregate a whole age of woe, wholly made up of instantaneous intensities; for even in their pointless centres, those noble natures contain the entire circumferences of inferior souls' (p. 451). At other times, his admiration is implicit and informs his consistent presentation of Ahab as 'a mighty pageant creature, formed for noble tragedies' (p. 71) and accounts for the figurative superiority given him in the drama he acts out. In other words, while Ahab in his own right possesses an intellectual superiority accorded him by his rare mind, and tragic vision and a social superiority accorded him by his rank, authority, and power, Ishmael figuratively enhances the latter in tribute to the former. In the process,

however, he ironically undercuts his idealization of democracy by presenting the crew as the knights, squires, and commoners of a feudal hierarchy" (Reynolds, "Kings and Commoners," 108-9).
53. Palfrey, *Poor Tom,* 149. Palfrey quotes from *Simone Weil: An Anthology,* 1-2.
54. Palfrey, *Poor Tom,* 149-50.
55. Person, "Gender and Sexuality," 236.
56. Brodhead, "Trying All Things," 9; Bode, "'Suckled by the Sea,'" 181.
57. Whitman, *Complete Poetry and Collected Prose,* 210.
58. Bode, "'Suckled by the Sea,'" 183.
59. Adelman, *Suffocating Mothers,* 104. When it comes to considering Melville's reworking of *Lear,* the evidence provided by his marginalia is extremely useful but not always revealing or explanatory. For example, on the page in the Hilliard, Gray, and Company edition of Shakespeare that Melville avidly plunged into in 1849, Melville left unmarked these lines from *Lear* cited by Adelman: "O, how this mother swells up toward my heart / *Hysterica passio!* down, thou climbing sorrow, / Thy element's below!" (2.2.246-48). Instead, Melville marks on the same page lines from the Fool that include the warning to Kent, "Let go thy hold, when a great wheel runs down / a hill lest it break thy neck with following it" (2.2.261-62). I mention this to establish that, invaluable resource though it is, the new digital archive is not exhaustive of Melville's possible meanings. This is a point I am making more generally as well.
60. Adelman, *Suffocating Mothers,* 104.
61. In *Melville's Anatomies,* Samuel Otter analyzes the scene of Ishmael and Queequeg's bedded intimacy closely, but does not discuss the significant figure of Ishmael's stepmother: "Awakening with Queequeg's arm around him, Ishmael compares his sensations to those he had while a child when he dreamed of unsettling contact with a supernatural hand" (162). To my mind, we lose a portion of the episode's resonance if we do not connect the supernatural hand to the presiding stepmotherly presence. Christopher Looby, in his essay "Strange Sensations: Sex and Aesthetics in 'The Counterpane,'" calls our attention to the "counterpane," or bedspread, that covers the two men lying in bed together and that, at some point, Ishmael mistakes for Queequeg's arm: "When Ishmael does come to be able to tell the difference between Queequeg's arm and the counterpane it rests upon—when, we might say, aesthetics and erotics split apart in this Melvillean micro-drama of closely observed sensory experience—we then have an emblem of the historical separation of 'sexuality' from sensuality, an emblem of the invention of sexuality as a newly constructed (and constricted) domain of experience, one that can no longer be confused with the broader domain of aesthetic perception" (81-82). Looby notes Ishmael's narcissistic self-regard and the fetishistic aspects of the episode, and acknowledges the traumatic aspect of Ishmael's childhood memory, reawakened by Queequeg's arm across his body, of his stepmother sending him to bed without supper as punishment for bad behavior. Looby, however, insists that he wants to "resist oedipalizing the story" and

psychoanalytically interpreting Ishmael's "distinctly un-Oedipal experience with Queequeg" (79). In the effort to eschew or avoid psychoanalytic interpretations, Looby leaves the stepmother's presence unexamined. For an opposing response to Looby's reading in terms of historical representations of same-sex desire, see Greven, *Gender Protest* (32–34).

62. John Halverson observes, "As M. O. Percival has shown (*A Reading of Moby-Dick* [Chicago, 1950], pp. 97 ff.), Pip offers Ahab the way to love. Ahab knows his 'fiery father,' but 'my sweet mother, I know not. Oh cruel! what hast thou done with her?' As if in answer to Ahab's plea to the 'clear spirit' to 'come in thy lowest form of love,' Pip appears to show the way to the 'compassionate feminine.' But Ahab repeatedly admonishes Pip to stay below; he will not raise him up to the deck level as Ishmael did Queequeg. Ahab remains master to the end, and Pip laments, 'Oh, master! master! I am indeed downhearted when you walk over me'" (443). Halverson, "Shadow in *Moby-Dick*," 443.

63. Fiedler, *Love and Death*, 389.

64. See Hiram Pérez, *A Taste for Brown Bodies: Gay Modernity and Cosmopolitan Desire, Sexual Cultures* (2007) for a treatment of the politics of race in Melville's evocations of homoerotic desire, in *Billy Budd* especially.

65. Otter, *Melville's Anatomies*, 162.

66. In *Herman Melville: The Tragedy of Mind*, Sedgwick calls *Moby-Dick* the work where Melville "had full command of himself," and that we experience Melville's "compassion for man, 'the thing itself,' as *Lear* called Mad [Poor] Tom: 'thou art the thing itself; unaccommodated man is no more but such a bare, forked animal as thou art.' It is this compassion which is signalized by the rites and ties of friendship between Ishmael and Queequeg." This compassion gives "Ahab his poignant humanity" and, however "battered" and "ruined" a likeness, a likeness to Prometheus (186). Sedgwick unfavorably compares *Moby-Dick* to *Pierre*, which he views as lacking any compassion save for its hero.

67. Sten, *Sounding the Whale*, 80.

68. Ishmael shares Ahab's self-understanding of being tethered to the Fates. The first chapter is called "Loomings," of course. The Ishmael of the present declares the "invisible police officer of the Fates" responsible for his decision to embark on his fateful whaling voyage with Ahab, "part of the grand programme of Providence that was drawn up a long time ago" (*MD*, 7). He then shifts gears, describing the Fates through a theatrical metaphor and making them, rather than their law enforcement agent, responsible for Ishmael's decision to enlist on the *Pequod*: "Though I cannot tell why it was exactly that those stage managers, the Fates, put me down for this shabby part of a whaling voyage, when others were set down for magnificent parts in high tragedies, and short and easy parts in genteel comedies, and jolly parts in farces—though I cannot tell why this was exactly; yet, now that I recall all the circumstances, I think I can see a little into the springs and motives which being cunningly presented to me under various disguises, induced me to set about performing the part I did, besides cajoling me into the delusion

that it was a choice resulting from my own unbiased freewill and discriminating judgment" (7). When Ahab and his elite force of dark-skinned exotics create the weapon that will be used to slay the White Whale, Ahab performs a Satanic parody of baptism, bathing the weapon in the blood of Tastego, Queequeg, and Daggoo. The weapon consists of "pole, iron, and rope," and "like the Three Fates" remains "inseparable" (489–90).

In chapter 47, "The Mat-Maker," Ishmael once again contends with the Fates. Ishmael notes that he was the "attendant or page of Queequeg" as he created a sword-mat: "As I kept passing and repassing the filling or woof of marline between the long yarns of the warp, using my own hand for the shuttle, and as Queequeg, standing sideways, ever and anon slid his heavy oaken sword between the threads, and idly looking off upon the water, carelessly and unthinkingly drove home every yarn; I say so strange a dreaminess did there then reign all over the ship and all over the sea, only broken by the intermitting dull sound of the sword, that it seemed as if this were the Loom of Time, and I myself were a shuttle mechanically weaving and weaving away at the Fates. There lay the fixed threads of the warp subject to but one single, ever returning, unchanging vibration, and that vibration merely enough to admit of the crosswise interblending of other threads with its own. This warp seemed necessity; and here, thought I, with my own hand I ply my own shuttle and weave my own destiny into these unalterable threads" (*MD*, 214–15). And in the epilogue, Ishmael reveals that "I was he whom the Fates ordained to take the place of Ahab's bowsman," an event that leads to Ishmael's lone survival of the destruction of the *Pequod* and all of her crew (573).

Regarding Ishmael's self-study in "The Mat-Maker," Edgar Dryden observes, "Here Ishmael first considers the possibility of creating the pattern of his own life rather than giving himself up to the workings of the universal loom. With the 'ball of free will' in his hands, he refuses to allow the Fates to knit him into the design of their fabric. Instead he weaves 'away at the Fates,' thereby achieving 'the last featuring blow at events' (213). This initial experience, however, is only momentary, for he drops the ball of free will and is caught up again in the flow of experience as soon as the first whale is sighted." Dryden, *Form of American Romance*, 106–7.

69. "Despite the aporetic evidences of Melville's text... virtually all commentators on Melville's elusive novel... have been tempted by the annunciatory aura of the beginning into assuming that the mysterious universe his narrator inhabits could reveal its integral wholeness by readings its differential but finally related shadowy signatures... [Melville offers] subversion by mockery" of the Calvinistic teleological form of typical nineteenth-century narratives. Spanos, *Errant Art of Moby-Dick*, 88.

70. Adapted from Hornstein, Edel, and Frenz, *Reader's Companion to World Literature* (2002). For an extended reading of the relevance of the Fates to Melville's work in a Miltonic context, see Engel, *Early Modern Poetics*, 39–45.

71. Olsen-Smith, Norberg, and Marnon, "*King Lear*" (*Melville's Marginalia Online*, 7.085).

72. Buell, *Emerson*, 140. Fuller would read in her room while Emerson spent the day in his study, coming out in the evening for dinner and discussions with Fuller and his wife about his work. Fuller believed strongly in fate: "That Fuller's story seems like that of a Greek figure whose tragedy has been preordained by fate would not surprise this woman who, at age twenty-nine, had depicted herself as Oedipus" (Murray, *Margaret Fuller*, 5). In commenting on the same painting of the Fates, Hawthorne noted "the terrible, stern, passionless severity, neither loving nor hating us, that characterizes these ugly old women. If they were angry, or had the least spite against human kind, it would render them the more tolerable. They are a great work, containing and representing the very idea that makes a belief in fate such a cold torture to the human soul. God give me the sure belief in his Providence!" See Hawthorne, 14:306, 334. In reference to this passage, Barriss Mills, in his essay "Hawthorne and Puritanism," wrote, "Hawthorne obviously preferred God's Providence to Fate, but which he believed in is not entirely clear" (100).
73. For a discussion of the history of Fata Morgana sightings and their significance as supernatural and miraculous events, see Warner, *Phantasmagoria*, 95–103. Of particular interest is Warner's observation that, with the rise of scientific explanations for the causes of such mirages, the "battle against divinatory significance provided the impetus from which a modern idea of the subject, an idea of radical personal vision, issued forth to replace supernatural causation" (102–3).
74. Foakes, *Coleridge on Shakespeare*, 102.

5. "FALTERING IN THE FIGHT"

1. A great deal of the loss and the grief inherent in the Oedipus complex stems from the repudiation of homoerotic feelings of identification *and* desire that this stage of development demands, as Judith Butler has shown in her remarkable work on what she calls "the melancholia of gender identification." The grief that inheres within the formation of proper gender identity—produced by the Oedipus complex—stems from the loss of the prior homoerotic attachment the subject feels towards the same-sex parent before the complex ensues, an attachment that will be replaced by feelings of murderous rivalry and enmity for the opposite sex parent. The male subject in particular must repudiate this attachment in order properly to identify with the father, for the subject cannot identify with and desire the father at once. (Identification has been one of the chief points of queer theory reconsiderations of the Oedipus-complex.) Moreover, identification is only possible in the symbolic realm of language and law—the Father's realm—and *identification must happen.* While establishing his identification with the father that makes a complete break with prior homoerotic attachment, the male child also develops exogamous heterosexual desire, realizing that the mother is the father's property, the father's terrifying threat of castration more than enough motivation for the boy to accept that he must renounce his desire for his mother and turn his

attention to girls and women outside the family, while making this turn towards nonfamilial female objects a lifelong preoccupation. See Butler's chapter "Melancholy Gender / Refused Identification" in *The Psychic Life of Power* (132-50).

2. William Shakespeare, *The Tragedy of Hamlet, Prince of Denmark*, second quarto, published in 1604-5. All quotations from this work are from the Arden edition and are parenthetically documented in the main text.

3. Sigmund Freud, *The Interpretation of Dreams*, trans. James Strachey (New York: Science Editions, 1961). This edition reprints vols. 4 and 5 of the Strachey-edited *Standard Edition of the Complete Psychological Works of Sigmund Freud* (London: Hogarth Press / Institute of Psycho-Analysis, 1953). Though first published in 1900, Strachey notes this was one of the works Freud most "systematically" updated as it went through its series of editions (xii).

4. Ibid., 265.

5. Michael Silk speaks to the uncanny similarities between Sophocles's and Shakespeare's tragedies. If, for readers born in a post-Freudian age, *Oedipus* haunts *Hamlet* for us, Silk makes it very clear that Sophocles was not available to the Elizabethan dramatist as a source: "To all intents and purposes, Shakespeare and Greece constitute the twin independent peaks of tragedy, with all other versions looking back to one, or both of these. This is no new thought." Despite famously having "small Latin and less Greek," as Ben Jonson put it in a memorial tribute poem to Shakespeare, Shakespeare has come to occupy a place of "parity with the Greeks" (indeed, he well exceeds them in general critical reception), and now exerts "a multifarious interpretive pull over them: not affinity ... but a kind of reverse, Eliotian influence." Silk, "Shakespeare and Greek Tragedy," 246.

6. As Brian Arkins notes, "for the dramatists of the Renaissance in France, in Italy, and in England, Classical tragedy means the ten Latin plays of Seneca, not Aeschylus, Sophocles, and Euripides.... Indeed Francis Meres sees Shakespeare as a new Seneca..... Seneca was in the Elizabethan air. Between 1551 and 1563 Cambridge was very Senecan, with two performances of *The Trojan Women*, two performances of *Medea*, and one of *Oedipus*; a landmark was clearly the staging of *The Trojan Women*, one of Seneca's best plays, in 1551. Then the first English tragedy *Gorboduc*, performed in 1562, was clearly Romanizing and was praised by Sidney as 'climbing to the height of Seneca his style.' And, not least, *The Tenne Tragedies* of Seneca were translated into English by Jasper Heywood and others between 1559 and 1581, when they were published as a single book. These translations ... exercised a substantial influence on Elizabethan dramatists." Arkins, "Heavy Seneca," 2.

7. In Bloomian terms, Shakespeare has already anticipated psychoanalytic appropriations of his work and provided the psychoanalytic reading. An immediate objection to this Bloomian reading is that psychoanalysis inherits a long-standing intertextual debate between *Hamlet* and the Oedipus myth; by the time psychoanalytic theory catches up to both of its source texts, the intertextual discussion has already been long since established.

8. Arac, *Impure Worlds*, 6. In the Romantic era, Shakespeare assumed the God-like power of the Bible; his works and the Bible were both seen as "the expression of an incomparable inner power requiring endless exegesis" (15).
9. For an analysis of the thoroughgoing importance of incest to literary production and social arrangements in the early republic and the antebellum period, see Connolly, *Domestic Intimacies*. Connolly draws on Butler's theory of the "melancholia of gender identification," noting that the incest prohibition, rooted in the prior ban on homosexual desire for the same-sex parent, establishes heteronormativity as norm. As he notes, however pervasive incest discourse was, it remained silent on the subject of same-sex incest: "Every iteration of incest in nineteenth century America presumed, and in doing so produced, heterosexual subjects" (17). For a related discussion, see Jackson, *American Blood*, 70–71.
10. In book 2 of *The Aeneid*, Virgil's version of the scene places quite different emphases. After Pyrrhus (here called Neoptolemus) kills one of Priam's other sons before Priam's eyes, Priam rebukes Pyrrhus, reminding him that Achilles gave him back the body of his beloved son Hector after Achilles killed him, an act of mercy that Pyrrhus has now desecrated. While Virgil places Hecuba within this book's fraught action—she attempts to stop Priam from going into battle—she is neither present at this moment between Priam and Pyrrhus nor when Pyrrhus annihilates the old man. Ovid emphasizes the maternal foundation of Hecuba's grief and rage. In book 13 of *The Metamorphoses*, Hecuba chiefly grieves over the murder of her last remaining child, her son Polydorus, by the Thracian king, Polymestor. After viciously gouging out Polymestor's eyes, with the help of the other Trojan women, behaving in the manner of Maenads, the snarling elderly Hecuba transforms into a barking dog. Lina Perkins Wilder makes the very interesting point that Hecuba, in her role as avenger in certain "Classical texts, and indeed to some extent in Marlowe's *Dido*," "is Hamlet's double as well as Gertrude's," which is to say, "neither clearly a passive female rememberer nor an active female revenger." See Wilder, *Shakespeare's Memory Theatre*, 116–17.
11. In the Globe's original production of *Hamlet*, "it is likely that miniature portraits would have been used." Wilder, *Shakespeare's Memory Theatre*, 124.
12. For a discussion of this textual history and its interpretive possibilities, see Garber, *Shakespeare After All*, 14.
13. The soundest way of interpreting texts from a psychoanalytic perspective, to my mind, is a comparative approach. A method that compares the findings of each kind of reading—rather like Hamlet does with the images of Claudius and his dead father, albeit with an open-minded sense of inquiry, unlike the absolutism of foregone conclusions that motivates him here—can shed light on both ways of thinking.
14. Bellour and Penley, *Analysis of Film*, 259.
15. Lupton and Reinhard, *After Oedipus*, 108–9.
16. I admire Catherine Belsey's treatment of these themes; although I share her fascination with the proliferation of images of the Cain and Abel story in the early

modern era, I do not see the narrative of Cain and Abel as being more significant to the play than the Adam and Eve narrative, and with it the primal narrative of heterosexuality. Similarly, while her focus on the figure of Death here is revelatory, I would argue that the Eros side outweighs the Thanatos side of the play's chief themes. See chapter 5, "Sibling Rivalry: *Hamlet* and the First Murder," in Belsey, *Loss of Eden*, 129-75.

17. As Milton will later depict in *Paradise Lost,* Adam rebukes Eve as the Serpent herself:

> Out of my sight, thou Serpent, that name best
> Befits thee with him leagu'd, thy self as false
> And hateful; nothing wants, but that thy shape,
> Like his, and colour Serpentine may shew
> Thy inward fraud, to warn all Creatures from thee
> Henceforth; least that too heav'nly form, pretended
> To hellish falsehood, snare them. (10.867-73)

18. As he comes to the realization that the "play's the thing / Wherein I'll catch the conscience of the king" (2.2.561-62), realizing that he can use the Players' presence to his advantage, Hamlet crafts a plot that derives from his own unacknowledged phantasy of reunion with his parents' union: "I'll have these players / Play something like the murder of my father / Before mine uncle. I'll observe his looks. / I'll tent him to the quick. If 'a do blench, / I know my course" (1.2.550-54). If, as I have been suggesting, the murder scene of Old Hamlet is a type of the primal scene, it follows that Hamlet wishes to place Claudius in his witnessing-child position: he will "observe" as Claudius observes the scene of his own crime; he will penetrate Claudius with his looks as Claudius penetrated the supine body of his father; he will derive a sense of mastery from Claudius's fearful flinching, or "blenching." Claudius's crime, over which the corrupted body of Gertrude looms, coalesces into the primal crime of Adam and Eve's fall into sexual shame, the awareness of the carnal capacities of their bodies, grotesquely signaled by the putrefaction ("vile and loathsome crust"), once he is penetrated ("in the porches of my ears did pour / The leprous distilment"), of the murdered King's body (1.5.60ff).

19. *Hamlet* verges on criminalizing sex. While the criminality of sex will become increasingly associated with nonnormative practices such as homosexuality, incest, and pedophilia, a quite fundamental association between heterosexual sexual intercourse and crime, synthesized in the Genesis tradition of Adam and Eve, inheres within long-standing cultural understandings of sexual morality. Milton will take great pains to depict the prelapsarian sexual relations between Adam and Eve as rapturously erotic, but he takes equally great pains to depict their postlapsarian sex as rank, pornographic in its abasement, the wedded pair pawing at each other like meat. As in *Hamlet,* idealized and repugnant depictions

of heterosexual eros serve as complementary aspects of the same sexual narrative, one an impossible, intangible state of bliss, the other a sordid evocation of revulsion. In both versions, sex is either transcended or rendered loathsome; in either version, sex can occur only in ideologically motivated form, unable to exist within a continuum of human experience. In much the same manner, Hawthorne in *The Marble Faun* will also isolate sex in this way, making it indistinguishable from crime, making it, indeed, the first or primal crime.

20. Bloom, *Invention of the Human*, 517.
21. Parker, *Herman Melville*, 2:632.
22. Higgins and Parker in *Reading Melville's Pierre* note that the romance tradition frequently depicts "golden-haired, blue-eyed heroines as so rarefied or almost disembodied in their beauty that they seem angelic" (46).
23. All quotations from *Pierre* are from the Northwestern-Newberry Edition and will be noted parenthetically in the main text.
24. Speaking to this question, Charlene Avallone asks, "What's a feminist to do with Melville?" Avallone, "What's a Feminist to Do."
25. As mirrors for male vanity, women consolidate male power and authority over the female sex, what Judith Butler, in dialogue with the French feminist Luce Irigaray, describes as "a spiritualized and desexualized desire for the form or reflection of a masculine self in another," which produces the "fantastic logic whereby men beget other men, reproducing and mirroring themselves at the expense of women and of their own reproductive origin in women/mothers." Butler, "Desire," in Lentricchia and McLaughlin, *Critical Terms for Literary Study*, 375.
26. Mitchell, *Mad Men and Medusas*, 343–44.
27. In the early American republic, one's countenance revealed "a permanent, essential, and involuntary sense of character . . . that no amount of individual performance could obscure." A now commonplace maxim from this era began to define American social relations: "there is a face that you put on before the public, and there is a face that the public puts on you." Lukasik, *Discerning Characters*, 10.
28. For a discussion of the "anti-Romantic" implications of these portraits, see Bell, *Hawthorne's View of the Artist*, 87–90.
29. Readings of the paternal portraits in *Pierre* include Creech, *Closet Writing/Gay Reading*, 130–52; Brown, *Domestic Individualism*, 153–54, 162; Higgins and Parker, *Reading Melville's Pierre*, 68–69 (the authors do make note of *Pierre*'s overlaps in other contexts with *Hamlet* and other Shakespeare works); Lukasik, *Discerning Characters*, 186–230; Dinius, *Camera and the Press*, 86–125. None of these treatments, however, sharp as they are, explore *Hamlet* as intertexts for Pierre. Sacvan Bercovitch, who makes surprisingly cursory note of valences between both texts in *The Rites of Assent*, observes that Pierre consists of characteristics of "a variety of Shakespearean heroes, most notably (and self-consciously) Hamlet but also Macbeth, Romeo, Coriolanus, and even for a moment (in the dialogue with Isabel) King Lear and his Fool." Bercovitch, *Rites of Assent*, 263.
30. Creech, *Closet Writing/Gay Reading*, 130–31.

31. Fredricks, *Melville's Art of Democracy*, 96.
32. Melville "knew Horace Walpole's *The Mysterious Mother* (1768), which he darkly alluded to in *White-Jacket* as dealing with the theme of incest," and probably "Matthew Gregory Lewis's piece of pornographic cruelty" *The Monk* (1796). Parker, *Herman Melville*, 2:54.
33. Haggerty, *Queer Gothic*, 87–88.
34. Arac, *Impure Worlds*, 41–42.
35. Pierre is yet another representation of a recurring antebellum figure, the sexually inviolate male, volitionally cut off from heterosexuality and male homosociality. For a study of the inviolate male in antebellum American fiction, see Greven, *Men beyond Desire*.
36. I am joined by critics Paula Miner-Quinn, in her essay, "Pierre's Sexuality," Michael Paul Rogin in *Subversive Genealogy*, and the great Newton Arvin in his 1950 study *Melville* in viewing Pierre and Isabel's marriage as platonic. As Rogin outlines, Pierre's decision to marry Isabel expresses a desire to destroy the romantic image of the father and to replace him. But the taboo on incest prevents him from sexually consummating the relationship; "he can only masquerade as the romantic father. His father's romance, outside of marriage, produced a child. Pierre, masquerading as a husband, is celibate." In keeping with the Medusa motif in the novel, Pierre is "encased in stone" because he "can neither possess Isabel, nor free himself from her." Rogin, *Subversive Genealogy*, 171.

    R. Scott Kellner, in his essay "Sex, Toads, and Scorpions," argues that Pierre and Isabel do sexually consummate their marriage, but that for Melville, "Sex is man's downfall. Man 'stoops' to sex. Pierre insists 'I do not stoop to thee, nor thou to me; but we both reach up alike to a glorious ideal!' (p. 192). This is a vision he is not able to maintain. In the end, the chivalrous knight Pierre wishes both Lucy and Isabel dead. 'For ye two, my most undiluted prayer is now, that from your here unseen and frozen; chairs ye may never stir alive' (p. 358). He has been ruined by his conflicting feelings about sex and women." Kellner, "Sex, Toads, and Scorpions," 19.
37. Braun, *Rise and Fall of the Femme Fatale*, 62–63. Braun discusses the romanticized femme fatale and realist novels such as Thackeray's *Vanity Fair*.
38. Many scholars have located the basis for the idea that all sexuality is incestuous in Michel Foucault's argument that given the centrality, at once, of the family and sexuality to modernity, incest "occupies a central place; it is constantly being solicited and refused; it is an object of obsession and attraction, a dreadful place and an indispensable pivot." Foucault, *History of Sexuality*, 109. But the thematization of incest in works such as *Hamlet*, *Paradise Lost*, *The House of the Seven Gables*, and *Pierre* hardly make such expedient use of the trope. The undermining of traditional concepts of the family, sexuality, and the couple in these works, complexly and diversely coordinated, refuses any stable deployment of incest themes even if they constitute a through line in these works. Which is to say, incest works specifically in each work while also adding to each work's resistant treatment of

sexuality. Why Foucault's tightly rigid schemas have proven so indispensable a pivot to contemporary scholarship is fodder for a different discussion.
39. If Hamlet and Ophelia had a sexual relationship, it was perhaps not conducted in the soft-core porn manner that Kenneth Branagh depicts in flashback in his 1996 film version of the play, in which he cast himself in the titular role.
40. This portrait, beloved in the nineteenth century, also figures prominently in Hawthorne's last published novel, *The Marble Faun* (1860). Beatrice Cenci, whose mild expression in the portrait was interpreted by nineteenth-century artists as indicative of great reserves of grief and violation, killed her father, who forced her to have incestuous relations with him. Her fair complexion has a seraphic quality, a blondeness "vailed by funereally jetty hair," which materializes the symbolic "black crape of the two most horrible crimes (of one of which she is the object, and of the other the agent) possible to civilized humanity—incest and parricide" (351). For a discussion of the influence of Shelley's closet drama *The Cenci* on Melville, see Mathews, "Enigma of Beatrice Cenci."
41. Findlay, "Enriching Echoes," 985. Jonathan Bate notes, in *Shakespeare and Ovid*, the millennium-long tradition of suppressing the erotic character of Ovid's works in favor of reading them allegorically, morally, and didactically, and this has relevance to the story of the giants' battle against the gods: "Allegorical and biblical interpretations were set beside moral ones; thus the revolt of the giants against the Olympian gods was made to represent the building of the tower of Babel, but also the pride of any human who rebels against the authority of God" (Bate, *Shakespeare and Ovid*, 25-26).
42. R. Lewis, *Hamlet and the Vision of Darkness*, 89.
43. Burton, "Hamlet, Osric, and the Duel," 6.
44. Fredricks, *Melville's Art of Democracy*, 96.
45. Ibid., 346.
46. Welsh, *Hamlet in His Modern Guises*, 150. Welsh notes that Freudian interpreters eager to maintain the "primacy of the Oedipus complex... tend to regard the half sister as a displacement of the mother and generally assume that Melville's glances at the 'wisely hidden' significance of *Hamlet* or the 'the hopeless gloom of its interior meaning' confirms some such reading" (50). While Freud's readings of *Oedipus* and *Hamlet* inform my own, I do not view Isabel as a displacement of Mary Glendinning. That would suggest that something subterranean was at work in Melville's depiction of Pierre's relationship with his mother, but the author goes quite far in making the incestuous dimensions of the mother-son relationship palpable and nearly explicit.
47. Shelley, *Shelley's Poetry and Prose*, 503-4.
48. Mellor, *Romanticism and Gender*, 25-26.
49. Bruhm, *Reflecting Narcissus*, 21-22.
50. DeLamotte, *Perils of the Night*, 87.
51. Kelley, "*Pierre*'s Domestic Ambiguities," 109.
52. Wai Chee Dimock argues that the quest for knowledge conducted by so many in

the novel is ultimately a fruitless one, the enterprise revealing its own futility. The quest for knowledge reflects the nineteenth century's investments in individualism: "the obsessed drama that emerges from the book—the drama of wanting to know and the plight of being known—ultimately registers a horizontal phenomenon: the emergence, organization, and deployment of knowledge as a technology of control, a technology at once consonant with and intrinsic to the institution of individualism." Dimock, *Empire for Liberty*, 157.

6. "A JEWISH ASPECT"

1. Joyce Carol Oates, "'Othello' is a great enough work of dramatic art...," Twitter, December 26, 2017, 9:51 a.m. https://twitter.com/JoyceCarolOates/status/945668312171798530.
2. Ibid.
3. As Evan Carton writes in reference to Hawthorne's account of the Lord Mayor's banquet, we must not ignore the racism and the antisemitism that Hawthorne "shared with most white Christians of his day." But as Carton also notes, the "the point of quoting his essays, letters, and notebook entries about blacks and Jews is not to indulge in fruitless moral condemnation of the prejudices of the long dead; in this instance, Hawthorne's image of Philip Salomons provides additional insight into the social grounds and implications of the theme of fatality or determinacy in *The Marble Faun*." See Carton, *Marble Faun*, 119.
4. All quotations from Hawthorne's works are taken from *The Centenary Edition of the Works of Nathaniel Hawthorne* (Columbus: Ohio State University Press, 1962).
5. Bercovitch, "Miriam as Shylock," 386.
6. As Evan Carton writes, "Salomons's religion had made his political career a difficult one, but with the help of a prominent and well-connected family he overcame the stigma of his Jewishness and such early humiliations as having been removed from his seat in the House of Commons when, in the oath of office, he substituted the words 'so help me God' for 'on the true faith of a Christian.'" Carton, *Marble Faun*, 117.
7. While the use of ostensibly private materials such as journals, letters, and so forth for literary study is not without its complications, on several levels, it is also true that famous artists, especially writers, must always have a sense of public interest in the private material that they produce. It is very likely that Hawthorne would have had some awareness that his private writing might one day be made public; even the coy line about the Lord Mayor's wife never being able to read what he has written about her, and that Hawthorne can therefore write unfavorably about her with impunity, suggests a kind of subversive awareness of his own impropriety that Hawthorne may have hoped someone would notice. Moreover, Hawthorne's penchant for ransacking his notebooks for materials that he would

then rework in his fictions reinforces the sense of slippages between Hawthorne's fictional and private writing identities.
8. See Philip Rahv's classic 1941 essay "The Dark Lady of Salem" (362–81).
9. In the famous tale "My Kinsman, Major Molineux" (1832), the young protagonist Robin Molineaux is described in a manner that evokes the classical model in newly imagined form: "He was a youth of barely eighteen years, evidently country-bred.... He was clad in a coarse grey coat, well worn, but in excellent repair; his under garments were durably constructed of leather, and sat tight to a pair of serviceable and well-shaped limbs.... Brown, curly hair, well-shaped features, and bright, cheerful eyes, were nature's gifts, and worth all that art could have done for his adornment" (11:209). Though leather-clad, Robin's body suggests an athlete in classical marble: his limbs and his features are both strong and "well-shaped." Echoing the Narcissus myth, a ferryman transports the Narcissus-like Robin to the underworld, or the nighttime city in which he will seek out his ill-fated uncle. "Rappaccini's Daughter" (1844) makes its Hellenic typing of male beauty even more explicit (and all the more interesting for occurring within a story ostensibly about a young man's unbreakable fixation with a beautiful young woman). At "an impulsive movement of Giovanni," Beatrice "drew her eyes to the window. There she beheld the beautiful head of the young man—rather a Grecian than an Italian head, with fair, regular features, and a glistening of gold among his ringlets—gazing down upon her like a being that hovered in mid-air" (10:104). This description echoes an earlier reference to the Roman god of the seasons, Vertumnus (represented as a beautiful young male figure), who attempts to seduce the chaste Pomona in Ovid's *Metamorphoses*.
10. Lewes, "Shylock's Humanity," 66–67.
11. Nathans, *Hideous Characters and Beautiful Pagans*, 139.
12. "It is often said that Jessica's conversion is easier than Shylock's because she perforce lacks the defining bodily mark of Judaism," circumcision. "But in fact the play worries the issue of blood more worrisomely in her case... Jessica's escape is everywhere compromised by the limiting specifics of her father's blood." Adelman, *Blood Relations*, 70.
13. Bridge, *Personal Reflections of Nathaniel Hawthorne*, 4.
14. "Neither his beauty nor his improvised tales had anything to do with his sobriquet of 'Oberon,'" writes Bridge, including the detail of his friend's physical beguilements even if only to classify them as ungermane in this particular instance. Ibid., 56.
15. Gollin, *Prophetic Pictures*, 31.
16. See, especially, Potts, *Flesh and the Ideal;* Painter, *History of White People*. Painter has importantly reopened the discussion of the racist logic of Winckelmann's white aesthetic.
17. Brickhouse, *Transamerican Literary Relations*, 181.
18. Wineapple, *Hawthorne*, 99.

19. J. Hawthorne, *Nathaniel Hawthorne and His Wife,* 120–21.
20. Person, "Man for the Whole Country," 4.
21. Denisoff, "'Men of My Own Sex,'" 153.
22. Ibid., 153.
23. Mosse, *Image of Man,* 65.
24. Ibid., 65–66.
25. As Louis Harap explains, when Miriam encounters the Model in the Catacombs of Saint Callixtus in Rome, Hawthorne evokes the legend of Memmius, one figure within the cluster of Wandering Jew types. Memmius had spied on the Christians hiding in the catacombs and had rejected the opportunity to accept the cross and "the holy light of the soul." For this he was condemned to wander forever in the catacombs. When he was able to induce someone to guide him into the daylight, he would perpetrate some evil and then return to the catacombs. Manifesting another trait of the Wandering Jew—his knowledge of things long past—the "specter" offers to teach Miriam "a long lost, but invaluable secret of old Roman fresco-painting." Harap, *Image of the Jew,* 114.
26. Gaer, *Legend of the Wandering Jew,* 105, italics in the original.
27. Leschnitzer, "Wandering Jew," 228.
28. Ibid., 229.
29. Maccoby, "Wandering Jew as Sacred Executioner," 256.
30. Greenwald, "Hawthorne and Judaism," 134.
31. Ragussis, *Figures of Conversion,* 15.
32. Harap, *Image of the Jew,* 27–28.
33. Here is Hawthorne's language of the Fortunate Fall: "Sin has educated Donatello, and elevated him. Is sin, then,—which we deem such a dreadful blackness in the universe,—is it, like sorrow, merely an element of human education, through which we struggle to a higher and purer state than we could otherwise have attained? Did Adam fall, that we might ultimately rise to a far loftier paradise than this?" (356–57).
34. Duplessis, "Romantic Thralldom in H. D.," 406.
35. In one of Freud's more controversial readings, he argues in his paper "The Taboo of Virginity" that women often find themselves sexually enthralled by the men to whom they lose their virginity. "The expression 'sexual thralldom' was adopted by von Krafft-Ebing in 1892 to denote the fact that one person may develop an unusually high degree of dependence and helplessness towards another with whom he has a sexual relationship." As Freud continues, "some degree of sexual thralldom is indeed indispensable in maintaining civilized marriage and restraining the polygamous tendencies that threaten to undermine it, and in our social communities this factor is regularly taken into account." See Freud, "Taboo of Virginity," 71.
36. Milbank, "Victorian Gothic," 159.
37. See Michie, *Sororophobia*.
38. Budick, "Perplexity," 461.

39. Ibid., 249.
40. Robert Milder reads this moment as reflective of Hawthorne's highly specific uses of Catholicism. For Hawthorne, the Pantheon symbolizes a "transsectarian Christianity." Milder makes the debatable point that Hawthorne "praises Catholicism for being *Protestant*" (his emphasis). See Milder, *Hawthorne's Habitations*, 239.
41. Hawthorne allows us to understand that the adulterous Hester, so forcefully shamed and shunned—though also sought out, in some ways—by her Puritan community, manipulates her own mind. Hawthorne illuminates the extent to which Hester has absorbed and made a part of her own psychic consciousness the cultural messages of the scarlet letter: "Earlier in life, Hester had vainly imagined that she herself might be the destined prophetess, but had long since recognized the impossibility that any mission of divine and mysterious truth should be confided to a woman stained with sin, bowed down with shame, or even burdened with a life-long sorrow. The angel and the apostle of the coming revelation must be a woman, indeed, but lofty, pure, and beautiful; and wise, moreover, not through dusky grief, but the ethereal medium of joy; and showing how sacred love should make us happy, by the truest test of a life successful to such an end. [New paragraph] So said Hester Prynne, and glanced her sad eyes downward at the scarlet letter" (1:263–64).

    Critics have rarely taken notice of Hester's internalized misogyny—her absorption of the cultural standards that make her feel she is unworthy of "the coming revelation"; that she is, indeed, "stained with sin, bowed down with shame." It is not incidental that Hawthorne describes Hester's grief as "dusky," given the relevance of her situation—her public shaming and exposure to the visual ravishment of the crowd—to slavery. One of the chief themes to emerge in Hawthorne's work is the powerful linkage he establishes between sexual otherness and racial otherness. Ultimately, the most inescapable thralldom is the one that binds phobically marked subjects to the systems of prejudice that render them as such. The sinful, because sexual, woman, the racially or ethnically marked nonwhite subject, and the figures of the converted Jewish woman and man in Hawthorne's work emerge, finally, as symbols of the subject's thralldom to its own oppression, and the ways in which this oppression becomes an indelible, essential, inescapable facet of lived, psychic, and also social experience. None of this is to exculpate Hawthorne for his deep prejudices. But it is to point out he also wielded the ability to pierce the seemingly impenetrable logic of prejudice with the probing light of empathetic inquiry.
42. Bacon, *Philosophy of the Plays of Shakspere Unfolded*, 59.
43. Hawthorne narrates Bacon's thought process thusly when she verged on making her long-anticipated and vindicating discovery: "But, in this apparently prosperous state of things, her own convictions began to falter. A doubt stole into her mind whether she might not have mistaken the depository and mode of concealment of those historic treasures; and after once admitting the doubt, she

was afraid to hazard the shock of uplifting the stone and finding nothing. She examined the surface of the gravestone, and, endeavored, without stirring it, to estimate whether it were of such thickness as to be capable of containing the archives of the Elizabethan club. She went over anew the proofs, the clues, the enigmas, the pregnant sentences, which she had discovered in Bacon's letters and elsewhere, and now was frightened to perceive that they did not point so definitely to Shakspeare's tomb as she had heretofore supposed. There was an unmistakably distinct reference to a tomb, but it might be Bacon's, or Raleigh's, or Spenser's; and instead of the Old Player, as she profanely called him, it might be either of those three illustrious dead, poet, warrior, or statesman, whose ashes, in Westminster Abbey, or the Tower burial-ground, or wherever they sleep, it was her mission to disturb." Hawthorne, "Recollections of a Gifted Woman."

44. Shapiro, *Shakespeare and the Jews*, 130.
45. Hirschfeld, "'We All Expect a Gentle Answer,'" 62.
46. Ibid., 67.
47. Ibid., 70.
48. Gross, *Shylock Is Shakespeare*, 77.
49. Adelman, *Blood Relations*, 4.
50. In chapter 16, "A Moonlight Ramble," Miriam gazes into the water in the Fountain of Trevi. She hears footsteps of the two men who have followed her—Donatello and the Model: "Corinne, it will be remembered, knew Lord Nelvil [Oswald, Lord Nelvil in the novel] by the reflection of his face in the water. In Miriam's case, however, (owing to the agitation of the water, its transparency, and the angle at which she was compelled to lean over,) no reflected image appeared; nor, from the same causes, would it have been possible for the recognition between Corinne and her lover to take place" (146). Miriam sees neither man's face in the water. But she also does not see her *own*. As she exclaims, "three shadows! Three separate shadows, all so black and heavy that they sink in the water! There they lie on the bottom, as if all three were drowned together" (147).

It is significant that the image of Miriam and the two males whose fates are inextricably linked with her own is one of drowning. Which is to say, the image *itself* is drowned. The significance of Miriam's own image being drowned is that Hawthorne adds this dimension to the intertext of de Staël's novel, where Nelvil sees Corinne's reflected image in water. If we view Miriam as an authorial imago, we can understand this moment as indicative of the work of influence. When Hawthorne makes influence explicit, as he does here by citing *Corinne* directly, the narcissistic encounter in which author beholds self in the image of the predecessor goes awry. The connection shatters, and the intertextual image dissolves. The literality of the citation blocks the flow of influence.

My reading has overlaps but also points of disagreement with Katharine Rodier's. Rodier assesses Hawthorne's uses of Corinne as "less than precise," citing the Miriam-Fountain of Trevi moment as an example. Rodier, "Hawthorne and *The Marble Faun*," 240. Rodier offers excellent insights into *Corinne*, but she views Hawthorne's reworking of the text as violations of the original's integrity. Fealty to the source text, to my mind, is not necessary for intertextual relations generally. Instead, it is the opportunity for creative reimagination that is crucial. If Hawthorne does not seize that opportunity here, he registers the failure as a blow to Miriam's autonomy, the denial of her the right to the gaze.

EPILOGUE

1. David Damrosch explains hypercanonicity thusly in his essay "World Literature in a Postcanonical, Hypercanonical Age."
2. See McKivigan, Stauffer, and Levine's introduction to Douglass, *Heroic Slave*, xii.
3. Stauffer, "Interracial Friendship," 134-58.
4. Anderson, "Textual Reproductions of Frederick Douglass," 61.
5. Ibid., 62.
6. Gustafson, "Eloquent Shakespeare," 83.
7. Ibid., 85.
8. Ibid., 86, 88.
9. Maxwell and Rumbold, *Shakespeare and Quotation*, 9.
10. Anderson, "Textual Reproductions of Frederick Douglass," 64.
11. Ibid., 66.
12. Ibid., 81-82.
13. Briggs, "Frederick Douglass's Appropriation of Shakespeare," 36.
14. Ibid., 38.
15. Ibid., 41.
16. de Stefano, "*Persona Ficta:* Frederick Douglass," 777.
17. Ibid., 794.
18. Khan and Nathans, "Introduction," 20.
19. Ibid., 21.
20. Ibid., 18.
21. Douglass, *Autobiographies*, 305.
22. William Aldis Wright and William George Clark, editors of the 1872 Clarendon edition of *Hamlet*, note that in Alexander Pope's 1723 edition of the play, he corrected the original "hoops of steel" to "hooks of steel," the version that Douglass cites. The metaphor comes from an enemy's boarding of a ship, which they "hook" or "grapple." Wright and Clark, however, dispute this change: "Pope's reading makes the figure suggested by 'grapple' the very opposite of what Shakespeare intended: grappling with hooks is the act of an enemy and not of a friend" (137n63). While it is likely that Douglass used the language in the edition of the text he read, we do well to keep in mind Briggs's point that Douglass "often uses phrases from Shakespeare in ways that do not resonate with their original contexts" (36).
23. Lee, "Intertextuality," 330.

24. Ibid., 335–36.
25. See, for example, John Stauffer et al., *Picturing Frederick Douglass: An Illustrated Biography of the Nineteenth Century's Most Photographed American* (2015); Maurice O. Wallace, *Constructing the Black Masculine: Identity and Ideality in African American Men's Literature and Culture, 1775–1995* (2002); Maurice O. Wallace and Shawn Michelle Smith, eds., *Pictures and Progress: Early Photography and the Making of African American Identity* (2012); Ginger Hill, "'Rightly Viewed': Theorizations of Self in Frederick Douglass's Lectures on Pictures"; Laura Wexler, "'A More Perfect Likeness': Frederick Douglass and the Image of the Nation"; Ansgar Nünning and Kai Marcel Sicks, eds., *Turning Points: Concepts and Narratives of Change in Literature and Other Media* (2012); Julia Faisst, "Turning a Slave into a Freeman: Frederick Douglass, Photography and the Formation of African American Fiction."
26. Wexler, "'More Perfect Likeness,'" 19.
27. Ibid., 20–21.
28. Faisst, "Turning a Slave into a Freeman," 222–23. Faisst explains the distinctions between the positive "portrait" and the problematic "figure" genres of photography: "daguerreotypes were believed to allow glimpses into the hidden parts of character, the inner workings of one's soul. Favouring the portrait genre, in other words, meant favouring one's own status, which was derived from outward as much as inward appearances. In marked contrast, the gaze directed towards 'figure' scenes was innately patronising. Those images could not depict the 'essence of man' since slaves and other members of the lower classes had to lack any interiority to speak of. Thus, again, Washington's dark face-as-mask stresses the underbelly of daguerreotypy, the figure genre" (221).
29. Douglass, *Heroic Slave*, 7.
30. For an analysis of Jacksonian-era gender standards, see Greven, "Gender Roles," 146–56.
31. Bassard, *Transforming Scriptures*, 21–22.
32. Ibid., 21.
33. Exum, *Song of Songs*, 8, 22.
34. Nohrnberg, "Naming Milton's Eve," 6.
35. Ibid., 6.
36. Wilburn, *Preaching the Gospel of Black Revolt*, 157–58.
37. Ibid., 172; Machacek, *Milton and Homer*, 21.
38. Clark, "Milton's Conception of Samson," 92.

BIBLIOGRAPHY

Adelman, Janet. *Blood Relations: Christian and Jew in the Merchant of Venice*. Chicago, IL: University of Chicago Press, 2008.
———. *Suffocating Mothers: Fantasies of Maternal Origin in Shakespeare's Plays, Hamlet to the Tempest*. New York: Routledge, 1992.
Adler, Eric. *The Battle of the Classics: How a Nineteenth-Century Debate Can Save the Humanities Today*. New York: Oxford University Press, 2022.
Ahmed, Sara. *Living a Feminist Life*. Durham, NC: Duke University Press, 2017.
Ailwood, Sarah, and Melinda Harvey. "'Like a Thousand Reflections of My Own Hands in a Dark Mirror': Katherine Mansfield and Literary Influence." In *Katherine Mansfield and Literary Influence*, edited by Melinda Harvey and Sarah Ailwood, 1–18. Edinburgh: Edinburgh University Press, 2015.
Allen, Graham. *Intertextuality*. London: Routledge, 2000.
Alvarez, Al. *Where Did It All Go Right?* New York: A&C Black, 2012.
Anderegg, Michael A. *Lincoln and Shakespeare*. Lawrence: University Press of Kansas, 2015.
Anderson, Douglas. "The Textual Reproductions of Frederick Douglass." *Clio: A Journal of Literature, History and the Philosophy of History* 27, no. 1 (1997): 57–87.
Arac, Jonathan. *Impure Worlds: The Institution of Literature in the Age of the Novel*. New York: Fordham University Press, 2011.
Arkins, Brian. "Heavy Seneca: His Influence on Shakespeare's Tragedies." *Classics Ireland*, no. 2 (1995): 1–8.
Armstrong, Nancy, and Leonard Tennenhouse. "Recalling Cora: Family Resemblances in *The Last of the Mohicans*." *American Literary History* 28, no. 2 (2016): 223–45.
Artese, Charlotte. "'You Shall Not Know': Portia, Power and the Folktale Sources of *The Merchant of Venice*." *Shakespeare* 5, no. 4 (2009): 325–37.
Arvin, Newton. *Herman Melville*. New York: Sloane, 1950.
Avallone, Charlene. "What's a Feminist to Do with Melville? [panel abstract, presented at MLA, Kailua, HI, 2007]" *Leviathan: A Journal of Melville Studies* 10, no. 2 (2008): 117–18. https://doi.org/10.1111/j.1750-1849.2008.01272_1.x.
Bacon, Delia. *The Philosophy of the Plays of Shakspere Unfolded, with a Preface by Nathaniel Hawthorne* (1857). Cambridge: Cambridge University Press, 2018.
Baker, William, and Brian Vickers. *The Merchant of Venice*. London: Bloomsbury, 2005.

Barrow, Rosemary. "Narcissus and Echo." In *A Handbook to the Reception of Classical Mythology,* 299-310. Hoboken, NJ: John Wiley & Sons, 2017.

Barthes, Roland. *S/Z.* 1st American ed. New York: Hill and Wang, 1974.

Barthes, Roland, and Stephen Heath. *Image, Music, Text.* New York: Hill and Wang, 1977.

Bassard, Katherine Clay. *Transforming Scriptures: African American Women Writers and the Bible.* Athens: University of Georgia Press, 2010.

Bate, Jonathan. *Shakespeare and Ovid.* Oxford: Oxford University Press; New York: Clarendon Press, 1993.

Bateman, Benjamin. *The Modernist Art of Queer Survival.* New York: Oxford University Press, 2018.

Bauer, Dale M. *Nineteenth-Century American Women's Serial Novels.* Cambridge: Cambridge University Press, 2020.

Baym, Nina. "*The Blithedale Romance:* A Radical Reading." *Journal of English and Germanic Philology,* no. 67 (October 1968): 545-69.

———. "The Heroine of 'The House of the Seven Gables'; or, Who Killed Jaffrey Pyncheon?" *The New England Quarterly* 77, no. 4 (2004): 607-18.

———. "The Women of Cooper's Leatherstocking Tales." *American Quarterly* 23, no. 5 (1971): 696-709.

Behdad, Ali. "Orientalist Desire, Desire of the Orient." *French Forum* 15, no. 1 (1990): 37-51.

Bell, Millicent. *Hawthorne's View of the Artist.* Albany: State University of New York Press, 1962.

Bellour, Raymond, and Constance Penley. *The Analysis of Film.* Bloomington: Indiana University Press, 2000.

Belsey, Catherine. "Disrupting Sexual Difference: Meaning and Gender in the Comedies." In *Alternative Shakespeares,* edited by John Drakakis, 166-90. London: Routledge, 1985.

———. *Shakespeare and the Loss of Eden: The Construction of Family Values in Early Modern Culture.* Basingstoke: Macmillan, 1999.

Bensick, Carol Marie. *La Nouvelle Beatrice: Renaissance and Romance in "Rappaccini's Daughter."* New Brunswick, NJ: Rutgers University Press, 1985..

Bercovitch, Sacvan. "Miriam as Shylock: An Echo from Shakespeare in Hawthorne's Marble Faun." *Forum for Modern Language Studies* 5, no. 4 (1969): 385-87.

———. *The Puritan Origins of the American Self.* New Haven, CT: Yale University Press, 1975.

———. *The Rites of Assent: Transformations in the Symbolic Construction of America.* New York: Routledge, 1993.

Berger, John. *Ways of Seeing* (1972). New York: Penguin, 1990.

Bergland, Renée. "A Damned Mob of Corinnes: Nathaniel Hawthorne and the Daughters of de Staël." *Nathaniel Hawthorne Review* 42, no. 1 (2016): 95-119. https://doi.org/10.5325/nathhawtrevi.42.1.0095.

Bergland, Renée. "Emily Dickinson 'in the Other's Eyes—.'" *Women's Studies* 47, no. 3 (2018): 259-62. https://doi.org/10.1080/00497878.2018.1451171.

Bersani, Leo. "Foreword: *A World Elsewhere.*" In *The Culture of Redemption.* Cambridge, MA: Harvard University Press, 1990.
———. *Homos.* Cambridge, MA: Harvard University Press, 1996.
Bewley, Marius. *The Complex Fate* (1952). New York: Gordian Press, 1967.
Blake, William. *The Marriage of Heaven and Hell: In Full Color.* United Kingdom: Dover Publications, 1994.
Bloom, Harold. *The Anxiety of Influence: A Theory of Poetry* (1973). 2nd ed. New York: Oxford University Press, 1997.
———. *A Map of Misreading.* New York: Oxford University Press, 1975.
———. *Shakespeare: The Invention of the Human.* New York: Riverhead Books, 1998.
———. *The Western Canon: The Books and School of the Ages.* New York: Harcourt Brace, 1994.
Blum, Hester, ed. *Turns of Event: Nineteenth-Century American Literary Studies in Motion.* Philadelphia: University of Pennsylvania Press, 2016.
Bode, Rita. "'Suckled by the Sea:' The Maternal in *Moby-Dick.*" *Melville and Women*, edited by Elizabeth Schultz and Haskell Springer, 181-98. Kent, OH: Kent State University Press, 2006.
Braun, Heather. *The Rise and Fall of the Femme Fatale in British Literature, 1790-1910.* Madison, NJ: Fairleigh Dickinson University Press, 2012.
Brickhouse, Anna. *Transamerican Literary Relations and the Nineteenth-Century Public Sphere.* New York: Cambridge University Press, 2004.
Bridge, Horatio. *Personal Reflections of Nathaniel Hawthorne* (1893). Honolulu, HI: University Press of the Pacific, 2004.
Briggs, John C. "Frederick Douglass's Appropriation of Shakespeare." In *Weyward Macbeth*, edited by Scott L. Newstok and Ayanna Thompson, 35-44. Basingstoke: Palgrave Macmillan, 2010.
Bristol, Michael D. *Shakespeare's America, America's Shakespeare.* London: Routledge, 1990.
Brodhead, Richard H. *Cultures of Letters: Scenes of Reading and Writing in Nineteenth-Century America.* Chicago, IL: University of Chicago Press, 1993.
———. "Trying All Things: An Introduction to *Moby-Dick.*" In *New Essays on Moby-Dick,* edited by R. H. Broadhead, 1-21. Cambridge: Cambridge University Press, 1986.
Brown, Gillian. *Domestic Individualism: Imagining Self in Nineteenth-Century America.* Berkeley: University of California Press, 1990.
Brown, Harry J. *Injun Joe's Ghost: The Indian Mixed-Blood in American Writing.* Columbia: University of Missouri Press, 2004.
Browne, Ray B. *Melville's Drive to Humanism.* Lafayette, IN: Purdue University Studies, 1971.
Bruhm, Steven. *Reflecting Narcissus: A Queer Aesthetic.* Minneapolis: University of Minnesota Press, 2001.
Bryant, John. *Herman Melville: A Half Known Life.* 2 vols. United Kingdom: Wiley, 2021.

Budick, Emily Miller. "Perplexity, Sympathy, and the Question of the Human: A Reading of *The Marble Faun*." In *The Cambridge Companion to Nathaniel Hawthorne*, ed. Richard Millington, 230-50. New York: Cambridge University Press, 2004.

Buell, Lawrence. *Emerson*. New ed. Cambridge, MA: Harvard University Press, 2003.

Burt, John. "Prosperity and Tyranny in Lincoln's Lyceum Address." In *Abraham Lincoln and Liberal Democracy*, edited by Nicholas Buccola, 13-43. Lawrence: University Press of Kansas, 2016. http://www.jstor.org/stable/j.ctt1c6v8j8.5.

Burton, J. Anthony. "Hamlet, Osric, and the Duel." *Shakespeare Bulletin* 2, no. 10 (1984): 5-25. Accessed July 17, 2021. http://www.jstor.org.pallas2.tcl.sc.edu/stable/26352578.

Butler, Judith. *The Psychic Life of Power: Theories in Subjection*. Stanford, CA: Stanford University Press, 1997.

Callaghan, Dympna, ed. *A Feminist Companion to Shakespeare*. Malden, MA: Blackwell, 2000.

Cambon, Glauco. "Ishmael and the Problem of Formal Discontinuities in *Moby-Dick*." *Modern Language Notes* 76, no. 6 (June 1961): 516-23.

Carby, Hazel V. *Reconstructing Womanhood: The Emergence of the Afro-American Woman Novelist*. Oxford: Oxford University Press, 1987.

Carton, Evan. *The Marble Faun: Hawthorne's Transformations*. New York: Twayne, 1992.

Castiglia, Christopher, and Christopher Looby, eds. "'Come Again?': New Approaches to Sexuality in Nineteenth-Century U.S. Literature." *ESQ: A Journal of the American Renaissance* 55, nos. 3-4 (2009): 195-209.

Castiglia, Christopher. *Interior States: Institutional Consciousness and the Inner Life of Democracy in the Antebellum United States*. Durham, NC: Duke University Press, 2008.

———. *The Practices of Hope: Literary Criticism in Disenchanted Times*. New York: New York University Press, 2017.

Castronovo, Russ. *Necro Citizenship: Death, Eroticism, and the Public Sphere in the Nineteenth-Century United States*. Durham, NC: Duke University Press, 2001.

Chai, Leon. *The Romantic Foundations of the American Renaissance*. Ithaca, NY: Cornell University Press, 1987.

Charry, Brinda. "'[T]he Beauteous Scarf': Shakespeare and the 'Veil Question.'" *Shakespeare* 4, no. 2 (2008): 112-26.

Chase, Richard Volney. *The American Novel and Its Tradition*. Garden City, NY: Doubleday, 1957.

Christy, Arthur. *The Orient in American Transcendentalism: A Study of Emerson, Thoreau, and Alcott*. New York: Octagon Books, 1963.

Clark, Evert Mordecai. "Milton's Conception of Samson." *Studies in English*, no. 8 (1928): 88-99. http://www.jstor.org/stable/20779391.

Clayton, Jay, and Eric Rothstein. "Figures in the Corpus: Theories of Influence and Intertextuality." In *Influence and Intertextuality in Literary History*, edited by Clayton and Rothstein, 3-36. Madison: University of Wisconsin Press, 1991.

Coiro, Ann Baynes, and Thomas Fulton, eds. *Rethinking Historicism from Shakespeare to Milton*. Cambridge: Cambridge University Press, 2012.
Colacurcio, Michael J. *The Province of Piety: Moral History in Hawthorne's Early Tales*. Cambridge, MA: Harvard University Press, 1984.
———. *Doctrine and Difference: Essays in the Literature of New England*. Routledge, 1997.
———. *Hawthorne's Histories, Hawthorne's World: From Salem to Somewhere Else*. New York: Anthem Press, 2022.
Coleridge, Samuel Taylor. *Lectures and Notes on Shakspere and Other English Poets* [1811-1819]. Bohn's Standard Library. London: George Bell and Sons, 1883.
Conley, Lacey. "'League with You I Seek': Inspiration and Narrative Control in *Paradise Lost*." *The Journal of the Midwest Modern Language Association* 44, no. 1 (2011): 13-28. Accessed July 1, 2020. www.jstor.org/stable/23621442.
Connolly, Brian. *Domestic Intimacies: Incest and the Liberal Subject in Nineteenth-Century America*. Philadelphia: University of Pennsylvania Press, 2014.
Cooper, James Fenimore. *Notions of the Americans: Picked up by a Travelling Bachelor*. 2 vols. London: H. Colburn, 1828.
———. *Pages and Pictures from the Writings of James Fenimore Cooper, with Notes by Susan Fenimore Cooper*. New York: W. A. Townsend, 1861.
———. *The Last of the Mohicans: A Narrative of 1757* Cooper, James Fenimore, 1789-1851. Works (1980). Albany: State University of New York Press, 1983.
Cooper, James Fenimore, and James Franklin Beard. *The Deerslayer; or, The First War-Path*. Cooper, James Fenimore, 1789-1851. Works (1980). Albany: State University of New York Press, 1987.
Cooper, Susan Fenimore. "Introduction." *Pages and Pictures from the Writings of James Fenimore Cooper, with Notes by Susan Fenimore Cooper*. 13-22. W. A. Townsend, 1861.
Coronato, Rocco. *Shakespeare, Caravaggio, and the Indistinct Regard*. New York: Routledge, 2018.
Cott, Nancy F. *The Bonds of Womanhood: "Woman's Sphere" in New England, 1780-1835*. New Haven: Yale University Press, 1977.
———. "Passionlessness: An Interpretation of Victorian Sexual Ideology, 1790-1850," *Signs* 4, no. 2 (Winter 1978): 219-36.
Cox, John F., ed. *Much Ado about Nothing*. By William Shakespeare Cambridge: Cambridge University Press, 1997.
Creech, James. *Closet Writing/ Gay Reading: The Case of Melville's Pierre*. Chicago, IL: University of Chicago Press, 1993.
Damrosch, David. "World Literature in a Postcanonical, Hypercanonical Age." In *Comparative Literature in an Age of Globalization,* edited by Haun Saussy, 43-53. Baltimore, MD: Hopkins University Press, 2006.
Dekker, George. *James Fenimore Cooper the Novelist*. London: Routledge and Kegan Paul, 1967.
Dekker, George, and John P. McWilliams. *Fenimore Cooper—the Critical Heritage*. London: Routledge and Kegan Paul, 1973.

DeLamotte, Eugenia C. *Perils of the Night: A Feminist Study of Nineteenth-Century Gothic*. New York: Oxford University Press, 1990.

Demson, Michael, and Derek Pacheco, eds. "Introduction to Transatlanticism and *The Blithedale Romance*." *Nathaniel Hawthorne Review* 43, no. 1 (2017): 1–18.

Denisoff, Dennis. "'Men of My Own Sex': Genius, Sexuality, and George Du Maurier's Artists." In *Victorian Sexual Dissidence*, edited by Richard Dellamora, 147–69. Chicago, IL: University of Chicago Press, 1999.

De Rocher, Cecile Anne, ed. *Elizabeth Manning Hawthorne: A Life in Letters*. Tuscaloosa: University of Alabama Press, 2006.

Derrida, Jacques. "Marx & Sons." In *Ghostly Demarcations: A Symposium on Jacques Derrida's Specters of Marx*, edited by Michael Sprinker. London: Verso, 1999.

De Stefano, Jason. "*Persona Ficta*: Frederick Douglass." *ELH* 85, no. 3 (2018): 775–800. https://doi.org/10.1353/elh.2018.0028.

Diamond, David B. *Psychoanalytic Readings of Hawthorne's Romances: Narratives of Unconscious Crisis and Transformation*. New York: Routledge, 2023.

DiBattista, Maria. "Introduction. American Shakespeare." *Memoria di Shakespeare: A Journal of Shakespearean Studies*, no. 8 (August 2021): 7–33. https://doi.org/10.13133/2283-8759/17609.

Dill, Elizabeth. "Angel of the House, Ghost of the Commune: Zenobia as Sentimental Woman in *The Blithedale Romance*." *Nathaniel Hawthorne Review* 37, no. 1 (2011): 62–87.

Dimock, Wai Chee. *Empire for Liberty: Melville and the Poetics of Individualism*. Princeton, NJ: Princeton University Press, 1989.

———. *Through Other Continents: American Literature across Deep Time*. Princeton, NJ: Princeton University Press, 2008.

Dinius, Marcy J. *The Camera and the Press: American Visual and Print Culture in the Age of the Daguerreotype*. Philadelphia: University of Pennsylvania Press, 2012.

Dirda, Michael. "Stephen Greenblatt's *The Swerve*, Reviewed by Michael Dirda." *The Washington Post*, September 21, 2011. https://www.washingtonpost.com/entertainment/books/stephen-greenblatts-the-swerve-reviewed-by-michael-dirda/2011/09/20/gIQA8WmVmK_story.html.

Donahue, Agnes McNeill. *Hawthorne: Calvin's Ironic Stepchild*. Kent, OH: Kent State University Press, 1988.

Douglas-Fairhurst, Robert. *Victorian Afterlives: The Shaping of Influence in Nineteenth-Century Literature*. Oxford: Oxford University Press, 2002.

Douglass, Frederick. *Autobiographies*. New York: Library of America, 1994.

———. *The Heroic Slave: A Cultural and Critical Edition*, edited by John R. McKivigan, John Stauffer, and Robert Steven Levine. New Haven, CT: Yale University Press, 2015.

Doy, Gen. *Picturing the Self: Changing Views of the Subject in Visual Culture*. London: I. B. Tauris / Palgrave Macmillan, 2005.

Dryden, Edgar A. *The Form of American Romance*. Baltimore, MD: Johns Hopkins University Press, 1988.

Dyer, Gary. "Irresolute Ravishers and the Sexual Economy of Chivalry in the Romantic Novel." *Nineteenth-Century Literature* 55, no. 3 (2000): 340-68.
Duplessis, Rachel Blau. "Romantic Thralldom in H. D." In *Signets: Reading H. D.*, edited by Susan Stanford Friedman. Madison: Wisconsin University Press, 1990.
Edelman, Lee. "Against Survival: Queerness in a Time That's Out of Joint." *Shakespeare Quarterly* 62, no. 2 (2011):148-69.
———. *Bad Education: Why Queer Theory Teaches Us Nothing.* Durham, NC: Duke University Press, 2023.
———. *Homographesis: Essays in Gay Literary and Cultural Theory.* New York: Routledge, 1994.
Edwards, Mary K. Bercaw. *Melville's Sources.* Evanston, IL: Northwestern University Press, 1987.
Eliot, T. S. "Tradition and the Individual Talent." 1919. In *Selected Prose of T. S. Eliot*, edited by Frank Kermode, 37-44. London: Faber, 1975.
Ellison, Ralph. *The Collected Essays of Ralph Ellison*, edited by John F. Callahan. New York: Modern Library, 1995.
Elsner, Jaś. *Roman Eyes: Visuality and Subjectivity in Art and Text.* Princeton, NJ: Princeton University Press, 2007.
Engel, William E. *Early Modern Poetics in Melville and Poe: Memory, Melancholy, and the Emblematic Tradition.* Farnham: Ashgate, 2012.
Erkkila, Betsy. *Mixed Bloods and Other Crosses: Rethinking American Literature from the Revolution to the Culture Wars.* Philadelphia: University of Pennsylvania Press, 2005.
Erlich, Gloria C. *Family Themes and Hawthorne's Fiction: The Tenacious Web.* New Brunswick, NJ: Rutgers University Press, 1984.
Exum, J. Cheryl. *Song of Songs: A Commentary.* Louisville, KY: Presbyterian Publishing Corporation, 2005.
Faisst, Julia. "Turning a Slave into a Freeman: Frederick Douglass, Photography and the Formation of African American Fiction." In *Turning Points: Concepts and Narratives of Change in Literature and Other Media,* edited by Ansgar Nünning and Kai Marcel Sicks, 222-23. Berlin: De Gruyter, 2012.
Farrell, Grace. "Mourning in Poe's *Pym*." In *Poe's Pym: Critical Explorations,* edited by Richard Kopley, 107-16. Durham: Duke University Press, 1992.
Fiedler, Leslie A. *Love and Death in the American Novel.* Rev. ed. New York: Stein and Day, 1966.
Findlay, L. M. "Enriching Echoes: Hamlet and Orpheus." *MLN* 93, no. 5 (1978): 982-89. Accessed July 17, 2021. https://doi.org/10.2307/2906454.
Fleming, Juliet. "The Ladies' Shakespeare." In *A Feminist Companion to Shakespeare,* edited by Dympna Callaghan, 3-20. Chichester: John Wiley and Sons, 2016.
Flory, Wendy Stallard. "Melville and Isabel: The Author and the Woman Within in the 'Inside Narrative' of *Pierre*." In *Melville and Women,* edited by Elizabeth Schultz and Haskell Springer, 121-40. Kent, OH: Kent State University Press, 2006.

Foakes, R. A. *Coleridge on Shakespeare: The Text of the Lectures of 1811-12*. New York: Routledge, 2005.
Foucault, Michel. *The History of Sexuality, Vol. 1: An Introduction*. Translated by Robert Hurley. Vintage, 1990.
Franklin, Wayne. *James Fenimore Cooper: The Early Years*. New Haven, CT: Yale University Press, 2007.
———. *The New World of James Fenimore Cooper*. Chicago, IL: University of Chicago Press, 1982.
Frans Van Dijkhuizen, Jan. *Devil Theatre: Demonic Possession and Exorcism in English Renaissance Drama, 1558-1642*. Boydell and Brewer, 2007.
Franson, J. Karl. "The Serpent-Driving Females in Blake's *Comus* 4." *Blake: An Illustrated Quarterly* 12, no. 3. Accessed June 30, 2020. http://bq.blakearchive.org/12.3.franson.
Fredricks, Nancy. *Melville's Art of Democracy*. Athens: University of Georgia Press, 1995.
Freedman, Estelle B. *Redefining Rape: Sexual Violence in the Era of Suffrage and Segregation*. Cambridge, MA: Harvard University Press, 2013.
Freud, Sigmund. "Mourning and Melancholia." 1917. *Standard Edition* 14:239-58.
———. "On Narcissism: An Introduction." 1914. *Standard Edition* 14:88-89.
———. *The Standard Edition of the Complete Psychological Works of Sigmund Freud*. Translated by James Strachey. Edited by James Strachey, Anna Freud, Alix Strachey, and Alan Tyson. 24 volumes. London: Hogarth Press / Institute of Psycho-Analysis, 1953-74.
———. "The Taboo of Virginity." 1918. Translated by Joan Riviere. In *Sexuality and the Psychology of Love*, edited by Philip Rieff, 70-86. New York: Collier Books, 1963.
———. "The Theme of the Three Caskets." 1913. *Standard Edition* 12:291-301.
———. *Three Essays on the Theory of Sexuality*. 1905. *Standard Edition* 7:125-245.
Friedrich, Paul. *The Gita within Walden*. Albany: SUNY Press, 2008.
Froula, Christine. "When Eve Reads Milton: Undoing the Canonical Economy." *Critical Inquiry* 10, no. 2 (1983): 321-47.
Fry, Paul H. *Theory of Literature*. New Haven, CT: Yale University Press, 2012.
Fuller, Margaret Ossoli. *Art, Literature, and the Drama*. Edited by Arthur B. Fuller. New York: Tribune Association, 1869.
Fuller, Randall. *Emerson's Ghosts: Literature, Politics, and the Making of Americanists*. New York: Oxford University Press, 2007.
Gaer, Joseph. *The Legend of the Wandering Jew*. New York: Mentor Book, 1961.
Gallop, Jane. *Reading Lacan*. Ithaca, NY: Cornell University Press, 1985.
Garber, Marjorie. *The Muses on Their Lunch Hour*. New York: Fordham University Press, 2017.
———. *Shakespeare After All*. New York: Anchor, 2005.
Gardiner, W. H. "Cooper's Novels: *The Last of the Mohicans*." *North American. Review*, no. 23 (July. 1826), 150-97. Reprinted (in part) in Dekker and McWilliams, *Fenimore Cooper—the Critical Heritage*, 104-18.

Garfield, Deborah M., and Rafia Zafar. *Harriet Jacobs and Incidents in the Life of a Slave Girl: New Critical Essays.* Cambridge: Cambridge University Press, 1996.

Gates, W. B. "Cooper's Indebtedness to Shakespeare." *PMLA* 67, no. 5 (1952): 716-31. Accessed August 19, 2020. https://doi.org/10.2307/460023.

Gilbert, Sandra M., and Susan Gubar. *The Madwoman in the Attic: The Woman Writer and the Nineteenth-Century Literary Imagination.* New Haven, CT: Yale Nota Bene, 2000.

Glazener, Nancy. "Print Culture as an Archive of Dissent: Or, Delia Bacon and the Case of the Missing Hamlet," *American Literary History* 19, no. 2 (Summer 2007): 329-49. https://doi.org/10.1093/alh/ajm009.

Goddu, Teresa. "The Circulation of Women in *The House of the Seven Gables.*" *Studies in the Novel* 22, no. 1 (1991): 120-21.

Goldberg, Jonathan. *The Seeds of Things: Theorizing Sexuality and Materiality in Renaissance Representations.* New York: Fordham University Press, 2009.

Gollin, Rita K. *Prophetic Pictures: Nathaniel Hawthorne's Knowledge and Uses of the Visual Art.* Westport, CT: Greenwood Press, 1991.

Gough, Melinda J. "'Her Filthy Feature Open Showne' in Ariosto, Spenser, and 'Much Ado About Nothing.'" *Studies in English literature, 1500-1900* 39, no. 1 (1999): 41-67.

Grant, William E. "Hawthorne's *Hamlet:* The Archetypal Structure of *The Blithedale Romance.*" *Rocky Mountain Review of Language and Literature* 31, no. 1 (1977): 1-15.

Gravil, Richard. *Romantic Dialogues: Anglo-American Continuities, 1776-1862.* New York: St. Martin's Press, 2000.

Greenblatt, Stephen. *Learning to Curse: Essays in Early Modern Culture.* New York: Routledge, 2007.

———. *The Swerve: How the World Became Modern.* New York: W. W. Norton, 2011.

Greenslade, William. "Shakespeare and Politics." In *Shakespeare in the Nineteenth Century,* edited by Gail Marshall, 229-50. Cambridge: Cambridge University Press, 2012.

Greenwald, Elissa. "Hawthorne and Judaism: Otherness and Identity in 'The Marble Faun.'" *Studies in the Novel* 23, no. 1 (1991): 128-38.

Greven, David. *The Fragility of Manhood: Hawthorne, Freud, and the Politics of Gender.* Columbus: Ohio State University Press, 2012.

———. *Gender Protest and Same-Sex Desire in Antebellum American Literature: Margaret Fuller, Edgar Allan Poe, Nathaniel Hawthorne, and Herman Melville.* New York: Routledge, 2014.

———. "Gender Roles." In *Nathaniel Hawthorne in Context,* edited by Monika Elbert, 146-56. Cambridge: Cambridge University Press, 2018.

———. *Intimate Violence: Hitchcock, Sex, and Queer Theory.* New York: Oxford University Press, 2017.

———. "Masculinist Theory and Romantic Authorship, or Hawthorne, Politics, Desire." *New Literary History* 39, no. 4 (2008): 971-87.

———. *Men beyond Desire: Manhood, Sex, and Violence in American Literature.* New York: Palgrave Macmillan, 2005.

———. "'Nothing Could Stop It Now!': Tennessee Williams, *Suddenly Last Summer*, and the Intersections of Desire." In *The Cambridge Companion to Erotic Literature*, edited by Bradford K. Mudge, 224–37. Cambridge: Cambridge University Press, 2017.

———. "Sex, the Body, and Health Reform." In *A Companion to American Literature*, vol. 2, edited by Susan Belasco, Theresa Strouth Gaul, Linck C. Johnson, and Michael Soto, 202–21. Hoboken, NJ: Wiley Blackwell, 2020.

Grey, Robin. *The Complicity of Imagination: The American Renaissance, Contests of Authority, and Seventeenth-Century English Culture.* Cambridge: Cambridge University Press, 1997.

———. "The Legacy of Britain." In *Blackwell's Companion to Melville*, edited by Wyn Kelley, 249–65. London: Blackwell's, 2006.

———. *Melville and Milton: An Edition and Analysis of Melville's Annotations on Milton.* Pittsburgh, PA: Duquesne University Press, 2004.

Gross, Kenneth. *Shylock Is Shakespeare.* Chicago, IL: University of Chicago Press, 2006.

Guillén, Claudio. "The Aesthetics of Literary Influence." In *Influx: Essays on Literary Influence.* Edited by Ronald Primeau, 49–73. Port Washington, NY: Kennikat Press, 1977.

———. *Literature as System: Essays toward the Theory of Literary History.* Princeton, NJ: Princeton University Press, 1971.

Gurr, Andrew. "*Measure for Measure*'s Hoods and Masks: The Duke, Isabella, and Liberty." *English Literary Renaissance* 27, no. 1 (1997): 89–105.

Gustafson, Sandra. "Eloquent Shakespeare." In *Shakespearean Educations*, edited by Coppelia Kahn, Heather S. Nathans, and Mimi Godfrey, 71–94. Newark: University of Delaware Press, 2011.

———. *Imagining Deliberative Democracy in the Early American Republic.* Chicago, IL: University of Chicago Press, 2011.

Haggerty, George E. *Queer Gothic.* Urbana: University of Illinois Press, 2006.

Halberstam, Jack. *The Queer Art of Failure.* Durham, NC: Duke University Press, 2011.

Halverson, John. "The Shadow in *Moby-Dick*." *American Quarterly* 15, no. 3 (1963): 436–46.

Hammond, Paul. *Milton's Complex Words: Essays on the Conceptual Structure as Paradise Lost.* Oxford: Oxford University Press, 2018.

Harap, Louis. *The Image of the Jew in American Literature: From Early Republic to Mass Immigration.* Philadelphia, PA: Jewish Publication Society of America, 1974.

Harding, J. Gregory. "'Without Distinction of Sex, Rank, or Color': Cora Munro as Cooper's Ideal and the Moral Center in *The Last of the Mohicans*." In *James Fenimore Cooper: His Country and His Art: Papers from the 1999 Cooper Seminar No. 12*, edited by Hugh C. MacDougall, 36–40. Oneonta: State University of New York at Oneonta, 2000.

Harkins, Gillian. *Everybody's Family Romance: Reading Incest in Neoliberal America.* Minneapolis: University of Minnesota Press, 2009.
Harris, Jonathan Gil. "Surviving *Hamlet.*" *Shakespeare Quarterly* 62, no. 2 (Summer 2011): 145–47.
Harvey, Melinda, and Sarah Ailwood. *Katherine Mansfield and Literary Influence.* Edinburgh: Edinburgh University Press, 2015.
Hawthorne, Elizabeth Manning. *Elizabeth Manning Hawthorne: A Life in Letters.* Edited and with an introduction by Cecile Anne de Rocher. Tuscaloosa: University of Alabama Press, 2006.
Hawthorne, Julian. *Nathaniel Hawthorne and His Wife: A Biography.* Vol. 1. 1884. Boston, MA: Houghton Mifflin, 1982.
Hawthorne, Nathaniel. *"The Blithedale Romance" and "Fanshawe."* Edited by Fredson Bowers. Vol. 3 of *The Centenary Edition of the Works of Nathaniel Hawthorne,* edited by William Charvat, Roy Harvey Pearce, and Claude M. Simpson. Columbus: Ohio State University Press, 1964.
———. *The Consular Letters, 1853–1857.* Vol. 21, *Centenary Edition.* 1962.
———. *The French and Italian Notebooks.* Vol. 14, *Centenary Edition,* edited by Thomas Woodson. 1980.
———. *The House of the Seven Gables.* Vol. 2, *Centenary Edition,* edited by William Charvat, Roy Harvey Pearce, and Claude M. Simpson. 1965.
———. *The Marble Faun; or, The Romance of Monte Beni.* Vol. 4, *Centenary Edition,* edited by William Charvat, Roy Harvey Pearce, and Claude M. Simpson. 1968.
———. *Miscellaneous Prose and Poetry.* Vol. 23, *Centenary Edition,* 1962.
———. "Rappaccini's Daughter." Vol. 10, *Centenary Edition,* edited by Fredson Bowers, L. Neal Smith, John Manning, and J. Donald Crowley, 91–128.
———. "Recollections of a Gifted Woman." *The Atlantic,* January 1863 issue. Accessed July 19, 2022. https://www.theatlantic.com/magazine/archive/1863/01/recollections-of-a-gifted-woman/539787/.
Heffernan, Teresa. *Veiled Figures: Women, Modernity, and the Spectres of Orientalism.* Toronto: University of Toronto Press, 2016.
Hellman, Caroline Chamberlin. *Children of the Raven and the Whale: Visions and Revisions in American Literature.* Charlottesville: University of Virginia Press, 2019.
Hemphill, C. Dallett. *Siblings: Brothers and Sisters in American History.* New York: Oxford University Press, 2011.
Herbert, T. Walter. *Dearest Beloved: The Hawthornes and the Making of the Middle-Class Family.* Berkeley: University of California Press, 1993.
Hermerén, Göran. *Influence in Art and Literature.* Princeton, NJ: Princeton University Press, 1975.
Higgins, Brian, and Hershel Parker. *Reading Melville's Pierre; or, The Ambiguities.* Baton Rouge: Louisiana State University Press, 2006.
Hill Collins, Patricia. *Black Sexual Politics: African Americans, Gender, and the New Racism.* New York: Routledge, 2005.
Hill, Ginger. "'Rightly Viewed': Theorizations of Self in Frederick Douglass's Lectures

on Pictures." In *Pictures and Progress: Early Photography and the Making of African American Identity,* edited by Maurice O. Wallace and Shawn Michelle Smith, 41-82. Durham, NC: Duke University Press, 2012.

Hirschfeld, Heather. "'We All Expect a Gentle Answer, Jew': The Merchant of Venice and the Psychotheology of Conversion." *ELH* 73, no. 1 (2006): 61-81.

Hollander, John. *Melodious Guile: Fictive Pattern in Poetic Language.* New Haven, CT: Yale University Press, 1988.

Hopkins, David. "Dryden and the Garth-Tonson Metamorphoses." *Review of English Studies* 39, no. 153 (1988): 64-74. http://www.jstor.org/stable/515478.

Hornstein, Lillian Herlands, ed. *The Reader's Companion to World Literature.* Rev. 2nd ed. Edited by Lillian Herlands Hornstein, Leon Edel and Horst Frenz. New York: Signet Classics, 2002.

Hughes, Raymond G. "Melville and Shakespeare." *The Shakespeare Association Bulletin* 7, no. 3 (1932): 103-12.

Hurh, Paul. "The Sound of Incest: Sympathetic Resonance in Melville's Pierre." *Novel* 44, no. 2 (2011): 249-67.

Hutcheon, Linda. "Literary Borrowing . . . and Stealing: Plagiarism, Sources, Influences, and Intertexts." *ESC: English Studies in Canada* 12, no. 2 (1986): 229-39. https://doi.org/10.1353/esc.1986.0020.

Hutchings, Kevin, and Julia M. Wright. *Transatlantic Literary Exchanges, 1790-1870: Gender, Race, and Nation.* Farnham: Ashgate, 2011.

Idol, John L., and Buford Jones. *Nathaniel Hawthorne: The Contemporary Reviews.* Cambridge: Cambridge University Press, 1994.

Inchbald, Elizabeth. *The British Theatre; or, A Collection of Plays.* Hildesheim, NY: Olms, 1970.

Irigaray, Luce. *This Sex Which Is Not One.* Ithaca, NY: Cornell University Press, 1985.

Jackson, Holly. *American Blood: The Ends of the Family in American Literature, 1850-1900.* New York: Oxford University Press, 2014.

Juvan, Marko. *History and Poetics of Intertextuality.* Translated by Timothy Pogačar. West Lafayette, IN: Purdue University Press, 2008.

Kahn, Coppélia, Heather S. Nathans, and Mimi Godfrey. *Shakespearean Educations: Power, Citizenship, and Performance.* Newark: University of Delaware Press, 2011.

Kahn, Coppélia and Heather S. Nathans. "Introduction." *Shakespearean Educations: Power, Citizenship, and Performance,* 13-29. Newark: University of Delaware Press, 2011.

Kelley, Wyn. "Hawthorne and Melville in the Shoals: 'Agatha,' the Trials of Authorship, and the Dream of Collaboration." In *Hawthorne and Melville: Writing A Relationship,* edited by Jana Argersinger and Leland S. Person. Athens: University of Georgia Press, 2008.

———. "Pierre's Domestic Ambiguities." In *The Cambridge Companion to Herman Melville,* edited by Robert S. Levine, 99-113. New York: Cambridge University Press, 1998.

Kellner, R. Scott. "Sex, Toads, and Scorpions: A Study of the Psychological Themes in Melville's Pierre." *Arizona Quarterly: A Journal Of American Literature, Culture, And Theory*, no. 31 (1975): 5-20.
Kennedy, J. Gerald, and Leland S. Person. 2014. *The Oxford History of the Novel in English: The American Novel to 1870.* Vol. 5. Oxford: Oxford University Press.
Kesselring, Marion Louise. *Hawthorne's Reading, 1828-1850: A Transcription and Identification of Titles Recorded in the Charge-Books of the Salem Athenaeum.* New York: New York Public Library, 1949.
Kesterson, David B. "Milton's Satan and Cooper's Demonic Chieftains." *The South Central Bulletin* 29, no. 4 (1969): 138-42.
Kilcup, Karen. "'Ourself behind Ourself, Concealed': The Homoerotics of Reading *The Scarlet Letter.*" *ESQ: A Journal of the American Renaissance* 42, no. 1 (1996): 1-28.
Kilgour, Maggie. *Milton and the Metamorphosis of Ovid.* Oxford: Oxford University Press, 2012.
Klein, Melanie. *Envy and Gratitude.* London: Tavistock, 1957.
Kofman, Sarah. *The Enigma of Woman: Woman in Freud's Writings.* Ithaca, NY: Cornell University Press, 1985.
Kohut, Heinz. *The Restoration of the Self.* Chicago, IL: University of Chicago Press, 2009.
Kolich, Augustus M. "Miriam and the Conversion of the Jews in Nathaniel Hawthorne's 'The Marble Faun.'" *Studies in the Novel* 33, no. 4 (2001): 430-43.
Kristal, Efrain. "The Circulation of Resentment in *The Merchant of Venice*: A Commentary Inspired by Peter Sloterdijk." In *The Polemics of Ressentiment: Variations on Nietzsche*, edited by Sjoerd van Tuinen, 227-41. London: Bloomsbury Academic, 2018.
Kristeva, Julia. *Desire in Language: A Semiotic Approach to Literature and Art.* New York: Columbia University Press, 1980.
———. *Powers of Horror. An Essay on Abjection.* New York: Columbia University Pres, 1982.
———. "Word, Dialogue, and Novel." In *Desire in Language: A Semiotic Approach to Literature and Art*, 52-80. New York: Columbia University Press, 1980.
Kraus, Natasha Kirsten. *A New Type of Womanhood: Discursive Politics and Social Change in Antebellum America.* Durham, NC: Duke University Press, 2008.
Lacan, Jacques. *Écrits: A Selection.* Translated by Alan Sheridan. New York: Norton, 1977.
———. *Freud's Papers on Technique 1953-1954. The Seminar of Jacques Lacan, Book 1.* Translated by John Forrester. Edited by Jacques-Alain Miller. New York: Norton, 1991.
Lathrop, George Parsons. *A Study of Hawthorne.* Boston: James R. Osgood and Co., 1876.
Lavery, Grace. "Trans Realism, Psychoanalytic Practice, and the Rhetoric of Technique." *Critical Inquiry* 46, no. 4 (Summer 2020): 719-44.

Lee, Julia. "Intertextuality." In *Frederick Douglass in Context,* edited by M. Roy, 329-40. Cambridge: Cambridge University Press, 2021. https://doi.org/10.1017/9781108778688.033.

Lefcowitz, Allan, and Barbara Lefcowitz. "Some Rents in the Veil: New Light on Priscilla and Zenobia in *The Blithedale Romance.*" *Nineteenth-Century Fiction* 21, no. 3 (1966): 263-75. https://doi.org/10.2307/2932589.

Lentricchia, Frank, and Thomas McLaughlin. *Critical Terms for Literary Study.* Chicago, IL: Chicago University Press, 1995.

Leschnitzer, Adolf F. "The Wandering Jew: The Alienation of the Jewish Image in the Christian Consciousness." In *The Wandering Jew: Essays in the Interpretation of a Christian Legend,* edited by Galit Hasan-Rokem and Alan Dundes, 227-36. Bloomington: Indiana University Press, 1986.

Levine, Robert S. *Race, Transnationalism, and Nineteenth-Century American Literary Studies.* Cambridge: Cambridge University Press. 2018.

———. *The Lives of Frederick Douglass.* Cambridge, MA: Harvard University Press, 2016.

Lewes, George Henry. "Shylock's Humanity." In *The Merchant of Venice: Shakespeare, The Critical Tradition,* edited by William Baker and Brian Vickers, 65-67. London: Bloomsbury, 2005.

Lewis, Ffrangcon. "Women, Death and Theatricality in *The Blithedale Romance.*" *The Journal of American Studies* 26, no. 1 (1992): 75-94.

Lewis, Rhodri. *Hamlet and the Vision of Darkness.* Princeton, NJ: Princeton University Press, 2017.

Lewis, R. W. B. *The American Adam: Innocence, Tragedy, and Tradition in Nineteenth-Century.* Chicago, IL: University of Chicago Press, 1959.

Lifton, Robert Jay. *Death in Life: Survivors of Hiroshima.* New York: Random House, 1967.

Long Hoeveler, Diane. "Beatrice Cenci in Hawthorne, Melville and her Atlantic-Rim Contexts." *Romanticism on the Net,* nos. 38-39 (2005).

Lilley, James D. *Common Things: Romance and the Aesthetics of Belonging in Atlantic Modernity.* New York: Temple University Press, 2013.

Looby, Christopher. "Strange Sensations: Sex and Aesthetics in 'The Counterpane.'" In *Melville and Aesthetics,* edited by Geoffrey Sanborn and Samuel Otter, 65-84. New York: Palgrave Macmillan, 2011.

Love, Heather. *Feeling Backward: Loss and the Politics of Queer History.* Cambridge, MA: Harvard University Press, 2007.

Low, Lisa Elaine, and Anthony John Harding. *Milton, the Metaphysicals, and Romanticism.* Cambridge: Cambridge University Press, 1994.

Luciano, Dana. *Arranging Grief: Sacred Time and the Body in Nineteenth-Century America.* New York: New York University Press, 2007.

Luciano, Dana, and Ivy Wilson. *Unsettled States. America and the Long 19th Century.* New York: New York University Press, 2014.

Ludot-Vlasak, Ronan. "Cartographies de l'imaginaire: La subversion du discours scientifique dans l'écriture Melvillienne." In *Discours et objets scientifiques: Dans l'imaginaire Américain eu xixe siècle,* Ronan Ludot-Vlasak and Claire Maniez, 113–31. Grenoble: ELLUG, 2010.

———. "Defamiliarising the Bard: The Resurgence of Shakespeare in *Moby-Dick /* Transactions en eaux troubles: Résurgence de la voix Shakespearienne dans *Moby-Dick.*" *Revue LISA/ LISA E-Journal,* vol. 7, no. 2 (2009): 104–16.

———. "Displacing Origin: Melville's Intertextual Veerings in *The Confidence-Man; His Masquerade,*" *Leviathan: A Journal of Melville Studies,* no. 1 (2022): 53–69.

———. "L'intertextualité à l'épreuve du tournant spatial: perspectives transdisciplinaires." In *Espaciaildades: Revisões do espaço na literatura,* edited by Ana Paula Coutinho, Gonçalo Vilas-Boas, Jorge Bastos Da Silva, Maria de Fátima Outeirinho, and Maria Hermínia Amado Laurel, 161–80. Porto: Instituto de Literatura Comparada Margarida Losa (FLUP) e Edições Afrontamento, 2019.

———. *La réinvention de Shakespeare sur la scène littéraire Américaine–1798-1857 / The reinvention of Shakespeare on the American literary scene (1798-1857).* Lyon: Presses Universitaires de Lyon; Grenoble: ELLUG, 2013.

———. "Le Théâtre de *Pierre:* Espace urbain et (inter)textualité dans *Pierre, Ou Les Ambiguïtés.*" *Anglophonia: French Journal of English Studies,* no. 25 (2009): 39–50.

Ludot-Vlasak, Ronan, Édouard Marsoin, and Cécile Roudeau. "Melville's Veerings." *Leviathan: A Journal of Melville Studies* 24, no. 1 (March 2022): 24–28.

Lueck, Beth Lynne, Brigitte Bailey, and Lucinda L. Damon-Bach. *Transatlantic Women: Nineteenth-Century American Women Writers and Great Britain.* Durham, NC: University of New Hampshire Press, 2012.

Luedtke, Luther S. *Nathaniel Hawthorne and the Romance of the Orient.* Bloomington: Indiana University Press, 1989.

Lukasik, Christopher J. *Discerning Characters: The Culture of Appearance in Early America.* Philadelphia: University of Pennsylvania Press, 2011.

Lupton, Julia Reinhard, and Kenneth Reinhard. *After Oedipus: Shakespeare in Psychoanalysis.* Ithaca, NY: Cornell University Press, 1993.

Lystra, Karen. *Searching the Heart: Women, Men, and Romantic Love in Nineteenth-Century America.* New York: Oxford University Press, 1989.

Maccoby, Hyam. "The Wandering Jew as Sacred Executioner." In *The Wandering Jew: Essays in the Interpretation of a Christian Legend,* edited by Galit Hasan-Rokem and Alan Dundes, 236–61. Bloomington: Indiana University Press, 1986.

MacCormack, Patricia. *Posthuman Ethics: Embodiment and Cultural Theory.* Taylor and Francis, 2012. ProQuest Ebook Central.

Machacek, Gregory. *Milton and Homer: "Written to Aftertimes."* Pittsburgh, PA: Duquesne University Press, 2011.

Mannoni, Octave. *Prospero and Caliban: The Psychology of Colonization.* 1950. Ann Arbor: University of Michigan Press, 1990.

Markels, Julian. *Melville and the Politics of Identity: From King Lear to Moby- Dick.* Urbana: University of Illinois Press, 1993.

Marshall, Gail. *Shakespeare in the Nineteenth Century.* Cambridge: Cambridge University Press, 2012.
Martindale, Charles, and A. B. Taylor. *Shakespeare and the Classics.* Cambridge: Cambridge University Press, 2004.
Mathews, James W. "The Enigma of Beatrice Cenci: Shelley and Melville." *South Atlantic Review* 49, no. 2 (1984): 31-41.
Matthiessen, Francis Otto. *American Renaissance: Art and Expression in the Age of Emerson and Whitman.* 1941. New York: Oxford University Press, 1968.
Maxwell, Julie, and Kate Rumbold, eds. *Shakespeare and Quotation.* Cambridge: Cambridge University Press, 2018.
McColley, Diane Kelsey. *Milton's Eve.* Urbana: University of Illinois Press, 1983.
McCoy, Richard C. "'Look Upon Me, Sir': Relationships in *King Lear.*" *Representations* 81, no. 1 (2003): 46-60.
McDonald, Ronan, ed. "Introduction." In *The Values of Literary Studies: Critical Institutions, Scholarly Agendas,* 1-12. New York: Cambridge University Press, 2015.
McEachern, Claire. "Fathering Herself: A Source Study of Shakespeare's Feminism." *Shakespeare Quarterly* 39, no. 3 (1988): 269-90.
McGill, Meredith L., ed. *The Traffic in Poems: Nineteenth-Century Poetry and Transatlantic Exchange.* New Brunswick, NJ: Rutgers University Press, 2008.
———. "Introduction." *The Traffic in Poems: Nineteenth-Century Poetry and Transatlantic Exchange,* 1-14. New Brunswick, NJ: Rutgers University Press, 2008.
McWilliams, John P. "'In the Face of the Fire': Melville's Prometheus, Classical and Romantic Contexts." In *The Call of Classical Literature in the Romantic Age,* by Kevin P. Van Anglen and James Engell, 241-66. Edinburgh: Edinburgh University Press, 2017.
———. *The American Epic: Transforming a Genre, 1770-1860.* Cambridge: Cambridge University Press, 1989.
———. *The Last of the Mohicans: Civil Savagery and Savage Civility.* New York: Twayne Publishers, 1995.
Mellor, Anne K. *Romanticism and Gender.* New York: Routledge, 1993.
Mellow, James R. *Nathaniel Hawthorne in His Times.* Boston, MA: Houghton Mifflin, 1980.
Melville, Herman. *Correspondence.* Edited by Lynn Horth. Evanston, IL: Northwestern University Press; Chicago, IL: Newberry Library, 1993.
———. "Hawthorne and His Mosses, by a Virginian Spending July in Vermont." In *The Piazza Tales and Other Prose Pieces, 1839-1860,* edited by Harrison Hayford, Alma A. MacDougall, and G. Thomas Tanselle, 239-53. Evanston, IL: Northwestern University Press; Chicago, IL: Newberry Library, 1987.
———. *Journals.* Edited by Howard C. Horsford with Lynn Horth. Evanston, IL: Northwestern University Press; Chicago, IL: Newberry Library, 1989.
———. *Moby-Dick; or The Whale.* 1851. Edited by Harrison Hayford, Hershel Parker, and G. Thomas Tanselle. Evanston, IL: Northwestern University Press; Chicago, IL: Newberry Library, 1989.

———. *Pierre; or The Ambiguities.* 1852. Edited by Harrison Hayford, Hershel Parker, and G. Thomas Tanselle. Evanston, IL: Northwestern University Press; Chicago, IL: Newberry Library, 1971.

Metzger, Mary Janell. "Edgar and Queer Affect in *King Lear.*" Paper presented at SAA Seminar, Lehman College and the Graduate Center, CUNY, 2018.

Michaels, Walter Benn. *The Gold Standard and the Logic of Naturalism: American Literature at the Turn of the Century.* Berkeley: University of California Press, 1987.

Michie, Helena. *Sororophobia: Differences among Women in Literature and Culture.* New York: Oxford University Press, 1992.

Milbank, Alison. "The Victorian Gothic in English Novels and Stories, 1830–1880." In *The Cambridge Companion to Gothic Fiction,* edited by Jerrold E. Hogle, 145–66. New York: Cambridge University Press, 2002.

Milder, Robert. *Exiled Royalties: Melville and the Life We Imagine.* New York: Oxford University Press, 2006.

———. *Hawthorne's Habitations: A Literary Life.* New York: Oxford University Press, 2013.

———. "The Last of the Mohicans and the New World Fall." *American Literature* 52, no. 3 (1980): 407–29.

Miller, Edwin Haviland. *Salem Is My Dwelling Place: A Life of Nathaniel Hawthorne.* Iowa City: University of Iowa Press, 1991.

Miller, Perry. *The New England Mind; the Seventeenth Century.* New York: Macmillan, 1939.

Mills, Barriss. "Hawthorne and Puritanism." *The New England Quarterly* 21, no. 1 (1948): 78–102.

Milton, John. *Milton: The Complete Shorter Poem.* 2nd ed. Edited by John Carey. New York: Longman, 1996.

———. *Paradise Lost.* 2nd ed. Edited by Alastair Fowler. London: Longman, 1998.

———. *The Prose Works of John Milton: With a Biographical Introduction.* Edited by Rufus Wilmot Griswold. Philadelphia, PA: H. Hooker, 1845.

Miner-Quinn, Paula. "Pierre's Sexuality: A Psychoanalytic Interpretation of Herman Melville's *Pierre, or, The Ambiguities.*" *Studies In Literature* 13, no. 2 (1981): 111–21.

Mishkin, Tracy. *Literary Influence and African American Writers: Collected Essays.* New York: Garland, 1996.

Mitchell, Juliet. *Mad Men and Medusas: Reclaiming Hysteria.* New York: Basic Books, 2000.

———. *Siblings: Sex and Violence.* Cambridge: Polity Press, 2003.

Mohamed, Feisal G. "I Love the Public Humanities, but . . ." *The Chronicle of Higher Education,* July 28, 2021. https://www.chronicle.com/article/i-love-the-public-humanities-but.

Moore, Jeanie Grant. "The Two Faces of Eve: Temptation Scenes in Comus and Paradise Lost." *Milton Quarterly* 36, no. 1 (2002): 1–19.

Morrison, Paul. *The Explanation for Everything: Essays on Sexual Subjectivity, Sexual Cultures.* New York: New York University Press, 2001.

Morrison, Toni. "Unspeakable Things Unspoken: The Afro American Presence in American Literature." In *Source of Self-Regard: Selected Essays, Speeches, and Meditations,* 161–98. New York: Alfred A. Knopf, 2019.

Mosse, George L. *The Image of Man: The Creation of Modern Masculinity.* New York: Oxford, 1996.

Mueller, Martin. "Shakespeare's Sleeping Beauties: The Sources of *Much Ado about Nothing* and the Play of Their Repetitions." *Modern Philology* 91, no. 3 (1994): 288–311.

Mullin, Emily. "Macready's Triumph: The Restoration of *King Lear* to the British Stage." *Penn History Review* 18, no. 1 (2010): article 3.

Murray, Meg McGavran. *Margaret Fuller, Wandering Pilgrim.* Athens: University of Georgia Press, 2008.

Mylander, Jennifer. "Instruction and English Refinement in America: Shakespeare, Antitheatricality, and Early Modern Reading." In *Shakespearean Educations,* edited by Coppelia Kahn, Heather S. Nathans, and Mimi Godfrey, 33–53. Newark: University of Delaware Press, 2011.

Nathans, Heather S. "'A Course of Learning and Ingenious Studies': Shakespearean Education and Theater in Antebellum America." In *Shakespearean Educations,* edited by Coppelia Kahn, Heather S. Nathans, and Mimi Godfrey, 54–70. Newark: University of Delaware Press, 2011.

———. *Hideous Characters and Beautiful Pagans: Performing Jewish Identity on the Antebellum American Stage.* Ann Arbor: University of Michigan Press, 2017.

Newstok, Scott L., and Ayanna Thompson. *Weyward Macbeth: Intersections of Race and Performance.* New York: Palgrave Macmillan, 2010.

Nohrnberg, James. "Naming Milton's Eve." *Milton Studies* 60, no. 1 (2018): 1–28. https://doi.org/10.1353/mlt.2018.0010.

Norberg, Peter, Steven Olsen-Smith, and Dennis C. Marnon. "Newly Recovered Erased Annotations in Melville's Marginalia to Milton's Poetical Works." *Leviathan* 17, no. 2 (2015): 59–73.

Norsworthy, Scott. "Melville's Notes from Thomas Roscoe's *The German Novelists.*" *Leviathan: A Journal of Melville Studies* 10, no. 3 (2008): 7–37.

Nünning, Ansgar, and Kai Marcel Sicks, eds. *Turning Points: Concepts and Narratives of Change in Literature and Other Media.* Berlin: De Gruyter, 2012.

Ochieng' Nyongó, Tavia Amolo. *The Amalgamation Waltz: Race, Performance, and the Ruses of Memory.* Minneapolis: University of Minnesota Press, 2009.

Ohge, Christopher, Steven Olsen-Smith, and Elisa Barney Smith, with Adam Brimhall, Bridget Howley, Lisa Shanks, and Lexy Smith. "'At the Axis of Reality': Melville's Marginalia in *The Dramatic Works of William Shakespeare.*" *Leviathan* 20, no. 2 (2018): 37–67.

Ohge, Christopher. "Digital Text Analysis of Herman Melville's Marginalia in Shakespeare [A Progress Report]." September 13, 2018. Accessed July 20, 2022. https://christopherohge.com/digital-text-analysis-of-herman-melvilles-marginalia-in-shakespeare-a-progress-report/.

Ohi, Kevin. *Dead Letters Sent: Queer Literary Transmission*. Minneapolis: University of Minnesota Press, 2015.

Olsen-Smith, Steven, Peter Norberg, and Dennis C. Marnon, eds. *Melville's Marginalia Online*. 2023. http://melvillesmarginalia.org/.

Olson, Charles. *Collected Prose*. Edited by Donald Allen and Benjamin Friedlander. Berkeley: University of California Press, 1997.

Otter, Samuel. *Melville's Anatomies*. Berkeley: University of California Press, 1999.

Ovid. *The Metamorphoses*. Translated by Dryden, John, Alexander Pope, William Congreve, Joseph Addison, and others, in *Classical Library*, vols. 20–21. New York: Harper and Bros., 1844.

Paglia, Camille. *Sexual Personae: Art and Decadence from Nefertiti to Emily Dickinson*. Vintage Books, 1991.

Painter, Nell Irvin. *The History of White People*. New York: W. W. Norton and Company, 2010.

Palfrey, Simon. *Poor Tom: Living King Lear*. Chicago, IL: University of Chicago Press, 2014.

Parker, Hershel. *Herman Melville: A Biography*. 2 vols. Baltimore, MD: Johns Hopkins University Press, 1996–2002.

Parvini, Neema. *Shakespeare's History Plays: Rethinking Historicism*. Edinburgh: Edinburgh University Press, 2012.

Pearce, Howard D. "Hawthorne's Old Moodie: *The Blithedale Romance* and *Measure for Measure*." *South Atlantic Bulletin* 38, no. 4 (1973): 11–15.

Percival, M. O. *A Reading of Moby-Dick*. Chicago, IL: University of Chicago Press, 1950.

Peretz, Eyal. *Literature, Disaster, and the Enigma of Power: a Reading of "Moby-Dick."* Stanford, CA: Stanford University Press, 2003.

Pérez, Hiram. *A Taste For Brown Bodies: Gay Modernity and Cosmopolitan Desire*. New York: New York University Press, 2007.

Person, Leland S. "Gender and Sexuality." In *A Companion to Herman Melville*, edited by Kelley (2015), 231–46. Malden, MA: Blackwell, 2006.

———. "A Man for the Whole Country: Marketing Masculinity in the Pierce Biography." In *The Nathaniel Hawthorne Review* 35, no.1 (2009): 1–23.

Pfister, Joel. *The Production of Personal Life: Class, Gender, and the Psychological in Hawthorne's Fiction*. Stanford, CA: Stanford University Press, 1991.

Pollak, Vivian R. *The Erotic Whitman*. Berkeley: University of California Press, 2000.

Porter, Carolyn. "Call Me Ishmael, or How to Make Double-Talk Speak." In *New Essays on Moby-Dick*, edited by Richard H. Brodhead, 73–108. Cambridge: Cambridge University Press, 1986.

Potts, Alex. *Flesh and the Ideal: Winckelmann and the Origins of Art History*. New Haven, CT: Yale University Press, 1994.

Prado, Ignacio M. Sánchez. "On Cosmopolitanism and the Love of Literature: Revisiting Harold Bloom through His Final Books." *Los Angeles Review of Books,* March 2, 2021. https://lareviewofbooks.org/article/on-cosmopolitanism-and-the-love-of-literature-revisiting-harold-bloom-through-his-final-books/.

Primeau, Ronald. *Influx: Essays on Literary Influence.* Port Washington, NY: Kennikat Press, 1977.

Quilligan, Maureen. *Incest and Agency in Elizabeth's England.* Philadelphia: University of Pennsylvania Press, 2005.

Ragussis, Michael. *Figures of Conversion: "The Jewish Question" and English National Identity.* Durham, NC: Duke University Press, 1995.

Rahv, Philip. "The Dark Lady of Salem," *Partisan Review* 8 (1941): 362–81.

Rans, Geoffrey. *Cooper's Leather-Stocking Novels: A Secular Reading.* Chapel Hill: University of North Carolina Press, 1991.

Rees, John O. "Shakespeare in *The Blithedale Romance*." *ESQ*, no. 71 (1973): 84–93.

Reno, Janet. *Ishmael Alone Survived.* Cranbury, NJ: Associated University Presses, 1990.

Reynolds, Larry. "Kings and Commoners in *Moby-Dick*," *Studies in the Novel* 12 (Summer 1980): 101–13.

Richardson, Alan. *The Neural Sublime: Cognitive Theories and Romantic Texts.* Baltimore, MD.: Johns Hopkins University Press, 2010.

Richardson, Donna. "Cooper's Revision of Paradise Lost and of Romantic Satanism in *The Last of the Mohicans*." *Literature in the Early American Republic: Annual Studies on Cooper and His Contemporaries*, no. 6 (2014): xiv–xv, 217–44.

Richmond-Garza, Elizabeth. "Translation Is Blind: Reflections on Narcissus and the Possibility of a Queer Echo." *Comparative Literature Studies* 51, no. 2 (2014): 277–97. https://doi.org/10.5325/complitstudies.51.2.0277.

Riffaterre, Michael. "Intertextual Representation: On Mimesis as Interpretive Discourse." *Critical Inquiry* 11, no. 1 (1984): 141–62. http://www.jstor.org/stable/1343294.

Ripley, George. "Review of *The House of the Seven Gables*." *Harper's New Monthly Magazine*, May 1851, 855–56. Collected in Idol and Jones, *Nathaniel Hawthorne: The Contemporary Reviews*, 167–68.

Robertson, Ben P. *Inchbald, Hawthorne and the Romantic Moral Romance: Little Histories and Neutral Territories.* Abingdon: Routledge, 2016.

Robertson, Fiona. "Walter Scott and the American Historical Novel." In *The Oxford History of the Novel in English*, vol. 5, edited by J. Gerald Kennedy and Leland S. Person, 107–23. Oxford: Oxford University Press, 2014.

Rodier, Katharine. "Nathaniel Hawthorne and *The Marble Faun:* Textual and Contextual Reflections of *Corinne, or Italy*." In *The Novel's Seductions: Stael's* Corinne *in Critical Inquiry*, edited by Karyna Szmurlo, 221–42. Lewisburg, PA: Bucknell University Press, 1999.

Rogers, Thomas. "An Artist's Queer Take on 'Moby-Dick.'" *New York Times*, February 20, 2023. https://www.nytimes.com/2023/02/20/arts/wu-tsang-moby-dick.html?smid=url-share.

Rogin, Michael Paul. *Subversive Genealogy: The Politics and Art of Herman Melville.* New York: Knopf, 1983.

Rosenthal, Debra J. *Race Mixture in Nineteenth-Century U.S. and Spanish American*

Fictions: Gender, Culture, and Nation Building. Chapel Hill: University of North Carolina Press, 2004.

Roudiez, Leon S. "Introduction." In *Desire in Language: A Semiotic Approach to Literature and Art,* by Julia Kristeva, translated by Thomas Gora, Alice Jardine, and Leon S. Roudiez, edited by Leon S. Roudiez, 1–20. New York: Columbia University Press, 1980.

Rubin, Gayle. "The Traffic in Women: Notes on the 'Political Economy' of Sex." In *Toward an Anthropology of Women,* edited by Rayna R. Reiter, 157–210. New York: Monthly Review, 1975.

Sale, George. *The Koran Commonly Called "The Alcoran of Mohammed"; Translated into English Immediately from the Original Arabic* [. . .]. London: Maiden, 1801.

Sale, Roger. *Literary Inheritance.* Amherst: University of Massachusetts Press, 1984.

Sanborn, Geoffrey. "James Fenimore Cooper and the Invention of the Passing Novel." *American Literature* 84, no. 1 (2012): 1–29. https://doi.org/10.1215/00029831-1540932.

———. "Lounging on the Sofa with Leigh Hunt: A New Source for the Notes in Melville's Shakespeare Volume." *Nineteenth-Century Literature* 63, no. 1 (2008): 104–15.

———. *Whipscars and Tattoos: The Last of the Mohicans, Moby-Dick, and the Maori.* New York: Oxford University Press, 2011.

Sandler, Matt. *The Black Romantic Revolution: Abolitionist Poets at the End of Slavery.* London: Verso Books, 2020.

Scheff, Thomas J. "Gender Wars: Emotions in *Much Ado about Nothing.*" *Sociological Perspectives* 36, no. 2 (1993): 149–66.

Schirmeister, Pamela. *The Consolations of Space: The Place of Romance in Hawthorne, Melville, and James.* Stanford, CA: Stanford University Press, 1990.

Schmidgall, Gary. *Containing Multitudes: Walt Whitman and the British Literary Tradition.* New York: Oxford University Press, 2014.

Schoenfeldt, Michael. "Gender and Conduct in *Paradise Lost.*" In *Sexuality and Gender in Early Modern Europe: Institutions, Texts, Images,* edited by James Grantham Turner. 310–38. Cambridge: Cambridge University Press, 1993.

Schultz, Karla. "In Defense of Narcissus: Lou Andreas-Salomé and Julia Kristeva," *German Quarterly* 67, no. 2 (1994): 185–96.

Schwarz, Kathryn. *What You Will: Gender, Contract, and Shakespearean Social Space.* Philadelphia: University of Pennsylvania Press, 2011.

Sedgwick, Eve Kosofsky. *Between Men: English Literature and Male Homosocial Desire.* New York: Columbia University Press, 1985.

———. "Paranoid Reading and Reparative Reading; or, You're So Paranoid, You Probably Think This Introduction Is about You." In *Novel Gazing: Queer Readings in Fiction,* edited by Eve Kosofsky Sedgwick, 1–37. Durham, NC: Duke University Press, 1997.

Sedgwick, William Ellery. *Herman Melville: The Tragedy of Mind.* Cambridge, MA: Harvard University Press, 1944.

Sensabaugh, George Frank. *Milton in Early America*. Princeton, NJ: Princeton University Press, 1964.

Serpell, Namwali. *The Furrows: An Elegy*. New York: Random House, 2022.

Shakespeare, William. *The Dramatic Works of William Shakespeare*. 7 vols. Boston, MA: Hilliard, Gray, and Company, 1837.

———. *Hamlet*. Edited by Ann Thompson and Neil Taylor. Arden Shakespeare. London: Bloomsbury, 2006.

———. *King Lear*. Edited by R. A. Foakes. Arden Shakespeare. London: Bloomsbury, 1997.

———. *Measure for Measure*. Edited by J. W. Lever. Arden Shakespeare. London: Bloomsbury, 2010.

———. *The Merchant of Venice*. Edited by John Drakakis. Arden Shakespeare. London: Bloomsbury, 2010.

———. *Much Ado about Nothing*. Edited by Claire McEachern. Arden Shakespeare. London: Bloomsbury, 2016.

———. *The Tempest*. Edited by Virginia Mason Vaughan and Alden T. Vaughan. Arden Shakespeare. London: Bloomsbury, 2011.

Shamir, Milette. *Inexpressible Privacy: The Interior Life of Antebellum American Literature*. Philadelphia: University of Pennsylvania Press, 2006.

Shapiro, James. *Shakespeare and the Jews*. New York: Columbia University Press, 1996.

———. *Shakespeare in a Divided America: What His Plays Tell Us about Our Past and Future*. New York: Penguin, 2020.

Shapiro, James, ed. *Shakespeare in America: An Anthology from the Revolution to Now*. New York: Library of America, 2014.

Shears, Jonathon. *The Romantic Legacy of Paradise Lost: Reading Against the Grain*. Farnham: Ashgate, 2009.

Shelley, Percy Bysshe. *Shelley's Poetry and Prose: Authoritative Texts, Criticism*. Norton Critical Edition. 2nd ed. Edited by Donald H. Reiman and Neil Fraistat. New York: Norton, 2002.

Sherwyn, Skye. "Ellen Gallagher's *Bird in Hand:* Slave Ships and Sunken Treasure." *The Guardian*, April 19, 2019. https://www.theguardian.com/artanddesign/2019/apr/19/ellen-gallagher-bird-in-hand.

Shiff, Richard, Carol Armstrong, Robin D. G. Kelley, Ellen Gallagher, and Ulrich Wilmes. *Ellen Gallagher: AxME*. New York: Harry N. Abrams, 2013.

Shoaf, Richard Allen. *Milton, Poet of Duality: A Study of Semiosis in the Poetry and the Prose*. New Haven, CT: Yale University Press, 1985.

Shoulson, Jeffrey S. "The Embrace of the Fig Tree: Sexuality and Creativity in Midrash and in Milton." *ELH* 67, no. 4 (2000): 873–903.

Showalter, Elaine. *Sister's Choice: Tradition and Change in American Women's Writing*. New York: Clarendon Press; Oxford: Oxford University Press, 1991.

Shurr, William. *Rappaccini's Children: American Writers in a Calvinist World*. Lexington: University Press of Kentucky, 1981.

Sicher, Efraim. *The Jew's Daughter: A Cultural History of a Conversion Narrative.* Lanham, MD: Lexington Books, 2017.
Siegel, Allen M. *Heinz Kohut and the Psychology of the Self.* London: Routledge, 1996.
Silk, Michael. "Shakespeare and Greek Tragedy: Strange Relationship." In *Shakespeare and the Classics,* edited by Charles Martindale and Albert Booth Taylor, 241–60. Cambridge: Cambridge University Press, 2004.
Silverman, Kaja. *The Threshold of the Visible World.* New York: Routledge, 1996.
Simms, William Gilmore. *Charleston and Her Satirists; A Scribblement by a City Bachelor.* Charleston: James S. Burges, 1848. Alexandria, VA: Literature Online / Chadwyck-Healey Inc., 1996.
Simon, Bennett. *Tragic Drama and the Family: Psychoanalytic Studies from Aeschylus to Beckett.* New Haven, CT: Yale University Press, 1988.
Skura, Meredith Anne. "Dragon Fathers and Unnatural Children: Warring Generations in *King Lear* and Its Sources." *Comparative Drama* 42, no. 2 (2008): 121–48.
Smith, Susan L. *The Power of Women: A "Topos" in Medieval Art and Literature.* Philadelphia: University of Pennsylvania Press, 1995.
Smith, Sydney. *The Works of the Rev. Sydney Smith.* 3 vols. London: Printed for Longman, Orme, Brown, Green, and Longmans, 1839.
Sobchack, Vivian Carol. *Carnal Thoughts: Embodiment and Moving Image Culture.* Berkeley: University of California Press, 2004.
Sorisio, Carolyn. *Fleshing Out America: Race, Gender, and the Politics of the Body in American Literature, 1833–1879.* Athens: University of Georgia Press, 2002.
Spanos, William V. *The Errant Art of Moby-Dick: The Canon, the Cold War, and the Struggle for American Studies.* Durham, NC: Duke University Press, 1995.
Spofford, H. P. *The Amber Gods and Other Stories.* Edited by A. Bendixen. New Brunswick, NJ: Rutgers University Press, 1989.
Stanton, Elizabeth Cady. *The Woman's Bible.* 1895–98. Edinburgh: Polygon Books, 1985.
Stauffer, John. "Interracial Friendship and the Aesthetics of Freedom." In *Frederick Douglass and Herman Melville: Essays in Relation,* edited by Robert S. Levine and Samuel Otter, 134–58. Chapel Hill: University of North Carolina Press, 2008.
Stauffer, John, Zoe Trodd, Celeste-Marie Bernier, Henry Louis Gates, and Kenneth B. Morris. *Picturing Frederick Douglass: An Illustrated Biography of the Nineteenth Century's Most Photographed American.* New York: Liveright Publishing Corporation, 2015.
Stein, Suzanne. *The Pusher and the Sufferer: An Unsentimental Reading of "Moby Dick."* New York: Routledge, 2014.
Sten, Christopher. *Sounding the Whale: Moby-Dick as Epic Novel.* Kent, OH: Kent State University Press, 1996.
Stevenson, R. Scott. "Milton and the Puritans." *The North American Review* 214, no. 793 (1921): 825–32. http://www.jstor.org/stable/25120913.
Stokes, John. "Shakespeare in Europe." In *Shakespeare in the Nineteenth Century,* edited by Gail Marshall, 296–314. New York: Cambridge University Press, 2012.

Stuckey, Sterling. *African Culture and Melville's Art: The Creative Process in Benito Cereno and Moby-Dick.* Oxford: Oxford University Press, 2009.

Sun, Emily. *Succeeding King Lear: Literature, Exposure, and the Possibility of Politics.* New York: Fordham University, 2010.

Suzuki, Mihoko. "Gender, Class, and the Ideology of Comic Form: *Much Ado about Nothing* and *Twelfth Night.*" In *A Feminist Companion to Shakespeare,* edited by Dympna Callaghan, 121-43. Chichester: John Wiley and Sons, 2016.

Sweet, Nancy. "'Man Needs It So': Roman Catholicism in *The Blithedale Romance.*" *Nathaniel Hawthorne Review* 48, no. 2 (December 2022): 195-217. https://doi.org/10.5325/nathhawtrevi.48.2.0195.

Takaki, Ronald T. *A Different Mirror: A History of Multicultural America.* 1st rev. ed. New York: Back Bay Books / Little, Brown, and Co., 2008.

Tassi, Marguerite A. *Women and Revenge in Shakespeare: Gender, Genre, and Ethics.* Selinsgrove, PA: Susquehanna University Press, 2011.

Taylor, Gary. *Reinventing Shakespeare: A Cultural History, from the Restoration to the Present.* New York: Weidenfeld and Nicolson, 1989.

Thorslev, Peter L. "Incest as Romantic Symbol." *Comparative Literature Studies* 2, no. 1 (1965): 41-58.

Tintner, Adeline R. *Edith Wharton in Context: Essays on Intertextuality.* Tuscaloosa: University of Alabama Press, 1999.

Tompkins, Jane P. *Sensational Designs: The Cultural Work of American Fiction, 1790-1860.* New York: Oxford University Press, 1985.

Tromly, Frederic B. *Fathers and Sons in Shakespeare: The Debt Never Promised.* Toronto: University of Toronto Press, 2010.

Turner, James. *Sexuality and Gender in Early Modern Europe: Institutions, Texts, Images.* Cambridge: Cambridge University Press, 1993.

Valman, Nadia. *The Jewess in Nineteenth-Century British Literary Culture.* Cambridge: Cambridge University Press, 2007.

Van Anglen, Kevin P. *The New England Milton: Literary Reception and Cultural Authority in the Early Republic.* University Park: Pennsylvania State University Press, 1993.

Van Anglen, Kevin P., and James Engell. *The Call of Classical Literature in the Romantic Age.* Edinburgh: Edinburgh University Press, 2017.

VanDette, Emily E. *Sibling Romance in American Fiction, 1835-1900.* New York: Palgrave Macmillan, 2013.

Vandiver, Edward P., Jr. "James Fenimore Cooper and Shakespeare." *Shakespeare Association Bulletin* 15, no. 2 (1940): 110-17.

Van Harn, Roger E. *The Lectionary Commentary: Theological Exegesis for Sunday's Texts, the First Readings.* Vol. 1. Grand Rapids: Wm. B. Eerdmans Publishing Company, 2005.

Vaughan, Alden T., and Virginia Mason Vaughan. *Shakespeare in America.* Oxford: Oxford University Press, 2012.

Vaughan, Virginia Mason. "Making Shakespeare American: Shakespeare's dissemination in nineteenth-century America." In *Shakespeare in American life*, edited by Virginia Mason Vaughan and Alden T. Vaughan, 22-33. Washington, DC: Folger Shakespeare Library; Seattle: University of Washington Press, 2007.

Versluis, Arthur. *American Transcendentalism and Asian Religions*. New York: Oxford University Press, 1993.

Walker, Julia M. *Medusa's Mirrors: Spenser, Shakespeare, Milton, and the Metamorphosis of the Female Self*. Delaware: University of Delaware Press, 1998: 158-87.

Wallace, Maurice O. *Constructing the Black Masculine: Identity and Ideality in African American Men's Literature and Culture, 1775-1995*. Durham, NC: Duke University Press, 2002.

Wallace, Maurice O., and Shawn Michelle Smith, eds. *Pictures and Progress: Early Photography and the Making of African American Identity*. Durham, NC: Duke University Press, 2012.

Warner, Marina. *Phantasmagoria: Spirit Visions, Metaphors, and Media into the Twenty-first Century*. Oxford: Oxford University Press, 2006.

Weil, Simone. *An Anthology*. Edited by Sian Miles. London: Penguin, 2005.

Weinstein, Cindy, and Christopher Looby. *American Literature's Aesthetic Dimensions*. New York: Columbia University Press, 2012.

Weinstein, Cindy. *Family, Kinship, and Sympathy in Nineteenth-Century American Literature*. Cambridge: Cambridge University Press, 2004.

Weisbuch, Robert. *Atlantic Double-Cross: American Literature and British Influence in the Age of Emerson*. Chicago, IL: University of Chicago Press, 1986.

Welsh, Alexander. *Hamlet in His Modern Guises*. Princeton, NJ: Princeton University Press, 2001.

Welter, Barbara. "The Cult of True Womanhood: 1820-1860." *American Quarterly* 18, no. 2 (1966): 151-74.

Westfall, Alfred Van Rensselaer. *American Shakespearean Criticism, 1607-1865*. New York: H. W. Wilson, 1939.

Wexler, Laura. "'A More Perfect Likeness': Frederick Douglass and the Image of the Nation." In *Pictures and Progress: Early Photography and the Making of African American Identity*, edited by Maurice O. Wallace and Shawn Michelle Smith, 18-40. Durham, NC: Duke University Press, 2012.

White, Edmund. *City Boy: My Life in New York during the 1960s and '70s*. 1st US ed. New York: Bloomsbury USA, 2009.

White, Patricia. *Rebecca*. London: British Film Institute / Bloomsbury, 2021.

Whitley, Edward. *American Bards: Walt Whitman and Other Unlikely Candidates for National Poet*. Chapel Hill: University of North Carolina Press, 2010.

Whitman, Walt. *Complete Poetry and Collected Prose*. With notes and chronology by Justin Kaplan. New York: Literary Classics of the United States / Viking Press, 1982.

Wilburn, Reginald A. *Preaching the Gospel of Black Revolt: Appropriating Milton in Early African American Literature*. State College: Pennsylvania State University Press, 2020.

Wilder, Lina Perkins, and Andrew Hiscock. *The Routledge Handbook of Shakespeare and Memory*. Abingdon: Routledge, 2018.

Wilder, Lina Perkins. *Shakespeare's Memory Theatre: Recollection, Properties, and Character*. Cambridge: Cambridge University Press, 2010.

———. "Veiled Memory Traces in *Much Ado about Nothing, Pericles*, and *The Winter's Tale*." In *The Routledge Handbook of Shakespeare and Memory*, edited by Lina Perkins Wilder and Andrew Hiscock, 239–52. Abingdon: Routledge, 2018.

Wilson, James. "Incest and American Romantic Fiction." *Studies in the Literary Imagination* 7, no. 1 (1974): 31.

Wineapple, Brenda. *Hawthorne: A Life*. New York: Alfred A. Knopf, 2003.

Wittreich, Joseph Anthony. *Why Milton Matters: A New Preface to His Writings*. New York: Palgrave Macmillan, 2006.

Woodberry, George Edward. *Nathaniel Hawthorne*. Boston: Houghton, Mifflin and Company, 1902.

Wright, William Aldis, William George Clark, and William Shakespeare. *Hamlet, Prince of Denmark*. United Kingdom: Clarendon Press, 1872.

Yarnall, Judith. *Transformations of Circe: The History of an Enchantress*. Urbana: University of Illinois Press, 1994.

Young, Philip. *Hawthorne's Secret: An Un-told Tale*. Boston, MA: DRGodine, 1984.

Young, Thelathia Nikki. *Black Queer Ethics, Family, and Philosophical Imagination*. New York: Palgrave MacMillan, 2016.

INDEX

abjection, 15, 54, 81, 109, 132, 140–41
Adelman, Janet, 113, 128, 137, 182, 204
adoption, 126
Aeneid, The (Virgil) 149, 255n10
aesthetics: contemporary study of, 6; Hellenic, 180, 184, 188
"Agatha" letters (Melville), 62, 244–45n15
aging, 73, 79, 82
agon, 5–6, 13, 16, 19, 20, 26, 28, 136, 207–8
Ahab (*Moby-Dick*): as father figure, 124, 126, 133–34; as king, 135; and King Lear, 123, 135–36, 140, 142; relationship with Pip, 129, 134, 139; as Satan figure, 4, 19, 134; and stepmother world, 139–41
amalgamation, 45, 63. *See also* miscegenation
"Ambitious Guest, The" (Hawthorne), 73
ambivalence: Eve's toward Adam, 63–64; and influence, 13; male heterosexual in *Hamlet*, 31, 148, 153; male heterosexual in *Pierre*, 31, 148
American literature: establishing legitimacy of, 33–34; influence and emergence of, 1, 20, 65–66; separation from European forbears, 4–6, 9, 20
American Men of Letters (Woodberry), 61
American Newness, 17
"American Scholar, The" (Emerson), 20

American Society for Meliorating the Condition of the Jews, 192
amor fati, 141
antebellum America: contexts for veiled woman, 98–99, 114–15; incest as affective trend, 67, 75; social problems, 34, 174
antihumanism, 7
antisemitism: and caricature, 42, 187–88; in 1850s Rome, 191, 193; gender of, 176, 183–88, 194, 197, 198; Hawthorne's, 176–77, 179, 180, 181, 189, 197, 201; internalized, 201–2; in *The Marble Faun*, 176; in *The Merchant of Venice*, 3, 40–42, 203–4
anxieties of influence: American, 5–6; and Bloom, 7, 17, 20, 223–24n25; and national literary identity, 9, 20–21
Anxiety of Influence, The (Bloom), 7, 17, 224n25
Apollo Belvedere (sculpture), 183
apophrades, 16
Arac, Jonathan, 121–22, 147, 163
archetype: beautiful Jewess, 180, 182, 205; dark lady, 179; lovers, 217; women, 101
Artese, Charlotte, folktales in *The Merchant of Venice*, 43–44, 45
Arvin, Newton, 5
askesis, 16
Atlantic, 202
autoeroticism, 88

Bacon, Delia: and Hawthorne, 202, 263–64n43; *Philosophy of the Plays of Shakspere Unfolded*, 202
Bacon, Francis, 202
Bakhtin, Mikhail, 9
Baldwin, Alice, 79
Banford, Isabel (*Pierre*), 31–32, 125; and incest, 148, 156–57, 163–64; and Milton's Eve, 26, 170–71; as muse, 164; and paternal image, 26, 170–71
Barthes, Roland, 10
bastardy, Edmund's, 126, 131
Bathsheba, 178
Baym, Nina, 55, 72, 100
Beatrice (*Much Ado about Nothing*), as intertext for Zenobia (*The Blithdale Romance*), 94–95, 98, 102–3, 240–41n29
beauty: Black male, 217, 219; and Jewish caricature, 187–88; male in Hawthorne, 77, 80, 180, 183–84, 186, 261n9; Zenobia's (*The Blithdale Romance*), 108, 179
belatedness: and Bloom, 14, 17–18; Satan's, 15–16, 18–19, 22
Benedick (*Much Ado about Nothing*): as intertext for Miles Coverdale (*The Blithdale Romance*), 94–95; misogyny of, 102–3
Bercovitch, Sacvan, 32, 176–77, 204
Berger, John, 73
Bersani, Leo, 9, 127–28, 246–47n26
Bewley, Marius, 4–5, 223n17
Billy Budd (Melville), 159, 251n64
Black American fiction, 208
Blake, William: *The Marriage of Heaven and Hell*, 4; on Milton, 4, 47, 70, 94
Blithedale Romance, The (Hawthorne), 30, 37, 59, 62–65, 89–95, 97, 99–107, 111, 113–16, 119–20, 179, 197; and *Comus*, 93–94; and *King Lear*, 90, 92, 103–9; and *Much Ado about Nothing*, 30, 37, 90–91, 93–95, 97–98, 101–3; Shakespearean influence, 89–90. *See also* Coverdale, Miles; Hollingsworth; Moodie; Priscilla; Zenobia
Bloom, Harold: *The Anxiety of Influence*, 7, 17, 224n25; belatedness, 14, 17–18, 22, 226n60; contemporary engagement with or opposition to, 7, 223–24n25; influence theory, 5–6, 11, 16; *A Map of Misreading*, 18–19, 224n25; misprision, 14, 16–18; on oedipal desire, 16, 27, 208; reparative reading, 14, 20, 223–24n25; on Shakespeare's influence, 2–3
Blum, Hester, 6
Bowdoin College, 177, 182, 186
Bridge, Horatio, 182–83, 184
Bristol, Michael D., 7
British Society for the Propagation of the Bible among the Jews, 192
Brodhead, Richard, 114, 136
Brook Farm, 114, 236–37n46, 242–43n56
Brown, Charles Brockden, 61, 66
Bumppo, Natty (*The Leatherstocking Tales*), 37, 51, 54, 55
Butler, Judith, 145, 154, 159, 253n1, 255n9, 257n25
Byronic hero, Madison Washington as (*The Heroic Slave*), 214

Cain and Abel, 153
canon, 8, 11, 174, 212, 221n3; American, 208, 223n17; reformation of, 6
Castiglia, Christopher, 80, 224n27
Castle of Otranto, The (Walpole), 163
Castronovo, Russ, 114–15
Catholicism: in *The Blithedale Romance*, 118; in *The Marble Faun*, 176, 194, 195, 200; sentiment against, 191
Cavendish, Margaret, *Sociable Letters*, 100
Cervantes, Miguel, *Don Quixote*, 2
Chamberlin Hellman, Caroline, 7, 10–11, 12

Circe, 48, 71, 93-94
Claudius (*Hamlet*): compared to brother, 150-51, 152; murder as homoerotic, 148, 151, 154-55
Clayton, Jay, and Eric Rothstein, 10
clinamen, 16-17, 226n57
Colacurcio, Michael, 89
Coleridge, Samuel Taylor, 61, 66; "Kubla Khan," 164; *Lectures on Shakespeare*, 38, 143-44
collaboration: artistic, 62; aspect of influence, 101; instead of enmity or agon, 6, 26, 208
Columbian Orator, The, 209, 219
compensatory approximation, in *The House of Seven Gables*, 84
compensatory pleasures, 81-84. See also Irigaray, Luce
Comus (Milton), 3, 30, 59, 93-94, 97. See also Cotytto
Confidence-Man, The (Melville), 142
consanguination (of literary lines), 63
Constitution, of United States, 209-10, 211
contemplation: as aspect of influence, 208, 218; of self within text, 22, 220
conversion, religious: of Jews, 176, 191, 198, 200, 203-4; as trauma, 182, 192, 203
conversion hysteria, 193-94, 200
conversion narrative, 181-82
Cooper, James Fenimore: on American and English culture and literature, 34-36; *The Deerslayer*, 51; *The Leatherstocking Tales*, 55; and Milton, 19, 34-36, 46-48, 50, 52-56, 58; *Notions of the Americans*, 34; *The Pathfinder*, 55; and Shakespeare, 28-29, 34-37, 39-46, 58. See also *Last of the Mohicans, The*
Cooper, Susan Fenimore, 36, 229n11
Cordelia (*King Lear*), 104-5, 130; as avenger, 241n34; compassion of, 109;

intertext for Cora Munro (*Last of the Mohicans*), 46; intertext for Priscilla (*The Blithdale Romance*), 106; as redeemer, 113, 140
Cotytto (*Comus*), 93-94; intertext for Zenobia (*The Blithdale Romance*), 101
Coverdale, Miles (*The Blithedale Romance*), 93, 180; and Benedick (*Much Ado about Nothing*), 94-95; and King Lear, 113; on Zenobia, 113, 179, 242n54
Cox, John, 96
Creole Mutiny, 208, 214
Cult of True Womanhood, 99, 114, 174, 240n21

daemonization, 16
Daniel Deronda (Eliot), 182, 192
Dante, 18, 168, 169; *The Divine Comedy*, 2
Death (*Paradise Lost*), 18, 19, 68, 70-71
Deerslayer, The (Cooper), 51. See also Bumppo, Natty
Dekker, George, 36-37, 40, 43, 46-47
Derrida, Jacques: on Echo, 27; Edelman's response to, 126
desire: female, 159; and female gaze, 87-88; in *The House of Seven Gables*, 26, 60, 68, 75-77, 82, 87; incestuous, 66, 153; intertextual influence as, 13-14, 21; Lacan on, 91; oedipal, 77, 80; queer, 68, 88
dialogue, 8, 28
Diana, 91, 93
DiBattista, Maria, 2-3
Dickens, Charles: *Great Expectations*, 197; *Oliver Twist*, 187
Dickinson, Emily, 13, 18, 208
Dido, Queen of Carthage (Marlowe and Nashe), 149
Dimmesdale, Arthur (*The Scarlet Letter*), 76, 77, 99, 112, 180, 197
Dimock, Wai Chee, 12, 221n2, 227n69, 259-60n52

INDEX

disguise: Edgar's (*King Lear*), 129, 134; in *King Lear* and *Moby-Dick*, 124. *See also* veil

Divine Comedy, The (Dante), 2

Donatello (*The Marble Faun*), 175, 183, 190, 192, 204–5; connection to Miriam Schaefer, 200; sensual form, 62–63, 180

Don Quixote (Cervantes), 2

Doré, Gustave, 188–89

Douglass, Frederick, 208–20; escape from enslavement, 211, 213; *The Heroic Slave*, 208, 213–16, 219; and Milton, 213–14, 218–20, 222–23n15; *My Bondage and My Freedom*, 208, 212; and photography, 215–16; and Portia (*The Merchant of Venice*), 211–12; and Shakespeare, 208–13, 214, 219–20; "What to the Slave Is the Fourth of July?," 209

Douglass, William, 61

Dramatic Works of William Shakespeare (Hilliard, Gray, and Company), 121, 122, 250n59

Dred Scott case, 211

Du Maurier, George, *Trilby*, 187

Dunham, Mabel (*The Pathfinder*), 55

Duyckinck, Evert, 121

Echo: as figure for writer, 27–28; myth, 23–24, 88

Edelman, Lee: on Eve's narcissism, 24; on *Hamlet*, 126–27

Edgar (*King Lear*): intertext for Ishmael, 123–24, 130, 133, 134–36, 245n17; misogyny, 131; as performer, 128–30, 132, 134; as survivor, 124–29

Edmund (*King Lear*), 31, 124, 130; bastardy, 126, 131, 132

effeminacy: disdain for, 103; Pierre's fear of, 158

Elaw, Zilpha, 217

Eliot, George: *Daniel Deronda*, 182, 192; and Hawthorne, 181

Eliot, T. S., 11, 18

Emerson, Ralph Waldo, 2, 18; "The American Scholar," 20; relationship with Hawthorne, 61–62, 186; *Representative Men*, 212; *The Three Fates* (Salviati painting), 142

emotional labor, 139

Enceladus, 167; in *Hamlet*, 157, 166–67; and incest, 166, 168; in *Pierre*, 32, 157, 158, 166, 168–69, 171

Enceladus Fountain, The (sculpture by Marsy), 168

English Notebooks, The (Hawthorne), 177

enmity, 5–6, 13, 207–8. *See also* agon

"Ethan Brand" (Hawthorne), 189

European cultural hegemony, 20

Eve (*Paradise Lost*): and American romantics, 19, 26; birth and reflection, 22–23, 63, 68, 87–88, 218; and Gertrude, 153; as model for women, 52; narcissistic desire, 23–24; reimagined by Hawthorne, 63–66; relevance to queer theory, 24; as wronged other, 4

Eve as intertext: for Isabel Banford (*Pierre*), 170–71; for Mary Glendinning (*Pierre*), 158; for Cora Munro (*Last of the Mohicans*), 47–56; for Hester Prynne, 59, 64; for Pyncheon women (*The House of Seven Gables*), 87–88; for Beatrice Rappaccini ("Rappaccini's Daughter"), 63–66

exile: as annihilation, 127; Edgar's (*King Lear*), 125, 132; in *The Tempest*, 37

exploitation: of Priscilla (*The Blithedale Romance*), 94, 106, 120; of women, 30, 54, 81

family: in Hawthorne, 81–82, 104; in *King Lear*, 105, 110–11. *See also* Irigaray, Luce

Fanshawe (Hawthorne), 61, 180

fantasy: of heroism, 166; of Jewishness, 190, 195, 203; male, of women, 98, 100, 101, 113, 118; of mother figure, 158, 160
Fata Morgana, 143–44, 253n73
Fates, the: for Hawthorne, 142; Ishmael and Ahab, 141–43, 251–52n68; and Lear's daughters, 142; in myth, 141–42; as opposed to fate, 141
fatherhood: idealized in *Hamlet*, 150, 153; idealized in *Pierre*, 157, 160–62, 172; in *King Lear*, 103–4, 110–11, 128, 133, 135–36; in *King Lear* and *The Blithedale Romance*, 107–8, 112–14; paternal narcissism, 103–14; and patriarchy, 110
fatherlessness, on the *Pequod*, 124
Faust (Goethe), 2
felix culpa, 32, 59, 69, 193
female gaze, 68, 85–88, 158, 205; through Eve, 26, 29, 87–88, 170–71
female rebellion, in Hawthorne's works, 65
female sexuality, 90, 114; and Eve, 22, 49; Freud on, 14, 87; and monstrosity, 101, 105, 112–13; and morality, 97; site of healing, 49; transgressive, in Hawthorne, 72; as veiled, 30; and visuality, 85
Female Society of Boston and Vicinity for Promoting Christianity among Jews, 192
female will, 90, 100, 102–3, 105
femininity: aging, 73, 79; antebellum, 56, 240n21; Freud on, 164; in *King Lear*, 105; and meaning, 102; and Miranda (*The Tempest*), 38; in *Moby-Dick*, 123, 124–25, 136–37, 143; as mysterious, 56–58, 96–97, 98, 101, 115, 117–18, 163–64, 194; in *Pierre*, 31, 124–25, 157–59, 163–64; and traffic in women, 76, 86, 95; and visuality, 84–85, 170–72.

See also "power of women" trope; stranger
feminist agency: dearth of, 27, 174; of Cora Munro (*The Last of the Mohicans*), 56, 58; and narcissistic woman, 24, 87; in *Pierre*, 158
feminist ethics, 59
femme fatale, 156, 163
femme fragile, 163
Fiedler, Leslie, 139
Fish, Stanley, 19
Flory, Wendy Stallard, 164
Ford, Christine Blasey, 243n67
Foucault, Michel, 258–59n38
Fredricks, Nancy, on *Hamlet* and *Pierre*, 161–62, 168
free indirect discourse, 82, 159
Freud, Sigmund: and the Fates, 142; on female sexuality, 14, 87, 197; on femininity, 164; *From the History of an Infantile Neurosis*, 152; in Hawthorne, 84, 87; *The Interpretation of Dreams*, 146; male homosexuality, 77, 84, 87; melancholia and influence, 21, 208; "Mourning and Melancholia," 21, 227n70; "On Narcissism: An Introduction," 21; renewed relevance, 225n46; reparative reading, 14; "The Theme of the Three Caskets," 142
friendship, literary, 61–62
From the History of an Infantile Neurosis (Freud), 152
Fry, Paul H., 11, 17–18
Fugitive Slave Act, 208–9
Fuller, Margaret, 3, 38; belief in the Fates, 142, 253n72; *Woman in the Nineteenth Century*, 102
Furrows, The (Serpell), 247–48n38

Garber, Marjorie, 9, 11, 117
Garrison, William Lloyd, 210–11
Gates, W. B., 36

gaze: in *The Marble Faun*, 204–5; white male, 172, 216. *See also* female gaze
gender: ambiguity, 75, 76; of antisemitism, 183–88; fluidity, 76, 77, 218; and Jewishness for Hawthorne, 176, 194, 198
Gertrude (*Hamlet*): and Eve, 153; and image, 171–72; as mother, 152–53, 159, 165; and narcissism, 159; sexuality, 153–54, 165
Giants, 167. *See also* Enceladus
Giles, Paul, 5
Gita, 2
Glazener, Nancy, 2
Glendinning, Mary (*Pierre*): intertexts from Milton, 158; as mother figure, 157–58; relationship with Pierre, 156, 159–60, 162, 170, 172, 259n46
Glendinning, Pierre (*Pierre*): incest, 156, 162; and male fantasy, 158, 160, 163, 166; masculinity, 159, 164
Gloucester (*King Lear*), 31, 124, 126, 128–31, 133–34, 136, 140, 142
Goddu, Teresa, 76
Goethe, 163; *Faust*, 2; *The Sorrows of Young Werther*, 2
Goneril (*King Lear*), 104–6, 113, 142, 241n34; as stepmother figure, 140; and Zenobia (*The Blithedale Romance*), 106, 109
Graham, Allen, 11
Great Expectations (Dickens), 197
Greek revival, 2
Greenblatt, Stephen, *The Swerve: How the World Became Modern*, 17
Griswold, Rufus, 3
Gross, Kenneth, 45, 203–4
Gustafson, Sandra, 209, 210

Hamlet (Shakespeare), 126–27, 145–55, 212–23; criminalization of sex, 165, 256n19; Douglass's quotation of, 212–13, 214, 219; influence on Gothic writers, 163; and *Pierre*, 147–48, 151, 157–59, 161–69, 171–72; and psychoanalysis, 145–47, 152–54, 255n13; and queer theory, 126–27; source material, 149. *See also* Claudius; Gertrude; Ophelia
Hawthorne, Elizabeth "Ebe," 60, 67
Hawthorne, Nathaniel: adolescence and development as writer, 60–61; "The Ambitious Guest," 73; appearance, 78, 186; and Delia Bacon, 202, 263–64n43; *The English Notebooks*, 177; "Ethan Brand," 189; family history, 62, 67, 77–78, 190, 234n14; *Fanshawe*, 61, 180; incestuous desire/motifs, 59–60, 67, 70, 75–77, 80–81, 190; as influence on Melville, 67, 148; literary friendships, 61–63; "The May-Pole of Merry Mount," 59; and Milton's influence, 59, 62–66, 68–72, 78, 84–85, 87–88, 90, 101–2, 193, 229n11; on the mind and body, 62–63; "The Minister's Black Veil," 91; "My Kinsman, Major Molineaux," 112, 180, 261n9; "The New Adam and Eve," 59; *Our Old Home*, 202; as politically inactive, 115; "Rappaccini's Daughter," 59, 63–66, 112, 185, 234n16; "Recollections of a Gifted Woman," 202; "Roger Malvin's Burial," 112; *Septimius Felton*, 180, 190; and Shakespeare's influence, 60–61, 89, 94–98, 101–3, 107, 111; *Twice-Told Tales*, 183; "A Virtuoso's Collection," 189. See also *Blithedale Romance, The*; *House of Seven Gables, The*; *Marble Faun, The*; *Scarlet Letter, The*
"Hawthorne and His Mosses" (Melville), 28, 123
Hayne, Robert, 209
Hecuba, 149, 255n10
Hellenism, 90, 180, 184, 188, 261n9
Henry VIII (Shakespeare), 122, 208
"hermeneutical Jew," 203

Hero (*Much Ado about Nothing*), 92–93, 96, 101, 110; intertext for Priscilla (*The Blithdale Romance*), 95, 99–100, 102
Heroic Slave, The (Douglass), 208, 213–16, 219; and Shakespeare, 214
Heyward, Duncan (*The Last of the Mohicans*), 42–43, 53–54
Hirschfeld, Heather, on *Merchant of Venice*, 203
Hollander, John, 21, 227n69; and "intertextual echoes," 8, 147
Hollingsworth (*The Blithedale Romance*), 76, 77, 98–100; views on women, 92, 112
Homer, 8, 18, 34, 48; *The Iliad*, 149
homoerotic: desire, 77; influence as, 19, 25
homoerotic intimacy: Ahab and Pip, 139; Kenyon and Donatello (*The Marble Faun*), 183; Pierre and Glen, 162; Queequeg and Ishmael, 138–39, 250n61
homoerotic oedipal connections: in *Hamlet*, 150–53, 155, 162; in *Pierre*, 151, 162
homophobia, 8, 174
homosexuality: historical emergence of, 80; incest as allegory for, 67–68, 75–76, 164–65; in *The House of Seven Gables*, 68, 75–77, 80–84
homosocial bonds: Hawthorne's, as bachelor, 185; negotiation, 95; Pierre's, 258n35
House of Seven Gables, The (Hawthorne), 59–60, 66–68, 71–88; grammatical problems, 83; and incest theme, 67–68, 75–76; Maule family, 76, 85; Alice Pyncheon, 26, 60, 72, 85–86, 158; Jaffrey Pyncheon, 71, 112; as queer text, 80. *See also* Pyncheon, Clifford; Pyncheon, Hepzibah; Pyncheon, Phoebe
humanism, 7, 200, 223n24. *See also* antihumanism

Hutcheon, Linda, 10
hypercanonicity, 207

Iliad, The (Homer), 149
Il Penseroso (Milton), 3
image: female, 32, 205; feminist and queer concerns, 22; importance of to influence, 16, 19, 21–23, 26–27, 70, 101, 213–14, 218–20
incest: as affective trend in antebellum America, 67, 75; as coded homosexuality, 164–65; in early American literature, 66–68, 75; and Enceladus, 168–69; in *King Lear*, 30, 242n49; in *Hamlet*, 148, 153, 159; and Hawthorne, 29, 66–67, 70, 190; and horror, 163; in *The House of Seven Gables*, 67–68, 75–77, 80–81; as metaphor for writers, 29, 66, 148, 162–63; in *Paradise Lost*, 29, 70–72; in *Pierre*, 67, 148, 156–57, 162–66, 168–69, 171, 259n46; opposing normative sexual order, 162–63; theorized through Melville and Milton, 169–72
Incidents in the Life of a Slave Girl (Jacobs), 102
influence: on American authors, 2, 65–66; and Bloom, 11–12; collaborative, 26, 208; and critical historical awareness, 115; feminist and queer in *Moby-Dick*, 137; as genealogical tie, 62; as homoerotic, 24–25; importance of, 7, 11, 207; and literary deep time, 12; Milton and Melville as theorists of, 24–28; narcissistic and melancholic, 21–22, 88, 208, 213–14; new scholarship on, 12–13; opposed to intertextuality, 10–11; problematic attitudes surrounding, 8; studies of, 1, 11, 209; turn away from, 1, 6–9, 174; uncanniness, 16
Interpretation of Dreams, The (Freud), 146

intersections, of identity and influence, 14
intertextual desire, 13-14, 21, 225n45
intertextuality, 7, 68, 209; and critical historical awareness, 115; feminist and queer in *Moby-Dick*, 137, 143; intertextual echoes, 8, 52, 147; Kristeva on, 9; opposed to influence, 10-11; possibilities, 9-13; Riffaterre on, 9-10
intimacy, lack of, in *The Marble Faun*, 198-99
intransigence, female, 63-65, 84, 90
Irigaray, Luce, 81-82, 257n25
Ishmael (biblical figure), as survivor, 133
Ishmael (*Moby-Dick*): and Edgar (*King Lear*), 123-24, 130, 133-36, 245n17; on man and mankind, 249-50nn51-52; as survivor, 124, 133-34, 155
Ivanhoe (Scott), 49, 182

Jacobs, Harriet, *Incidents in the Life of a Slave Girl*, 102
Jessica (*The Merchant of Venice*), 181-83; conversion, 182; intertext for Miriam Schaefer (*The Marble Faun*), 181, 199
Jewish character, closeted, 177
Jewish masculinity: caricature, 187-88; Hawthorne on, 176, 180, 185, 187. *See also* Wandering Jew
Jew of Malta, The (Marlowe), 182
"Jezebel" figure, 51
Job (biblical figure), as survivor, 31, 124, 133
Jonah (biblical figure), as survivor, 133
Juif errant (Wandering Jew), 188-89
Julius Caesar (Shakespeare), 173, 208-9, 212
Juvan, Marko, 11

Kavanaugh, Brett, 243n67
Kean, Edmund, 104
Kelley, Wyn, 171, 244-45n15
kenosis, 16

Kenyon (*The Marble Faun*), 183, 196-97, 199-201
King Lear (Shakespeare), 103-14, 122-36; and *The Blithedale Romance*, 90, 103-9; influence on Hawthorne, 104; intertext for *Moby-Dick*, 122-24, 133-36; Macready's production, 131, 248n45; plot, 104; queer reading, 127-28. *See also* Cordelia; Edgar; Edmund; Gloucester; Goneril; Regan
King Lear (*King Lear*): intertext for Ahab, 123, 135-36, 140, 142; intertext for Miles Coverdale (*The Blithedale Romance*), 113
King Leir, 111, 137
Kohut, Heinz, 84
Kristeva, Julia: on abjection and maternal body, 140-41; on intertextuality, 9; "Word, Dialogue, and Novel," 9
"Kubla Khan" (Coleridge), 164
Kyd, Thomas, *The Spanish Tragedy*, 149

Lacan, Jacques, mirror stage, 21-22, 24, 227n71; veil, 91
L'Allegro (Milton), 3
Larsen, Nella, *Passing*, 198
Last of the Mohicans, The (Cooper), 28-29, 34-58; Duncan Heyward, 42-43, 53-54; and *The Marble Faun*, 175; and *The Merchant of Venice*, 28-29, 34, 40-46, 175; and *Paradise Lost*, 46-48, 50, 52-56; Shakespeare's influence, 34-37, 58; and *The Tempest*, 37, 39-40; and *Uncle Tom's Cabin*, 34, 229n4. *See also* Bumppo, Natty; Magua; Munro, Cora
Lathrop, George Parsons, 62
Leatherstocking Tales, The (Cooper), 55. *See also* Bumppo, Natty
Lewes, George Henry, 181
Lewis, R. W. B., 54
"Ligeia" (Poe), 102, 164
Lincoln, Abraham, 186, 187, 215

literariness, 9, 224n27
literary forbears, American authors' engagement with, 2, 4–5
London Society for Promoting Christianity amongst the Jews, 192
Lorenzetto, 201
Luciano, Dana, 6, 50
Lucina. *See* Diana
Ludolf, Hiof, influence on Hawthorne, 61
"Lycidas" (Milton), 17–18

Macbeth (Shakespeare), 173, 209–11
Macready, William Charles, 131, 248n45
Magua (*The Last of the Mohicans*): and Caliban, 37–38, 40, 52–53; and Cora Munro, 26, 39–40, 41, 44, 50–51, 53; as poet/Satan figure, 19, 47, 231–32n44; like Shylock, 41, 175
maiden, 56–58
Malbone, Edward Greene, 75, 80
Manning, Mary, 61
Manning, Robert, 77–78
Map of Misreading, A (Bloom), 18–19, 224n25
Marble Faun, The (Hawthorne) 32, 49, 59, 63–64, 65–66, 69, 72, 174–77, 179–84, 188–205; criminalization of sex, 256n19; gender, 176, 198; Jewishness, 174–77, 179–85, 188–201; Kenyon, 183, 196–97, 199–201; and *The Last of the Mohicans*, 175; and *The Merchant of Venice*, 175–76, 181–83, 203–4; and Milton, 59, 69, 193; otherness, 192–93. *See also* Donatello; Model, the; Schaefer, Miriam
marginalia: Coleridge's, 143–44; Melville's, 68, 121, 122, 123, 142, 250n59. *See also* Melville's Marginalia Online
marketplace, sexual, 78
Marlowe, Christopher: *Dido, Queen of Carthage*, 149; *The Jew of Malta*, 182
Marriage of Heaven and Hell, The (Blake), 4
Marsy, Gaspard, 168

masculinity: in *Moby-Dick*, 136; refusal of traditional in *Pierre*, 164. *See also* Jewish masculinity
mask. *See* veil
maternal figures: absence in *King Lear*, 137; in *Hamlet*, 152–53, 159, 165; presence and deprivation in *Moby-Dick*, 137–40; relationship in *Pierre*, 125, 157. *See also* motherlessness; stepmother figures
Mather, Cotton, 61
Mather, Increase, 61
Matthiessen, F. O.: on American literary tradition, 2, 221–23n3; and gay male critical tradition, 5, 223n17; on Hawthorne, 62, 94; responses to, 249n50
Maule family (*The House of Seven Gables*), 76, 85
"May-Pole of Merry Mount, The" (Hawthorne), 59
McColley, Diane Kelsey, 23
McDonald, Rónán, 12
McEachern, Claire, 103, 110–11
McGill, Meredith L., 5
Measure for Measure (Shakespeare), 90, 115–19; intertext for *The Blithedale Romance*, 90, 115–19
Medusa, 116, 118, 258n36
melancholia, 20–22, 26–27, 208, 214, 219–20, 227n70
Mellor, Anne K., 170
Melville, Herman: *Billy Budd*, 159, 251n64; *The Confidence-Man*, 142; "Hawthorne and His Mosses," 28, 123; importance of Salviati painting *The Three Fates*, 142–43; influence theorized through comparison with Milton, 26, 28; on Narcissus, 24–26, 28, 170; *Redburn*, 187; relationship with Hawthorne, 67, 148; Shakespearean intertexts, 136, 141–44, 147–48, 151, 157, 159, 161–66, 172; *Timoleon, Etc.*, 159; views of Shakespeare, 121–23.

Melville, Herman (*continued*)
See also *Moby-Dick; or, The Whale*; *Pierre; or The Ambiguities*
Melville's Marginalia Online, 121, 122
Merchant of Venice, The (Shakespeare), 28-29, 30-37, 39-44, 142, 175-77, 179, 181-83, 203-4, 211; intertext for *The Last of the Mohicans*, 28-29, 34, 40-46, 175; intertext for *The Marble Faun*, 175-76, 181-83, 203-4. See also Jessica
mesmerism, 72, 95, 106, 115, 196
Metamorphoses, The (Ovid), 23-24, 25-26, 70-71, 93, 147, 149, 167
Michaelangelo, 143. See also Salviati, Francesco; *Three Fates, The*
Michie, Helena, 100, 166, 199
Midsummer Night's Dream, A (Shakespeare), 37
Milder, Robert, 134
Milton, John: in antebellum America, 2, 3-4; and British Romantics, 4, 29; *Comus*, 3, 30, 59, 93-94, 97; and Cooper, 19, 46-48; and Douglass, 213-14, 218-20, 222-23n15; and Hawthorne, 68-72, 84-85, 87-88, 101-2, 193; *Il Penseroso*, 3; *L'Allegro*, 3; "Lycidas," 17-18; and Melville, 158; misogyny, 49-50, 54-55; *Paradise Regained*, 219; as poet, 18; Puritanism, 3-4, 69; revision of Ovid, 23-24, 26, 88; *Samson Agonistes*, 214, 219; as template for later authors, 1-2. See also *Paradise Lost*
Miltonic-Melvillean theory of influence, 24-28
mirror: and female artists, 74; and female narcissism in Hawthorne, 73-74, 87; and female vanity, 73, 158, 159; women as, 117, 158-59, 169-70, 257n25. See also Pyncheon, Hepzibah
miscegenation, 44, 45, 50, 63, 66
misogyny: antebellum American, 174; early modern, 102; internalized, 202, 263n41; in *King Lear*, 90, 92, 105, 125, 131-32, 137; masculine Romantic 169-70; Milton's, 49-50, 54-55; in Shakespeare and Hawthorne, 90, 97, 99-100, 102-3, 112, 118
misprision (misreading): and American romance, 14; and influence, 17; six forms, 16
Mitchell, Juliet, 159-60
Moby-Dick; or, The Whale (Melville), 24-25, 28, 122-44, 155, 170; class in 134-35; femininity and motherlessness, 136-38; and *King Lear*, 122-24, 130, 133-36, 137; stepmother world, 125, 139-41; Queequeg, 124-25, 136, 138-39; Starbuck, 139-41. See also Ahab; Ishmael; Pip
Model, the (*The Marble Faun*): and Christian redemptive feeling, 204; connection to Miriam Schaefer, 175, 181, 190-91, 195-99; death, 192-93; seducer, 64
"Monsieur Schaeffer," 184-85, 187
Moodie (*The Blithedale Romance*), 95, 99; and Lear, 104, 107, 112-14; relationship with Zenobia, 108-9, 113
motherlessness: in Hawthorne, 77, 113; Jewish father-daughter trope, 182; in *King Lear*, 38-39, 113, 125; in *Moby-Dick*, 31, 125, 136-38, 148; in *The Tempest*, 38-39. See also maternal figures; stepmother figures
"Mourning and Melancholia" (Freud), 21, 227n70
Much Ado about Nothing (Shakespeare), 30, 37, 91, 95-98; Beatrice as intertext for Zenobia (*The Blithdale Romance*), 94-95, 98, 102-3, 240-41n29; misogyny in, 101-3; productions of, 94. See also Benedick; Hero
Munro, Cora (*The Last of the Mohicans*): and Cordelia (*King Lear*), 46;

description, 230n30; and Eve, 47-56; and Magua, 26, 39-40, 41, 44, 50-51, 53, 175; and Miranda (*The Tempest*), 38, 37-38, 40, 52-53, 56; and Portia (*The Merchant of Venice*), 43-46, 175; as racial-ethnic other, 42-43, 53-54, 56, 180, 204, 232n57; sexuality, 50-52; unknowability as stranger maiden, 56-58

muse: Satan's, 18; woman as, 164

My Bondage and My Freedom (Douglass) 208, 212

"My Kinsman, Major Molineaux" (Hawthorne), 112, 180, 261n9

Mysterious Mother, The (Walpole), 163, 258n32

narcissism: centrality to Romanticism, 169-70; in *Pierre*, 158-59; male in Hawthorne, 60, 108, 109, 237n62; maternal, 158; paternal, 103-14; psychoanalytically linked to homosexuality, 68, 75, 80; represented by incest, 70, 80-81

narcissism, female, 24, 73; in *Hamlet*, 159; in Hawthorne, 73-74, 87

narcissistic encounter: influence as, 21-22, 88; with texts, 19

Narcissus, 22; in art, 24-25; and Douglass, 218, 220; female, 88; for Melville, 170

Narrative of Arthur Gordon Pym (Poe), 136

Nashe, Thomas, *Dido, Queen of Carthage*, 149

"New Adam and Eve, The" (*Hawthorne*), 59

nonrecognition of kin: in *The Blithedale Romance*, 106; in *King Lear*, 105

Notions of the Americans (Cooper), 34

Oates, Joyce Carol, 173-74

oedipal conflict: in *Hamlet*, 146-47, 152-55; and influence, 13, 16, 20, 27, 207-8

Oedipus complex, 77, 80, 145-47, 152-53, 155, 253n1, 259n46. *See also* Freud, Sigmund

Oedipus Tyrannus (Sophocles), 145, 147

Ohge, Christopher, and Steven Olsen-Smith, 122, 123

Ohi, Kevin, 13-14

Old Drift, The (Serpell), 247-48n38

Old Manse (Hawthorne home), 61

Oliver Twist (Dickens), 187

Olson, Charles, 30, 123

"On Love" (Shelley), 169

"On Narcissism: An Introduction" (Freud), 21

Ophelia (*Hamlet*): complex, 89; as Hamlet's victim, 145, 162; intertext for Isabel Banford (*Pierre*), 31-32; representation in film, 259n39; and sexual disgust, 152, 154, 165

Orientalism: in *The Blithedale Romance*, 91, 239n7; in *The House of Seven Gables*, 79

Othello (Shakespeare), 173-74, 210; and race, 173-74, 210

otherness, 14; in *The Last of the Mohicans*, 29; in *The Marble Faun*, 192-93

Our Old Home (Hawthorne), 202

Ovid, 259n41; and *Hamlet*, 147, 166; and Hawthorne, 78, 88, 93; and Melville, 25-26, 166; *The Metamorphoses*, 23-24, 25-26, 70-71, 93, 147, 149, 167; and Milton, 23-24, 70-71, 88, 218; and Oedipus, 147

Paglia, Camille, 67-68

Palfrey, Simon, 127, 135. *See also* Edgar

Paradise Lost (Milton), 4, 15-16, 18-19, 22-24, 29, 46-49, 52-53, 68-72, 158, 219; Blake on, 4; Death, 18, 19, 68, 70-71; incest theme, 29, 68-72; and intertextual practices, 70; Sin, 18, 19,

Paradise Lost (Milton) (*continued*) 29, 68, 70-71, 78, 79, 158. *See also* Eve; Satan
Paradise Regained (Milton), 219
Parvini, Neema, 7
Passing (Larsen), 198
passing, religious, 198-200
paternal image, 26, 163, 170-71; paternal narcissism, 103-14. *See also* fatherhood
Pathfinder, The (Cooper), 55. *See also* Bumppo, Natty
patriarchy, 90; Renaissance, 110
Peabody, Sophia, 61
Pearce, Howard D., 89-90, 115-16
Peretz, Eyal, 27, 126
Person, Leland S., 136, 186-87
Philosophy of the Plays of Shakspere Unfolded (Bacon), 202
photography, 215-16
phrenology, 99, 114
Pierce, Franklin, 177; handsomeness of, 186-87
Pierre; or The Ambiguities (Melville), 26, 31, 66-67, 125, 147-48, 155-66, 168-72; Stanley Glendinning, 156-57; and *Hamlet*, 147-48, 151, 157-59, 161-69, 171-72; male sexuality, 164-66, 258nn35-36; reception, 155. *See also* Banford, Isabel; Glendinning, Mary; Glendinning, Pierre; Tartan, Lucy
Pip (*Moby-Dick*): relationship to Lear, 136; relationship with Ahab, 129, 134, 139; as survivor, 129
piracy, 227n66
pleasure, 3; in *The House of Seven Gables*, 60, 73, 79, 80, 81-84
Poe, Edgar Allan, 62, 66, 236n35; "Ligeia," 102, 164; *Narrative of Arthur Gordon Pym*, 136
poet, figure of: Bloom on, 17; and influence, 13; Satan as, 15-16, 18-19
Poor Tom. *See* Edgar

portraits: of Empress Josephine, 184-85; in *Hamlet*, 161-63, 171, 255n11; in *The House of Seven Gables*, 75, 80, 160; Miriam's in *The Marble Faun*, 204-5; in *Pierre*, 26, 31-32, 160-63, 170-71, 257n29; queer implications, 161; of Madison Washington (*The Heroic Slave*), 216
Portia (*The Merchant of Venice*): as ambiguous character, 40-41, 42, 45; and Douglass, 211-12; intertext for Cora Munro (*Last of the Mohicans*), 43-46, 175
postcolonial theory, and *The Tempest*, 39, 230n22
"power of women" trope, 90, 92-93
predation, male, in Hawthorne, 112
prejudice: Hawthorne's, religious, 179, 180; hazards of, 1; internalized, 201-2; and the law, 193
primal scene: Bloom's "scene of instruction," 18-19; Freud, 148, 151-52; in *Hamlet*, 148-49, 152, 154, 256n18
Priscilla (*The Blithedale Romance*), 108; ambivalent veiled personality, 119-20; and Cordelia, 106; and Hero, 95, 99-100, 102; sexuality and spectacle, 99, 115; as "The Veiled Lady," 30, 95, 99, 115, 119-20
Protestantism, in *The Marble Faun*, 200-201
protofeminism, Hawthorne's, 114
Prynne, Hester (*The Scarlet Letter*), 59, 64, 72, 99, 177-78, 202, 263n41
"psychotheology," 203
purity, feminine, 91, 93, 99
Pyncheon, Alice (*The House of Seven Gables*), 26, 60, 72, 85-86, 158
Pyncheon, Clifford (*The House of Seven Gables*): beauty, 78, 80, 81, 180; gender and sexuality, 29, 68, 75, 76; and loss, 82; undesirability, 59-60, 84

Pyncheon, Hepzibah (*The House of Seven Gables*): erotic agency, 81; gaze, 87–88; love for brother, 75; name, 236n40; sexuality, 72–74; shame and inadequacy, 79; sympathetic ambivalence toward, 29, 71–72; undesirability, 59–60, 78, 84; will, 102
Pyncheon, Jaffrey (*The House of Seven Gables*), 71, 112
Pyncheon, Phoebe (*The House of Seven Gables*), 60, 76; as gendered visual object, 83

Queequeg (*Moby-Dick*), 124–25, 136, 138–39
queer ethics, 59
queer resilience, Edgar (*King Lear*) as example of, 132–33
queer survivors, 31, 245–46n24. *See also* survival
quotation, 209
Qur'an, 2

race: and American literature, 33–34, 174; anxiety and American culture, 34, 63; in *The Last of the Mohicans*, 34, 43, 45–46, 52–54, 56; in productions of *The Merchant of Venice*, 41–42, 181; and *Othello*, 173–74, 210
Rachel (biblical figure), as survivor, 133
racism, 8, 34, 51, 174, 176; Duncan Heyward's (*The Last of the Mohicans*), 42, 53–54
Radcliffe, Anne, 163
Rappaccini ("Rappaccini's Daughter"), 64, 112
Rappaccini, Beatrice ("Rappaccini's Daughter"): as allegory for influence, 65, 234n16; influenced by Milton's Eve, 63–66
"Rappaccini's Daughter" (Hawthorne), 59, 63–66, 112, 185, 234n16; as allegory of influence and race, 63

Rebecca (*Ivanhoe*): as beautiful Jewess archetype, 182; influence on Hawthorne and Cooper, 182; intertext for Cora Munro (*Last of the Mohicans*), 49
"Recollections of a Gifted Woman" (Hawthorne), 202
Redburn (Melville), 187
redeemer, woman as, 113. *See also* Cordelia
Regan (*King Lear*), 142, 241n34; as stepmother figure, 140
Representative Men (Emerson), 202
repugnance, 178–79, 180, 192, 199, 201
Reynolds, Larry, 134–35
Richmond-Garza, Elizabeth, 27–28
Rilke, Rainer Maria, 28
Ripley, George, 75
"Roger Malvin's Burial" (Hawthorne), 112
romance, American form, 17
Romanticism: American, 4, 7, 58, 66, 87, 147; masculine, 169–70; non-Western influences, 2, 221n2; representational practices, 2
Romantic tradition, and lateness, 18
Roudiez, Leon, 9

Salomons, David (Lord Mayor of London), 176, 177
Salomons, Emma Abigail Montefiore: Hawthorne's descriptions of, 178–79; as template for Miriam Schaefer (*The Marble Faun*), 179, 195, 205
Salomons, Philip, 178–79, 181, 185–86, 187, 189, 194
Salviati, Francesco, *The Three Fates*, 142–43
Samson Agonistes (Milton), and Douglass, 214, 219
Satan (*Paradise Lost*): as belated poet, 15–16, 18, 19, 22; and Bloom, 15, 18–19; physical decay, 219; and Clifford Pyncheon (*The House of Seven Gables*),

Satan (*Paradise Lost*) (*continued*) 78; queerness, 15-16; as symbol for Cooper, 19, 47, 231-32n44; temptation of Eve, 47-49, 53, 56, 153; as wronged other, 4

Scarlet Letter, The (Hawthorne), 59, 63, 69, 72, 73, 99, 112, 177-78, 202, 263n41; internalized misogyny, 202, 263n41; and Milton, 59, 69. *See also* Dimmesdale, Arthur; Pyrnne, Hester

Schaefer, Miriam (*The Marble Faun*): connection to Donatello, 200; connection to the Model, 175, 181, 190-91, 195-99; heritage, 174-75, 176, 179, 180, 190-91, 194-95, 199, 205; and Jessica (*The Merchant of Venice*), 181, 199; and Cora Munro (*Last of the Mohicans*), 180, 204; reflection and drowning, 264-65n50; self-portrait of, 204-5; sexuality, 72; and Shylock, 32, 175-76, 204

Schmidgall, Gary, 7, 13, 17, 18

Schoenfeldt, Michael, 49

Schwarz, Kathryn, 102, 105

Scott, Walter, 61; *Ivanhoe*, 49, 182

Scottish Anti-Slavery Society, 211

Scylla (*The Metamorphoses*), 71

"Secret Jew," 195, 199; in Victorian England, 191

Sedgwick, Eve Kosofsky, 14-15

Seneca, 147, 149, 254n6

Septimius Felton (Hawthorne), 180, 190

Serpell, Namwali: *The Furrows*, 247-48n38; *The Old Drift*, 247-48n38

Shakespeare, William: in antebellum America, 2-3, 212, 239n3; and Cooper, 28-29, 34, 36-46, 58; as cultural authority, 45; and Hawthorne, 60-61, 89, 94-98, 101-3, 107, 111; *Henry VIII*, 122, 208; influence on American romantics, 147-48; *Julius Caesar*, 173, 208-9, 212; knowledge of Greek drama, 147, 149, 25n4n5-6; *Macbeth*, 173, 209-11; and Melville, 121-25, 147-48, 151, 161-69, 171-72; *A Midsummer Night's Dream*, 37; and Sophocles's *Oedipus Tyrannus*, 145, 147; and Edmund Spenser, 92-93; as template for later authors, 1-2, 123. *See also Hamlet; King Lear; Measure for Measure; Merchant of Venice, The; Much Ado about Nothing; Othello; Tempest, The*

Shapiro, James, 203

shattering, 127-28, 246n26. *See also* Bersani, Leo; Palfrey, Simon

Shelley, Percy Bysshe, 61, 66; "On Love," 169

Shoulson, Jeffrey, 22-23; on Milton and midrash, 49

Shylock (*Merchant of Venice*), 179; Jewish identity, 175, 203-4; and Magua, 41, 175; and Miriam Schaefer (*The Marble Faun*), 175-76; as sympathetic, 40-41

siblings. *See* incest

Sicher, Efraim, 181

Simms, William Gilmore, 52

Sin (*Paradise Lost*), 18, 19, 29, 68, 70-71, 78, 79, 158

slavery, 33-34, 197, 209, 211, 213, 237n57

Smith, Sydney, 20, 33

Sociable Letters (Cavendish), 100

social abjection, 81. *See also* Irigaray, Luce

Song of Songs, gender politics, 217-18

Sophocles: and Elizabethan drama, 147, 254n5; *Oedipus Tyrannus*, 145, 147

sororophobia, 100, 166, 199. *See also* Michie, Helena

Sorrows of Young Werther, The (Goethe), 2

Spanish Tragedy, The (Kyd), 149

Spenser, Edmund, 30; and Hawthorne,

61, 62, 90; and Milton, 70; and Shakespeare, 92–93
Stanley, Glendinning (*Pierre*), 156–57
Stanton, Elizabeth Cady, 98–99
Starbuck (*Moby-Dick*), 139–41
stepmother figure: lack of critical attention in *Moby-Dick*, 251n61; stepmother world, 125, 139–41. See also maternal figures
Stowe, Harriet Beecher, *Uncle Tom's Cabin*, 34, 229n4
stranger, 26, 171–72; Biblical figure of, 57–58; maiden, 56–58; the Model as (*The Marble Faun*), 204
Sue, Eugène, 188
Suffering Jew, in Victorian England, 191
suicide: Gloucester's (*King Lear*), 128; in *Hamlet*, 151, 166
survival: in *King Lear* and *Moby-Dick*, 30–31, 123–24; in *Moby-Dick*, 133–36; and queer theory, 124, 126–27, 245–46n24
survivor: Edgar as (*King Lear*), 31, 125–26, 129; Horatio as (*Hamlet*), 155; Ishmael as, 31, 124, 129, 133–36
swerve, 16, 17, 65, 226n57. See also *clinamen*; misprision
Swerve, The: How the World Became Modern (Greenblatt), 17

Tartan, Lucy (*Pierre*); as femme fragile, 163; relationship with Pierre, 156–57, 163, 171
Tate, Nahum, 131
Tempest, The (Shakespeare), 36, 37–40, 52–53, 229–30n16; feminist response to, 38; intertext for *The Last of the Mohicans*, 34, 36–40, 52–53, 56, 229–30n16; postcolonial theory, 39, 230n22
temporality: and Freud, 151–52; and intertextuality, 12

tessera, 16
"Theme of the Three Caskets, The" (Freud), 142
Thoreau, Henry David, 36, 185–86, 187
thralldom: in Dickens, 197; female authority in *Moby-Dick*, 141–43; Freud on, 197, 262n35; Matthew Maule over Alice Pyncheon in *The House of Seven Gables*, 197; the Model over Miriam Schaefer in *The Marble Faun*, 190, 196–97, 198–99; Westervelt over Zenobia and Priscilla in *The Blithedale Romance*, 94, 197
Three Fates, The (Salviati painting), 142–43
Timoleon, Etc. (Melville), 159
"Tintern Abbey" (Wordsworth), 17–18
transatlantic literary studies, 5–6
transmission, term, 13
trauma, 97, 237n62; religious conversion as, 182, 192, 203
Trilby (Du Maurier), 187
Tsang, Wu, 248n38
Twice-Told Tales (Hawthorne), 183

utopia: in *Blithedale Romance*, 93; failed in *Pierre*, 164–65, 166. See also Brook Farm

Van Anglen, K. P., and Milton's legacy, 4
Vandiver, Edward P., Jr., 40
veil: biblical, 91; antebellum context for veiled woman, 98–99, 114–15; in *Comus*, 93–94; in Hawthorne, 91–93, 95, 118, 201; and male fantasy, 92, 101, 118; in *Measure for Measure*, 30, 116–69; metaphor of, 91–92; in *Much Ado about Nothing*, 30, 96, 98; and Muslim women, 91–92, 117; and mysterious femininity, 58; and Priscilla or "The Veiled Lady" (*The Blithdale Romance*), 30, 95, 99, 115, 119–20; and Miriam

veil (*continued*)
  Schaefer (*The Marble Faun*), 201;
  unveiling, 92-93, 117; veiled women, 90
violence: between men, 153; misogynistic, 84-85, 96-97, 100-101; paternal, 107
virago, 113
Virgil, *The Aeneid*, 149, 255n10
"Virtuoso's Collection, A" (Hawthorne), 189
visuality: and Douglass, 215-17; female, 84-85

Walpole, Horace: *The Castle of Otranto*, 163; *The Mysterious Mother*, 163, 258n32; incest as theme, 163
Wandering Jew: as cultural legend, 189-90; Hawthorne's gothic Romantic aesthetic, 188, 190; in Hawthorne's journal, 178; and Hawthorne's Model, 189-90, 262n25; and Jewish masculinity, 187
Washington, Madison (*The Heroic Slave*), 214, 216, 218-20
Webster, Daniel, 209
Weekes, Princess, 173
Weil, Simone, 135
Weisbuch, Robert, 5-6

"What to the Slave Is the Fourth of July?" (Douglass), 209
Whitman, Walt: and Bloom, 17, 226n60; and British literary tradition, 7, 212
Wilder, Lina Perkins, 91, 96, 98
Williams, Tennessee, 225n45
Wilson, Ivy, 6
Winckelmann, Johann Joachim, 183-84, 188
Wineapple, Brenda, 60-61, 185
witchcraft, 61, 76
Wolf-Man, The (Freud), 152
Woman in the Nineteenth Century (Fuller), 102
Woodberry, George, *American Men of Letters*, 61
"Word, Dialogue, and Novel" (Kristeva), 9
Wordsworth, William, "Tintern Abbey," 17-18

Zenobia (*The Blithedale Romance*): and Beatrice (*Much Ado about Nothing*), 94-95, 98, 102-3, 240-41n29; and Goneril and Regan (*King Lear*), 106, 109; Moodie's appraisal of, 108-9; rebellion, 65, 103; sexuality, 62-63, 72, 97-98, 113, 114, 179, 242n54; and the veil, 118, 201

www.ingramcontent.com/pod-product-compliance
Lightning Source LLC
Chambersburg PA
CBHW021648230426
43668CB00008B/549